CAMBRIDGE STUDIES IN
INTERNATIONAL AND COMPARATIVE LAW: NEW SERIES

General Editor:
SIR ROBERT Y. JENNINGS, *Judge of the International Court of Justice, formerly Whewell
Professor of International and Comparative Law, University of Cambridge*

TORTIOUS LIABILITY FOR UNINTENTIONAL HARM IN THE COMMON LAW AND THE CIVIL LAW

VOLUME II

TORTIOUS LIABILITY FOR UNINTENTIONAL HARM IN THE COMMON LAW AND THE CIVIL LAW

Volume II: Materials

BY

F. H. LAWSON

D.C.L., F.B.A.

of Gray's Inn, Barrister;
Formerly Professor of Comparative Law, Oxford

B. S. MARKESINIS

D.IUR. (ATHEN.), M.A., PH.D. (CANTAB.)

of Gray's Inn, Barrister;
Fellow of Trinity College, Cambridge;
Lecturer in Law of the University of Cambridge

CAMBRIDGE UNIVERSITY PRESS

CAMBRIDGE

LONDON   NEW YORK   NEW ROCHELLE

MELBOURNE   SYDNEY

Published by the Press Syndicate of the University of Cambridge
The Pitt Building, Trumpington Street, Cambridge CB2 IRP
32 East 57th Street, New York, NY 10022, USA
296 Beaconsfield Parade, Middle Park, Melbourne 3206, Australia

First Published 1982

Printed in Great Britain at
the University Press, Cambridge

Library of Congress catalogue card number: 81–10230

British Library Cataloguing in Publication Data
Lawson, F.H.
Tortious liability for unintentional harm in
the Common law and the Civil law. – (Cambridge studies
in international and comparative law. New Series)
Vol. II: Materials
1. Torts – Law and legislation – Europe
1. Title II. Markesinis, B.S.
342.36'094
ISBN 0 521 235863

CONTENTS

Contents

Contents

Contents

GENERAL EDITOR'S FOREWORD
TO THE NEW SERIES

A series of *Cambridge Studies in International and Comparative Law*, under the general editorship of H.C. Gutteridge, H. Lauterpacht and Sir A.D. McNair, was launched in 1946 with the first edition of Professor Gutteridge's important monograph on *Comparative Law: An Introduction to the Comparative Method of Legal Study and Research*. In a general introduction to the series the editors explained that it was designed to fill certain gaps in that part of English legal literature which is concerned with international relations: and that it would involve public international law, private international law and comparative law. In fact all the subsequent volumes of the distinguished series save the last, contributed by Dr B.S. Markesinis and dealing with the controversial issue of Dissolution of Parliament, were to do with public and international law.

In the 1970s there was a gap during a time when the Syndics were persuaded that books on law should be left to commercial publishers. Happily, counsels more apt to the Press of Maitland's university have now prevailed, and the series is being revived. The intention is to publish monographs mainly on public international law; but it is a happy coincidence that this first work of the revived series is again about the comparative method of legal study and research.

The general editors of the original series said, in April 1946, that 'at present the literature of Comparative Law is scattered, fragmentary and often difficult of access'. The aim of the present volumes is precisely to make an important part of that material readily available to scholars and students, and to provide an authoritative commentary and guide to understanding it.

We are most fortunate that the new Cambridge series thus begins with work by that most distinguished Oxford scholar and teacher, Professor F.H. Lawson, in partnership with a Cambridge scholar and teacher, Dr Basil Markesinis.

Cambridge
April 1981

R.Y.J.

PREFACE

This is the second volume of a work which we have entitled *Tortious Liability for Unintentional Harm in the Common Law and the Civil Law* and one must seek in the preface of the first volume and the pages that follow it the history of its genesis and its detailed aims. But both the authors and the publisher felt that it might be useful to make the second volume available on its own and so, for the sake of the reader who has not purchased or consulted the first volume, a few introductory remarks about what follows may not be out of place.

In one sense, this book is a 'companion volume' to the first, in which we have attempted to give some of the general principles related to our subject and make some observations which, in varying degrees, apply to all the systems under comparison. The aim of this second volume was therefore to provide the interested reader with some basic texts and extracts from decisions which would enable him to pursue his study more deeply and, at the same time, question or develop some of our assumptions and conclusions. For this reason, the material in this volume follows closely the pattern and contents of the first and it would be futile to pretend that the reader will not get greater benefit if he uses the two volumes side by side.

But the material of this volume also aspires to independent status and could easily have been entitled *Cases and Materials on Comparative Torts*. To strengthen this element of self-sufficiency we have added some material of our own which either sketches for the reader the judicial background in France and Germany or provides a brief commentary on the law found in the case extracts.

The greater part of this second volume is devoted to the *modern* Civil law. But in the first volume we included a fairly long historical chapter giving an account of the *lex Aquilia* and tracing in briefest outline the development of the law from Roman times to the modern codes. In view of this and because we feel that Roman law has a strong pedagogic value we have included in this volume some of those classic texts. Reasons of space dictated that this be done in translation form only. While the omission of the Latin originals should not cause undue hardship to the serious Roman lawyer (who can easily trace them elsewhere), it did make room for more of the modern law. Given today's emphasis on the modern Civil law, this, we hope, will counter the disadvantage of omitting the original texts.

The texts that follow aim at giving the reader some familiarity with some of the basic civil codes such as an educated Common lawyer ought, in our opinion, to possess. These are followed by extracts from decisions from German and French Courts and once again we wish to thank Messrs Carl Heymanns Verlag KG, C.H. Beck'sche Verlags-buchandlung and the editors of Recueil Dalloz-Sirey, *La Semaine Juridique* and the *Gazette du Palais* for permission to translate or reproduce here their original texts.

The topics discussed in this volume are *roughly* those considered in the first. In neither volume, however, have we wished or tried to discuss *every* topic from the point of view of *every* system. The emphasis has thus alternated depending on a variety of factors, the importance of a particular decision being only one of them. Our main effort was to select not only the *leading* case but also the case which was factually equivalent to one which our Common law student would have met while studying his own system, so that he will be able to compare the two with greater profit. We hope that within the strict confines of a short book we have succeeded in showing that French and German lawyers have been called upon to solve problems almost identical to ours; that their solutions have been remarkably similar; and that their reasoning has often been as tortuous if not as unsatisfactory as ours. Above all, however, we hope to have shown how useful it can be for a lawyer studying his own system to study how *foreign* colleagues have handled similar problems. This, in our opinion, is the first and arguably the greatest benefit one can derive from the use of the comparative method.

One final word should be added as an explanation rather than as an apology. The preponderance of French material in this volume is justified partly by the knowledge that French law is the most commonly taught 'foreign system' in this country, and partly because we find that in its study one encounters an admirable ability to blend the theoretical and the practical while it always strives for elegance and symmetry. Thus, though the French system appears (to our eyes at least) less rigorous and less 'worked on' than the German, it has managed to avoid some of the theoretical excesses which can be found in the otherwise admirable Germanic legal literature. At the same time, however, it has avoided the opposite extreme found in the Common law which, in the words of the great Holmes, 'decides the case first and determines the principle afterwards'.

F.H. Lawson   B.S. Markesinis

ABBREVIATIONS

ABGB	Austrian General Civil Code.
A.C.	Law Reports, Appeal Cases (Decisions of the House of Lords and the Privy Council from 1891).
AcP	*Archiv für die civilistische Praxis.*
A.E.F.	Cour d'appel de l'Afrique Equatoriale française.
A.J.Comp.L.	*American Journal of Comparative Law.*
A.L.J.R.	Australian Law Journal Reports.
All E.R.	All England Law Reports.
AMG	Arzneimittelgesetz.
Amos and Walton	Sir M.S. Amos and F.P. Walton, *Introduction to French Law*, 3rd edn (1967) by F.H. Lawson, A.E. Anton and L. Neville Brown.
Am. Rep.	American Reports.
App. Cass.	Law Reports, Appeal Cases (1875–90).
ATF	*Recueil officiel d'arrêts du Tribunal fédéral suisse* (can also be referred to as *BGE* – *Entscheidungen des schweizerischen Bundesgerichts*).
Atiyah	P.S. Atiyah, *Accidents, Compensation and the Law*, 2nd edn (1975).
B.	*Basilica.*
BB	*Betriebsberater.*
Beseler	G. Beseler, *Beiträge zur Kritik der Römischen Rechtsquellen*, I (1910); II (1911); III (1913); IV (1920); V (1931).
Bet.	*Der Betrieb.*
BGB	Bürgerliches Gesetzbuch (German Civil Code).
BGBl.	*Bundesgesetzblatt.*
BGE	*Entscheidungen des schweizerischen Bundesgerichtes* (can also be referred to as *ATF* – *Recueil officiel d'arrêts du Tribunal fédéral suisse*).
BGHZ	*Entscheidungen des Bundesgerichtshofes in Zivilsachen* (Decisions of the West German Supreme Court in civil matters).

Buckland, *Slavery*	W.W. Buckland, *The Roman Law of Slavory* (1908, 1970).
Buckland, *Text-book*	W.W. Buckland, *A Text-book of Roman Law from Augustus to Justinian*, 3rd edn revised by P. Stein (1963).
Buckland and McNair	W.W. Buckland and A.D. McNair, *Roman Law and Common Law*, 2nd edn revised by F.H. Lawson (1952 reprinted 1965, 1974).
Bull.civ.	*Bulletin des arrêts de la Cour de cassation, chambres civiles* (official reports).
Bull.crim.	*Bulletin des arrêts de la Cour de cassation, chambre criminelle* (official reports).
C.	*Codex Iustinianus.*
C.A.	Decision of the English Court of Appeal.
Cal.L.Rev.	*California Law Review.*
Cal. Reptr. 2d.	California Reporter, 2nd series (American law reports).
Cal. Reptr. 3d.	California Reporter, 3rd series (American law reports).
Cass.	Cour de cassation.
CC	Civil Code.
C.E.	Conseil D'Etat.
Ch.	Law Reports, Chancery Division (from 1891).
Ch. Civ.	Cour de cassation, Chambre Civile.
Ch. Civ. 2^e	Cour de cassation, second Chambre Civile.
Ch. Comm.	Cour de cassation, Chambre Commercielle.
Ch. Crim.	Cour de cassation, Chambre Criminelle.
Ch. D.	Law Reports, Chancery Division (1875–90).
Ch. Mixte	Cour de cassation, Chambre Mixte.
Ch. Req.	Cour de cassation, Chambre des Requêtes.
Ch. Réun.	Cour de cassation, Chambres Réunies.
C.L.J.	*Cambridge Law Journal.*
C.L.R.	Commonwealth Law Reports.
Coll.	*Mosaicarum et Romanarum Collatio*, ed. Hyamson, 1913.
D.	Recueil Dalloz (1945–64).
D	*Iustiniani Digesta.*
D.C.	Dalloz, recueil critique de jurisprudence et de législation (1941–4).
D. Chron.	Dalloz chronique.

Deutsch, *Haftungsrecht*	E. Deutsch, Haftungsrecht, I, 5th edn (1976).
de Visscher	F. de Visscher, *Le Régime romain de la noxalité* (1947).
D.H.	Dalloz Hebdomadaire (1924–40).
D.L.R.	Dominion Law Reports.
D.P.	Dalloz périodique (1825–1940).
D.S.	Recueil Dalloz et Sirey (1965–).
D. StR.	Deutsches Steuerrecht.
EG. BGB.	Einführungsgesetz zum BGB (Introductory law to the BGB).
Encyclopedia	*International Encyclopedia of Comparative Law*, gen. ed. A. Tunc (1975).
Esser-Schmidt, *Schuldrecht*	J. Esser and E. Schmidt, *Schuldrecht*, 5th edn, I, *Allgemeiner Teil*, (1975), II, *Besonderer Teil* (1976).
Ex. D.	Law Reports, Exchequer Division (1875–80).
Fleming	John G. Fleming, *The Law of Torts*, 5th edn (1977).
F. Supp.	Federal Supplement (American law reports).
F. 2d.	Federal Reporter, 2nd series (American law reports).
G.	*Gai Institutiones.*
GG	Grundgesetz (the Constitution of Western Germany).
Giffard	A.E. Giffard and R. Villers, *Droit romain et ancien droit français* (*obligations*), 4th edn (1976).
G.P.	*Gazette du Palais.*
Grueber	E. Grueber, *The Lex Aquilia* (1866).
GVG	Gerichtsverfassunggesetz.
H. & C.	Hurlstone and Coltman (private reports 1862–6).
Hart and Honoré	H.L.A. Hart and A.M. Honoré, *Causation in the Law* (1959).
Heimbach	C.G.E. Heimbach, *Basilicorum Libri LX*, vol. v (1850).
HGB	Handelsgesetzbuch (West German Commercial Code).
Holdsworth	Sir W.S. Holdsworth, *History of English Law*, 12 vols.
Honoré, *Encyclopedia*	*International Encyclopedia of Comparative Law* (chief ed. A. Tunc), XI, ch. 7, 'Causation and Remoteness of Damage' by A.M. Honoré.

I.C.L.Q.	International and Comparative Law Quarterly.
J.	Iustiniani Institutiones.
J.C.L.	Journal of Comparative Legislation and International Law, 3rd series.
J.C.P.	Juris-Classeur Périodique (also referred to as S.J. (La Semaine Juridicue).
Jolowicz, *De Furtis*	H.F. Jolowicz, Digest XLVII. 2, De Furtis (1940).
Jolowicz and Nicholas	H.F. Jolowicz and B. Nicholas, Historical Introduction to the Study of Roman Law, 3rd edn (1972).
Josserand	L. Josserand, Cours de droit civil positif français, 2nd edn (1933).
J.S.P.T.L.	Journal of the Society of Public Teachers of Law.
JuS	Juristische Schulung.
JW	Juristische Wochenschrift.
JZ	Juristenzeitung.
Kaser, *R. PR.*	Max Kaser, Das römische Privatrecht, I, 2nd edn (1971).
K.B.	Law Reports, King's Bench (1901–52),
Larenz, *Schuldrecht*	K. Larenz, Lehrbuch des Schuldrechts, 11th edn, I, Allgemeiner Teil (1976), II, Besonderer Teil (1977).
LebMG	Lebensmittelgesetz
Lenel, *Ed.*	O. Lenel, Das Edictum Perpetuum, 3rd edn (1927).
LK	Leipziger Kommentar.
LM	Lindenmaier, Möhring et al.(Commentary on decisions of BGH).
L.Q.R.	Law Quarterly Review.
L.R. Ch. App.	Law Reports, Chancery Appeal Cases (1865–75).
L.R.C.P.	Law Reports, Common Pleas Cases (1868–75).
L.R. Ex.	Law Reports, Exchequer Cases (1865–75).
L.R.H.L.	Law Reports, English and Irish Appeals (1866–75).
L.R.Q.B.	Law Reports, Queen's Bench (1865–75).
L.T.	Law Times Reports (1859–1947).
Macq.	Macqueen (Sc.) H.L. (private reports 1851–65).
M. & W.	Meeson and Welsby Ex. (private reports 1836–47).

Mazeaud and Mazeaud	Henri, Léon et Jean Mazeaud, *Traité théorique et pratique de la responsabilité civile délictuelle et contractuelle*, II, 6th edn (1970).
Mazeaud and Mazeaud, *Leçons*	Henri, Léon et Jean Mazeaud, *Leçons de droit civil*, II, part I, 6th edn (1978) by F. Chabas.
Mazeaud and Tunc	Henri et Léon Mazeaud et A. Tunc. *Traité theorique et pratique de le responsabilité civile délictuelle et contractuelle*, I, 6th edn (1965).
McKerron	R.G. McKerron, *The Law of Delict*, 7th edn (1971).
M.D.R.	*Monatschrift für Deutsches Recht*.
Medicus	Dieter Medicus, *Bürgerliches Recht*, 9th edn (1979).
M.L.R.	*Modern Law Review*.
Monier	R. Monier, *Manuel élémentaire de droit romain*.
Monro	C.H. Monro, *Digest IX. 2, Lex Aquilia* (1898).
N.E.	North Eastern Reporter (American law reports).
N.I.L.Q.	*Northern Ireland Legal Quarterly*.
NJW	*Neue Juristische Wochenschrift*.
N.W.	North Western Reporter (American law reports).
OGH	Oberster Gerichtshof (Austrian Supreme Court).
OLG	Oberlandesgericht a German Court of Appeal).
OR	Swiss Code of Obligations.
P.	Law Reports, Probate Division (1891–).
Pas.	*Pasicrisie Belge* (Belgian law reports).
Pernice	A. Pernice, *Die Lehre der Sachbeschädigungen* (1867).
Planiol et Ripert	M. Planiol et G. Ripert, *Traité pratique de droit civil*, 14 vols., tome VI par P. Esmein (1952).
Prosser	W.L. Prosser, *Law of Torts*, 4th edn (1971).
P. 2d.	Pacific Reporter, 2nd series (American law reports).
Q.B.	Law Reports, Queen's Bench (1891–1900; 1952–).
Q.B.D.	Law Reports, Queen's Bench Division (1875–90).

Rabels Z.	*Rabels Zeitschrift für ausländisches und internationales Recht.*
Rev. crit. jur. Belge	*Revue critique de jurisprudence Belge.*
Rev. crit. lég. et jur.	*Revue critique de législation et de jurisprudence.*
Rev. gén. ass. terr.	*Revue générale des assurances terrestres.*
Rev. hist. dr. fr. et é.	*Revue historique de droit français et étranger.*
Rev. int. dr. ant.	*Revue internationale des droits de l'antiquité* (3rd series, 1954–).
Rev. int. dr. comp.	*Revue internationale de droit comparé.*
Rev. trim. dr. civ.	*Revue trimestrielle de droit civil.*
RGBl.	*Reichsgesetzblatt.*
RGSt.	*Amtliche Sammlung der Entscheidungen des Reichgerichts in Strafsachen.*
RGZ	*Entscheidungen des Reichsgerichts in Zivilsachen* (Decisions of the German Imperial Court in civil matters).
Rotondi, *Scr. Giur.*	G. Rotondi, *Scritti Giuridici* (1922).
RVO	Reichsvericherungsordnung (German Imperial Insurance Ordinance).
S.	*Recueil Sirey.*
S.A.L.J.	*South African Law Journal.*
Savatier	R. Savatier, *Traité de la responsabilité civile en droit français*, 2nd edn (1951).
S.C.	Session Cases (Scottish law reports).
S.D.H.I.	*Studia et Documenta Historiae et Iuris.*
Seuff Arch	Seuffert's Archiv.
S.J.	*La Semaine Juridique* (also referred to as J.C.P. (*Juris-Classeur périodique*)).
S.L.T.	*Scots Law Times.*
So.	Southern Reporter (American law reports).
Somm.	*Sommaire* (summary of French decisions in D.).
So. 2d.	Southern Reporter, 2nd series (American law reports).
StGB	Strafgesetzbuch (German Criminal Code).
StVG	Strassenverkehrsgesetz (German Road Traffic Act).
Starck	Boris Starck, *Droit civil, obligations* (1972).
S.W.	South Western Reporter (American law reports).
Trib. Civ.	Tribunal Civil.
XII T.	The Twelve Tables.
U. of P.L. Rev.	*University of Pennsylvania Law Review.*
Va.L.Rev.	*Virginia Law Review.*

Vand.L.Rev.	*Vanderbilt Law Review.*
VersR.	*Versicherungsrecht.*
Weill and Terré	*Droit civil.* 2nd end (1975).
Weir, *Encyclopedia*	*International Encyclopedia of Comparative Law* (gen. ed. A. Tunc), XI, ch. 12, 'Complex Liabilities' by Tony Weir.
Winfield and Jolowicz	Winfield and Jolowicz on Tort, 11th edn by W.V.H. Rogers (1979).
W.L.R.	Weekly Law Reports.
WM	*Wertpapier-Mitteilungen.*
ZPO	Zivilprozessordnung (Code of Civil Procedure).
Z.S.S.	*Zeitschrift der Savigny-Stiftung für Rechtsegeschichte, Romanistische Abteilung.*
Zweigert and Kötz	K. Zweigert and H. Kötz, *An Introduction to Comparative Law*, II, *The Institutions of Private Law* (translated by Tony Weir, 1977).

PART IA
Digest 9,2 on the *lex Aquilia*

1. ULPIAN *in the 18th book on the Edict*. The *lex Aquilia* partially repealed every preceding statute which spoke of unlawful damage, whether it was the Twelve Tables or any other enactment. These statutes need not now be mentioned. s. 1. Now the *lex Aquilia* is a plebiscite, Aquilius, a tribune of the plebs, having procured its enactment by the plebs.

2. GAIUS *in the 7th book on the Provincial Edict*. The *lex Aquilia* provides in its first chapter: 'If anyone kills unlawfully a slave of either sex belonging to another or a four-footed animal of the kind called *pecudes*, let him be ordered to pay the owner whatever was the highest value of the victim in that year': s. 1. and then below this stands a provision that the action against a defendant who denied liability should be for double the value. s. 2. Thus it appears that the statute assimilates to our slaves four-footed animals which belong to the class of *pecudes* and are kept in herds, such as sheep, goats, horses, mules, and asses. But there is a question whether pigs are included under the term *pecudes*: and Labeo rightly holds that they are. But a dog does not fall within *pecudes*. Still less are wild beasts in that class, such as bears, lions, and panthers. Elephants, however, and camels are so to speak 'mixed', for on the one hand they do service as draught animals but on the other are wild by nature, and so they should be included in the first chapter.

3. ULPIAN *in the 18th book on the Edict*. If a slave of either sex is killed unlawfully, the *lex Aquilia* applies. It is rightly added that the killing must be wrongful; for killing is not enough, it must have been done wrongfully.

4. GAIUS *in the 7th book on the Provincial Edict*. So if I kill your slave who is lying in wait to rob me, I shall be safe: for natural reason allows a person to defend himself against danger. s. 1. The law of the Twelve Tables allows one to kill a thief caught at night, provided that warning is given by a shout: but it allows one to kill a person caught by day only if he defends himself with a weapon, provided still that warning is given by a shout.

5. ULPIAN *in the 18th book on the Edict*. Further, if one kills anyone else, whoever he may be, who is going for him with a sword, he will not be held to kill wrongfully: and if in fear of death one kills a thief, assuredly he will not be liable under the *lex Aquilia*. But if when he could have arrested him, he preferred to kill him, the better opinion is that he should be held to have acted unlawfully: accordingly he will also be liable under the *lex Cornelia*. s. 1. Now we must not understand *iniuria* here as some kind of insult, as in the *actio iniuriarum*, but as something that is done not according to law, in short, contrary to law, that is, if one kills negligently (*culpa*): and so the two actions, on the *lex Aquilia* and for *iniuriae*, sometimes concur, but there will be two assessments of damages, one for damage, the other for insult. We shall therefore take *iniuria* to mean here damage caused negligently (*culpa*) even by one who intended no harm. s. 2. Hence the question, whether there is an action on the *lex Aquilia* if a lunatic does damage. Pegasus denies it: for what negligence, he asks, can there be in him, seeing that he is not in his right mind? This is perfectly true. Accordingly the Aquilian action will fail, just as it fails if an animal does damage or a tile falls. Further, we must say the same if an *infans* does damage. But if it is done by an *impubes*, Labeo says that, since he is liable for theft, he is also liable to the Aquilian action: and this I regard as correct, if he is able to distinguish right from wrong. s. 3. If a teacher in the course of instruction wounds or kills a slave, is he liable under the *lex Aquilia* as having done unlawful damage? Julian writes that a man was held liable under the *lex Aquilia* who had put out a pupil's eye in the course of instruction: much more therefore must the same view be taken if he kills him. Now he puts the following case: a shoemaker, he says, when a boy who was learning under him, a freeborn *filiusfamilias*, did rather badly what he gave him to do, struck at his neck with a last, so that the boy's eye was put out. Accordingly Julian says that the *actio iniuriarum* does not lie, because he struck the blow not intending to insult but to correct and instruct: he inclines to think that the *actio ex locato* lies, since only slight punishment is permitted to a teacher: but I have no doubt that an action can be brought on the *lex Aquilia*:

6. PAUL *in the 22nd book on the Edict*. For excessive brutality in a teacher is counted as negligence.

7. ULPIAN *in the 18th book on the Edict*. And in this action he says that the father will recover his prospective loss of profit from the son's services through the eye being destroyed, and the expenses incurred in

medical attendance. s. 1. Now we must take killing to mean whether someone hit him with a sword or even a stick or other weapon or the hands (if, for instance, he strangled him) or kicked or butted or in any way whatever. s. 2. But if one who is overloaded throws down his burden and kills a slave, the Aquilian action lies: for it was in his discretion not to burden himself so. For even if a man slips and crushes another's slave with his burden, Pegasus says that he is liable under the *lex Aquilia*, provided he loaded himself unduly or carelessly walked through a slippery place. s. 3. Hence if a man does damage through being pushed by another, Proculus writes that neither is the one who pushed liable, because he did not kill, nor the one who was pushed, because he did not do the damage unlawfully: and on this view an action *in factum* must be given against the one who pushed. s. 4. If one man kills another in wrestling or in the *pancratium*, or in a boxing-match, if the one kills the other in a public contest, the Aquilian action does not lie, because the damage is held to have been done in the cause of fame and valour, not of wrongdoing. However, this does not operate in the case of a slave, since it is the custom only for freeborn persons to enter the contest: but it operates if a *filiusfamilias* is wounded. Of course, if a man wounds one who has given in, the Aquilian action lies, or if he kills a slave not a party to a contest, except where it happens in a case where the master puts the slave up to fight: for then the Aquilian action fails. s. 5. But if one gives a slight blow to a sick slave and he dies, Labeo rightly says that he is liable under the *lex Aquilia*, because different things are fatal to different people. s. 6. Now Celsus says it makes a great deal of difference whether a person kills or furnishes a cause of death, seeing that one who furnishes a cause of death is liable, not to the Aquilian action but to an action *in factum*. Thus he mentions the case of a man who gave poison instead of medicine and says that he furnished a cause of death, just like one who holds out a sword to a lunatic: for this man is not liable under the *lex Aquilia* either, but to an action *in factum*. s. 7. But if a man throws someone off a bridge, Celsus says that, whether he dies from the impact or is at once drowned, or is overcome by the force of the current and dies from exhaustion, the offender is liable under the *lex Aquilia*, just as if someone had dashed a boy against a stone. s. 8. Proculus says, if a doctor operates unskilfully on a slave, an action lies either *ex locato* or under the *lex Aquilia*.

8. GAIUS *in the 7th book on the Provincial Edict.* The law is the same if he makes a wrong use of a drug. Moreover, one who operates

properly and then omits further treatment will not get off free but is considered guilty of negligence. s. 1. Again, where a mule-driver through inexperience is unable to hold in his mules, if they run over another's slave, he is commonly said to be liable on the ground of negligence. The same is said also if he cannot hold his mules on account of weakness; and it does not seem unjust that weakness should be accounted negligence, since no one should undertake a task in which he knows or ought to know that his weakness will be dangerous to another. The law is the same for one who through inexperience or weakness cannot hold in a horse on which he is riding.

9. ULPIAN *in the 18th book on the Edict*. Again if a midwife gives a woman a drug from which she dies, Labeo draws this distinction, that if she administered it with her own hands, she is held to have killed. but if she gave it to the woman for her to take it herself, an action *in factum* must be given; and this opinion is correct, for she furnished a cause of death rather than killed. s. 1. If, by force or suasion, one administers a drug to anyone, whether by draught or by injection, or rubs him with a poisonous preparation, he is liable under the *lex Aquilia*, just as the midwife is liable who administers a drug. s. 2. If a man starves a slave to death, Neratius says he is liable to an action *in factum*. s. 3. If my slave is riding a horse and by frightening the horse you cause him to be thrown into a river so that he perishes, Ofilius writes that an action *in factum* must be given: just as if my slave is led into an ambush by one man and killed by another. s. 4. But if persons are throwing javelins by way of sport and a slave is killed, the Aquilian action lies: but if when others are throwing javelins in a field, a slave crosses it, the Aquilian action fails, because he ought not to have made his way at an inopportune time across the field used for javelin-throwing. However, anyone who deliberately aims at him is, of course, liable to the Aquilian action;

10. PAUL *in the 22nd book on the Edict*. For negligence also includes taking part in a mischievous sport.

11. ULPIAN *in the 18th book on the Edict*. Again Mela writes: if, when people were playing at ball, one of them hit a ball rather hard and knocked it against the hands of a barber so that a slave whom the barber was shaving had his throat cut by reason of the razor being jerked against it, in such a case whoever of them is negligent is liable under the *lex Aquilia*. Proculus says the negligence is the barber's; and certainly if he was shaving at a place where people were accustomed to play or where there was heavy traffic, some blame must be attributed

to him; though it is well said that if a person entrusts himself to a barber who has his chair in a dangerous place, he has only himself to blame. s. 1. If one man held a slave and another killed him, the one who held him is liable to an action *in factum*, on the ground that he furnished a cause of death. s. 2. But if several persons strike a slave, let us see whether all are liable as having killed him. And if it appears by whose blow he perished, that person is liable as having killed him: but if it does not, Julian says that all are liable as having killed him, and if one is sued, the others are not released; for under the *lex Aquilia* what one man pays does not relieve another, since what is paid is a penalty. s. 3. Celsus writes that if one man gives a slave a mortal wound, and another afterwards deprives him of life, the former is not liable as having killed, but as having wounded, because he died of a different wound, but the latter is liable as having killed. And Marcellus agrees with this and it is the better view. s. 4. If several persons let fall a beam and crush a slave, the older jurists held that they are all equally liable under the *lex Aquilia*. s. 5. Again, Proculus gave an opinion that an action on the *lex Aquilia* lay against a person who had incited a dog and caused it to bite someone, even though he was not holding it: but Julian says that only a person who holds it and causes it to bite someone is liable to the Aquilian action: but if he did not hold it, the action must be *in factum*. s. 6. Now the action on the *lex Aquilia* belongs to the *erus*, that is, the owner. s. 7. If wrongful damage is done to a slave whom I was about to restore to you by way of redhibition, Julian says that I have the action on the *lex Aquilia* and I shall assign it to you when I proceed to make the redhibition. s. 8. But if a slave is in the service of a *bona fide* possessor, has the latter the Aquilian action? And the better view is that the action to be given is *in factum*. s. 9. Julian says that one to whom clothes have been lent cannot bring the Aquilian action if they are torn, but the action belongs to the owner. s. 10. Julian discusses whether a usufructuary or a usuary has the action on the *lex Aquilia*: I think it is better to give an *actio utilis* in these circumstances.

12. PAUL *in the 10th book on Sabinus.* Moreover, if the owner wounds or kills a slave in whom I have the usufruct, I ought to be given an action against him on the analogy of the *lex Aquilia* according to the proportionate value of my usufruct, in such a way that even the part of the year before I had the usufruct is to be taken into account in assessing the penalty.

13. ULPIAN *in the 18th book on the Edict.* A freeman has a *utilis actio*

on the *lex Aquilia* on his own account; he has not a direct action, since no one is considered owner of his own limbs. However, the owner has one on account of a runaway slave. s. 1. Julian writes that, if a free man acts as a *bona fide* slave to me, he is liable to me under the *lex Aquilia* in his own person. s. 2. Where a slave belonging to an inheritance is killed, it is a question who may bring the Aquilian action, seeing that such a slave has no owner. And Celsus says the *lex* meant the damage to be made good to the owner, and therefore the inheritance will be regarded as owner. Accordingly once the inheritance has been entered on, the heir can sue. s. 3. If a slave who has been left as a legacy is killed after the inheritance has been entered on, the action on the *lex Aquilia* belongs to the legatee, provided he did not accept the legacy after the death of the slave: but if he refused it, Julian says that it follows that the action belongs to the heir.

14. PAUL *in the 22nd book on the Edict*. But if the heir himself kills him, it has been said that an action must be given against him to the legatee.

15. ULPIAN *in the 18th book on the Edict*. From the passage in Julian it follows that, if the bequeathed slave is killed before entry is made on the inheritance, the Aquilian action acquired through the inheritance remains with the heir. But if he is wounded before the entry, the action remained part of the inheritance, but the heir must assign it to the legatee. s. 1. If a mortally wounded slave afterwards, by the fall of a house or a shipwreck or some other kind of blow, dies sooner than he would have done, an action cannot be brought for killing, but for wounding; but if he dies from the wound after being manumitted or alienated, Julian says an action can be brought for killing. And the reason for the difference is that the truth is that he was killed by you at the time when you wounded him, though this came to light only when he died; whereas in the former case the fall of the house did not allow it to come to light whether he was killed. But if you direct that he shall be free and your heir, and he then dies, his heir cannot sue on the *lex Aquilia*.

16. MARCIAN *in the 4th book of rules*. Because the matter reached a stage where an action cannot arise.

17. ULPIAN *in the 18th book on the Edict*. If a master kills his own slave, he will be liable in an action *in factum* to a *bona fide* possessor or pledgee.

18. PAUL *in the 10th book on Sabinus*. Moreover if a pledgee kills or wounds a slave, he can be sued both under the *lex Aquilia* and by the

action of pledge, but the plaintiff will have to be content with one of the two actions.

19. ULPIAN *in the 18th book on the Edict*. But if a man kills a slave whom he owns in common with another, Celsus says he is liable to the Aquilian action; it is the same if he wounds him:

20. ULPIAN *in the 42nd book in Sabinus*. That is, in proportion to the share that belongs to the plaintiff.

21. ULPIAN *in the 18th book on the Edict*. The *lex* says: 'whatever was the highest value of that slave in that year'. And this clause contains the method of valuing the damage done. s. 1. Now the year is reckoned backwards from the time when a man was killed: but if he was mortally wounded and died later after a long interval, we shall, according to Julian, reckon the year from the time when he was wounded, though Celsus writes to the contrary. s. 2. But do we value only his person, at what it was worth when he was killed, or rather our interest in his not being killed? And the rule we follow is to value the interest.

22. PAUL *in the 22nd book on the Edict*. Thus if you have killed a slave whom I have promised to deliver under a penalty my interest comes into account in this action. s. 1. Further, elements of value attaching to the object are taken into account, if one kills one of a troupe of actors or singers, or one of twins or of a chariot team or of a pair of mules; for not only must a valuation be made of the object destroyed, but account must also be taken of the amount by which the other objects have been depreciated.

23. ULPIAN *in the 18th book on the Edict*. Hence Neratius writes that if a slave who has been instituted heir is killed, the value of the inheritance comes into account too. s. 1. Julian says, if a person has directed that a slave shall be free and his heir, and the slave is killed, neither the substitute nor the statutory heir will recover in the action on the *lex Aquilia* the value of the inheritance, which the slave himself did not manage to acquire; and this view is correct. Therefore he says that only his market value will be taken into account, because that alone would be considered to be the substitute's interest; however, I think that not even the market value is taken into account, since if he had become heir he would also have been free. s. 2. The same Julian writes that, if I am instituted heir on condition of manumitting Stichus and Stichus is killed after the testator's death, I shall also recover as part of the damages the value of the inheritance; for the condition failed by reason of the killing. But if he is killed in the testator's

lifetime, there is no valuation of the inheritance, since we look backwards for the highest value. s. 3. The same Julian writes that the valuation of the slave killed is made with reference to the time when he was worth most in that year; and so even if a valuable painter has his thumb cut off and within a year of the injury is killed, the owner can bring the Aquilian action and the slave must be valued at his price before he had lost his thumb and with it his skill. s. 4. Moreover, if a slave is killed who had committed great falsifications in my accounts and whom I had intended to put to torture in order to extract the names of his accomplices, Labeo very properly writes that he must be valued at the interest I had in discovering the slave's frauds, that is, those committed through him, not at the value of the harm done by that slave. s. 5. Moreover, if an honest slave changes his character within the year and is killed, his value will be reckoned at what he was worth before he changed his character. s. 6. In short, we must say that all such advantages as would make the slave more valuable within the year in which he was killed are added to his value. s. 7. If a child under a year old is killed, the better opinion is that this action will meet the case, the valuation being referred to the part of the year he lived. s. 8. It is settled that this action is also given to the heir and all other successors: but this action will not be given against the heir, etc., since it is penal, unless the heir should happen to become richer through the damage. s. 9. If a slave is killed maliciously, it is settled that the owner can also proceed under the *lex Cornelia*; and if he sues under the *lex Aquilia*, the Cornelian action ought not to be prejudged. s. 10. This action lies against one who confesses for simple damages, for double against one who denies liability. s. 11. If a person wrongly confesses that he has killed a slave who is still alive and is afterwards prepared to show that he is alive, Julian writes that the Aquilian action fails, although he confessed that he killed; for the action on a confession only relieves the plaintiff of the necessity of showing that the person who killed was the defendant: but it is required that the slave should have been killed by someone or other.

24. PAUL *in the 22nd book on the Edict*. This is more obvious in the case of a wounded slave; for if a party confesses that he wounded, but the slave was not wounded, what wound shall we value, or what time are we to go back to?

25. ULPIAN *in the 18th book on the Edict*. Thus if the slave was not killed, but is nevertheless dead, the better view is that the party is not liable in respect of the dead slave, although he has confessed. s. 1. If a

procurator or tutor or curator or anyone else confesses that the absent principal did the wounding, an *actio utilis* on a confession must be given against them. s. 2. It should be noted that in this action which is given against one who confesses, the judge is appointed not in order to decide the case, but to assess the damages; for there is no scope for the function of deciding in proceedings against those who confess.

26. PAUL *in the 22nd book on the Edict.* For suppose that the defendant confesses that he has killed and is prepared to pay the sum assessed, but his adversary assesses his claim at a very high figure.

27. ULPIAN *in the 18th book on the Edict.* If a slave carries off and kills another's slave, both Julian and Celsus write that the actions both of theft and of wrongful damage lie. s. 1. If a common slave, that is, belonging to you and me, kills my slave, the *lex Aquilia* applies against you, if he did it with your consent; and Urseius reports that this was Proculus' view. But he adds that if he acted without your consent, there is no noxal action, lest it should be in the power of the slave to serve you alone; which I think correct. s. 2. Again, if a slave common to you and me is killed by Titius' slave, Celsus writes that if either of the owners sues, either he will recover a proportion of the value assessed or noxal surrender will have to be made to him of the slave as a whole, since such a proceeding does not admit of division. s. 3. Now if a slave kills, it is the owner who is liable on his account, but not a person whom he is serving in good faith. But it is a question whether the owner is liable on account of a fugitive slave; Julian says he is liable, and this is perfectly true, since even Marcellus agrees. s. 4. The second chapter of this *lex* has become obsolete. s. 5. Now in the third chapter the *lex Aquilia* goes on to say: 'In respect of all other things, besides slaves or cattle killed, if anyone does damage to another by wrongfully burning, breaking or breaking off, whatever the matter in issue shall turn out to be worth in the next thirty days, so much let him be condemned to pay to the owner.' s. 6. If therefore a man does not kill, but burn, fracture, or break a slave or cattle, there is no doubt that it is under these words of the *lex* that the action must be brought. Accordingly if you throw a torch at my slave and scorch him, you will be liable to me. s. 7. Again if you set fire to my plantation or country house, I shall have the Aquilian action. s. 8. If someone intended to burn down my tenement house and the fire spreads to that of a neighbour, he will be liable in the Aquilian action to the neighbour also; he will also be liable no less to the tenants on account of any of their goods that have been burnt. s. 9. If a tenant's slave, a stoker, fell

asleep at the furnace and the country house is burnt down, Neratius writes that the tenant must fulfil his obligation under the contract of letting and hiring, supposing he was negligent in his choice of labour; but if one man lit the furnace and another watched it negligently, will the one who lit it be liable? For the one who watched it did nothing, while the one who lit it in the proper way was not at fault. What then are we to say? I think that an *actio utilis* lies against both the man who fell asleep at the furnace and the man who negligently watched it; nor can anyone say that the man who fell asleep was overtaken by a natural human weakness, because his duty was either to put out the fire or to make certain that it should not spread. s. 10. If you have an oven against a wall held in common with your neighbour, are you liable for wrongful damage? And Proculus says there can be no action, because there would be none against one who had a fire-place; and so I think the fairer course is to give an action *in factum*, supposing, that is, the wall is burnt down. If, however, you have not yet done me any damage, but you keep your fire in such a way as to cause me to fear that you will do me damage, I think the undertaking against threatened damage will suffice. S. 11. Proculus says that where the slaves of a tenant have burnt down the country house, the tenant is liable either on the contract of letting and hiring or on the *lex Aquilia*, the tenant being at liberty to make noxal surrender of the slaves; and if the matter is decided in one action, the other can no longer be brought. But this applies only if the tenant was not at fault: if, on the other hand, he had slaves who were likely to do harm, he is liable for wrongful damage, because he had that kind of slave. The same rule must be observed, he writes, as to the tenants in a tenement house. s. 12. If my bees fly off to join yours, and you fire them, Celsus says that the action on the *lex Aquilia* lies. s. 13. The *lex* says '*ruperit*'. Almost all the older jurists understood the word to mean '*corruperit*' (spoils). s. 14. And so Celsus asks, if you sow tares or wild oats in another's crop, so that you spoil it, not only can the interdict *quod vi aut clam* be brought by the owner or, if the field is let, the tenant, but there is also an action *in factum*, and if the *colonus* brings it, he must give an undertaking that there will be no further proceedings, that is, lest the owner should give further trouble; for it is one kind of damage to spoil or alter something in itself, so as to give ground for an action on the *lex Aquilia*, and quite another where, without altering the thing itself, something else is added which it would be a nuisance to have to separate. s. 15. Of course the Aquilian action, Celsus says, can be brought against a man who adulterates wine or spills it or turns it into vinegar or otherwise worsens it, because even spilling and turning into vinegar are included in the term *corrumpere* (spoil). s. 16. And he admits that fracturing and burning are included in the term 'spoiling' but he says that there is nothing new in a statute enumerating certain things specifically and then adding a general word which embraces the specific things; and this opinion is correct. s. 17. We shall certainly hold that the term *rumpere* applies to one who wounds, or strikes with a rod or a lash or his fist or a weapon or anything else, so as to cut a slave's skin, or makes a bruise, but only if he causes loss. But if he makes the slave in no way less valuable or useful, the Aquilian action does not apply and only the *actio iniuriarum* will have to be brought; for in the Aquilian action one can claim only for those cases of breaking which cause loss. It also follows that if, although the slave has not been rendered less valuable, expense has been incurred in restoring him to health and safety, to this extent, in my opinion, damage has been done; and so an action can be brought under the *lex Aquilia*. s. 18. If a man tears or spots clothes, he is liable to the Aquilian action, for breaking. s. 19. Moreover, if a man pours out my millet or corn into a river, an action on the *lex Aquilia* is applicable. s. 20. Again, if a man mixes sand or something else with corn, so that it is hard to separate them, an action can be brought as it were for spoiling. s. 21. If a man knocks coins out of my hand, Sabinus thinks there is an action for wrongful damage, provided they are lost so that they come into nobody's hands, for instance if they fall into a river or the sea or a drain; but if they come into anybody's hands, an action lies for aiding and abetting a theft; and the old jurists held this too. The same writer says that an action *in factum* can also be given. s. 22. If a slave woman or a mare has a miscarriage from your blow, Brutus says you are liable to an Aquilian action as it were for breaking. s. 23. And he adds that if a man overloads a mule and breaks part of its body, the Aquilian action lies. s. 24. If a man scuttles a merchant vessel, there is an action on the *lex Aquilia* for breaking, so Vivianus writes. s. 25. If a man picks unripe olives or cuts an unripe crop or grapes, he will be liable to the Aquilian action; but if they are ripe, the Aquilian action does not lie; for no wrong has been done, since he has made you a present of the expense that is incurred in gathering such a crop. But if he removes the crop he has gathered, he is liable for theft. As for the grapes, Octavenus adds, 'unless he threw them on the ground so that they became a total loss'. s. 26. He writes the same about coppice, that if it is immature, he is liable to the Aquilian action, but if he takes twigs which are ready for cutting, he is liable for theft and for cutting trees by stealth. s. 27. If you cut mature pollard willows so as not to injure the trunk, the Aquilian action does not lie. s. 28. And if a man castrates a slave boy, and so increases his value, Vivian writes that the Aquilian action does not lie, but one should bring the *actio iniuriarum* or sue under the edict of the aediles or for four times the value. s. 29. If you give a cup to a jeweller to be filigreed, he will be liable for wrongful damage if he breaks it through lack of skill, but if he broke it not from lack of skill but because it had cracks which made it unsuitable, he may be excused; and so workmen usually contract, when things of this kind are entrusted to them, that they shall not do it at their own risk, and this takes away any right of action on the contract of letting and hiring or under the *lex Aquilia*. s. 30. If a husband gives his wife unstrung pearls for her use and against the will or without the knowledge of her husband she pierces them, in order, when bored through, to wear them on a string, she is liable under the *lex Aquilia*, whether she is divorced or is still married. s. 31. If a man breaks down or breaks open my doors or demolishes the building itself, he is liable under the *lex Aquilia*. s. 32. If a man demolishes my aqueduct, although the materials which are demolished are mine, yet because the land over which I bring the water is not mine, it is better to say that an *actio utilis* should be given. s. 33. If a stone falls from a cart and breaks to pieces or fractures something, it is agreed that the carter is liable to an action on the *lex Aquilia*, if the stones fell because he packed them badly. s. 34. If a man hires a slave to drive a mule and entrusts it to him, and, the slave having tied the mule to his thumb by its halter, the mule breaks away so violently as to tear the slave's thumb off and dash itself over a height, Mela writes that if an inexperienced slave was let out as an experienced one, an action can be brought on the contract of hiring against his owner for the breaking or disabling of the mule; but if the mule was excited by someone striking or frightening it, then the owner, that is, the mule's, as well as the owner of the slave, will have an action on the *lex Aquilia* against the man who excited it. It seems to me, however, that in the case where there is an action on the contract of letting, the action on the *lex Aquilia* also lies. s. 35. Again, if you let out a cistern full of wine to a plasterer to be mended and he makes a hole in it so that the wine runs out, Labeo writes that an action *in factum* should be brought.

28. PAUL *in the 10th book on Sabinus.* Those who make pits in

order to catch bears and deer are liable under the *lex Aquilia* if they have made them where people pass and something falls in and is injured; but if they have made them in other places where it is customary to make them, they are not liable. s. 1. However, this action will be given only for cause shown, that is if there was no warning and the plaintiff was unaware of and could not foresee the danger; and many cases of the kind are to be found where the plaintiff is defeated, if he could have avoided the danger;

29. ULPIAN *in the 18th book on the Edict.* as where you set traps in a place where you had no right to set them, and a neighbour's cattle fall into them. s. 1. If you cut off a projecting roof of mine which I had without any right over your house, Proculus writes that I can sue you for wrongful damage; for you ought to have brought an action against me claiming that I had no right to have the projection; nor is it fair that I should suffer damage from your cutting off my beams. A different decision is contained in a rescript of the Emperor Severus, who ruled that a person through whose house a water-pipe had been laid without any servitude could of his own right break it up, and very properly, the difference being that the former made the projection on his own land, whereas the latter did what he did on another's. s. 2. If your ship collides with my boat and causes me damage, the question has been asked which action I have. And Proculus says that if it was in the power of the sailors to avoid the collision and it happened through their negligence, an action can be brought against the sailors under the *lex Aquilia*, since it matters little whether you do damage by driving your ship at my boat or by steadying your helm too soon or with your own hands, since in all these ways I suffer damage directly caused by you; but if a rope broke or the ship collided when it was under nobody's control, no action can be brought against the owner. s. 3. Again, Labeo writes that if a ship is driven by the force of the wind against the anchor-ropes of another and the sailors cut the ropes, no action should be allowed if the ship could be got loose in no other way than by cutting the ropes. And Labeo and Proculus took the same view about fishermen's nets in which a fishing-vessel had become caught. Of course if it had happened through the negligence of the sailors, an action can be brought under the *lex Aquilia*. But where an action is brought for wrongful damage to nets, no valuation is made of the fish that were not caught on account of the injury, since it is uncertain whether they would have been caught. The same is true of hunters and bird-catchers. s. 4. If a ship runs down another coming

towards it, Alfenus says that an action for wrongful damage lies against the steersman or the captain; but if the ship was being driven with such force that it could not be controlled, no action is to be given against the owner; but if it happened through the negligence of the sailors, I think the Aquilian action is available. s. 5. If a man cuts a rope by which a ship was moored, an action *in factum* can be brought for the ship which is lost. s. 6. The action under this chapter of the *lex* can be brought for damage to all animals which are not *pecudes*, for instance a dog; and the same can be said of boars and lions and all other wild beasts and birds. s. 7. Municipal magistrates can be made liable to the Aquilian action if they do wrongful damage. Also if one of them takes cattle in execution and starves them to death, refusing to let you take food to them, an action must be given *in factum*. Again, if he thinks he is levying execution under a statute but does not really act under the statute, and he returns the goods in a worn and spoilt condition, the *lex Aquilia* is said to apply; indeed the same must be said even if he did levy execution under the statute. If, however, a magistrate acts rather violently against one who resists, he will not be liable to the Aquilian action; for even where he has taken a slave in execution and the latter hangs himself, no action is given. s. 8. It is settled that the words 'whatever was the value in the last thirty days', although they lack the word 'highest', must nevertheless be understood in that sense.

30. PAUL *in the 22nd book on the Edict*. A man who kills someone else's slave taken in the act of adultery will not be liable under this *lex*. s. 1. If a slave who has been given as a pledge is killed, the debtor has the action. But it is asked whether the creditor also should be given an *actio utilis*, because he may have an interest on the ground that the debtor is insolvent or his own action on the debt is barred by lapse of time. But it is unfair that the defendant should be liable to both owner and creditor; unless one should consider that in a case like this the debtor will suffer no wrong, since the satisfaction of the creditor is of advantage to him so far as the amount of the debt is concerned, and he will recover the surplus from the wrongdoer, or perhaps the debtor ought to be given an action from the start for the amount by which the damages exceed the debt. And so in those cases in which the creditor is to be given an action because of the poverty of the debtor or because his action has been barred, the creditor will have the action on the *lex Aquilia* up to the amount of the debt, so that this benefits the debtor, but the debtor himself has the action on the *lex Aquilia* for the excess over the amount of the debt. s. 2. If a man consumes another's wine or

corn, he does not appear to do wrongful damage, and so an *actio utilis* ought to be given. s. 3. In this action also which arises from this title malice and negligence are punished; and so if a man sets fire to his stubble or thorns in order to burn them up, and the fire escapes and spreads so as to harm another's crop or vineyard, we are to ask whether it occurred through his want of skill or negligence. For if he did it on a windy day, he is guilty of negligence (for even a person who furnishes an opportunity for damage is held to do damage): the same charge can be brought against one who did not see to it that the fire did not spread. But if he saw to everything he should have done or a sudden gust of wind spread the fire, he is free from negligence. s. 4. If a slave is wounded, but not mortally, and he dies from neglect, the action will be for wounding, not killing.

31. PAUL *in the 10th book on Sabinus.* If a pruner by throwing down a branch off a tree or a man on a scaffolding kills a passing slave, he is liable only if it falls on to a public place and he failed to shout so that the accident could be avoided. But Mucius said that even if the same thing happened on private property, an action can be brought on the ground of negligence; for he held it to be negligence where what could have been foreseen by a diligent man was not foreseen or warning was given too late for the danger to be avoided. On this reasoning it does not matter much whether the victim was making his way across public or private land, as people commonly enough make their way across private places. But if there is no path, he ought to be liable only for malice, so that he must not aim at one whom he sees passing; for he is not to be held to account for negligence, when he could not have guessed that someone would pass through that place.

32. GAIUS *in the 7th book on the Provincial Edict.* It has been asked whether the proconsul's practice in relation to a theft committed by a gang of slaves (that is, that a demand for the penalty is not to be allowed in respect of each slave, but that it is enough if payment is made of what would have been paid had one free man committed the theft) ought also to be observed in an action for wrongful damage. But the opinion has prevailed that the same rule should be observed, and rightly; for the reasoning in regard to theft is that the owner ought not to lose his whole household on account of one delict, and this reasoning applying likewise to the action for wrongful damage, it follows that the same assessment should be made, especially as this form of delict is sometimes less serious, as when the damage is done negligently and not maliciously. s. 1. If the same person wounds the

same slave and afterwards also kills him, he will be liable for both wounding and killing; for there are two delicts. This case is different from that where a person kills somebody by inflicting several wounds in the course of the same attack; for then there will be one action for killing.

33. PAUL *in the 2nd book on Plautius*. If you kill my slave, I do not think that personal feelings should be taken into account, as if someone kills your natural son whom you would be willing to buy for a high price, but only what he would be worth to all the world. Sextus Pedius agrees that the prices of things are taken not in accordance with the personal feelings or convenience of individuals, but in a general way; and accordingly that one who possesses his natural son is none the richer because he would be prepared to redeem him for a very large sum if someone else possessed him, nor has a man who possesses another's son got an amount of wealth equivalent to what he could sell him for to his father. For under the *lex Aquilia* we recover the amount of damage; and we shall be held to have lost either what we could have gained or what we are forced to expend. s. 1. For damage which is not included in the *lex Aquilia* an action is given *in factum*.

34. MARCELLUS *in the 20th book of digests*. Stichus was bequeathed to Titius and Seius; while Seius was making up his mind, but after Titius had vindicated the legacy, Stichus was killed; then Seius repudiated the legacy. Titius can sue just as if he were sole legatee,

35. ULPIAN *in the 18th book on the Edict*. Because his ownership by accrual is held to relate back:

36. MARCELLUS *in the 20th book of digests*. For just as where a legatee repudiates a legacy the heir has an action as if the slave had not been bequeathed, so Titius has the action as if he were sole legatee. s. 1. If the owner orders that a slave mortally wounded by Titius be free and his heir, and afterwards Maevius becomes heir to the slave, Maevius will not have an action under the *lex Aquilia* against Titius, not, that is, according to the opinion of Sabinus, who thought that an action could not be transmitted to the heir which could not have been available to the deceased; and indeed it would be an absurd result that the heir should recover for the killing of the person to whom he succeeded as heir. But if he orders the slave to be part-heir and free, the latter's co-heir will be able to sue under the *lex Aquilia* on his death.

37. JAVOLENUS *in the 14th book from Cassius*. If a free man has committed an injury with his own hand by the order of another, the

action under the *lex Aquilia* lies against the one who gave the order, provided he had a right to command; but if he had not, the actual doer must be sued. s. 1. If a quadruped on account of which an action lay against the owner on the ground of *pauperies* has been killed and an action is brought against the wrongdoer, the assessment must be made in relation, not to the quadruped's physical but to its juristic condition, in which the action for *pauperies* is involved, and the person who killed it must be condemned in the action under the *lex Aquilia* to pay the amount by which it would have benefited the owner to make noxal surrender rather than pay the assessed damages.

38. JAVOLENUS *in the 9th book of letters.* If during the time when my slave whom you bought in good faith was in your service, he was wounded by a slave of yours, it is agreed that in any case I can properly sue you under the *lex Aquilia*.

39. POMPONIUS *in the 17th book on Quintus Mucius.* Quintus Mucius writes: a mare was grazing in another's field and, being pregnant, miscarried while she was being driven off: it was asked whether her owner could sue under the *lex Aquilia* the man who had driven her off, for injuring the mare in striking her. If he had struck her or purposely driven her too violently, it was held that the owner could sue. s. 1. Pomponius. Although a person finds someone else's cattle on his land, he is bound to drive them off in the same way as if what he had found was his own, since if he has suffered any damage from them, he has the appropriate actions. And so a person who finds another's cattle on his land has no right to impound them and is not allowed to drive them otherwise than as we have said above, that is, as if they were his own; he must either drive them off without harming them or give notice to the owner to come and get them.

40. PAUL *in the 3rd book on the Edict.* Under the *lex Aquilia*, if I allege that a chirograph of mine has been erased in which it was recorded that a sum of money was owed me on a condition, and for the time being I am able to prove this by witnesses as well, who may not be available when the condition is fulfilled, and if after a brief exposition I can bring the judge to presume the truth of the story, I ought to win; but the execution of the judgment will be permitted only when the condition of the debt is fulfilled, and if it fails, the judgment will have no effect.

41. ULPIAN *in the 41st book on Sabinus.* If a man erases a will, let us see if the action for wrongful damage lies. And Marcellus in the fifth book of his *Digest* after hesitation denies that it lies; for how, says he,

are you going to make a start with the assessment of damages? I made a note in his book to the effect that this was indeed true of the testator, because his interest could not be valued, but that on the other hand it was different for the heir or the legatees, to whom wills are almost equivalent to chirographs. In the same place Marcellus writes that the action under the *lex Aquilia* lies when a chirograph is erased. Moreover, if a man erases or reads out in the presence of several people the tablets of a will which have been deposited with him, the better plan is to bring an *actio in factum* or an *actio iniuriarum*, if he published the secrets of one's last will with an insulting intention. s. 1. Pomponius neatly remarks that it sometimes happens that a man does not make himself liable for theft by erasing a document, but only for wrongful damage, for example, if he did it intending to commit not a theft, but only wrongful damage; for he will not be liable for theft, since theft requires the act to be accompanied by an intent to steal.

42. JULIAN *in the 48th book of digests.* If a person who has had deposited with him the tablets of a will or some document of title erases it so that it cannot be read, he is liable to an action of deposit and also *ad exhibendum*, on the ground that he returned or produced the thing in a spoilt condition. The action under the *lex Aquilia* also lies in the same case; for it is also truly said of a man who has falsified a document that he has spoilt it.

43. POMPONIUS *in the 19th book on Sabinus.* For damage done to property belonging to an inheritance before you entered on the inheritance you have an action under the *lex Aquilia*, although it happened after the death of the person whose heir you are; for the *lex Aquilia* applies the term 'owner' not simply to the one who was owner when the damage was done; for in that way the action could not even be transmitted to the heir from the person whose heir he is; and you could not after your return by *postliminium* sue for what had been done whilst you were in the power of the enemy; nor could a different rule be laid down without great injustice to posthumous children who become heirs to their fathers. We shall say the same also about trees secretly cut during the same period. I think the same can be said also of the action *quod vi aut clam*, provided a person acts after being told not to, or it is shown that he ought to have understood that he would be warned by those to whom the inheritance belonged, if they had known of his intention.

44. ULPIAN *in the 42nd book on Sabinus.* Under the *lex Aquilia* even the slightest negligence counts. s. 1. Whenever a slave wounds or kills

with the knowledge of his master, there is no doubt that the master is liable to the Aquilian action.

45. PAUL *in the 10th book on Sabinus.* We take knowledge to mean here sufferance, so that a person who could have prevented an act is liable if he did not. s. 1. An action can be brought under the *lex Aquilia* even if a wounded slave is cured. s. 2. If you kill my slave, thinking him to be free, you will be liable under the *lex Aquilia.* s. 3. As two slaves were jumping over a heap of burning straw, they collided and both fell, and one of them was burnt to death: no action can be brought on that account, if it is not known which was upset by which. s. 4. Persons who do damage because they cannot otherwise defend themselves are innocent; for all statutes and legal systems allow one to repel force by force. But if in order to defend myself I throw a stone at my adversary, but hit, not him but a passer-by, I shall be liable under the *lex Aquilia*; for one is allowed to strike only the person who uses force, and then only when it is done for the purpose of protection and not revenge as well. s. 5. One who removes a good wall is liable for wrongful damage to its owner.

46. ULPIAN *in the 50th book on Sabinus.* If an action is brought under the *lex Aquilia* when a slave is wounded, none the less can an action be brought under the *lex Aquilia* if he afterwards dies of the wound.

47. JULIAN *in the 86th book of digests.* But if a valuation has been made in the former action, and afterwards, when the slave dies, the owner starts an action for killing, then. if the *exceptio doli mali* is raised, he will be debarred from recovering any more in both actions than he would have recovered had he started by suing for the death of the slave.

48. PAUL *in the 39th book on the Edict.* If a slave does damage to property belonging to an inheritance before entry is made on the inheritance and then does damage to that property after he has become free, he will be liable to both actions, because these matters depend on the two different acts respectively.

49. ULPIAN *in the 9th book of disputations.* If by raising smoke a man drives away or even kills another's bees, he is held rather to have furnished a cause of death than to have killed, and so he will be liable to an action *in factum.* s. 1. The saying that in the Aquilian action one can sue for damage done wrongfully must be taken to mean that damage is held to be done wrongfully when it inflicts wrong along with the damage; which happens unless it is done under the

compulsion of *vis major*, as in the case which Celsus gives of a man who pulled down an adjoining house in order to keep off a fire; for he writes that there is no action under the *lex Aquilia* since he pulled down the adjoining house under the reasonable fear that the fire would reach himself; and whether the fire reached him or was put out first, he thinks that there is no action under the *lex Aquilia*.

50. ULPIAN *in the 6th book of opinions*. If a person demolishes another's house without the owner's consent and builds baths on the site, then apart altogether from the rule of natural law that erections belong to the owner of the soil, he is also exposed to an action on the ground of the damage done.

51. JULIAN *in the 86th book of digests*. A slave was wounded so severely that it was certain that he would die of the blow; then in the meantime he was instituted heir and afterwards died of a blow from another assailant: I ask whether an action can be brought against both under the *lex Aquilia* for killing. He answered: a person is popularly said to have killed if he furnished a cause of death in whatever way, but he is held to be liable under the *lex Aquilia* only if he furnishes a cause of death by applying force and, so to speak, with his own hand; the word, that is to say, being interpreted as from *caedere* and *caedes*. Again liability under the *lex Aquilia* is understood to attach not only to those who wound in such a way as to deprive at once of life, but also to those who inflict a wound of which it is certain that someone will die. If therefore a person inflicts a mortal wound on a slave and another person strikes the same slave after a while, so that he is put an end to earlier than he would have died of the former wound, we must decide that both of them are liable under the *lex Aquilia*. s. 1. And this is in keeping with the authority of the older jurists, who, where the same slave was wounded by several persons in such a way that it was not clear of whose blow he died, decided that all are liable under the *lex Aquilia*. s. 2. Now the valuation of the dead slave will not be the same for both persons; for the one who wounded him first will pay whatever was the highest value of the slave in the past year, counting back three hundred and sixty-five days from the day of the wound, the later assailant will be liable for the highest price the slave could have been sold for in the year next before he departed this life, and in this the value of the inheritance will be included. Accordingly, for the killing of the same slave one will pay a higher and the other a lower valuation, which is not surprising since each of them is taken to have killed the slave under different circumstances and at a different time.

But if anyone should think that we have given an absurd ruling, let him reflect that it would be a far more absurd ruling that neither should be liable under the *lex Aquilia*, or one rather than the other, for on the one hand misdeeds should not go unpunished and on the other it is not easy to decide which of the two is more clearly liable under the *lex*. The fact is that it can be proved by countless examples that many solutions have been accepted by the civil law contrary to logic for the general convenience; I shall content myself for the moment with one. Where several persons, with intent to steal, remove another's beam which any one of them could not have carried, and are held to be liable to an action of theft, although the fine point might be taken that no one of them is liable because no one of them really removed it.

52. ALFENUS *in the 2nd book of digests*. If a slave dies from blows and this occurred owing neither to the ignorance of a doctor nor to the neglect of his owner, an action may properly be brought for killing him wrongfully. s. 1. A shopkeeper had placed his lantern at night on a stone by the road; a passer-by had carried it off; the shopkeeper followed him demanding the lantern and held him back when he tried to escape. The man, to make him let go, started to beat the shopkeeper with a whip that he had in his hand, in which was a spike. This gave rise to a serious scuffle in which the shopkeeper put out the eye of the man who had carried off the lantern; he asked for my opinion whether he might be held not to have done wrongful damage, seeing that he had first been struck with the whip. I replied that unless he had deliberately put out the eye he could not be held to have done wrongful damage, for the fault rested with the one who had first struck with the whip; but if he had not first been beaten by him, but had started the scuffle when he was trying to snatch away the lantern, it must be held to have happened through the shopkeeper's fault. s. 2. Mules were dragging two loaded carts up the Capitoline steep; the drivers of the front cart, which had got tilted back, were holding it up to make it easier for the mules to drag; meanwhile the upper cart began to go back, and when the drivers, who were between the two carts, left their place, the rear cart, being struck by the front one, moved backwards and ran over someone's slave boy. The boy's owner asked my opinion whom he ought to sue. I replied that the law depended on the circumstances; for if the drivers who held up the upper cart got out of the way of their own accord and that was the reason why the mules could not hold the cart and were dragged back by its weight, no action lies against the owner of the mules, but an

action can be brought under the *lex Aquilia* against the men who had been holding up the cart which had got tilted back; for a man does damage none the less because he lets go intentionally something he is holding up, so that it hits someone; for example if a person failed to hold in an ass he was driving, he would do wrongful damage just as if he discharged a missile or anything else from his hand. But if, I said, the mules shied at something and the drivers left the cart fearing they would be crushed, there will be no action against the men, but there will against the owner of the mules. But if neither the mules nor the men were responsible, but the mules could not hold up the weight or whilst struggling to do so slipped and fell, so that the cart went back, and the men could not hold up the weight as the cart was tilted back, there is no action against either the owner of the mules or the men. One thing at least was certain, that whatever the circumstances, no action lies against the owner of the mules behind, since they fell back not of their own will but because they were hit. s. 3. A man sold some oxen, it being a term of the contract that he should let the buyer have them on trial; then he let him have them on trial; a slave of the buyer while trying them was struck by one of the oxen with its horn; it was asked whether the seller ought to make good the damage to the buyer. I answered that if the buyer had bought the oxen, the seller was not bound to make it good; but if he had not bought them, then, if it was the slave's fault that he was struck by the ox, the seller ought not to pay, but if it was due to some vice in the ox, he ought. s. 4. A number of people were playing at ball, and one of them pushed a little slave boy when he was trying to pick up the ball, and the boy fell and broke his leg. It was asked whether the slave's owner could sue under the *lex Aquilia* the one whose push made him fall. I answered that he could not, as it seemed to have been done accidentally rather than by negligence.

53. NERATIUS *in the first book of sketches.* You drove another's oxen into a narrow place with the result that they fell over a precipice; an action *in factum* on the analogy of the *lex Aquilia* will be given against you.

54. PAPINIAN *in the 37th book of questions.* An action under the *lex Aquilia* is available to the debtor when the stipulator wounds the promised animal before the debtor is in default; the same is true also if he kills the animal. But if the promisee kills it after default on the part of the promisor, while the debtor is released, he will have no right in this case to proceed under the *lex Aquilia*; for the creditor is held to have

done wrong to himself rather than anyone else.

55. PAUL *in the 22nd book of questions.* I promised Titius either Stichus or Pamphilus, Stichus being worth ten thousand, Pamphilus twenty; the promisee killed Stichus before I was in default; a question was asked about the action under the *lex Aquilia.* I answered: since he is assumed to have killed the cheaper, for the purposes of this discussion the creditor differs not at all from an outsider. Then what will be the valuation: ten thousand, that is, the value of the slain Stichus, or the value of the one I am under an obligation to hand over, in short, the value of my interest? And what shall we say if Pamphilus dies too without default in delivery on my part? Will the value of Stichus now be decreased because the promisor is released? It will be enough to say that he was worth more when he was killed or within the year. On this principle even if he is killed within the year after the death of Pamphilus, he will be held to have been worth more.

56. PAUL *in the 2nd book of decisions.* If a woman does damage to her husband's property, she can be sued in accordance with the *lex Aquilia.*

57. JAVOLENUS *in the 6th book of Labeo's posthumous works.* I lent you a horse; as you were riding it and several persons were riding with you, one of them bumped against your horse and threw you off, and in the accident the horse's legs were broken. Labeo says that there is no action against you, but if it happened through the horseman's negligence, there would be against him; of course, he says, no action can be brought against the owner of the horse. I agree.

Extracts from other Roman texts

Institutes of Gaius

Book 3

s. 202. Sometimes a person is liable for theft who has not himself committed a theft, such as one by whose aid and counsel a theft has been committed. To this class belongs one who has struck coins out of your hand for another to carry off, or has got in your way, so that another could carry them off, or has set your sheep or oxen on the run for another to make away with them. The instance the older jurists gave of this was a man scattering a herd by means of a red rag; but if it was done wantonly and not with the intent that a theft should be committed, we shall have to see whether an analogous action ought to be given, since by the *lex Aquilia*, which was passed to deal with damage, negligence also is punished.

s. 210. The action of wrongful damage is given by the *lex Aquilia*, in the first chapter of which it is provided that if anyone wrongfully kills another person's slave or four-footed animal which is included in the class of cattle, he is to be condemned to pay to the owner the highest value the thing had in that year. s. 211. Now a person is understood to kill wrongfully when the death occurs through his wilful intent or negligence, nor is damage caused without wrongfulness punished by any other statute; and so one who commits damage through some accident, without wilful intent or negligence, goes unpunished. s. 212. In the action under this statute account is taken not only of the body of the victim; but undoubtedly, if by the killing of the slave the master receives damage over and above the market value of the slave, that too is taken into account, for instance if a slave of mine, instituted heir by someone, is killed before he makes cretion of the inheritance by my order; for not only is his own market value taken into account, but also the amount of the lost inheritance. Again, if one of twins or of a band of actors or musicians is killed, account is taken not only of the one killed, but besides this the amount is also reckoned by which the survivors are depreciated. The rule is the same if one of a pair of mules or again one of a team of chariot horses is killed. s. 213. Anyone whose slave has been killed is free to choose whether he will make the killer defendant on a capital charge or sue for damages under this statute. s. 214. Now the insertion in this statute of the words 'the highest value the thing had in that year' has this effect, that if a person kills, say, a lame or one-eyed slave who was whole within that year, account is taken, not of his value when he was killed, but of his highest value in that year; the result of which is that a person sometimes recovers more than the damage done to him.

s. 215. In the second chapter an action is given against an adstipulator who gives a receipt for money in fraud of his stipulator, for the value of the amount in issue. s. 216. In this part of the statute also it is clear that the action was introduced on the score of damage; but there was no need for the provision, since the action of mandate would meet the case, except for the fact that the action under this statute is for double against one who denies liability.

s. 217. In the third chapter provision is made for all other damage. And so if someone wounds a slave or a four-footed animal which is included in the class of cattle, or kills or wounds a four-footed animal which is not included in the class of cattle, such as a dog, or a wild beast such as a bear or lion, an action is allowed under this chapter. Further, with respect to all other animals, as well as everything devoid of life, damage done wrongfully is redressed under this part of the statute. For if anything is burnt or broken or fractured, an action is allowed under this chapter, though the term 'broken' would by itself have met all these cases; for anything spoilt in any way is understood to be broken. Hence not only things burnt or broken or fractured, but also things torn and bruised and spilled and deteriorated by being damaged or destroyed in any way, are comprised in this word. s. 218. Under this chapter, however, the person who has done damage is condemned to pay not the value the thing had in that year, but the value it had in the last thirty days. And the word 'highest' is not inserted either; and so some people have thought that the judge is free to refer the valuation to the time within the thirty days when the thing had its highest value or to a time when it had a lower one. But Sabinus held that it must be taken as though the word 'highest' had been inserted in this part of the statute also; for he said that the author of the statute had been satisfied with the use of the word in the first part of it. s. 219. It is also accepted that an action lies under this statute only if a person does damage with his own body, and so for damage done in any other way analogous actions are given, for instance if someone shuts up another person's slave or cattle and starves it to death, or drives a beast of burden so violently that it is ruptured; again, if someone persuades another person's slave to climb a tree or go down a well, and he falls on the way up or down and either dies or is injured in some part of his body. Again, to take a converse case, if someone pushes another person's slave from a bridge or bank into a river and he is drowned, it is not difficult to recognize here that he has done damage with his own body, inasmuch as he pushed him in.

s. 223. Under the law of the Twelve Tables the penalty for injuries was, for destroying a limb, retaliation; on the other hand, for breaking or bruising a bone the penalty was 300 *asses*, if the broken bone had been a freeman's; but if a slave's then of 150; for all other injuries, however, a penalty of 25 *asses* had been fixed. In those days of great poverty these money penalties appeared sufficient.

Book 4

s. 9. But we sue for both our right and a penalty in those cases, for example, in which we sue for double against a defendant who denies liability; which occurs in an action on a judgment debt, an *actio depensi*, an action for wrongful damage under the *lex Aquilia*, or on account of legacies of a definite amount which have been left *per damnationem*.

s. 11. The actions which the older generation used were called *legis actiones*, whether because they were made available by statutes (for in those days the edicts of the praetors, by which many actions have been introduced, were not yet in use), or because they were adjusted to the very words of statutes and so were treated as no less immutable than statutes. Hence it was held that a person who in suing for the cutting down of vines, called them vines in his action, had lost his claim, because he ought to have called them trees, since the law of the Twelve Tables, on which the action for the cutting down of vines lay, spoke generally of the cutting down of trees.

s. 37. ... Similarly if a foreigner sues or is sued for wrongful damage under the *lex Aquilia*, an action is given with a fiction of Roman citizenship.

s. 76. Now noxal actions have been established either by statutes or by the praetor's edict: by statutes, as for theft by the law of the Twelve

Table, for wrongful damage by the *lex Aquilia*; by the practor's edict, as for injuries and robbery with violence.

Sentences of Paul

Book 1 [19. How claims are doubled by denial of liability]

1. Certain actions are for double if the defendant denies liability, for instance on a judgment debt, an *actio depensi*, an action to recover a legacy left *per damnationem*, for wrongful damage under the *lex Aquilia*.... 2. Those claims which are doubled by denial of liability cannot be settled by agreement.

Collatio of the Mosaic and Roman laws[1]

Title 2 of Aggravated Outrage

4.1. ULPIAN *in the 18th book on the Edict.* We shall certainly hold that the term *rumpere* applies to one who wounds, or strikes with a rod or a lash or his first, or cuts a slave's skin with a weapon or by the application of any other kind of force, or makes a bruise: but only if he causes loss. But if he makes the slave in no way less valuable or useful, the Aquilian action does not apply and the *actio iniuriarum* will have to be brought. It also follows that if, although the slave has not been rendered less valuable, expense has been incurred in restoring him to health and safety, to this extent an action cannot, in my opinion, be brought under the *lex Aquilia* for damage.

5.5 PAUL *in the single book and title on injuries.* The action for injuries is either statutory or magisterial. If statutory, it comes from the law of the Twelve Tables: whoever does injury to another, is subjected to a penalty of twenty-five sesterces. This law is general in character; there were also special laws, for instance, if he fractures a bone with his hand or a stick, if it is freeman's, he is subjected to a penalty of 300 *sesterces*, if a slave's, of 150.

Title 7 of Thieves and Their Punishment

3.1. ULPIAN *in the 18th book on the Edict.* It is rightly added that the killing must be wrongful; for killing is not enough, it must have been done wrongfully. So if a man kills a slave caught in a robbery, he is not liable under the *lex Aquilia*, because he did not kill wrongfully, s. 2. Further, if one kills anyone else, whoever he may be, who is going for him with a sword, he will not be held to kill wrongfully. Likewise if one kills a thief operating by night, whom the law of the Twelve Tables allows one to kill in any case, or one operating by day, whom that law also allows one to kill, but only if he defends himself with a weapon, let us see if he is liable under the *lex Aquilia*. And Pomponius doubts this law is not in use. s. 3. And if a man kills a thief by night, we do not doubt that he is not liable under the *lex Aquilia*; but if when he could have arrested him, he preferred to kill him, the better opinion is that he should be held to have acted unlawfully; accordingly he will also be liable under the *lex Cornelia*. s. 4. Now we must not understand *iniuria* here as some kind of insult, as in the *actio iniuriarum*, but as something that is done not according to law, in short, contrary to law, that is, if one kills negligently (*culpa*), etc.

Title 12 of Incendiaries

7.1. ULPIAN *in the 18th book on the Edict*. Again if you damage by fire or set fire to my tenement house, I shall have the Aquilian action, and the same rule also applies if you do it to my plantation or country house. s. 2. But if anyone burns down a tenement house, he is also punished capitally as an incendiary. s. 3. Again if someone intended to burn down a tenement house and the fire spreads to that of a neighbour, he will be liable under the *lex Aquilia* to the neighbour also; and no less to the tenants on account of any of their goods which have been burnt; and thus Labeo reports in the fifteenth book of his *Responses*. s. 4. But if you burn stubble in your field and the fire spreads and reaches a neighbour's land and burns it, the question was raised whether the *lex Aquilia* applies or the action is *in factum*. s. 5. But several authorities hold that the *lex Aquilia* does not apply, and so Celsus writes in the thirty-seventh book of his *Digests*. He says: 'If a fire lit by a person burning stubble escapes, he is not liable under the *lex Aquilia*, but an action must be brought *in factum*, because he did not do the burning directly, but the fire spread whilst he was doing something else.' s. 6. His opinion is also approved by a rescript of the late Emperor Severus in the following words: 'You propose suing in a noxal action on the analogy of the *lex Aquilia* on account of a fire lit for the purpose of preparing a pasture, which spread through the fault of

Veturia Astilia's slaves and, as you say, laid waste your field. An assessment of the damage is allowed and a trial can take place.' Obviously the Aquilian action was held not to lie. s. 7. If the slave of a tenant of a house or of a tenant farmer happened to fall asleep at a furnace and the country house is burnt down, Neratius writes that the tenant must fulfil his obligation under the contract of letting and hiring, supposing he was negligent in his choice of labour. But if one man lit the furnace and another watched it negligently, is he liable? For the one who did not watch it did nothing, while the one who lit it in the proper way was not at fault; just as when a doctor operates properly on a slave, but either the doctor himself or someone else is negligent in the after-treatment, the Aquilian action does not lie. What then are we to say? Here I think an action ought to be allowed on the analogy of the Aquilian action against the man who fell asleep at the furnace or watched it negligently just as against the doctor who was negligent in the after-treatment, whether the slave died or was disabled. Nor can anyone say that the man who fell asleep was overtaken by a natural human weakness, because his duty was either to put out the fire or to take precautions so that it did not spread. s. 8. Again it is reported in the sixth book from Vivianus: If you have an oven against a wall held in common with your neighbour, are you liable for wrongful damage? And [Proculus] says there can be no action under the *lex Aquilia*, because there would be none against one who had a fire-place; and so I think the fairer course is to give an action *in factum*. But he does not put the case of the wall being burnt down. The question may indeed be asked whether if you have not yet done me any damage but you keep your fire in such a way as to cause me to fear that you will do me damage, it is right that I should obtain in the interim an action, that is, *in factum*. Perhaps that was what Proculus felt. Unless it be said that the undertaking against threatened damage will suffice. s. 9. Moreover, if a tenant's slaves had burnt down a tenement house, Urseius in his tenth book reports Sabinus as having replied that the master should be sued in a noxal action under the *lex Aquilia* on his slaves' account; but he denies that the master is liable on the contract of letting and hiring. Proculus, however, replied that where the slaves of a tenant have burnt down the country house, the tenant is liable either on the contract of letting and hiring or on the *lex Aquilia*, the tenant being at liberty to make noxal surrender of the slaves, and if the matter is decided in one action, the other can no longer be brought. s. 10. Again Celsus in the twenty-seventh book of his *Digests* writes: If my bees fly off to join yours, and you fire them, some jurists, among them Proculus, deny that the action under the *lex Aquilia* lies on the ground that the bees were not in my ownership. But Celsus says that that view is wrong, since bees are accustomed to return and are a source of profit to me. But Proculus is moved by the consideration that they are neither tame nor shut up. However Celsus himself says that there is no difference between them and pigeons, which, though they escape from the hand, nevertheless fly home.

Notes

1. The *Collatio*, as it is called for short, is a juxtaposition of extracts from the Old Testament and from the Roman jurists on certain topics, made by unknown authors somewhere between 292 and 438. It is particularly interesting to Roman lawyers because it contains extracts from the classical jurists in a form unaffected by the operations of the compilers of the *Digest*. But it almost certainly contains interpolations and glosses, and sometimes it appears that the *Digest* is nearer than the *Collatio* to the original text of the classical jurists. It happens that the *Collatio* contains a considerable number of passages which reappear in the *Digest* title on the *lex Aquilia* in more or less altered form. Thus *Coll.* 2, 4 corresponds to h.t. 27, 17; *Coll.* 7, 3, 1 to h.t. 3; *Coll.* 7, 3, 2.3.4 to h.t. 5pr. and the beginning of 5, 1; *Coll.* 12, 7 to h.t. 27, 7–12; but *Coll.* 12, 7, 2.4.5.6 are not found in the *Digest*, *Coll.* 12, 7, 2 doubtless because it refers to criminal law.

Institutes of Justinian

Book 3

Tit. 27. Of actions *quasi ex contractu*

s. 7. In some cases, however, there can be no recovery of money paid by mistake when not due. For the older jurists laid down the rule: in cases where the amount recoverable is increased by denial of liability there can be no recovery of a payment made without being due, for instance under the *lex Aquilia*....

Book 4

Tit. 1. Of obligation which arise from delict

s. 11. Sometimes a person is liable for theft who has not himself committed a theft, such as one by whose aid and counsel a theft has been committed. To this class belongs one who has struck coins out of your hand for another to seize, or has got in your way so that another could make away with them, or has set your sheep or oxen on the run for another to make away with them; and the instance the older jurists gave of this was a man scattering a herd by means of a red rag. But if any of these acts was done wantonly and not with the intent that a theft should be committed, an action *in factum* ought to be given.

Tit. 3. Of the *lex Aquilia*

The action of wrongful damage is given by the *lex Aquilia*, in the first chapter of which it is provided that if anyone wrongfully kills another person's slave or four-footed animal which is included in the class of cattle, he is to be condemned to pay to the owner the highest value the thing had in that year, s. 1. Now from the fact that it does not provide for four-footed animals absolutely, but only for such as are included in the class of cattle, it follows that we are to understand to provision to relate not to wild animals or dogs, but only to those which are properly said to graze, such as horses, mules, asses, oxen, sheep, goats. The same view is also held of swine; for swine also are comprised in the term 'cattle', because they also graze in herds. And so in fact Homer says in the *Odyssey*, as Aelius Marcianus Quotes in his *Institutes*:

> You will find him sitting with his swine, as they graze by the Raven's Crag, at the spring called Arethusa.

s. 2. Now a person is understood to kill wrongfully who kills without any right. And so one who kills a robber is not liable, that is to say, if he could not escape danger in any other way s. 3. And not even is a person who kills by accident liable under this statute, provided no negligence is found in him; however, everyone is liable under this statute for wilful wrongdoing as well as for negligence. s. 4. Accordingly if someone, in the course of playing or practising with javelins, runs your slave through as he passes by, a distinction is made. If the act was committed by a soldier on a parade ground where practising is usual, he is understood not to be negligent; if anyone else does the like, he is guilty of negligence. The same rule applies to a soldier if he did it in any other place than one appropriated to military exercises. s. 5. Again, if a pruner throws a branch down from a tree and kills your slave as he passes by, he is guilty of negligence if this occurred near a public or occupation road and he did not call out so that the accident could be avoided; if he did call out and the slave did not trouble to take care, the pruner is free from negligence. He is understood to be equally free from negligence if he was cutting, say, at a distance from the road or in the middle of a field, even though he did not call out, because no stranger had any right to be on the spot. s. 6. Further, if a doctor who has operated on your slave omits further treatment and the slave dies in consequence, he is guilty of negligence. s. 7. Lack of skill, too, is accounted negligence, for instance if a doctor kills your slave by operating on him badly or giving him a wrong medicine. s. 8. So too if your slave is run down by the onset of mules which the muleteer could not hold in for lack of skill, the muleteer is guilty of negligence. But even if he could not hold them in through lack of strength, he is equally liable for negligence, provided another stronger person could have held them in. The same views are held of a person on horseback who cannot control the horse's career through his lack of strength or sill. s. 9. Now the words of the statute 'the highest value the thing had in that year' convey the meaning that if someone kills a slave of yours who is now lame or one-eyed or maimed, but was whole or valuable within that year, he is liable to pay not what he is now worth, but his highest value in that year. On this ground the action under the statute has been supposed to be penal, since a person is bound to pay not only the amount of the damage he has done, but sometimes much more; and so it is agreed that the action does not pass against his heir, as it would have done if the amount recoverable never exceeded the damage. s. 10. It has been decided, not on the wording of the statute, but by interpretation, that account is to be taken, according to what we have said, not only of the body that has perished, but over and above that of whatever damage has been done to you in addition by the loss of the body, for instance if a man kills a slave of yours, instituted heir by someone, before he enters on the inheritance by your order; for it is agreed that account must be taken of the lost inheritance also. Again, if he kills one of a pair of mules or one of a team of chariot horses, or one slave from a band of actors is killed; account is taken not only of the one killed, but besides this the amount is also reckoned by which the survivors are depreciated. s. 11. It is open to one whose slave has been killed, both to sue for damages in a private action under the *lex Aquilia* and to make the wrongdoer defendant on a capital charge.

s. 12. The second chapter of the *lex Aquilia* is not in use.

s. 13. In the third chapter provision is made for all other damage. And so if someone wounds a slave or a four-footed animal which is included in the class of cattle, or kills or wounds a four-footed animal which is not included in the class of cattle, such as a dog or wild beast, an action is allowed under this chapter. Further, with respect to all other animals, as well as everything devoid of life, damage done wrongfully is redressed under this part of the statute. For if anything is burnt or broken or fractured, an action is allowed under this chapter, though the term 'broken' will by itself meet all these cases; for anything spoilt in any way is understood to be broken. Hence not only things burnt or fractured, but also things torn and bruised and spilled and destroyed and deteriorated in any way, are comprised in this word. Finally it has been decided that if a person puts something into another person's wine or oil, by which the natural goodness of the wine or oil is spoilt, he is liable under this part of the statute. s. 14. It is clear that, just as each person in liable under the first chapter only if the slave or animal has been killed by his wilful wrongdoing or negligence, so he is liable for all other damage under this chapter on the ground of wilful wrongdoing or negligence. Under this chapter, however, the person who has done damage is bound to pay not the value the thing had in that year, but the value it had in the next thirty days. s. 15. And the word 'highest' is not inserted either. But Sabinus rightly held that the account must be taken as though the word 'highest' had been inserted in this part of the statute also; for he said that the Roman plebs, which passed this statute on the motion of the tribune Aquilius, had been satisfied with the use of the word in the first part of it.

s. 16. But it is accepted that an action lies under this statute only if a person, beyond all doubt, does damage with his own body. And so analogous actions are allowed against one who does damage in any other way; for instance if someone shuts up another person's slave or cattle, so that it starves to death, or drives a beast of burden so violently that it is ruptured, or scares a herd to such an extent that it rushes over a precipice, or if someone persuades another person's slave to climb a tree or go down a well, and he dies or is injured in some part of his body on the way up or down, an analogous action is given against him. But if someone pushes another person's slave from a bridge or bank into a river and he is drowned, it will not be difficult to recognise that he has done damage with his own body, inasmuch as he pushed him in, and so he is liable under the *lex Aquilia* itself. But if damage has not been done with the body nor has physical injury been done to a body, but damage has happened to someone in some other way, inasmuch as neither the direct nor an analogous Aquilian action applies, it is agreed that the person responsible is liable to an action *in factum*; for instance if someone moved by compassion sets free the fettered slave of another person, to enable him to escape.

Tit. 4. Of injuries

s. 7. Under the law of the Twelve Tables the penalty for injuries was, for destroying a limb, retaliation; on the other hand, for breaking a bone money penalties were fixed corresponding to the great proverty of our ancestors. . . .

Tit. 6. Of actions

s. 19. . . . Moreover the action for damage under the *lex Aquilia* is a mixed one, not only where it is brought for double value against one who denies liability, but sometimes even if a person sues for the simple value. For instance if someone kills a lame or one-eyed slave who was whole and worth a high price within the year; for he is condemned to pay the highest value of the slave in that year, according to the distinction already reported. . . .

Tit. 8. Of noxal actions

s. 4. Now noxal actions have been established either by statutes or by the praetor's edict: by statutes, as for theft by the law of the Twelve Tables, for wrongful damage by the *lex Aquilia*; by the praetor's edict, as for injuries and robbery with violence.

Digest

2.14 of Pacts

7. s. 13. ULPIAN *in the 4th book on the Edict.* If I agree that no action shall be brought, whether on a judgment debt or for the burning of a house, the agreement is valid.

4.3 of *Dolus Malus*

7. . . . s. 7. ULPIAN *in the 11th book on the Edict.* Labeo asks whether, if you set free my fettered slave, to enable him to escape, an *actio doli* ought to be given. And Quintus in his notes on Labeo says that if you acted not moved by compassion, you are liable for theft; but if you were so moved, an action *in factum* ought to be given.

35. ULPIAN *in the 30th book on the Edict*. If after a testator's death a person has erased or in some other way spoilt the tablets of a will that had been deposited with him, the instituted heir will have an *actio doli* against him. Moreover, an *actio doli* ought to be given to the legatees also.

6.1 of the Vindication of a Thing

38. CELSUS *in the 3rd book of digests*. On land belonging to a third party which you had bought without notice, you built or planted, and then it is recovered from you: in such a case a good judge will decide differently according to the circumstances of the parties and the facts. Suppose the owner too would have done the same as you: then, in order to get back the land, he must make good your expenses, but only to the extent that it has been made more valuable, and even if more has been added to the value of the land, only what has been actually spent. Or suppose he is a poor man who, if he is bound to make that good, will have to relinquish his household gods and the graves of his forefathers: then it will be enough if you are allowed to take away what you can of what was yours, provided the land be not left worse than if no building had ever taken place. But we lay down that if the owner is prepared to pay as much as the possessor would have gained by taking the things away, he shall be allowed to do so; and no concession is to be made to your spiteful feelings, if for instance you want to scrape off plaster which you have put on or paintings, when you stand to gain nothing but to cause trouble. Or suppose the case to be that of an owner who is about to sell the recovered land directly; then unless he pays what we have said ought to be paid in the first case above, you must be condemned to pay only the balance after deducting that amount.

7.1 of Usufruct and How it is Exercised

13 s. 2. ULPIAN *in the 18th book on Sabinus*. For items of damage already done the usufructuary is also liable under the *lex Aquilia* and to the interdict *quod vi aut clam*, as Julian says; for it is certain that the usufructuary is also liable to these actions, and for theft too, like anyone else who does anything of the kind to another man's property. Moreover, being asked in consultation what was the use of the praetor's promising a special action when the action on the *lex Aquilia*

36

lies, he replied that it was because there are cases where there is no action on the *lex Aquilia* that a judge is appointed, so that the usufructuary may exercise his right subject to the judge's decision; for a person who does not plough up land or plant fresh vines, or again lets water-courses go to ruin, is not liable under the *lex Aquilia*. The same must be said of a usuary too.

9.1 of the Alleged Commission of *Pauperies* by a Four-Footed Animal

3. GAIUS *in the 7th book on the Provincial Edict*. There is no doubt that an action can be brought on this statute on account of free persons also, for instance if a quadruped wounds a *paterfamilias* or *filiusfamilias*; not, that is to say, that disfigurement is to be taken into account, for no valuation can be made of a free man's body, but account is to be taken of expenses incurred for medical treatment and for his actual and prospective loss of employment through being disabled.

9.4 of Noxal Actions

2. ULPIAN *in the 18th book on the Edict*. If a slave kills with the knowledge of his master, he binds his master in full, for the master himself is considered to have killed; if, however, the master did not know, the action is noxal, for he ought not to be liable for more than noxal surrender on his slave's wrongdoing. s. 1. One who did not forbid the act is liable in this action, whether he remains owner or has ceased to be owner; for it is enough if he was owner at the time when he did not forbid the act, to such an extent that Celsus thinks that if the slave is alienated wholly or partly or is manumitted, the noxal liability does not follow the person; on the ground that a slave who obeyed his master's order committed no wrong. And clearly if he did give an order, this view can be taken; but if he simply did not forbid it, how shall we excuse the slave's act? However, Celsus distinguishes between the *lex Aquilia* and the law of the Twelve Tables; for under the old statute, if a slave has committed a theft or done any other harm with the knowledge of the master, the action is a noxal one on the slave's account and the master is not liable on his own account, whereas under the *lex Aquilia*, he says, the master is liable on his own account, not the slave's. The rationale of the two statutes he gives as being that the Twelve Tables intended slaves not to obey their masters in such a case, but the *lex Aquilia* forgave a slave who obeyed his

master, since it would be the worse for him if he did not. But if we are to accept the opinion given by Julian in his eighty-sixth book, that the words 'if a slave has committed a theft or done some harmful act' applies also to subsequent statutes, it will be possible to hold that a noxal action also can be brought against the master on the slave's account, so that the giving of the Aquilian action against the master does not excuse the slave but throws a burden on the master. We, however, have settled the point in Julian's favour, his opinion having right on its side and being approved by Marcellus also in discussing Julian.

6. Moreover the slave himself is liable too when manumitted.

11.5 of Gamblers

2. PAUL *in the 19th book on the Edict*. s.1. A *senatusconsultum* forbade playing for money, except where the contest is one of throwing javelins or pikes or running, jumping, wrestling, or fighting to prove one's valour.

19.2 of the Actions of Letting and Hiring

11. ULPIAN *in the 32nd book on the Edict*. Let us see if a lessee is bound to answer for the negligence both of his slaves and of those whom he admits to the premises. And how far does his answering extend, to surrendering his slaves noxally or, on the contrary, to liability on his own account? And will he merely assign any actions he has against those whom he has admitted or will he be liable as if he had himself been negligent? My own opinion is that he answers on his own account for the negligence of those whom he has admitted, even if there has been no agreement to that effect, provided, however, that he was guilty of negligence in admitting them, that is, by having such persons whether as members of his own family or as guests: and Pomponius confirms this view in his sixty-third book on the Edict.

13. ULPIAN *in the 32nd book on the Edict*. s. 4. Again, Julian wrote in the eighty-sixth book of his *Digests* that if a shoemaker, when a boy does his work badly, strikes at his neck so violently that the boy's eye is put out, the boy's father has an action on the letting and hiring; for although slight punishment is permitted to masters, yet the shoe-

maker did not keep within the limit. We have already spoken about the further point of the *lex Aquilia*. However, Julian says that the action for *iniuria* does not also lie, because he did it not with intent to commit an injury, but to instruct. s. 5. Suppose that a gem is handed over to be set or cut and it is broken, then if it happened through a flaw in the gem itself, there will be no action on the contract of letting, but if through want of skill on the part of the workman, then there will be such an action. To this opinion must be added the qualification, unless the workman also took the risk upon himself; for then there will be an action on the contract of letting even if it happened through a flaw in the gem.

25. GAIUS *in the 10th book on the Provincial Edict* . . . . s. 7. If a man has accepted a column for carriage, and it is broken whilst being removed or carried or re-erected, he undertakes the risk if the breakage occurs through the negligence of himself and of those whose services be used: there is, however, no negligence if everything has been done that the most careful of men would have paid attention to. The same must of course be understood if someone accepts jars or timber for carriage; and the same principle can be applied to all other things too.

30. ALFENUS *in the 3rd book of digests epitomised by Paul.* s. 2. A person who had let out mules to be loaded only up to a certain weight sought an opinion as to the action he ought to bring when the hirer had injured them by overloading. He [Alfenus] answered that he could properly sue either on the *lex Aquilia* or on the letting, on the *lex Aquilia*, however, only against the man who had driven the mules at the time in question, on the letting against the hirer, even if someone else had injured them.

19.5 of Actions *Praescriptis Verbis* and *in Factum*

11. POMPONIUS *in the 39th book on Quintus Mucius.* The list of actions being incomplete, it followed in general that actions *in factum* are required. Moreover, where actions have been provided by statutes and the statute is just and fills a need, the praetor makes good gaps in the statute; he does this in the *lex Aquilia* by giving actions *in factum* adjusted to the *lex Aquilia*, as the reason of that statute demands.

14. ULPIAN *in the 41st book on Sabinus.* One who has thrown

another's goods overboard in order to save his own goods is not liable to any action; but if he did it without cause he is liable *in factum*, if maliciously, for *dolus*. s. 1. Moreover, if a person strips another's slave and he dies of cold, an action of theft can be brought on account of the clothes, but an action *in factum* on account of the slave, without prejudice to the criminal penalty against the wrongdoer. s. 2. Moreover, if a person throws overboard another's silver cup intending to do damage and not for purposes of gain, Pomponius in his seventeenth book on Sabinus writes that no action of theft or wrongful damage lies, but an action *in factum* must be brought. s. 3. If acorns fall from your tree on to my land and I send in my cattle and consume them, Aristo writes that there is no appropriate statutory action which you can bring. For no action can be brought either under the law of the Twelve Tables for the pasturing of cattle (since it did not take place on your land) or for *pauperies* or for wrongful damage; and so an action *in factum* must be brought.

23. ALFENUS *in the 3rd book of digests epitomised by Paul.* Whilst two men were walking along the Tiber, one of them at his companion's request held out to him a ring; the ring fell out of the latter's hand and rolled into the Tiber. His [Alfenus'] opinion was that an action *in factum* could be brought against him.

39.3 of Water and the Action for Keeping off Rainwater

1. ULPIAN *in the 53rd book on the Edict.* ...s. 12. Then Marcellus writes that no action can be brought against one who by digging on his own land intercepts another's spring, not even the *actio doli*; and certainly he ought not to have it, if he did it not with the intension of hurting his neighbour but of making his own land better.

41.1 of the Acquisition of Ownership

55. PROCULUS *in the 2nd book of Letters.* ...But if you had released to his natural liberty a wild boar which had become mine, and he had thereby ceased to be mine, an action *in factum* ought to be given to me, according to the opinion given when one man had thrown another's cup overboard.

43.24 of the Interdict *Quod Vi Aut Clam*

7. ULPIAN *in the 71st book on the Edict.* ...s. 4. There is also another defence, though Gallus doubts whether it can be set up: for instance if I demolish a neighbour's house to prevent the spread of fire, and proceedings are brought against me *quod vi aut clam* or for wrongful damage. Gallus doubts whether the defence ought to be allowed: 'the act not having been done to restrain a fire'. Servius, however, says that if a magistrate did it, the defence ought to be admitted, but that it should not be allowed to a private person; if nevertheless the act was complained of as being done *vi aut clam* and the fire had not reached the neighbour's house, he says that recovery is of the simple value; if it had reached so far, he ought to be acquitted. He says the result is the same if the action should be for wrongful damage, on the ground that he is not regarded as doing either wrong or damage to a house which was going to perish in any case. But if you do it when there is no fire, but a fire starts up afterwards, the decision will not be the same, because Labeo says that the question whether damage has or has not been done must be answered not *ex post facto* but according to the state of affairs at the time.

47.2 of Thefts

27. ULPIAN *in the 41st book on Sabinus.* ...s. 2. Further, if a receipt is stolen, we must likewise say that the action of theft is only for the amount of the party's interest, but that seems to me to be nothing, if there is other evidence that the money has been paid. s. 3. But if someone has not carried away such documents, but merely falsified them, not only the action of theft, but also that on the *lex Aquilia* lies; for mere spoiling is covered by the word 'to break'.

31. ULPIAN *in the 41st book on Sabinus.* Moreover, if someone erases a picture or a book, he too is liable for wrongful damage, as having spoilt it....
32. PAUL *in the 9th book on Sabinus* ....s. 1. For the *lex Aquilia* it is a still more important question how the amount of the plaintiff's interest can be proved; for if it can be proved in some other way, he suffers no damage. What then if, for example, he has lent money on a

condition, and for the time being he has plenty of witnesses to prove it, but they may die while the condition is still unfulfilled? Or suppose I have sued to recover a loan and have been defeated and lost my money because I could not produce witnesses and signatories who remembered the transaction; but now, when I sue for theft, I can produce them and use their recollection to warrant the truth of the loan.

50. ULPIAN *in the 37th book on the Edict.* . . .s. 4. An action of theft lies against one who holds up a red rag and scatters a herd so that they fall into the hands of thieves, provided he acts maliciously; but even if he acts with no intention of causing a theft, so ruinous a sport ought not to go unpunished; accordingly Labeo writes that an action ought to be given *in factum*.

51. GAIUS *in the 13th book on the Provincial Edict.* For it is also the case that if cattle are driven over a precipice, an *actio utilis* will be given for unlawful damage on the analogy of the *lex Aquilia*.

47.8 of Robbery and Riot

2. ULPIAN *in the 56th book on the Edict.* . . .s. 20. If a tax farmer takes away my cattle, thinking I have done something contrary to the taxing statute; even though he has made a mistake, Labeo says that no action can be brought against him for taking goods by force; for clearly he was free from wrongful intent. If, however, he shut them up to prevent them from grazing and in order that they should die of hunger, he will also be liable to a *utilis actio* on the analogy of the *lex Aquilia*.

47.9 of Pillage on the Occasion of Fire, Collapse of Building, Wreck, or the Seizure of a Raft or Ship

3. ULPIAN *in the 56th book on the Edict.* . . .s. 7. What the praetor says about the doing of damage applies only if the damage is done maliciously; for if malice is absent, the edict has no effect. How then does it follow, as Labeo writes, that if on the starting up of a fire I pull down a neighbour's building in self-defence, an action ought to be given against me on my own account and on that of those in my household? For seeing that I acted to protect my own house, I am of course free from malice. Accordingly I think that what Labeo writes is

not true. But can such a person be sued under the *lex Aquilia*? I do not think he ought to be, for a person who intended to defend himself did not act wrongfully when he could not do otherwise. And that is what Celsus writes.

9. GAIUS *in the 4th book on the law of the Twelve Tables*. Anyone who burns a house or a heap of corn placed next to a dwelling is ordered to be first bound and scourged and then burnt to death, provided he did it consciously and knowingly. But if he has done it by accident, that is, by negligence, he is ordered to make good the damage or, if he is not capable of this, is punished more lightly. Under the term house all kinds of building are included.

47. 10 of Outrages and Defamatory Writings

7. ULPIAN *in the 57th book on the Edict*. ...s. 1. If a slave is said to have been killed wrongfully, surely the praetor ought not to allow the *lex Cornelia* to be prejudged by a private action? And is not the same true if someone wishes to sue on the ground 'that you administered poison in order to kill a slave'? Thus he will be better advised not to allow such an action. However, we are accustomed to say that where a case can give rise to a public action we ought not to be prevented from suing privately also. This is indeed true, but only where the main cause of action does not allow of public prosecution. What then is our view of the *lex Aquilia*? For this action too has as its main cause that a slave has been killed. But the killing of the slave is not really the main cause, for the main cause of action is the damage which has been done to the master, whereas in the *actio iniuriarum* the point is to seek redress for the actual blow or poisoning, not compensation for damage. What then if someone wishes to bring the *actio iniuriarum* on the ground that his head has been broken by a sword? Labeo says that he is not to be stopped; for clearly nothing, he says, is included in the claim which could give rise to public punishment. But this is not true; for who can doubt that this sort of wrongdoer too can be proceeded against under the *lex Cornelia*?

13. ULPIAN *in the 57th book on the Edict*. s. 1. One who exercises a public right is not considered to do it for the sake of doing wrong; for the execution of the law does not amount to wrong.

17. s. 7. If a slave does an injury by his master's order, clearly the

master can be sued too on his own account. But if the slave is assumed to have been manumitted, Labeo's opinion is that an action should be given against him, both because the liability follows the person and because a slave ought not to obey his master in all things; but even if he kills by his master's order, we shall excuse him from liability under the *lex Cornelia*.

48.8 of the lex Cornelia Concerning Assassins and Poisoners

9. ULPIAN *in the 33rd book on the Edict.* If a person kills a thief operating by night, he will not be punished for his blow if he could not have spared him without danger to himself.

50.16 of the Meaning of Words

102. MODESTINUS *in the 7th book of rules.* A statute can suffer 'derogation' or 'abrogation': derogation when part of it is taken away, abrogation when it is completely repealed.

50.17 of Divers Rules of the Old Law

36. POMPONIUS *in the 27th book on Sabinus.* Meddling with something that does not belong to one amounts to *culpa*.

55. GAIUS *in the 2nd book on wills to the Urban Edict.* No one is regarded as acting with wrongful intent if he is exercising his right.

151. PAUL *in the 64th book on the Edict.* No one does damage except in doing what he has no right to do.

115. PAUL *in the 65th book on the Edict. s. 1.* A person is not regarded as using force if he exercises a right of his and has recourse to a regular action.

169. PAUL *in the 2nd book on Plavtius.* A person who orders the doing of damage id held to do it himself; but the one who is bound to obey is not guilty of *culpa*.

203 POMPONIUS *in the 8th book on Quintus Mucius.* Where a person suffers damage through his own fault, he is not understood to suffer damage at all.

Basilica[2]
Scholion on *D* 9.2. 11 pr.

Hagiotheodoreta. Where, he says, these two men are at fault, both the barber shaving in such a spot and the one who entrusted himself to such a barber, the one who was shaved ought to have come off worse and to have it said of him that he has only himself to blame, and to have no action against the barber. However, we prefer to make the barber come off worse, and we make him liable to an action on two grounds: the one is, lest in the result we should injure the slave's master, who was not at all at fault but was in complete ignorance, and should deprive him of his double penalty, whilst letting off the barber scot-free, which would be unjust: the other is that, even if the one who had his throat cut had not been a slave, but free, it is just, of two evils, to prefer the removal of the greater to the punishment of the less. For if we do not punish the barber, that sort of man will harm many others in that sort of way. That is clearly the greater danger, which ought to be averted, so that one barber may not be at liberty to damage a large crowd of people, even if the crowd is inattentive. It is therefore just, and we shall act accordingly and punish the barber, and not shut out the one who was shaved from his remedy: which would have happened if the lesser evil had been chosen for punishment. We shall therefore punish the barber, and free many from harm to come, deriving support for this from the rule in book 2, title 3, which says: when something cannot be done without damage, we choose the lesser injustice. But in the case immediately preceding this the only person at fault was the one who passed by where people were playing at javelin-throwing; for those who were throwing javelins on a parade-ground were not at all at fault.

Note

2. This is a twelfth- or thirteenth-century scholion to the Basilica, for which see generally Jolowicz, 510–11, and Lawson, 'The Basilica', 46 *L.Q.R.* 486 and 47 *L.Q.R.* 536. It is one of the corner-stones of the theory that an earlier objective doctrine of responsibility, based mainly on causation, gave way, probably in post-classical times, to a subjective doctrine based on moral blameworthiness. But, apart altogether from its very late date, we have to note that the scholion is much more concerned with preventing future harm than punishing a wrongdoer. The two evils are assessed not in accordance with their moral blameworthiness but with their capacity for harm. This is certainly not causation, as usually applied to the solution of problems in tort, but it is not particularly moral. Indeed it is not incompatible with liability without fault.

PART II
Extracts from foreign codes

Prussian Code[1]
(Allgemeines Landrecht für die preussischen Staaten)

Title 6 Of the Duties and Rights which arise out of Unlawful Acts

5. Advantages which anyone would have obtained if a particular act or omission had not taken place are reckoned *lucrum cessans*.

6. Nevertheless, in the ascertaining of *lucrum cessans* regard is paid only to such advantages as might reasonably have been expected either according to the usual run of things and of the transactions of civil life, or by virtue of particular preparations and provisions which had already been made.

7. Complete satisfaction comprises compensation for the whole damage and *lucrum cessans*.

10. Anyone who injures another by intent or gross negligence must render him full satisfaction.

11. The same obligation attaches to anyone who by intent or gross negligence omits to perform a duty owed to another, and thereby causes damage to him.

12. Anyone who injures another by act or omission through only moderate negligence is liable only for the actual damage from it.

13. Nevertheless, the person causing the injury must also make compensation for the *lucrum cessans* which the victim would have obtained through the normal use of that faculty in respect of which he had been injured, if the injury had not taken place.

14. In such a case the *lucrum cessans* must be compensated for even if the actual damage is incapable of assessment.

15. In cases where even slight negligence must be answered for, the person doing the damage is liable for the immediate damage arising from such negligence.

16. Damage arising accidentally from an act must be made good only if the act itself is contrary to a statutory prohibition; or if the doer has through such unlawful conduct placed himself in the situation by which he was caused to do the act.

18. The party causing the injury is not released by the contributory negligence of the victim from making good damage which was immediately caused by intent or gross negligence.

19. On the other hand, mediate damage and *lucrum cessans* need not be made good if the victim has made himself responsible for gross negligence in respect of its occurrence.

20. Such gross negligence on the part of the victim makes him forfeit all indemnification if the damage arose from a moderate or slight negligence on the part of the party causing the damage.

21. Compensation for mediate damage arising from moderate or slight negligence and for *lucrum cessans* is disregarded if the victim could have avoided the damage by the application of ordinary care.

22. If two or more persons have injured each other each one is liable to the other for the damage caused, according to the measure of the blame which falls to his charge.

23. If persons sharing in an unlawful act have done damage to each other in the course of it, each one must bear his own damage.

41. If lunatics and imbeciles or children under the age of seven years injure anyone, compensation for immediate damage only can be demanded from their estate.

42. Nevertheless, the estate of such persons is liable only if the victim cannot obtain compensation from the estate of persons charged with their supervision or of their parents.

43. Further, the wrongdoer's estate is liable only so far as the wrongdoer is not deprived thereby of necessary maintenance and, if he is a child, of the means for an education in accordance with his station.

44. If the victim has through his own negligence, even though it was only slight, caused such persons to do the injurious act, he cannot have recourse to their estate.

79. If damage has taken place everything must be restored as far as possible to the situation in which it was before the damage took place.

Note

1. This famous code, which came into force in 1794 and governed the greater part of the Kingdom of Prussia untill 1900, no longer operates anywhere.

It has, however, been thought worth while to include a few extracts in translation as specimens of a mode of treating responsibility which is highly characteristic and has had considerable influence on later law. The code contains what is, almost certainly, the first statutory provisions for the payment of damages out of the estates of persons, such a lunatics, to whom no fault can be attributed. But its most striking feature is to be found in a grading of negligence in three degrees, to each of which separate effects are attributed in the assessment of damages and the interlocking of which, according as they are attributed to the wrongdoer and his victim, allows a more subtle treatment of the problems of contributory negligence and of contribution between joint tortfeasors than would otherwise have been possible without admitting a wide exercise of discretion by the courts. For, as has often been remarked (Vinogradoff, *Common Sense in Law*, 88), the whole spirit of the code was unfavourable to discretionary action except on the part of the sovereign himself and accordingly rules were enunciated in the most precise form. Perhaps we should see in § 15 the starting-point of a line of thought that culminates in the possibility of mitigating damages allowed in § 44 of the Swiss Code of Obligations.

French Civil Code

Art. 1149. Les dommages et intérêts dûs au créancier sont, en général, de la perte qu'il a faite et du gain dont il a été privé, sauf les exceptions et modifications ci-après.

Art. 1150. Le débiteur n'est tenu que des dommages et intérêts qui ont été prévus ou qu'on a pu prévoir lors du contrat, lorsque ce n'est point par son dol que l'obligation n'est point exécutée.

Art. 1151. Dans le cas même ou l'inexécution de la convention résulte du dol du débiteur, les dommages et intérêts ne doivent comprendre à l'égard de la perte éprouvée par le créancier et du gain dont il a été privé, que ce qui est une suite immédiate et directe de l'inexécution de la convention.

Chapitre II *Des délits et des quasi-délits*

Art. 1382. Tout fait quelconque de l'homme, qui cause à autrui un dommage, oblige celui par la faute duquel il est arrivé, à le réparer.

Art. 1383. Chacun est responsable du dommage qu'il a causé non seulement par son fait, mais encore par sa négligence ou par son imprudence.

Art. 1384. On est responsable non seulement du dommage que l'on cause per son propre fait, mais encore de celui qui est causé par le fait des personnes dont on doit répondre, ou des choses que l'on a sous sa garde.

(L. 7 novembre 1922) Toutefois, celui qui détient, à un titre quelconque, tout ou partie de l'immeuble ou des biens mobiliers dans lesquels un incendie a pris naissance ne sera responsable, vis-à-vis des tiers, des dommages causés par cet incendie que s'il est prouvé qu'il doit être attribué à sa faute ou à la faute des personnes dont il est responsable.

'Cette disposition ne s'applique pas aux rapports entre propriétaires et locataires, qui demeurent régis par les articles 1733 et 1734 du Code civil.'

(L 4. juin 1970) Le père en la mère en tant qu'ils exercent le droit de garde sont solidairement responsables du dommage causé par leurs enfants mineurs habitant avec eux;

Les maîtres et les commettants, du dommage causé par leurs domestiques et préposés dans les fonctions auxquelles ils les ont employés;

'Les instituteurs et les artisans, du dommage causé par leurs élèves et apprentis pendant le temps qu'ils sont sous leur surveillance.'

(L. 5 avril 1937) 'La responsabilité ci-dessus a lieu, à moins que les père et mère et les artisans ne prouvent qu'ils n'ont pu empêcher le fait qui donne lieu à cette responsabilité.

'En ce qui concerne les instituteurs, les fautes, imprudences ou négligences invoquées contre eux comme ayant causé le fait dommageable, devront être prouvées, conformément au droit commun, par le demandeur à l'instance.'

Art. 1385. Le propriétaire d'un animal, ou celui qui s'en sert, pendant qu'il est à son usage, est responsable du dommage que l'animal a causé, soit que l'animal fût sous sa garde, soit qu'il fût égaré ou échappé.

Art. 1386. Le propriétaire d'un bâtiment est responsable du dommage causé par sa ruine, lorsqu'elle est arrivée par une suite du défaut d'entretien ou par le vice de sa construction.

Code de l'aviation civile

Art. 141–2 L'exploitant d'un aéronef est responsable de plein droit des dommages causés par les évolutions de l'aéronef ou les objets qui s'en détacheraient aux personnes et aux biens situés à la surface. – Cette responsabilité ne peut être atténuée ou écartée que par la preuve de la faute de la victime.

Austrian Civil Code[1]

§ 1304. If the victim by his fault contributes to the infliction of damage he bears the damage proportionately with the person causing it; and if the proportion cannot be ascertained, in equal shares.

§ 1306a. If anyone causes damage under force of necessity in order to avert from himself or from another an immediately threatening danger, the judge must decide whether and to what extent the damage is to be made good having regard to whether the victim forebore to avert it out of consideration for the danger threatening the other person, as well as of the relation of the magnitude of the damage to this danger or finally to the estate of the person doing the damage and that of the victim.[2]

§ 1308. If lunatics or imbeciles or minors[3] do damage to anyone who has himself through some fault on his part given occasion for it, he cannot claim any compensation.

§ 1309. Apart from this case he is entitled to compensation from those persons to whom the damage can be attributed owing to their neglect of the care entrusted to them over such persons.

§ 1310. If the victim cannot obtain compensation in such a way, the judge must decide to award the whole compensation or at least an equitable portion of it having regard to the circumstances, that is to say whether the person doing the damage, notwithstanding that he is not normally *compos mentis*, was not, nevertheless, in the particular case to blame, or again whether the victim did not forego defending himself because he wished to spare the person causing the damage, or finally out of regard for the estate of the person doing the damage and that of the victim.

Notes

1. This Code of 1811, one of the greatest products of the Enlightenment, was in force throughout the Austrian portions of Austria–Hungary until 1918. It is still in force in Austria and was until very recently, at any rate, in Czechoslovakia. It was greatly influenced by both the Prussian and the French Codes, and itself exerted considerable influence on both the German and Swiss Codes. Three so-called *Teilnovellen* were enacted in 1914–16, to incorporate in it more recent developments, especially as shown in the German and Swiss Codes.
2. This paragraph was added to the Code in 1916 by Nov. III, § 156.
3. This word was added to the Code in 1916 by Nov. III, § 158.

Belgian Civil Code[1]
De la réparation du dommage causé par les anormaux

§ 1386 bis. L. 16 avril 1935, art. 1er.

Lorsqu'une personne se trouvant en état de démence, ou dans un état grave de déséquilibre mental ou de débilité mentale la rendant incapable du contrôle de ses actions, cause un dommage à autrui, le juge peut la condamner à tout ou partie de la réparation à laquelle elle serait astreinte si elle avait le contrôle de ses actes.

Le juge statue selon l'équité, tenant compte des circonstances et de la situation des parties.]

Note

1. The Belgian Civil Code is on all other relevant matters identical with the French, except that it contains nothing comparable to the laws of 7 November 1922 and 5 April 1937.

Quebec Civil Code[1]

Chapitre III *Des Délits et Quasi-délits*

§ 1053. Toute personne capable de discerner le bien du mal, est responsable du dommage causé par sa faute à autrui, soit par son fait, soit par imprudence, négligence, ou inhabileté.

§ 1054. Elle est responsable non seulement du dommage qu'elle cause par sa propre faute, mais encore de celui causé par la faute de ceux dont elle a le contrôle, et par les choses qu'elle a sous sa garde.

Le père, et aprés son décès, la mère, sont responsables du dommage causé par leurs enfants mineurs;

Les tuteurs sont également responsables pour leurs pupilles;

Les curateurs ou autres ayant légalement la garde des insensés, pour le dommage causé par ces derniers;

L'instituteur et l'artisan, pour le dommage causé par ses élèves ou apprentis, pendant qu'ils sont sous sa surveillance;

La responsabilité ci-dessus a lieu seulement lorsque la personne qui y est assujettie ne peut prouver qu'elle n'a pu empêcher le fait qui a causé le dommage;

Les maîtres et les commettants sont responsables du dommage causé par leurs domestiques et ouvriers dans l'exécution des fonctions auxquelles ces derniers sont employés.

§ 1055. [Animals and buildings.]

§ 1056. Dans tous les cas ou la partie contre qui le délit ou quasi-délit a été comms décède en conséquence, sans avoir obtenu indemnité ou satisfaction, son conjoint, ses ascendants et ses descendants ont, pendant l'année seulement à compter du décès, droit de poursuivre celui qui en est l'auteur ou ses représentants, pour les dommages-intérêts résultant de tel décès.

Au cas de duel, cette action peut se porter de la même manière non seulement contre l'auteur immédiat du décès, mais aussi contre eux qui ont pris part au duel soit comme seconds, soit comme témoins.

En tout cas, il ne peut être porté qu'une seule it même action pour tour ceux qui ont droit à l'indemnité et le jugement fixe la proportion de chacun dans l'indemnité.

Ces poursuites sont indépendantes de celles dont les parties peuvent être passibles au criminel, et sans préjudice à ces dernières.

§ 1056a. Nul ne peut exercer les recours prévus par ce chapitre s'il s'agit d'un accident visé par la Loi des accidents du travail, 1931, excepté dans la mesure où ladite loi le permet.

§ 1056b. Sous la réserve des dispositions de la loi du barreau dans le recouvrement d'une indemnité exigible en vertu du présent chapitre troisième aucun mandataire ou intermédiaire ne peut recevoir à titre de rémunération, ou se faire transporter en garantie collatérale ou autrement, en tout ou en partie, l'indemnité à laquelle peuvent prétendre la victime ou ses représentants, ni acquérir de quelque façon que ce soit un intérêt personnel dans le montant de cette indemnité.

Tout arrangement, verbal ou, écrit, formel ou implicite, conclu en violation du présent article, est nul de plein droit et celui qui paye une partie de l'indemnite en vertu de tel arrangement, a droit de répétition contre celui qui la reçoit.

Lors de l'exercice d'un recours prévu par ce chapitre le tribunal, sur demande de toute partie en cause, peut permettre la preuve qu'il existe un arrangement fait en violation du présent article.

Note

1. This code was drafted by three commissioners, one English-speaking and the other two French-speaking, and passed by the Parliament of United Canada in 865. The commissioners were instructed to codify the then existing law, but in matters of form to follow the model of the French Civil Code. Thus the substance of the Quebec Code is not always identical with that of the French. Here, however, it would seem that, apart from the provision imposing vicarious liability on tutors and curators, the two codes had the same intentions.

In addition to the French version of the Quebec Code, the English version has, in theory, equal authority. However, although this portion of the code was drafted by the English-speaking commissioner, it is obvious that he was thinking of the French Civil Code and so if either of the two versions can be considered the original, it must be the French.

Attention is particularly directed to the reports of the commissioners, published in English and French in three volumes at Quebec in 1865. They provide much the easiest means of ascertaining the sources of the detailed provisions, not only of the Quebec but also of the French Civil Code.

Dans les cas de recours en dommages-interets resultant de biessures corporelles, les quittances it les règlements et les declarations écrites obtenues de la victime dans les quinze jours de la date du délit ou du quasi-délit ne peuvent lui être opposés si elle en souffre lésion.

German Civil Code (BGB)

General part

Exercise of rights. Self-defence. Self-help.

§ 226. The exercise of a right is inadmissible if it can only have the purpose of causing damage to another.

§ 227. An act required by self-defence is not unlawful.

Self-defence is that defence which is necessary in order to ward off from oneself or another an actual unlawful attack.

§ 228. Anyone who damages or destroys a thing belonging to another in order to ward off from himself or another a danger threatened by it, does not act unlawfully, if the damage or destruction is necessary to ward off the danger and the damage is not out of proportion to the danger. If the person acting is to blame for the danger, he is bound to make good the damage.

§ 229. Anyone who for purposes of self-help takes away, destroys, or damages a thing or for purposes of self-help apprehends an obligor suspected of intending flight or overcomes the resistance of the obligor to an act which the latter is bound to suffer, does not act unlawfully if the help of the authorities cannot be obtained in good time and there is danger that unless he acts at once the realisation of the claim will be frustrated or appreciably impeded.

§ 230. Self-help must not go tarther than is necessary to ward off the danger.

In case of the seizure of things, in so far as compulsory execution is not effected, leave to distrain must be applied for.

In case of the apprehension of the obligor, in so far as he is not set free again, leave for the precautionary detention of his person must be applied for to the District Court in whose district the apprehension has taken place; the obligor must be brought before the Court without delay.

If the application is delayed or rejected, the restitution of the things seized and the liberation.of the person apprehended must follow without delay.

§ 231. Anyone who does one of the acts specified in § 229 under the mistaken assumption that the necessary presuppositions for the exclusion of illegality are in existence, is bound to compensate the other party, even if the mistake is not due to negligence.

§ 249. The person who is bound to make compensation must restore the situation which would exist if the circumstance making him liable to compensate had not occurred. If compensation is to be made for injury to a person or damage to a thing the creditor may demand, instead of restitution in kind, the sum of money necessary to effect such restitution.

§ 250. The creditor may by notice to the person liable to compensate, fix a reasonable period for the restitution in kind with a declaration that he will not accept restitution after the expiration of the period. After the expiration of the period, the creditor may demand the compensation in money if the restitution is not effected in due time; the claim for restitution is barred.

§ 251. In so far as restitution in kind is impossible, or is insufficient to compensate the creditor, the person liable must compensate him in money.

The person liable may compensate the creditor in money if restitution in kind is possible only through disproportionate outlay.

§ 252. The damage to be made good includes also lost profits. Profit is deemed to have been lost which would have been expected with probability according to the ordinary course of things, or according to the particular circumstances, in particular, according to the preparation and provisions made.

§ 253. For an injury which is not an injury to property compensation in money may be demanded only in the cases specified by law.

§ 254. If any fault of the injured party has contributed to the occurrence of the damage, the duty to compensate and the extent of the compensation to be made depend upon the circumstances, especially upon how far the injury has been caused predominantly by the one or the other party.

This applies also if the fault of the injured party was limited to omission to call the attention of the debtor to the danger of unusual serious damage, of which the debtor neither knew nor ought to have known, or to an omission to avert or mitigate the damage. The provision of § 278 applies *mutatis mutandis*.

§ 255. The person who is to make compensation for the loss of a thing or of a right is bound to make compensation only upon an assignment to him of the claims which belong to the person entitled to compensation by virtue of his ownership of the thing or by virtue of his right against third parties.

§ 276. The debtor is responsible, unless otherwise provided, for recklessness and negligence. A person who does not exercise the care required in ordinary intercourse acts negligently. The provisions of §§ 827 and 828 apply.

The debtor may not be released beforehand from responsibility for recklessness.

§ 277. The person who is answerable only for such care as he is accustomed to exercise in his own affairs is not relieved from liability for gross negligence.

§ 278. A debtor is responsible for the fault of his statutory agent, and of persons whom he employs in fulfilling his obligation, to the same extent as for his own fault. The provision of § 276, par. 2, does not apply.

Promise of performance for the benefit of a third party

§ 328. (1) A contract may stipulate for performance to a third party, so that the third party acquires a right to demand performance.

(2) In the absence of express stipulation it is to be deduced from the circumstances, especially from the object of the contract, whether the right of the third party shall arise forthwith or only under certain conditions, and whether any right shall be reserved to the contracting parties to take away or modify the right of the third party without his consent.

§ 329. If in a contract one party binds himself to satisfy a creditor of the other party without assuming the debt, it is not to be presumed, in case of doubt, that the creditor shall acquire a direct right to demand satisfaction from him.

§ 330. If, in a contract for life insurance or an annuity, payment of the insurance or annuity to a third party is stipulated for, it is to be presumed, in case of doubt, that the third party shall directly acquire the right to demand the performance. The same rule applies, if in a gratuitous transfer of property the duty to perform the act to a third party is imposed upon the recipient, or if a person, on taking over the whole of another person's property or goods, promises an act of performance to a third party for the purpose of settling the latter's debts.

§ 331. (1) If the performance to the third party is to be made after the death of the person to whom it was promised, in case of doubt the third party acquires the right to the performance upon the death of the promisee.

(2) If the promisee dies before the birth of the third party, the promise to perform to the third party can be revoked or altered only if the right to do so has been reserved.

§ 676. A person who gives advice or a recommendation to another is not bound to compensate for any damage arising from following the advice or the recommendation, without prejudice to his responsibility resulting from a contract or delict.

Unlawful acts

§ 823. A person who wilfully or negligently injures the life, body, health, freedom, property, or other right of another contrary to law is bound to compensate him for any damage arising therefrom.

The same obligation attaches to a person who infringes a statutory provision intended for the protection of others. If according to the purview of the statute infringement is possible even without fault, the duty to make compensation arises only if some fault can be imputed to the wrongdoer.

§ 824. A person who maintains or publishes, contrary to the truth, a statement calculated to endanger the credit of another, or to injure his earnings or prospects in any other manner, must compensate the other for any damage arising therefrom, even if he does not know of its untruth, provided he ought to know.

A communication the untruth of which is unknown to the person making it does not thereby render him liable to make compensation, if he or the recipient of the communication has a justifiable interest in it.

§ 825. A person who by fraud or threats, or by an abuse of the relation of dependence, induces a woman to permit illicit cohabitation is bound to compensate her for damage arising therefrom.

§ 826. A person who wilfully causes damage to another in a manner *contra bonos mores* is bound to compensate the other for the damage.

§ 827. A person who does damage to another in a condition of unconsciousness, or in a condition of morbid disturbance of the mental activity, incompatible with a free determination of the will, is not responsible for the damage. If he had brought himself into a temporary condition of this kind by spirituous liquors or similar means, he is responsible for any damage which he in this condition unlawfully causes in the same manner as if negligence were imputable to him; the responsibility does not arise if he has been brought into this condition without fault.

§ 828. A person who has not completed his seventh year of age is not responsible for any damage which he does to another.

A person who has completed his seventh year but not his eighteenth year of age is not responsible for any damage which he does to another, if he at the time of committing the damaging act did not have the understanding necessary for realising his responsibility. The same rule applies to a deaf mute.

§ 829. A person who in any one of the cases specified in §§ 823–6 is by virtue of §§ 827, 828 not responsible for any damage caused by him, must, nevertheless, to the extent that compensation cannot be obtained from a third party charged with the duty of supervision, make compensation for the damage in so far as according to the circumstances, in particular according to the relative positions of the parties, equity requires indemnification, and he is not deprived of the means which he needs for his own maintenance according to his station in life and for the fulfilment of his statutory duties to furnish maintenance to others.

§ 830. If several persons have caused damage by an unlawful act committed in common, each is responsible for the damage. The same rule applies if it cannot be discovered which of several participants has actually caused the damage.

Instigators and accomplices are in the same position as joint-doers.

§ 831. A person who employs another to do any work is bound to compensate for damage which the other unlawfully causes to a third party in the performance of his work. The duty to compensate does not arise if the employer has exercised ordinary care in the choice of the employee, and, where he has to supply appliances or implements or to superintend the work, has also exercised ordinary care as regards such supply or superintendence, or if the damage would have arisen, notwithstanding the exercise of such care.

The same responsibility attaches to a person who takes over the charge of any of the affairs specified in par. 1, sentence 2, by contract with the employer.

§ 832. A person who is bound by law to exercise supervision over a person who needs supervision on account of minority, or of his mental or physical condition, is bound to make compensation for any damage which the latter unlawfully does to a third party. The duty to compensate does not arise if he fulfils his duty of supervision, or if the damage would have occurred notwithstanding the proper exercise of supervision.

The same responsibility attaches to a person who takes over by contract the exercise of supervision.

§ 833. If a person is killed, or the body or health of a person is injured, or a thing is damaged by an animal, the person who keeps the animal is bound to compensate the injured party for any damage arising therefrom. The duty to make compensation does not arise if the damage is caused by a domestic animal which is intended to serve the profession, the business activities, or the support of the keeper of the animal and if the keeper of the animal has either exercised the requisite care in supervising the animal or if the damage would have occurred notwithstanding the exercise of such care.

§ 834. A person who undertakes to supervise an animal under a contract with the keeper of the animal is responsible for any damage which the animal causes to a third party in the manner specified in § 833. The responsibility does not arise if he has exercised the requisite care in the supervision of the animal, or if the damage would have occurred notwithstanding the exercise of such care.

§ 835. [Repealed]

§ 836. (1) If, by the collapse of a building or other structure attached to a piece of land, or by the detachment of parts of the building or structure, a person is killed, or the body or health of a person is injured, or a thing is damaged, and if the collapse or the detachment was caused by defective construction or inadequate maintenance, the possessor of the land is bound to compensate the injured party for any damage arising therefrom. The duty to make compensation does not arise if the possessor has exercised the requisite care for the purpose of averting danger.

(2) A former possessor of the land is responsible for the damage if the collapse or the detachment occurs within one year after the termination of his possession, unless during his possession he exercised the requisite care, or unless a subsequent possessor could have averted the danger by the exercise of such care.

(3) The possessor within the meaning of these provisions is the proprietary possessor.

§ 837. If a person in the exercise of a right possesses a building or other structure on the land of another, the responsibility specified in § 836 attaches to him instead of the possessor of the land.

§ 838. A person who undertakes for the possessor the maintenance of a building or a structure attached to land, or who has to maintain the building or the structure by virute of a right of use belonging to him, is responsible in the same manner as the possessor for any damage caused by the collapse or the detachment of parts.

§ 839. (1) If an official wilfully or negligently commits a breach of official duty incumbent upon him towards a third party, he shall compensate the third party for any damage arising therefrom. If only negligence is imputable to the official, he may be held liable only if the injured party is unable to obtain compensation otherwise.

(2) If an official commits a breach of his official duty in giving judgment in an action, he is not responsible for any damage arising therefrom, unless the breach of duty is subject to a public penalty to be enforced by criminal proceedings. This provision does not apply to a breach of duty consisting of refusal or delay in the exercise of the office.

(3) The duty to make compensation does not arise if the injured party has wilfully or negligently omitted to avert the injury by making use of a legal remedy.

§ 840. If several persons are together responsible for damage arising from an unlawful act, they are liable, subject to the provision of § 835, par. 3, as joint debtors.

If, in addition to the person liable under §§ 831, 832 to make compensation for the damage caused by another, that other person is also liable, as between themselves only the latter is liable, or in the case provided for by § 829, only the person who has the duty of supervision.

If, in addition to the person liable under §§ 833–8 to make compensation for any damage, a third party is also liable for the damage, as between themselves only such third party is liable.

§ 842. The obligation to make compensation for damage on account of an unlawful act directed against the person of another extends to the detriment which the act occasions to his earnings or prospects.

§ 843. If, in consequence of an injury to body or health, the earning capacity of the injured party is destroyed or diminished or an increase of his necessities arises, compensation must be made to the injured party by the payment of a money annuity.

The provisions of § 760 apply to the annuity. Whether, in what manner, and to what amount, the person bound to make compensation has to give security is determined according to the circumstances.

Instead of an annuity the victim may demand a lump sum settlement, if a serious reason exists for it.

The claim is not excluded by the fact that another person has to furnish maintenance to the injured party.

§ 844. In the case of causing death the person bound to make compensation must make good the funeral expenses to the person on whom the obligation of bearing such expenses lies.

If the deceased at the time of the injury stood in a relation to a third party by virtue of which he was or might become bound by law to furnish maintenance to him, and if in consequence of the death such third party is deprived of the right to claim maintenance, the person bound to make compensation must compensate the third party by the payment of a money annuity, in so far as the deceased would have been bound to furnish maintenance during the presumable duration of his life; the provisions of § 843, pars. 2 to 4 apply *mutatis mutandis*. The obligation to make compensation arises even if at the time of the injury the third party was only *en ventre sa mère*.

§ 845. In the case of causing death, or of causing injury to body or health, or in the case of deprivation of liberty, if the injured party was bound by law to perform services in favour of a third party in his household or industry, the person bound to make compensation must compensate the third party for the loss of services by the payment of a money annuity. The provisions of § 843, pars. 2 to 4, apply *mutatis mutandis*.

§ 846. If, in the cases provided for by §§ 844, 845, some fault of the injured party has contributed to cause the damage which the third party has sustained, the provisions of § 254 apply to the claim of the third party.

§ 847. In the case of injury to body or health, or in the case of deprivation of liberty, the injured party may also demand an equitable compensation in money for the damage which is not a pecuniary loss. The claim is not transferable and does not pass to the heirs, unless it has been acknowledged by contract, or an action on it has been commenced.

A like claim belongs to a woman against whom a crime or offence against morality is committed, or who is induced by fraud, or by threats, or by an abuse of a relation of dependence to permit illicit cohabitation.

§ 851. If a person bound to make compensation for any damage on account of the taking or damaging of a moveable compensates the person in whose possession the thing was at the time of the taking or damage, he is discharged by so doing even if a third party was owner of the thing, or had some other right in the thing, unless the right of the third party is known to him or remains unknown in consequence of gross negligence.

Substance of ownership

§ 903. The owner of a thing may, to the extent that it is not contrary to the law or the rights of third parties, deal with the thing as he pleases and exclude others from any interference.

§ 904. The owner of a thing is not entitled to forbid the interference of another with the thing, if the interference is necessary for the averting of a present danger and the threatened damage is disproportionately great in comparison with the damage to the owner arising from the interference. The owner can demand compensation for the damage caused to him.

Swiss Code of Obligations[1]

Chapter II Des obligations résultant d'actes illicites

A. Principes Généraux

I. *Conditions de la responsabilité*

41. Celui qui cause, d'une manière illicite,[2] un dommage à autrui, soit intentionnellement, soit par négligence ou imprudence, est tenu de le réparer.

Celui qui cause intentionnellement un dommage à autrui par des faits contraires aux mœurs est également tenu de le réparer.

II. *Fixation du dommage*

42. La preuve du dommage incombe au demandeur.

Lorsque le montant exact du dommage ne peut être établi, le juge le détermine équitablement en considération du cours ordinaire des choses et des mesures prises par la partie lésée.

III. *Fixation de l'indemnité*

43. Le juge détermine le mode ainsi que l'étendue de la réparation, d'après les circonstances et la gravité de la faute.[3]

Des dommages-intérêts ne peuvent être alloués sous forme de rente que si le débiteur est en même temps astreint à fournir des sûretés.

IV. *Réduction de l'indemnité*

44. Le juge peut réduire les dommages-intérêts, ou même n'en point allouer, lorsque la partie lésée a consenti à la lésion ou lorsque des faits dont elle est responsable ont contribué à créer le dommage, à l'augmenter, ou qu'ils ont aggravé la situation du débiteur.

Lorsque le préjudice n'a été causé ni intentionnellement ni par l'effet d'une grave négligence ou imprudence, et que sa réparation exposerait le débiteur à la gêne, le juge peut équitablement réduire les dommages-intérêts.

V. *Cas particuliers.* 1. *Mort d'homme et lésions corporelles*

a. Dommages-intérêts en cas de mort

45. En cas de mort d'homme, les dommages-intérêts comprennent les frais, notamment ceux d'inhumation.

Si la mort n'est pas survenue immédiatement, ils comprennent en particulier les frais de traitement, ainsi que le préjudice dérivant de l'incapacité de travail.

Lorsque, par suite de la mort, d'autres personnes ont été privées de leur soutien, il y a également lieu de les indemniser de cette perte.

b. Dommages-intérêts en cas de lésions corporelles

46. En cas de lésions corporelles, la partie qui en est victime a droit au remboursement des frais et aux dommages-intérêts qui résultent de son incapacité de travail totale ou partielle, ainsi que de l'atteinte portée à son avenir économique.

S'il n'est pas possible, lors du jugement, de déterminer avec une certitude suffisante les suites des lésions corporelles, le juge a le droit de réserver une revision du jugement pendant un délai de deux ans au plus à compter du jour où il a prononcé.

c. Réparation morale

47. Le juge peut, en tenant compte de circonstances particulières, allouer à la victime de lésions corporelles ou, en cas de mort d'homme, à la famille une indemnité équitable à titre de réparation morale.

48. [Repealed.]

3. *Atteinte aux intérêts personnels*

49. Celui qui subit une atteinte dans ses intérêts personnels peut réclamer, en cas de faute, des dommages-intérêts, et, en outre, une

somme d'argent à titre de réparation morale lorsque celle-ci est justifiée par la gravité particulière du préjudice subi et de la faute. Le juge peut substituer ou ajouter à l'allocation de cette indemnité un autre mode de réparation.

VI. *Responsabilité plurale*

1. *En cas d'acte illicite*

50. Lorsque plusieurs ont causé ensemble un dommage, ils sont tenus solidairement de le réparer, sans qu'il y ait lieu de distinguer entre l'instigateur, l'auteur principal et le complice.

Le juge appréciera s'ils ont un droit de recours les uns contre les autres et déterminera, le cas échéant, l'étendue de ce recours.

Le receleur[4] n'est tenu du dommage qu'autant qu'il a reçu une part du gain ou causé un préjudice par le fait de sa coopération.

2. *Concours de diverses causes du dommage*

51. Lorsque plusieurs répondent du même dommage en vertu de causes différentes (acte illicite, contrat, loi), les dispositions légales concernant le recours de ceux qui ont causé ensemble un dommage s'appliquent par analogie.

Le dommage est, dans la règle, supporté en première ligne par celle des personnes responsables dont l'acte illicite l'a déterminé et, en dernier lieu, par celle qui, sans qu'il y ait faute de sa part ni obligation contractuelle, en est tenue aux termes de la loi.

VII. *Légitime défense, cas de nécessité, usage autorisé de la force*

52. En cas de légitime défense, il n'est pas dû de réparation pour le dommage causé à la personne ou aux biens de l'agresseur.

Le juge détermine équitablement le montant de la réparation due par celui qui porte atteinte aux biens d'autrui pour se préserver ou pour préserver un tiers d'un dommage ou d'un danger imminent.

Celui qui recourt à la force pour protéger ses droits ne doit aucune réparation, si, d'après les circonstances, l'intervention de l'autorité ne pouvait etre obtenue en temps utile et s'il n'existait pas d'autre moyen d'empêcher que ces droits ne fussent perdus ou que l'exercice n'en fût rendu beaucoup plus difficile.

VIII. *Relation entre droit civil et droit pénal*

53. Le juge n'est point lié par les dispositions du droit criminel en

matière d'imputabilité, ni par l'acquittement prononcé au pénal, pour décider s'il y a eu faute commise ou si l'auteur de l'acte illicite était capable de discernement.

Le jugement pénal ne lie pas davantage le juge civil en ce qui concerne l'appréciation de la faute et la fixation du dommage.

B. Responsabilité des personnes incapables de discernement

54. Si l'équité l'exige, le juge peut condamner une personne même incapable de discernement à la réparation totale ou partielle du dommage qu'elle a causé.

Celui qui a été frappé d'une incapacité passagère de discernement est tenu de réparer le dommage qu'il a causé dans cet état, s'il ne prouve qu'il y a été mis sans sa faute.

C. Responsabilité de l'employeur

55. L'employeur est responsable du dommage causé par ses travailleurs ou ses autres auxiliaires dans l'accomplissement de leur travail, s'il ne prouve qu'il a pris tous les soins commandés par les circonstances pour détourner un dommage de ce genre ou que sa diligence n'eût pas empêché le dommage de se produire.

L'employeur a son recours contre la personne qui a causé le préjudice, en tant qu'elle est responsable du dommage.

56 and 57 [Animals]
58 and 59 [Buildings]
60 [Prescription]
61 [Responsibility of public officers]

---

1. These extracts are from the revised code enacted in 1911. Of the three equally authoritative versions, the French, German, and Italian, the first has been chosen here to avoid the necessity of translation.
2. The German version is *widerrechtlich*, which means merely 'contrary to law', and seems to emphasise, not the wrongful method but the absence of just cause or excuse.
3. The German version is *mach Ermessen des Richters*, 'according to the judge's discretion'.
4. This word means 'receiver'. The German *Begünstiger*, 'favourer', 'encourager', and the Italian *favoreggiatore* seem to show that something much wider is intended.

Civil Code for The
Mexican District and Territories[1]

Chapter V Of the obligations arising from wrongful acts

Art. 1910. Anyone who, by conduct wrongful or *contra bonos mores*, causes damage to another, is obliged to repair it, unless he shows that the damage arose in consequence of the fault or unexplainable negligence of the victim. (*Soviet C.C. art. 403; Swiss C.O. art. 41. § 2*)

Art. 1911. Anyone under a disability who causes damage must repair it, unless the responsibility falls on the persons charged with his supervision, in accordance with the provisions contained in articles 1919, 1920, 1921, and 1922. (*Swiss C.O. art. 54 ref.*)

Art. 1912. When damage is caused to another by the exercise of a right, there is an obligation to make it good if it is proved that the right was exercised only in order to cause the damage, without any advantage to the person entitled to the right. (*German C.C. § 226 ref.*)

Art. 1913. When a person makes use of mechanisms, instruments, apparatus, or materials dangerous either in themselves, or by the speed they develop, or by their explosive or inflammable nature, or by the energy of the electric current they conduct, or for other analogous reasons, he is obliged to answer for the damage which he causes, even if he does not act unlawfully, unless he shows that this damage was produced by the fault or inexcusable negligence of the victim. (*This article is new.*)

Art. 1914. When damage is produced without the employment of mechanisms, instruments, etc. referred to in the preceding article, and without fault or negligence in any of the parties, each one of them shall bear them without any right to be indemnified. (*This article is new.*)

Art. 1915. The reparation of the damage must take the form of the re-establishment of the pre-existing situation, and where that is impossible, of the payment of damages. (*Penal Code of 1871, art. 302 ref.*)

Art. 1916. Independently of the damages, the judge may grant in favour of the victim of the wrongful act, or of his family if he dies, an equitable indemnity, by way of moral reparation, which the person responsible for the act shall pay. This indemnity shall not exceed one-third of the amount for which he is civilly liable. The provision contained in this article shall not apply to the State in the case provided for in article 1928. (*Swiss C.O. arts. 47 and 49 refs.*)

Art. 1917. Persons who have caused damage in common are under a solidary responsibility to the victim for the reparation which they are obliged to make according to the provisions of this Chapter. (*C.C. of 84. art. 1474 ref.; Swiss C.O. art. 50.*)

Art. 1918. Juristic persons are responsible for the damage caused by their legal representatives in the exercise of their functions. (*C.C. of 84, art. 1481 ref.; Swiss C.O. art. 55; German C.C. §31.*)

Art. 1919. Those who exercise parental power are obliged to answer for the damage caused by the acts of minors who are under their power and live with them. (*C.C. of 84, art. 1481; Penal C. of 1871, art. 329. frac. I.*)

Art. 1920. The responsibility referred to in the preceding article ceases when minors do the acts giving rise to it while they are under the care and authority of other persons, such as heads of schools, work-shops, etc., since in that event those persons shall assume the responsibility in question. (*Argentine C.C., art. 1116 ref.*)

Art. 1921. The provisions contained in the two preceding articles apply to guardians in respect of the persons under disability whom they have under their care. (*C.C. of 84, art. 1481; Penal C. of 1871, art. 329, frac. II.*)

Art. 1922. Neither parents nor guardians are obliged to answer for damage caused by persons under disability subject to their care and vigilance, if they prove that they were unable to prevent it. This impossibility does not result from the mere circumstance of the act's having taken place outside their presence, if it appears that they have not exercised sufficient vigilance over the persons under disability. (*Argentine C.C. art. 1117 ref.*)

Art. 1923. Master craftsmen are responsible for the damage caused by their journeymen in the execution of the task which they entrust to them. In this case also the provisions contained in the preceding article apply. (*Penal C., art. 329, frac. III.*)

Art. 1924. The masters and owners of mercantile establishments are obliged to answer for damage caused by their workmen or dependants in the exercise of their functions. This responsibility ceases if they show that no fault or negligence can be imputed to them in the doing of the damage. (*Brazilian C.C., art. 1521, frac. III.*)

Art. 1925. Occupiers of houses or keepers of hotels or lodging-houses are obliged to answer for damage caused by their servants in the course of their employment. (*Argentine C.C., art. 1118 ref.*)

Art. 1926. In the cases provided for in articles 1923, 1924, and 1925, the person who suffers the damage can exact reparation directly from the person responsible, according to the terms of this Chapter. (*Argentine C.C., art. 1122 ref.*)

Art. 1927. Anyone who pays for the damage caused by his servants, employees or workmen may recover from them anything he may have paid. (*Argentine C.C., art. 1123. ref.*)

Art. 1928. [Responsibility of State for its servants]

Arts. 1929. and 1930 [Animals]

Art. 1931. [Buildings – as in French C.C.]

Art. 1932. Likewise owners of property answer for damage caused:

I. by the explosion of machines or the kindling of explosive material;

II. by smoke or gases, noxious to persons or property;

III. by the fall of their trees, when it is not occasioned by *force majeure*;

IV. by emanations from sewers or stores of tainted materials;

V. by collections of water which affect with damp a neighbour's party-wall or leak on to his property;

VI. by the weight or motion of machines, by the bringing together of materials or animals noxious to health or by any cause whatever from which damage originates without right. (*C.C. of 84 art. 1478 and 1479 refs; Spanish C.C. 1908.*)

Art. 1933. Heads of families who dwell in a house or part of a house are responsible for damage caused by things which are thrown or fall from it. (*Spanish C.C. art. 1910.*)

Note

1. Extracts from this highly eclectic code published in 1932 are given here to show the goal to which certain modern developments seem to tend.

Italian Civil Code[1]

1223. *Reparation of damage.* The reparation of damage caused by failure to perform or delay in performance is to include the loss suffered by the creditor[2] as well as his loss of profit, provided they are its immediate and direct consequence (see arts. 2056–9).

1226. *Equitable assessment of damage.* If proof of the damage cannot be brought to a precise figure, the judge fixes it by an equitable assessment (2056–2059).

1227. *Contributory negligence of the creditor.* If the negligence of the creditor has contributed to cause the damage, the reparation is reduced in accordance with the degree of negligence and the extent of the consequences flowing from it.

Reparation is not due for damage which the creditor could have avoided by using normal diligence.

Title IX Of wrongful acts[3]

2043. *Reparation for wrongful act.* Any malicious or negligent act which causes unjustifiable damage to another obliges the person who has committed the act to make good the damage.

2044. *Lawful defence.* No responsibility attaches to one who causes damage in lawful defence of himself or of others.

2045. *Case of necessity.* When the person who has committed the act causing damage was constrained thereto by the need of preserving himself or someone else from the present danger of serious personal injury, and the danger has not been caused voluntarily by himself and was not otherwise avoidable, the injured party is entitled to an indemnity the measure of which is left to the equitable assessment of the judge.

2046. *Imputability of the act causing damage.* No responsibility for the consequences of the act causing damage attaches to one who had no capacity for intention or volition at the moment when he committed it, unless the state of incapacity arose from his own fault.

2047. *Damage caused by one under incapacity.* In case of damage caused by a person incapable of intention or volition, reparation is due from the person who is responsible for the supervision of the incapable, unless he proves that he was unable to prevent the act.

2048. *Responsibility of parents, guardians, teachers, and masters of apprentices.* The father and mother, or the guardian, are responsible for the damage caused by the wrongful acts of the minor unemancipated children or wards living with them. The same provision applies to a foster parent.

Teachers and those who impart a trade or an art are responsible for damage caused by the wrongful act of their pupils and apprentices during the time when they are under their supervision.

The persons indicated in the foregoing paragraphs are freed from responsibility only if they prove that they were unable to prevent the act.

2049. *Responsibility of masters and principals.* Masters and principals are responsible for the damage arising from the wrongful act of their servants and agents in the exercise of the tasks for which they are employed.

2050. *Responsibility for the exercise of dangerous activities.* Whosoever causes damage to another in the carrying out of an activity which is dangerous by its own nature or by the nature of the means employed in it, is responsible for reparation, unless he proves that he has taken all the appropriate measures to avoid the damage.

2051. *Damage caused by things in one's care.* Everyone is responsible for damage caused by the things he has in his care, unless he proves inevitable accident.

2054. *Vehicular traffic.* The driver of a vehicle not on rails is obliged to repair damage done to persons or things by the movement of the vehicle, unless he proves that he has done everything possible to avoid the damage.

In the case of a collision between vehicles it is presumed, in the absence of evidence to the contrary, that each driver contributed equally to produce the damage sustained by the several vehicles.

The owner of the vehicle, or, in his stead, the usufructuary or the acquirer subject to a reservation of ownership, is jointly liable with the driver, unless he proves that the movement of the vehicle took place against his will.

In every case the persons indicated in the foregoing paragraphs are responsible for damage arising from faulty construction or defective upkeep of the vehicle.

2055. *Joint responsibility.* If the act causing damage is imputable to more than one person, all are under a solidary liability to repair the damage.

The one who has made reparation for the damage has recourse against each of the others, in a measure determined by the degree of their respective faults and the extent of the consequences flowing from them.

In the absence of evidence to the contrary, the several faults are presumed to be equal.

2056. *Assessment of damages.* The reparation due to the injured party is to be determined according to the provisions of articles 1223, 1226, and 1227.

The *lucrum cessans* is assessed by the judge on an equitable appreciation of the circumstances of the case.

2057. *Permanent damage.* Where the damage to a person is of a permanent character, the assessment may be made by the judge in the form of an annuity, account being taken of the position of the parties and the nature of the damage. In such a case the judge sees that appropriate security is furnished.

2058. *Specific reparation.* The injured party may claim to be specifically restored to his former position wherever it is possible, in whole or in part.

The judge may, however, decide that reparation shall take the form only of an equivalent sum of money, if specific restitution would prove excessively burdensome to the debtor.

2059. *Damage not of a patrimonial character.* Damage which is not of a patrimonial character gives rise to a claim for reparation only in the cases provided for by statute.

Notes

1. This Code of 1942, which superseded the Code of 1865, on this topic a mere reproduction of the French Civil Code, is the most up-to-date legislative treatment of responsibility as a whole. The influence of the German Civil Code and the Swiss Code of Obligations is apparent in many places.
2. The word 'creditor', in Italian as well as French and German law, has a much wider meaning than in English, and means anyone who is entitled to the benefit of an obligation.
3. This word is used for convenience of translation; but the Italian word *fatto* includes omissions and has no subjective connotation. It is used to show that it has no connexion with the 'will-theory' of obligation.

The (New) Netherlands Civil Code

Book 6. General Part of the Law of Obligations
(not yet in force)
Chapter 3. Tort

Section 1 General provisions

Art. 6.3.1.–1. A person who commits towards another a tort attributable to him is bound to make good the loss that other suffers in consequence thereof.

2. By a tort is meant an infringement of a right or an act or omission contrary to a statutory duty or to what is dictated by unwritten law in social intercourse, without prejudice, however, to the existence of a ground justifying it.

3. A tort can be attributed to the doer if it is due to his fault or to a

cause for which he is liable by virtue of statute or opinions prevailing in society.

Art. 6.3.1.2. No duty to compensate exists if the norm infringed does not purport to protect against such damage as the injured party has suffered.

Art. 6.3.1.2a. An act of a child who has not yet reached the age of fourteen years cannot be attributed to him as a tort.

Art. 6.3.1.2b.–1. The circumstance that an act of a person of fourteen years or over was done under the influence of a mental or bodily shortcoming is no obstacle to attributing it to the doer as a tort.

2. If a third person is liable to the injured party by reason of insufficient supervision, that third person is bound to the doer to contribute to compensate him for the whole extent of his liability to the injured party.

Art. 6.3.1.5.–1. If one among a group of persons unlawfully causes damage and the risk of thus causing it ought to have restrained those persons from so acting in a group, then they are jointly liable if those acts can be attributed to them.

2. Among themselves they must contribute towards the damage in equal parts, unless in the circumstances of the case equity requires a different apportionment.

Art. 6.3.1.5a.–1. When one person is liable to another under this chapter on account of a publication incorrect or misleading through an incomplete statement of its basis in fact, the court may, on the other's application, order him to publish a rectification in a manner to be indicated by the court.

2. The same applies if there is no liability because the publication is not attributable to the doer as a tort because he is unaware of its incorrectness or incompleteness.

3. In the case dealt with in paragraph 2, the court that grants the application may provide that the costs to be fixed by it of the case and of publishing the rectification shall be borne in whole or in part by the applicant.

Art. 6.3.1.5b.–1. The court may reject a demand for the prohibition of an unlawful act on the ground that act should be tolerated for serious social reasons. The injured party retains his right to compensation for the damage in accordance with the present chapter.

2. In the case dealt with in article 6.3.2.2. the servant is not liable for this damage.

3. If a judgment for damages or the provision of security therefor is not satisfied, the court may impose a prohibition against the act.

Section 2 Liability for persons and things

Art. 6.3.2.1.–1. For damage done to a third party by an act of a child who has not yet reached the age of fourteen years and to whom, under article 6.3.1.2a, that act is not attributable, the person who exercises parental power or guardianship over the child is liable.

2. For damage done to a third party through the fault of a child who has reached the age of fourteen years but not yet sixteen years, the person who exercises parental power or guardianship over the child is liable, unless it cannot be shown that he did not prevent the act of the child.

Art. 6.3.2.2.–1. For damage to a third party through the fault of a servant the person in whose service the servant executes his task is liable, if the risk of the fault was increased by the assignment of the task to be performed and the person in whose service he was had by virtue of the relevant legal relationship between them a say over the acts to which the fault was attributed.

2. If the servant was in the service of a natural person and was not acting in the interest or business of that person, the latter is liable only if the servant when committing the fault was acting in fulfilment of the task assigned to him.

3. If the servant and the person in whose service he was were both liable for the damage, the servant need not, as between them, contribute to the making good of the damage, unless the damage was in consequence of his wilfulness or conscious recklessness or, having regard to their relationship, a different result is implied in the circumstances of the case.

Art. 6.3.2.3. If a person who is not a servant but acts under the instruction of another person for the furtherance of his business, is liable to a third party for a fault committed in that activity, that other person is also liable to the third party.

Art. 6.3.2.4. If an agent is at fault towards a third party in the execution of the authority conferred on him as such, the principal also is liable to the third party.

Art. 6.3.2.5.–1. The possessor of a thing of which it is known that, if it does not satisfy the requirements that may be had in the circumstances, it constitutes a special danger to persons or things, is liable if the danger materialises, unless there would have been no liability under the foregoing section, even if he ought to have known of the danger at the time when it arose.

2. The first paragraph does not apply to buildings, animals, motor vehicles, ships or aircraft.

Art. 6.3.2.6.–1. The possessor of a substance known to have such characteristics that it constitutes a special danger to persons or things that cannot be avoided by taking the usual precautions, is liable if the danger materialises, unless the damage has its origin in the use of the material and in the circumstances in question even in a known dangerous use there can be no liability under the foregoing section.

2. If the material is in the custody of a storekeeper whose business it is to store such material, the liability under the first paragraph is on him.

3. A material is regarded as conforming to the description in the first paragraph if it is indicated as such in a general administrative decree.

Art. 6.3.2.7.–1. The possessor of a building which does not satisfy the requirements that may be laid down in the given circumstances and therefore constitutes a special danger to persons and things, is liable, if the danger materialises, unless even if he ought to have known of the danger at the time when it arose, there would have been no liability under the foregoing section.

2. In the case of long leases the liability falls on the lessee. In the case of public highways it falls on the authority charged with keeping the highway in repair, in the case of mains on the manager, except in so far the main is under a building or factory and serves for the supply or discharge for the benefit of that building or factory.

3. Buildings in this article are understood to comprise structures and works which are permanently fixed to the land, whether directly or through incorporation in other structures or works.

4. A person who is registered in the public registers as owner of the building is presumed to be the possessor of the building.

Art. 6.3.2.8. The possessor of an animal is liable for the damage done by the animal, unless there would have been no liability under the foregoing section even if he would have had control over the activity of the animal by which the damage was caused.

Art. 6.3.2.9.–1. In the cases covered by articles 5–8 co-possessors are jointly liable.

2. Where the transfer of a thing is conditional on the fulfilment of a

counter-performance the liability under articles 5–8 falls on the acquirer from the time of that transfer.

Art. 6.3.2.10.–1. If the things, materials, buildings or animals mentioned in articles 5–8 are used in the conducts of a business, the liability under article 5 paragraph 1, article 7 paragraph 1 and paragraph 2 first sentence, and article 8 falls on the person who conduct the business, unless it concerns a building and the occurrence of the damage has no connection with the conduct of the business.

2. If the things, materials, buildings or animals are used in the conduct of a business by placing them at the disposal of another for use in the conduct of his business, that other is indicated as the person liable under the foregoing paragraph.

Art. 6.3.2.11.–1. As regards liability under this section a defendant cannot invoke his youth or mental or bodily shortcomings.

2. Anyone exercising parental power or guardianship over a child who has not yet reached the age of fourteen years is liable in his stead under article 5, 6 and 8 for the things, materials and animals there mentioned, unless they are used in the conduct of a business.

Art. 6.3.2.12. With a view to limiting liability under articles 1–11 to whatever can reasonably be covered by insurance, amounts may be fixed by general administrative decree which the liability is not to exceed.

PART III
Extracts from German Cases
A BIRD'S EYE VIEW OF
THE ORGANISATION OF
THE GERMAN COURTS
IN CIVIL MATTERS[1]

The idea of a German Supreme Court can trace its origins to at least the end of the fifteenth century and the creation in 1495 of the Reichskammergericht of the Holy Roman Empire which originally sat in Frankfurt. The prevailing political fragmentation, however, prevented it from exercising any effective influence, especially in the area of the unification of the law, and even the Emperor himself held his own court in Vienna which often competed with the Reichskammergericht. A truly central supreme court had thus to await the unification of Germany which was eventually realised under Bismarck's strong hand in 1871. Even then it was some years later that the Reichsgericht came into being on 1 October 1879, this time, however, sitting in Leipzig. This was truly the first supreme court for the whole of Germany and, though other high federal courts subsequently saw the light of day, jurisdiction at the highest level was never divided. The Reichsgericht thus survived until the end of the Second World War (1945). During the next few years, while Germany lay in ruins and under foreign occupation, there was no Federal Supreme Court and, as a result, there followed an immediate and disturbing fragmentation of the law administered in the different parts of the country. The first attempts to re-establish some semblance of unity were made in 1947 in the British occupied zone when a special Court of Justice was entrusted with this task. However, it was not until 1 October 1950, a year after the enactment of the Constitution of Bonn, that the Bundesgerichtshof was established, this time in Karlsruhe. The scene was thus set for a 'judicial recovery' from the traumatic years of the Nazi period and the post-war chaos – a recovery which, in some respects, is as admirable as the more publicised 'economic miracle' of the 1950s which so symbolises the tenacity and determination of the German people.

Though in most respects modelled on the Reichsgericht, the Bundesgerichtshof was no longer accepted as the *unique*, supreme, federal court. The desire for increased specialisation, which is an important characteristic of the German judicial structure, meant that along with the Bundesgerichtshof, which became the Supreme Court for civil and criminal matters, *four* other Supreme Courts also came into being (each at the head of a separate set of courts with its own organisation and personnel) dealing respectively with administrative law, financial matters, labour matters and social legislation. Alongside these, the Supreme Constitutional Court (Bundesverfassungsgericht) was entrusted with the task of ensuring the preservation of the new constitution and the control of the constitutionality of legislation (articles 93, 94 GG). This proliferation of supreme courts, however, brought with it the possibility of jurisdictional conflicts, positive or negative in nature (e.g. two or more courts asserting or denying jurisdiction over the same dispute, now largely regulated by the Gerichtsverfassungsgesetz as amended in 1960) as well as the likelihood of a diverging case law on matters of substance. To resolve this latter conflict, and in order to ensure the unity of the federal law, article 95 of the Constitution of Bonn provided for the creation of a Highest Federal Court (Oberstes Bundesgericht) but this, in fact, never came into being and a constitutional amendment of 1968 provided instead for a 'Common Senate' (Gemeinsamer Senat) composed of judges from the other five supreme courts. The task of this court is to rule whenever one of the Supreme Courts proposes to depart from the case law of another Supreme Court or a holding of the Common Senate. Since in this work our emphasis has been on the civil law the remaining observations will be devoted to the organisation of the civil courts and the civil side of the Bundesgerichtshof.

The lowest court on civil matters is the Amtsgericht of which there are a large number (approximately six hundred). They have limited and specifically ascribed jurisdiction which includes disputes up to the value of 3,000 DM. In addition they deal with such varied matters as disputes between landlords and tenants; claims for financial support arising from marital or extra-marital relationships; the supervision of guardians, executors and trustees in bankruptcy and the handling of various registers including the all-important land register. Since 1977 all family matters, especially those associated with divorce proceedings, are heard by a special division of the court, the Familiengericht, and from there an appeal lies directly to the appropriate Oberlandesgericht. Though hierarchically an inferior court (and, in some respects, analogous to our own county court), the Amtsgericht is thus a court of singular importance to the average citizen who in his lifetime is usually spared the agony and the cost of the more prolonged or difficult type of litigation.

It is in the Landgericht, however, that one finds the equivalent of our High Court, and their large number (approximately one hundred) brings out clearly the second important characteristic of the German judicial organisation, namely, the considerable decentralisation in the administration of justice. The Landgericht is a court of *general* jurisdiction and sits as either a trial court or a court of review from any Amtsgericht of its district. It is usually divided into sections (or chambers) each of which includes a presiding judge and two associates (all three being professional and academically trained judges except for the Kammer Für Handelssachen (the commercial division) which is composed of one professional judge as president and two laymen experienced in commercial matters). From these courts an appeal lies to one of the Courts of Appeal (of which there are nineteen), which is called the Oberlandesgericht except for the one that sits in Berlin, which has always been known as the Kammergericht. Some Länder (namely, Bremen, Hamburg, Hessen, Saarland and Schleswig-Holstein) have only one Court of Appeal; others (e.g. Bavaria) have more. Quite exceptionally, a Court of Appeal can be by-passed and an appeal against a decision of the Landesgericht can be lodged directly with the Bundesgerichtshof. This, however, is likely to occur only where the facts of the case are not in dispute and the parties, desirous of an early solution to their dispute, are *both* willing to utilise this leap-frogging procedure (§ 566 ZPO).

The Bundesgerichtshof stands, as already stated, at the apex of the judicial hierarchy in civil and criminal matters. It is divided into ten Civil Senates (sections) and five Criminal Senates (of which one always sits in West Berlin). Each Senate specialises in different matters. The sixth Civil Senate, for example, deals with problems of delictual liability; the seventh Civil Senate with various types of contract and cases of unjust enrichment; the eighth Civil Senate handles disputes related to sales of goods, leases, etc. When deciding a case each Senate is composed of one presiding judge and four other Supreme Court judges and the entire Bundesgerichtshof is now staffed by over one hundred Supreme Court judges who are aided by specialist staff.

The large number of sections makes it once again necessary to provide for a mechanism which will solve potential conflicts between them and ensure the unity of the case-law at the highest level. This task is entrusted to the Great Senate (Gross Senat für Zivilsachen) and there is also a Great Senate for criminal matters which performs a similar function for the five criminal Senates. The Great Senate is composed of the President of the entire court and eight other judges and is seized of a dispute whenever one of the Civil senates wishes to depart from the case-law of another Civil Senate or the case-law of the Great Civil Senate itself. Before this happens, however, the Senate about to embark on a different course will inquire of the other Senate whether the latter wishes to abide by its jurisprudence. If it does not, then there is no reason to convene the Great Senate; but if the latter Senate does not wish to alter its case-law, then the Great Civil Senate becomes seized of the dispute. The Great Civil Senate may also become involved in a case even where there is no dispute in a narrow sense between various Senates of the court but one of them is anxious that the Great Civil Senate pronounce its opinion on a matter of particular significance. For the development of the law or its uniform application a conflict between one of the Civil Senates on the one hand and of the Criminal Senates on the other (or between one of them and the Supreme Civil Senate of the other branch) is resolved by the Combined Great Senates (Vereinigten Grossen Senate) which includes judges from both civil and criminal section of the court.

The decision to take a case to the Bundesgerichtshof can only be taken by one of the litigants, so that if both of them are content with or acquiesce in the result reached by the Court of Appeal the case can never reach the Supreme Court (even where a gross and obvious error of law has been made at the lower level). But though the parties decide whether they will take their case to a higher level, the decision whether their appeal will be admissible does not rest with them. There is a right of appeal (or, more technically, of a revision) only if the case was for technical reasons deemed inadmissible by the Court of Appeal, the reason for this being to ensure that all parties have at least two chances of having their case heard by a court of law. Review is also available as of right where the Court of Appeal has departed from a decision of the Bundesgerichtshof or of the Common Senate of the highest courts. Otherwise a distinction is made between pecuniary and non-pecuniary disputes. The former include cases which refer to a dispute estimable in money terms (e.g. disputes over contracts, delicts etc.); the latter relate to cases such as marriage or filiation proceedings etc. In non-pecuniary cases and in pecuniary cases which do not exceed 40,000 DM, the admissibility of the review depends on permission being granted by the Court of Appeal. This will be granted where the legal issues involved are of fundamental importance (§ 546 ZPO), but not otherwise, the idea being to shield the Supreme Court from overwork. In pecuniary matters exceeding 40,000 DM, the lodging of an appeal does not depend on the permission of the lower court. The Supreme Court itself may refuse to consider the case if the matter of law is not of fundamental importance (§ 544b. ZPO). If it is, the review will take place and a motivated judgment will be delivered either rejecting the appeal, or accepting it and remitting the case to the lower court for retrial or, finally, substituting the court's own judgment in the place of the decision that is quashed. If the legal point involved is not of great significance, the court has a discretion whether to hear the review or not. Its decision may be influenced by a variety of factors including the gravity of any procedural errors attributed to the decision under attack and, according to some authors, the volume of the work before the court. The decision is taken by the Senate appropriate for the particular kind of dispute and the revision cannot be denied if at least two of the five judges vote in favour of its being considered. The rejecting decision, however, is not, as a rule, accompanied by any reasons and, once again, this saves a great deal of time for the court.

Note

1. For a more detailed discussion, see: Kern, *Gerichtsverfassungsrecht* (1965); Vogel, 'Die Revision in Zivilsachen,' 28 NJW 1975, 1297; Schneider, 'Das neue Revisionsrecht aus der Sicht des Anwalts', 28 NJW 1975, 1537, and for statistical information H. Salger (and others) 'La cour fédérale de justice de la république fédérale d'Allemagne', in *Rev. int. dr. comp.* (1978), 811. Many of the points made in this section are also discussed in greater detail in the standard text-books on the law of Civil Procedure (Zivilprozessordnung).

NOTES TO THE GERMAN CASES

The chicken fowlpest case (case 1) marks for the German law of products liability the kind of turning point that *MacPherson* v *Buick Motor Co.* and *Donoghue* v *Stevenson* represent for the Common law. But it is reproduced here for the additional reason that it offers an excellent illustration of the thorough and systematic method the German Supreme Court will adopt, first, in rejecting the argument advanced by counsel in the case or the reasons given by a lower court for its decision, and then in advancing its own solution to the problem and the reasons for it. The Common lawyer should also note how the first answers offered to the problem of defective products were almost instinctively sought in the area of contract. Equally interesting is the similarity between some of these proposed solutions with those advocated by, say, American lawyers grappling with the same problems (e.g. the implied warranty approach). Others, however, have a strong German flavour about them; the Drittschadensliquidation approach, being one of the methods utilised to solve the problem, is briefly explained in a note to the decision.

The next four cases deal with the 'new' rights brought by the courts under the protective umbrella of para. 823 I BGB. Case 2 deals with the familiar 'cable cases' and the resulting pure economic loss as well as the repeated attempts to treat this conduct as an interference with the 'right of an established and operating business' and thus make it actionable under para. 823 I BGB; but the case also deals with possible liability under para. 823 II BGB and the difficulties to which that sub-paragraph gives rise. The judgment is also noteworthy for its open allusion to the kind of policy considerations which can have such influence on the outcome of this type of litigation.

Cases 3, 4, and 5 deal with the other 'new right'–the right to one's personality. Case 3 is, in one sense, the leading case and illustrates, amongst other things, how the general constitutional framework can affect the development and interpretation of the Civil Code. Case 4 – Germany's *Tolly* v *Fry* – takes this process a step further by acknowledging the possibility of monetary compensation (in addition to the granting of an injunction not to publish the defamatory material). Given the limitations of paras. 253 and 847 BGB the solution was quite a daring one and, though criticised in some quarters, it succeeded in setting the pattern of subsequent developments. Finally, case 5 also deals with the same topic and contains dicta which suggest that through the notion of 'satisfaction' German law may have come quite close to our penal damages. The point however is hotly disputed.

Cases 6, 7, 8, 9, and 10 deal with problems of causation. Case 6 rather laconically accepts the adequate cause theory but it has been referred to many times since. However, it must always be understood in the light of the gloss put upon this term by the BGH in 1951 (*BGHZ* 3, 261, 267). There, the Supreme Court said that 'only if the courts remain conscious of the fact that the question is not really one of causation but of fixing of the limits within which the author of a condition can fairly be made liable for its consequences.... can they avoid schematising the adequate cause formula and guarantee correct results'.

Cases 7 and 8 are, in a sense, of less significance, but they are reproduced here, the first to show how the adequate cause theory is applied in practice; the second in order to illustrate how problems, which in the Common law would be treated under the heading of duty, in the Civil law fall naturally to be considered under the heading of legal cause. It will be noticed that though the conceptual approach is different the underlying ideas are very similar.

By contrast, cases 9 and 10 are particularly important for they show the use made of the more normative theory of causation – the 'scope of the rule' approach – adopted as a result of growing disillusionment with the limiting capability of the more traditional theories of causation. But this theory, too, is incapable of universal application (see volume I, Chapter 3).

Cases 11 and 12 deal with *culpa in contrahendo* and these two cases, along with cases 13 and 14, show how the law of contract can be used to perform the functions of the law of tort. Case 12 also shows how a contractual and delictual action can be cumulated without the kind of difficulties experienced by French law.

Case 15 is a decision of the Grosse Senat which deals with the thorny question of unlawfulness (see chapter 2 of volume I and Nipperdey in *NJW* 1957, 1777). The theoretical interest of this decision is great and it has given rise to a very large literature. In practice, however, the decision has had little effect. In this respect it could be taken as exemplifying the German interest in theoretical constructions.

Case 16 and 17 are the exact equivalents to *Dutton* and *Anns*. The superiority of the German reasoning, however, must be noted. The kind of harm suffered by the plaintiff is rightly described as financial and, even though this is recoverable in principle in actions under para. VI. 839 BGB, the plaintiff's claim is here dismissed. The disadvantage of being too theoretical has been noted. Here, however, we see one of the advantages of clear doctrinal thinking. The German legal mind could not (and did not) tolerate the sloppy confusion between damage done *by* the defective thing and damage *to* the defective thing itself. The result is, surely, fortunate. Finally, case 19 is one of very many cases dealing with the problem of negligent mis-statements. It has been chosen for inclusion partly because it brings out very clearly the importance attached to the plaintiff's reliance on the defendant's statements and partly because it happens to be one of the latest pronouncements on this point. Once again, however, the emphasis on the law of contract rather than the law of tort must be noted.

1. Decision of the 6th Civil Senate of 26 November 1968 (BGHZ 51, 91)[1]

(a) If in using an industrial product for its proper purpose a person or thing is injured through its defective manufacture, the manufacturer must prove that he was not at fault in respect of the defect.

(b) If the manufacturer fails to produce that proof, he is liable according to the principles governing delict. An intermediate acquirer cannot claim on the basis of the law of contract the damage suffered by a third party.

BGB §§§ 823, 249

VI. Zivilsenat judgment of 26 November 1968 in Re: S.V. GmbH (Defendant) v.B. (Plaintiff) VI ZR 212/66

I. Landgericht Mönchengladbach

II. Oberlandesgericht Düsseldorf

On 19 November 1963 the plaintiff, who ran a chicken farm, had her chickens inoculated against fowlpest by the vet, Dr H. A few days later fowlpest broke out. More than 4,000 chickens died and over 160 had to be slaughtered.

The plaintiff claimed compensation for the damage from the defendants, vaccine manufacturers, whose vaccine 'XY' had been used by the vet. This the vet had acquired from the defendants in 500 ccm bottles at the beginning of November 1963. The bottles came from batch 'ALD 210', which the defendant company had had inspected on 18 October 1963 at the public Paul-Ehrlich Institute in Frankfurt-am-Main; and the batch had been released by them for public use. The defendant had subsequently and in the course of its business poured the contents into receptacles normally used in commerce. As regards receptacles with lower than 500 ccm capacity that is done by airtight closure under negative pressure; larger bottles were filled by the defendants 'openly' but in a closed room under ultraviolet radiation.

When a few days later, on 22 November 1963, Dr H inoculated the chickens at B's farm, fowlpest broke out there. At about this time this happened also in three other poultry farms in Württemberg which had had their chickens inoculated with the defendant company's vaccine from batch 'ALD 210'. When the Stuttgart Veterinary Inspection Office had several bottles of that batch inspected by the Federal Research Institute for Virus Diseases in Animals, there were found in some bottles bacterial impurities and still active ND (Newcastle Disease) viruses, which had not been sufficiently immunised.

Moreover, the Paul-Ehrlich Institute established that some of the bottles sent to it for inspection were not sterile and ND virus could be detected in them.

The defendant company disputed the claim that the outbreak of fowlpest was to be traced to the use of its vaccine; and in any case the defective sterility of the bottles was not the cause. For this it invoked the opinion supplied to it by Dr E of the Federal Research Institute for Virus Diseases. It put forward evidence exonerating it from liability for its workers in and the director of its virus section.

The Landgericht and the Oberlandesgericht declared the claim well founded. The defendant company's appeal was unsuccessful for the following reasons:

The Court of Appeal started by finding that the vaccine supplied to Dr H was contaminated by bacteria, and that the outbreak of fowlpest was to be traced to it. Even the defendant company's expert, Professor Dr E, could not exclude the possibility that the contamination had arisen through carelessness on the part of persons employed by the defendant company in the bottling. For their fault the defendant company must be liable under § 278 BGB to the vet, the buyer of the vaccine. He, however, was entitled to be compensated for the damage done to the plaintiff. Since he had assigned his claim for compensation to the plaintiff, the action was well founded.

I. The principles governing the claims for damage suffered by a third person (Drittschadensliquidation)[2] cannot be applied to the present case.

1. In principle the only person who can claim compensation for damage under a contract is the one to whom the damage occurred in fact and who, in law, has to bear it. If the damage occurs to a third party, the doer of it is liable to him – apart from certain exceptions- only in delict. This distinction between the more favourable liability in contract and the more restricted liability for delict is imbedded in the existing system of liability law and is not a mere theoretical dogma. Only in special cases have the courts admitted exceptions, namely, where special legal relations between the creditor under the contract and the beneficiary of the protected interest cause the interest to be 'shifted' on the third party, so that as a matter of law the damage is done to him, and not to the creditor. From it the doer can derive no benefit to the third party's detriment: he must make good to the creditor the damage to the third party. That applies–apart from the rare cases of responsibility for risks (*BGHZ* 40, 91, 100)–where the

creditor has contracted for the third party's account (*BGHZ* 25, 250, 258), or where the thing that the debtor promised to take care of belonged not to the creditor but to the third party (*BGHZ* 15, 224).

(a) This is no such exceptional case. No 'union of interests' between the vet (who made the contract) and the third party (i.e. the plaintiff) is created by indirect agency. Dr H had not bought the vaccine to the order or for the benefit of the plaintiff. When he ordered and obtained it from the defendant company he did not yet know for which farmer he would use it. A vet invariably buys his medicines for himself like a contractor in respect of his materials and not for his patients or employers, even if he requires them to perform an order already given him.

Moreover, this is not one of the cases where the thing placed in the debtor's care belonged not to the creditor but to a third party. Of course Dr H may have had imposed on him a 'duty of care' (Obhutspflicht) concerning the plaintiff's chickens. But it is a condition for claiming for damage suffered by a third party (Drittschadensliquidation) that the duty of care exists between creditor and debtor (*BGHZ* 40, 101). That was not the case here.

(b) The Court of Appeal also acts on these principles. It is also aware that in principle the manufacturer and supplier of a thing which has been sold again to a third party does not need, merely on the basis of the contract of sale, to make good damage occurring to a third party (*BGHZ* 40, 104, 105). All the same it believed that in the present case it could permit the claim in respect of the damage suffered by the third party. Here the faultless condition of the vaccine was of special interest to the plaintiff, on whose chickens it was to be used. The vet could not check the condition of the vaccine, but had to rely on careful manufacture by the defendant company. The latter must therefore have proceeded on the assumption that a duty of faultless delivery rested on it in favour not merely of the vet but also of whoever happened to keep chickens.

(c) These considerations do not justify treating this as a case for claiming damage as suffered by a third party (Drittschadensliquidation). Already in its judgment *BGHZ* 40, 90[3] the Bundesgerichtshof has emphasised that a contract of sale cannot be interpreted in accordance with the requirement of good faith so as to afford a basis for compensation to a third party injured through defects in the thing bought. In that decision it departed from the judgment of the Reichsgericht in *RGZ* 170, 246. The Court of Appeal has also established no concrete basis for holding that the defendant company had been ready and willing to afford to the other party to the contract (namely, the vet) claims to compensation more extensive than under the statutory law of sale. Moreover, it is a condition of claiming for damage suffered by a third party that only *one* damage shall have taken place, which would have been suffered by the creditor unless the protected legal interest was that of a third party. There can be no question here of 'shifting' the damage. It occurred here to the plaintiff in fact as well as in law, whereas in a genuine 'shifting' of damage it occurs to the creditor in fact, though not in law. It could not occur either to the vet or to the chicken farmer, but only to the latter, and not – which is the decisive point – to him instead of to the vet.

The cases of claims for damage suffered by a third party (Drittschadensliquidation) so far admitted by the courts cannot be extended to cover a case like the present one. Otherwise the manufacturer and supplier of necessaries and luxuries, of toiletries and medicines, etc. would have to make good damage to the ultimate user not only in delict but also on the contract of sale. For he also knows, like his buyer, the wholesaler, and intermediate and retail dealers, that any damage would show itself, in the hands not of the dealer, but of the ultimate recipient. This does not lead to the conclusion, however, that the producer is liable in contract to the ultimate recipient. The question how these interests are to be protected cannot, therefore, be solved by allowing a claim for damage suffered by a third party (Drittschadensliquidation).

2. The Court of Appeal also based its opinion on the principle that a duty of care on the part of the manufacturer towards the third party arises from the meaning and purpose of the contract. That might be interpreted in the sense that the Court of Appeal is willing to allow the plaintiff a claim to compensation on a *contract with protective effects for third parties*.[4] That consequence also cannot be approved.

(a) The Bundesgerichtshof has, indeed, allowed claims to compensation on this legal theory and under specified circumstances, to a third person not a party to a contract (*BGHZ* 33, 247, 249 and 49, 350, 351 with references). Those principles, however, cannot be called in aid here.

In no way can everyone who has suffered damage through a failure of care on the part of a debtor derive his own claim to compensation from the contract between creditor and debtor (Senate judgment of 30 April 1968–VI ZR 29/67 *NJW* 1968, 1323). The Senate in its judgment of 18 June 1968 (vi ZR 120/67 *NJW* 1968, 1929) indicated afresh that the law distinguishes between persons suffering direct and indirect damage and that liability under a contract is, on principle, bound up with the bond that binds the debtor to creditor (cf. also BGH judgment of 9 October 1968–viii ZR 173/66). Otherwise there is a danger that the debtor can no longer calculate the risk that he undertakes in making a contract. Hence it would no longer accord with the principle of good faith, out of which the contract with protective effect for third parties has been developed, for the debtor to be liable for such extensive consequences of his breach of contract. That can be admitted only if the creditor shares, so to say, in the responsibility for the welfare of the third party, because damage to the latter affects him also, since he is under a duty to afford him care and protection. It is this internal relation between creditor and the third party, ordinarily marked by legal relations of a personal character, and not the relation between the parties to the contract, that is the reason for the protection of the third party. Such a relation does not, as a rule, exist in a contract of sale or a contract for the doing of a job.

(b) Moreover, in the present case there are no such close relations between the creditor (the vet) and his clients.

II. If therefore the judgment under attack cannot be supported by the foregoing reasoning, we must inquire whether it can be upheld on other lines. The plaintiff not only based her action on claims derived from the contract made by Dr H with the defendant company, but also invoked §§ 823 *et seq.* BGB. In addition, she prayed in aid the question exhaustively argued in recent times, above all at the Deutscher Juristentag of 1968, concerning the direct liability of the manufacturer of goods to the ultimate user ('products liability').

1. Even the advocates of an extensive liability of the producer start as a rule from the proposition that it can be based neither on a claim for damage suffered by a third party (Drittschadensliquidation) or on a contract with protective effects for third parties. They prefer to provide the user with his own claim for damages, not one dependent on the contract between the manufacturer and buyer, and not brought against the manufacturer as an 'action directe' – like the claim for damages based on §§ 823 *et seq.* BGB. But they consider this claim in delict no longer satisfactory or appropriate, bacause it does not, as a rule, cover purely economic damage and, above all, because it leaves open to the producer the possibility of exonerating himself, especially where there is a mere slip in the productive process.

The case to be decided here affords no occasion for examining the question whether we should adhere to the rule developed by the courts that the producer can invoke § 831 BGB when there are defects in the actual production... and that such defects raise no presumption of fault against the manufacturer (Senate judgment of 21 April 1956–VI ZR 36/55). For it is not established here that it was because the defendant company's staff had made a mistake that the vaccine contained reactivated viruses. That may also be due to causes that are inherent in the company's methods of production, and in particular in the method of bottling. In the present case there is no need to adopt a comprehensive attitude to the problems of products liability. Here, only the following considerations apply.

(a) The claim in the action could be granted without further discussion if the view of Diederichsen[5] could be followed, that the manufacturer must be liable for every kind of defect in the product without reference to fault, as in the liability for risks or results ('strict liability'). He believes that this can be derived from the existing law by 'considerations of legal sociology or legal theory'. It is however doubtful whether his standpoint can be supported on grounds of legal policy and, at any rate, liability without fault is incompatible with the present law of (civil) liability. To extend the liability for risks regulated in particular enactments – mostly subject to different ceilings – to products liability is forbidden to judges. It is rather for the legislator to decide whether and how far a stronger objective liability should be imposed on the manufacturer.[6]

(b) Nor is it legally possible–apart from special cases–to afford to the ultimate recipient a direct claim for damages on the assumption that a contract of warranty was concluded directly, albeit tacitly, between him and the producer. The fact that the producer allows his goods to be distributed as his invention, that is to say with his label, in original packaging, with his trade name or trade mark, and so on, cannot, as a rule, be considered as a declaration that he intends to make himself responsible to users for careful manufacture (cf. *RGZ* 87/1). Normally, even the advertisement of branded goods which are advertised with particular emphasis on the ultimate user, contains no indication of any willingness to be liable for any defects in the goods (*BGHZ* 48, 118, 122/3). Moreover, that cannot be assumed even when the appreciably wider question is asked whether the manufacturer is willing to be directly liable to the ultimate user of his product.

(c) There is also no question of a claim for damages being accorded for a breach of alleged duties of protection consequent on a 'social contact'. No business relations exist between manufacturer and recipient, nor are they intended to be started and, eventually, to be concluded. The relations which certainly exist on the sociological plane have not enough legal weight for claims for liability to be made from a special legal relation. That applies also to Weimar's attempt to derive a producer's liability from the general rule in § 242 BGB.[7]

2. Especial consideration is merited by the idea that recognition should be given to a special quasicontractual relation between manufacturer and user, resting on statute and developed from the notion of confidence. In fact the relations that have come into existence between the buyer of a dangerous product and its manufacturer, before the occurrence of the damage, would seem to be closer than those that bring the latter into relations with 'everyman' when—and not before—he is actually injured. To refer 'everyman' to his claim in delict is sound. As regards the claims for compensation of a buyer, on the other hand, it should be considered whether they also arise from contract law if he bought the goods not directly from the manufacturer but through a dealer.

(a) Starting from the special legal relationship between manufacturer and acquirer of goods, Lorenz[8] at the Karlsruhe forum 1963 was the first to state the opinion that the manufacturer must be liable under § 122 BGB to answer for the confidence in his product, strengthened by advertising, that he has awakened in its users. Those ideas were mentioned by the eighth Civil Senate of the Bundesgerichtshof at the close of its judgment of 13 July 1963 (BGHZ 40, 91, 108), but without committing itself to any position. In its judgment *BGHZ* 48, 118, it declined to accept advertisement as a possible source of liability. In the struggles for the all-important customer (König Kunde), advertisements have become more and more extensive and more and more significant from a business point of view. This, however, does not yet mean that they have acquired the meaning of a promise of legal liability. Moreover, no reasonable user understands it to be so: and Lorenz has not followed up his idea.

(b) Lorenz's basic idea provided the foundation for the attempts to derive the manufacturer's liability from a duty to satisfy the confidence placed by the user and made the basis for a claim corresponding to the legal principles developed for *culpa in contrahendo*.

It is however doubtful whether these considerations can hold water, so as to afford the user a claim for damages which, like the claim in delict, cannot be excluded automatically, but on the other hand would not be threatened by exoneration under §831 BGB. The Senate has already, in its judgment of 21 March 1967 (VI ZR 164/65) reacted against the attempts to base the liability of a third person, not a party to a supposed contract, on the fact that his confidence was sought; and it emphasised that they would break, with dire consequences, through the boundary drawn between liability based on a contractual obligation and that arising from delict. Whether the doubt there expressed against an extension of liability for 'positive breach of contract' ('positiver Vertragsverletzung')[9] tells also against a subjection of the producer to a liability on the analogy of contractual liability need not be finally decided in this case. Nor need the question be gone into of how such a quasi-contractual claim should be afforded to a person injured by the product if he did not buy it but damage occurred through its use by himself or another person. In the case now to be decided there is no question of a number of legally successive sale contracts in which the seller, in fact, is often the mere 'distributor' of the manufacturer, in which case a breaking of the veil suggests itself. Here between the plaintiff and the defendant company stood a vet, who had alone to decide which vaccine to use. The plaintiff had placed her confidence in him and not in any advertisement. She was not, herself, in a position to buy the vaccine directly or in the market: the defendant company could deliver it only to the vet and only he might use it... That, of itself, excludes the idea that a quasi-contractual relation existed between the parties. The plaintiff was not a 'consumer' of the vaccine, nor even a 'user' of it, but, from a legal point of view, 'only' a sufferer of damage. As such she is limited to her claim in delict.

III. According to the Court of Appeal's findings of fact the conditions of liability under §823 BGB are fulfilled. The vaccine supplied by the defendant company was defective and the cause of the disease to the chickens. Even if, as explained above, the rules of contract law are not applicable, nevertheless the starting-point must be that the defendant company has committed a fault. If anyone when using an industrial product for its declared purpose suffers injury in one of the legal interests protected by §823 1 BGB, through the defective manufacture of the product, it is for the manufacturer to explain the antecedents that caused the defect and thereby to show that he was not to blame for it.

1. It is not in question that even in 'products liability' the injured party must prove that the damage was caused by a defect in the product. The plaintiff had therefore to show that the fowlpest broke out among her chickens because the vaccine originated with the defendant company and contained active viruses when delivered.

That proof was considered by the Court of Appeal to have been furnished. (An explanation followed.)

2. The Court of Appeal, having to ascertain why the vaccine contained live viruses, started from the fact that both the Paul-Ehrlich Institute and the Federal Research Institute found bacteria in the bottles examined by them. It based its conclusions in essence of Professor Dr E's opinion. He declared it highly probable that the bacteria had found their way into the bottles at the manual pouring of the vaccine from the large containers into the bottles. It has been observed on various occasions that viruses which–as here–have been killed by the addition of formaldehyde can, under certain conditions, become reactivated. It was therefore possible that the bacteria here had reactivated the virus. On the basis of these explanations of the expert, the Court of Appeal believed it could find that the contamination of the bottles by bacteria was the cause of reactivation. It pointed out also that no damage arose from the part of the batch that was not contaminated by bacteria, whereas that was the case with the bottles used by Dr H and in the district of Heilbronn, and in which the bacteria were found. Even Dr E held it possible that the contamination of the vaccine was caused by 'human error' on the part of one of the persons employed by the defendant company in bottling the vaccine.

3. The appellant attacked this conclusion of the Court of Appeal, but without success.

It is indeed correct that the Court of Appeal considered no fault of the defendant company itself as proved. It accepted that it was probably only an employee that was to blame for the damage. A liability of the defendant company, cannot, as we have seen, be established by applying the law of contract, as set out in § 278 BGB. That does not, however, necessitate sending the dispute back to the judge of fact. For it would still be for the defendant company to exonerate itself even if the plaintiff can rely on § 823 BGB.

(aa) This results from the fact that the plaintiff's claim for compensation is also based on § 823 II BGB. For the defendant company, by delivering the dangerous bottles of vaccine infringed a protective enactment. This vaccine, a medicine in the sense of the Medicines Act of 16 May 1961 (§ 3 III AMG), was capable of producing in the chickens injurious, even fatal, effects. §6 AMG prohibits the putting of such vaccines into circulation. That provision – like 3 LebMG (cf. *RGZ* 170, 155, 156 on §4 LebMG) which applies to foods dangerous to health – constitutes an enactment for the protection of endangered human beings or animals. If, however, an infringement of a protective enactment is proved, it is presumed to be the result of fault. The infringer therefore must produce facts sufficient to disprove his fault (Senate judgment of 12 March 1968–VI ZR 178/66). The owner of the business did not produce that proof so long as a possible cause, falling within the scope of his responsibility and which might point to fault, remained unelucidated (Senate judgments of 3 January 1961–VI ZR 67/60 and 4 April 1967–VI ZR 98/65).

(bb) This rule governing the burden of proof would, however, also apply if the plaintiff could base her claim for damages only on § 823 I BGB. In that case, also, it would be for the defendant to exonerate itself. It is true that the injured party who relies on § 823 I BGB will have to allege and if necessary prove not only the causal connection between his damage and the conduct of the doer, but also his fault (*BGHZ* 24, 21, 29). However, the possibility of proving the subjective conditions depends appreciably on how far the injured party can elucidate the detailed course of events. That is however especially difficult when it relates to antecedents which played a part in the business of manufacturing the products. The courts for a long time came to the help of the injured party by contenting themselves with proof of a chain of causation, which, according to human experience, indicates an organisational fault in the manufacturer. All the same, one cannot stop at this point in considering claims for damages for 'products liability'. All too often the owner of a business can show that the defect in the product might have been caused in a way that does not point to his fault – evidence which generally relies on activities in his business and which is difficult for the injured party to disprove. In consequence, when damage has arisen within the range of the manufacturer's business risks, he cannot be regarded as exonerated merely because he points out that the defect in the product might have arisen without any organisational fault of his. This is required in the area of 'products liability' in order to protect the interests of the injured party – whether ultimate acquirer, user or third party; on the other hand, the interests of the producer allow him to demand that he may prove his lack of fault.

This rule of evidence indeed only operates as soon as the injured party has proved that his damage falls within the scope of the manufacturer's organisation and risks, and indeed is satisfied by the existence of an objective defect or of unbusinesslike conduct. This proof is required of the injured party even when he sues the doer of damage for breach of protective and subsidiary duties arising from a contract or the negotiations for one (Senate judgments of 16 September 1961–VI ZR 92/61 and 18 January 1966–VI ZR 184/64). It is the same if he claims against the producer for breach of his duty of care. However, once he has provided this evidence, the producer is better able to explain the facts or to bear the consequences of being unable to offer an explanation. He surveys the field of production, determines and organises the manufacturing process and the control of delivering the finished products. The size of the business, its complicated, departmentalised organisation, its involved technical, chemical or biological processes and the like make it practically impossible for the injured party to ascertain the cause of the defect. He is therefore unable to lay the facts before the judge in such a way that he can decide with certainty whether the management is to be blamed for neglect or whether it is a case of a mistake in manufacture for which a workman is at fault, or a single breakdown that may happen at any time, or defect in development that was unforeseeable in the existing state of technology or science. But if the cause of inexplicability lies within the scope of the producer, it is also within the scope of his risks. In that case it is appropriate and expected of him that the risk of not being able to prove his innocence should lie with him.

Such rules of evidence have always been applied to contractual or quasi-contractual relations of a special legal character between injured party (creditor) and doer of damage (debtor) (*BGHZ* 48, 310, 313). No obvious reason can be given why they should not also apply to delict, if the reasons for them apply. In certain connections § 831 BGB already imposes on the employer the proof of exoneration–the same applies to liability cases under §§ 832, 833, 834 BGB, and, above all, to §§ 836 *et seq*. Here, indeed, the law requires a person damaged through the collapse of a building to prove that the damage was 'the consequence of defective erection or defective maintenance', but lays on the possessor etc. the burden of proving that he had done everything to avoid the dangers that could attach to his building. The reversal of the burden of allegation and proof ordered in these provisions does not always proceed from a presumption of fault in the doer of damage. It rests in the main on the thought that the doer is in a better position than the injured party to throw light on the events relevant to the charge of negligence, so that it is just to impose on him the risk of being unable to do so. The Senate has already in its judgment of 1 April 1953 (VI ZR 77/52) indicated that the plaintiff cannot be required to prove – as a rule an almost impossible task – that the thing that caused the damage came into circulation through the fault of the owner of the business or his agents. Above all, the Senate has already in its judgment of 17 October 1967 (VI ZR 70/66) declared that it is for the producer to exonerate himself, if the injured party can give no detailed information about the management's blameable breaches of duty. The modern development of production, which is distributed among persons or machines which are hard to identify at a subsequent stage and rests on finishing processes capable of being inspected and controlled only by specialists, demands a development of the law of evidence in the direction already indicated in § 836 BGB...

In any case – as with the recognised shifting of the burden of proof for 'positive breach of contract' – it always depends on the interests at stake in the groups of cases from time to time under consideration. The question whether the assumption of the risk of proof can be imputed in the case of the owner of a small business, where the manufacturing processes can be easily surveyed and examined (family and one-man businesses, agricultural producers and the like), need not be considered here. In cases of the present kind it is in any case for the manufacturer to exonerate himself.

4. The defendant company has not furnished that proof of exoneration.

(a) According to Professor Dr E's opinion submitted by the defendant company, it is possible that carelessness on the part of someone concerned with the bottling led to the contamination of the bottles. He considered the process of filling containers of over 500 ccm by manual pouring and not, as happens with the smaller containers, by means of an apparatus as an 'older method' which was indeed 'tolerable', but needing improvement. For this manual pouring there must at least be constructed a correspondingly superior 'clean work bench' with UV radiation. In addition the 'modest apparatus outfit' of the business must be increased by installing dry sterilisers, so that the larger containers could be better sterilised, above all without long interruption. He also pointed out that in the process of autoclave without a temperature and pressure gauge no control could be

95

exercised over whether the high temperature needed for the sterilisation under pressure was really attained. Moreover, he recommended the use of tubes showing changes of colour. He also advised that the filling room be examined for its germ content from time to time by exposing dishes of agar or blood.

The expert then was of opinion that in spite of these suggestions for improvement, the manufacturing methods of the defendant company were 'not unsatisfactory' and 'fulfilled the normal requirements'. Moreover, the method of bottling guaranteed a sufficient degree of security, even though it need to be improved. Finally, he was of opinion that the defendant company had not carelessly neglected any of the necessary precautions. The bacterial contamination could indeed have been caused by defective observance of the required precautions, but could have occurred even if they had been observed.

(b) The expert's view of the required degree of care cannot be approved. Even he starts by saying that in the manufacture of vaccines in which the effect of living viruses must be immunised 'the highest possible security' must be required. For that very reason vaccine works are subjected to strict public supervision (§ 10 AMG together with the provisions of Land law still operative under § 5). The defects mentioned by him in the equipment of the defendant company's business, above all as regards manual bottling, are in conflict with a finding that the management were not guilty of careless conduct. The improvements recommended by him were not at all far-fetched and imposed on the company requirements that were neither technically nor financially excessive. The possibility cannot be excluded that those additional precautions would have averted the bottling of dangerous vaccine.

Notes

1. This judgment, with its frequent references to a multitude of theories advanced to solve the problems arising from defective products, may prove especially difficult for the uninitiated reader. In order to help him in his task we have generously annotated the text of this decision with notes of our own but the complexity of some of these theories is such that the notes must be treated as *inevitably incomplete generalisations.* For further information, the advanced reader may consult any or all of the following works:

     For mainly German law: E. v. Caemmerer, 'Products liability in *Ius Privatum Gentium*', *Festschrift für Max Rheinstein* (1966) pp. 659 *et seq.*; *idem*, 'Das Problem des Drittschadensersatzes', repr. in *Gesammelte Schriften*, 1 (1969, pp. 597 *et seq.*); C.W. Canaris, 'Die Produzentenhaftpflicht in dogmatischer und rechtspolitischer Sicht', *JZ* 1968, 494 *et seq.*; U.Diederichsen, *Die Haftung des Warenherstellers* (1967); J. Gernhuber, 'Drittwirkungen im Schuldverhältnis kraft Leistungsnähe', *Festschrift für*

Extracts from German cases

Nikisch (1958), pp. 249 *et seq.; K.Larenz*, 'Culpa in contrahendo, Verkehrssicherungspflicht und "sozialer Kontakt"', in *M.D.R.* 1954, 515 *et seq.*; W.Lorenz, 'Rechtsvergleichendes zur Haftung des Warenherstellers und Lieferanten gegenüber Dritten', *Festschrift für Hermann Nottarp* (1961) pp. 59 *et seq.*; *idem*, 'Warenabsatz und Vertrauensschutz', *Karlsruher Forum* (1963), pp. 8 *et seq.*; E.Lukes, 'Produzentenhaftung und Maschinenschutz', *JuS* 1968, 345 *et seq.*; *idem, Reform der Produkthaftung* (1979); R.H. Mankiewiez, 'Products liability – a judicial breakthrough in West Germany', 19 *I.C.L.Q.* (1970), 99 *et seq.*; S.Simitis, 'Soll die Haftung des Produzenten gegenüber dem Verbraucher durch Gesetz, kann sie durch richterliche Fortbildung des Rechts geordnet werden? In welchem Sinne?' Gutachten für den 47. *Deutschen Juristentag* (1968); *idem, Grundfragen der Produzentenhaftung* (1965); W. Posch and B.Schilcher, eds., *Rechtsentwicklung in der Produkthaftung*, (1981).

For *Romanistic (mainly French Law)*: P.Malinvaud, 'La reponsabilité du vendeur a raison des vices de la chose', *J.C.P.* 1968,1.2153; *idem*, 'La responsabilité civile du fabricant en droit français', *G.P.* 1973, 2.463; H.Mazeaud, 'La responsabilité civile du vendeur-fabricant', *Rev. trim. dr. civ.* 1956, 611; J.F. Overstake, 'La responsabilité du fabricant de produits dangereux', *Rev. trim. dr. civ.* 1972, 485; G.Petitpierre, *'La responsabilité du fait des produits'* (1974).

For *the Common law*: A selection from the huge, mainly periodical, literature can be found in M.A. Franklin's *Tort Law and Alternatives*, 2nd ed (1979), ch. 5, and in Prosser, Wade and Schwartz, *Torts, Cases and Materials* (1976), ch. 15. For a recent English monograph, see Miller and Lovell, *Product Liability* (1977):

For *comparative works, see*: Tebbens, *International Product Liability. A study of comparative and international legal aspects of product liability* (1979); Stucki and Altenburger, *Product Liability: A manual of practice in selected nations* (2 vols., 1980); Faculté de droit d'Aix en Provence, *La responsabilité du fabricant dans les états membres du Marché commun* (1974); Schmidt-Salzer, *Produkthatung im französischen, belgischen, deutschen, schweizerischen, englischen, kanadischen und us-amerikanischen Recht sowie in rechtspolitischer sicht* (1975); C.Szladits, Comparative aspects of products liability, 16 *Buffalo Law Review* (1966–7), 229.

2. Drittschadensliquidation is a mainly judge-made doctrine which allows a *creditor* to a contract to claim (in contract) for loss resulting from the non-execution or bad execution of the contract, but falling not upon him (the creditor) but upon a third party. The doctrine is based on the all-pervading concept of good faith and is meant to prevent circuity of actions and, above all, to ensure that the defaulting party in the contract does not benefit from the fact that in these cases the loss has been shifted (Gefahrverlagerung, Schadensverlagerung) from the creditor to the third party. (On the whole matter see, amongst others, v.Caemmerer in *Gesammelte Schriften*, 1, 597 *et seq.*; W. Lorenz, 'Die Einbeziehung Dritter in vertragliche Schuldverhältnisse', *JZ* 1960, 108 *et seq.*; W. Selb, 'Kritik formaler Drittschadensthesen', *NJW* 1964, 1765.) If this exception to the notion of relativity of contracts had not been accepted, the defaulting party would not be liable to his creditor (since the latter has suffered no loss); nor would he be liable (in contract) to the third party in the absence of any *vinculum iuris* between them. Like all judge-made rights, however, this right is kept under close scrutiny lest it get out of control and expose the contractual debtor to an unlimited number of claims. Thus, the third party will be allowed to rely on the doctrine only where special relations between him and the creditor to the contract cause the interest (and the loss) to be shifted on to him. Example: A, acting as C's

97

'indirect agent', buys a chattel from B. German law does not recognise the notion of undisclosed agency, so C acquires no interest in the chattel at this stage and is under no obligations towards B. Through B's fault, the chattel cannot be delivered to A but A, being guilty of no fault, is not himself responsible to C (internal relations). If Drittschadensliquidation was not permitted in this case, B, though guilty of fault, would be relieved of all liability since A cannot sue him (since he has suffered no loss) and C cannot sue him since he has no contract with him. (For further examples in English, see E.J. Cohn, *Manual of German Law*, I (1968), nos. 165,205.)

One further point should be noted. We shall see (note 4, below) that German law recognises two variations of contracts *in favorem tertii* which come close to achieving practical results similar to those obtained by the application of the notion of Drittschadensliquidation. Yet between them there are some differences including the requirement that in the former type of action the *third party* has a personal right to claim directly from the debtor, whereas in the latter type of action the *creditor* must bring the action on behalf of the third party which has suffered the loss. Yet this may be more theoretical than practical, since in practice the creditor cedes (and, according to §281 BGB, is obliged to cede) his action to the third party.

3. It must, however, be noted that in this earlier case the court was dealing with the sale of *defective raw materials* (unprocessed leather) by A which caused (different kinds of) damage: to B (a belt manufacturer) who bought it from A; to C (a retailer of ladies' garments) who bought the belts from B and placed them on his products; and to D, the ultimate purchaser of the complete garment. The present case seems to extend the earlier refusal to rely on Drittschadensliquidation to the case of *defectively manufactured products*. For a discussion of the earlier case see Klaus Müller, 'Zur Haftung des Warenherstellers gegenüber dem Endverbraucher', *AcP* 1965, 285, 297–8; Diederichsen, *Die Haftung des Warenherstellers, pp.* 107 *et seq.*

4. In addition to contracts in favour of third parties (Vertrag zugunsten Dritter) which are regulated by the BGB in §§ 328 *et seq.*, and which entitle a specified third party to require performance of the contract concluded between creditor and debtor (cf. the point made in the last para. of note 1, above), German law has (under the influence of Karl Larenz) come to accept a new variant commonly referred to as Vertrag mit Schutzwirkung zugunsten Dritter (contracts with protective effects in favour of third parties). In this variation the debtor owes his 'principal' obligation not to the third party but to the creditor. But in addition to the 'principal' obligation, he also owes *de lege* (i.e irrespective of the wills of the parties) a number of 'subsidiary' obligations which include duties of care towards certain third parties which are directly enforceable by them. However, this new concept, which is once again justified by reference to article 242 BGB and the all-pervading principle of good faith, is kept closely under control, as the judgment above clearly shows. The way the courts achieve this is by insisting on the presence of some kind of close relationship (personenrechtliches Fürsorgeverhältnis) between the contractual creditor and the third party before the latter is given a contractual right to compensation (Thus *BGHZ* 15, 224; 25, 250; BGH NJW 1964, 33,4; and cf. case 13, below). It is noteworthy that even those authors who have argued in favour of expanding the circle of 'protected' third parties have refused to apply this theory in the case of products liability. Thus, see Canaris, 'Die Produzentenhaftpflicht', pp. 499 *et seq;* Gernhuber, 'Haftung des Warenherstellers', *Karlsruher Forum* 1963, 2 *et seq.*

5. Die Haftung des Warenherstellers, pp. 297 *et seq.*, 327 *et seq.*, 345 *et seq.*

Diederichsen's theory can, for present purposes, be reduced to two basic propositions: first, that the basic relationship that has to be considered in these cases is that between manufacturer and ultimate consumer, which is one of 'reliance' irrespective of any awareness of any advertisements of the manufacturer; second, that this 'relation' is *sui generis* (Warenkauf), not regulated by the written law, which must be determined in its details by the judge. A corollary of this is that the liability is strict. It is worth noting how summarily the civilian court deals with a theory which tends to give it wide powers which do not appear to be based on any specific provision of the Code. Equally interesting is the court's hostility towards any idea of strict liability, for which see the next note.

6. Apart from an isolated example (§ 833 BGB) strict liability has not been incorporated in the BGB and has, instead, been the subject of many separate enactments. One consequence of such a multitude of enactments, each containing its own divergent rules and presuppositions for strict liability, has been the view held by the German courts for a long time now (see, for example, *RGZ* 78, 171, 2) that the imposition of strict liability should be left to the legislator and the courts should not attempt it through analogical extension of existing statutes. This, however, is not an 'unavoidable' consequence for any system which opts for strict liability through the medium of special enactments since the Austrian Oberste Gerichtshof, for example, has never had the same qualms about analogical extension of particular provisions to other forms of 'dangerous' operations (thus, *OGH* 10 Sept. 1947, SZ XXI 46; 20 Feb. 1958, SZ XXXI 26).

7. This paragraph of the judgment deals in a summary fashion with a cluster of theories which appear to have met with little support in Germany. Their common starting-point appears to be the undoubtedly sound distinction between the debtor's 'primary' obligations (e.g. in the case of sale of goods to deliver the goods) and his 'subsidiary' obligations (Schutzpflichten, Aufklärungs-pflichten) which may be owed to persons other than the creditor (see note 4, above). According to the authors of these theories, such 'subsidiary' obligations may arise not only from contractual but from other 'relations', as well, and this is particularly likely to happen whenever the parties are in a 'social contact' from which it is clear that one of them is relying on the other. As already stated, such reasoning has met with little success in the context of products liability, though analogous reasoning fared better in the case of liability for negligent statements (cf. case 18, below). R. Weimar's theory, which is being rejected by the court, can be found in his book *Untersuchungen zum Problem der Produktenhaftung* (1967); the other main theory is by C.W. Canaris, 'Die Produzenten-haftpflicht'.

8. Lorenz's theory (Karlsruher Forum, pp. 8 *et seq.* especially p. 14) has many common points with some of the theories mentioned earlier and equally dismissed by the court. He too, for example, puts the emphasis on the relationship between producer and ultimate consumer and he, also, is prepared to attach considerable significance to the reliance that one person (the consumer) places on the conduct of another (the manufacturer). Like other writers, Lorenz also accepts that we are here faced with a *lacuna* in the written law which must be filled in a way that will ensure that the plaintiff is given equal (if not greater) protection to that enjoyed by contracting parties (moving towards strict liability). Unlike other authors, however, Lorenz makes a clearer attempt to base his solution on a specific provison in the code and this, in his opinion, is § 122 BGB. § 122 BGB provides that if a declaration of

intention is void either because it was made in error or because it was not seriously intended, the person who made the declaration must compensate the other party for the damage he has sustained as a result of relying upon the validity of the declaration. (The damages here extend only to the reliance interest and do not include the expectation interest.) This provision, according to Lorenz, can be analogically extended to cover the present problem, since the manufacturer, through the advertising of his products, leads the ultimate consumer to expect that his product will be free of all defects. In its judgment the Supreme Court directs its criticism mainly towards Lorenz's point about the significance of modern advertising techniques and the effect that they can be taken to have on the ultimate purchaser. It is submitted, however, that Lorenz's view has two further weaknesses: first, it is by no means clear (to an outsider, at any rate) that § 122 BGB, which envisages an entirely different situation, is capable of analogical extension; second, even if it is, the acceptance of this theory (which is based on §§ 118, 119 and 122 BGB) would lead to the imposition of *strict* liability on the manufacturer towards the *ultimate* consumer with whom the manufacturer has no contract), but to liability based only on fault (in accordance with the law of sale) towards his *immediate* purchaser, a solution which must be indefensible. (In this sense, also, M.Manghivas, *The Liability of the Manufacturer of Mass-Produced Products* (1978) (in Greek), pp. 99 *et seq.*)

9. The German BGB and indeed, the other Germanic systems (e.g. Swiss, Greek etc.) have only provided in their Codes for 'impossibility' of performance or 'delay'. But the debtor may (and usually does) perform, but performs 'badly', and the Germanic families have described such cases of bad performance with the inelegant phrase 'positive breaches of contract', which dates back to the seminal work of H. Staub, *Die positiven Vertragsverletzungen* (1904).

2. Decision of the 6th Civil Senate of 8 June 1976 (BGH NJW 1976, 1740)[1]

The defendant company, which conducted a building enterprise, was on 23 November 1973 making excavations on private property in the Württemberg town W. An electric cable was negligently damaged. This led to a twenty-seven minute interruption of the current used in the plaintiff's manufacturing business. The plaintiff estimated that the interruption led, through a failure of production, to a loss of 1157.66 DM. The plaintiff claims that amount as damages from the defendant.

Both lower instances reject the claim. The plaintiff is granted leave to apply for review, but is unsuccessful for the following reasons:

I.1. The appellate court is of opinion that:

(a) The claim can find no support in § 823 1 BGB; for no property of the plaintiff's was damaged or destroyed by the electricity failure. Moreover, no legal injury was done to the plaintiff's right of an established and operating business, since there was no direct interference with it.

(b) Moreover, the appellate court rejects a claim for compensation under § 823 II BGB; for the defendant's contravention of §18 III of the Baden–Württemberg Building Regulations did not constitute a breach of an enactment designed for the plaintiff's protection. That provision says:

Public spaces, supply, run-off and warning apparatuses and also hydrants, survey marks and boundary marks must be protected during the process of building and, where necessary, be kept accessible subject to the necessary precautions.

In essentials the appellate court says: the language of this provision contemplates damage only to things, not persons. Moreover, the Regulations as a whole belong to the law of *public* security and order. § 18 III cannot be assumed to afford to electricity users a claim to compensation not otherwise provided for, all the more since it would lead to a great and intolerable extension of liability. It would also be consistent with the fact that § 1 II No. 1 of the Regulations affords no private law right to compensation where a similar accident occurs in the course of building in places open to public traffic. This reasoning is in open conflict with the BGH decision of 12 March 1968 about the corresponding regulations of Land Nordrhein-Westfalen.

It is against this reasoning (i.e. of BGH *NJW* 1968, 1279) that this appeal is lodged. In support of the appeal a question is raised whether, contrary to the principles laid down by *BGHZ* 29, 65, 74 = *NJW* 1959, 479, an interruption of electricity supply is not to be regarded as an invasion of the right of an established and operating business, in the sense of § 823 I BGB.

II. The appeal is unsuccessful.

1. The Senate deciding the case agrees with the appellate court in holding that the plaintiff cannot invoke § 18 III 1 of the Regulations as a protective enactment for the purposes of § 823 II BGB. In so far as this runs counter to the principles of the aforementioned decision of the BGH of 12 March 1968, the court rejects them. The Hessen decision of 12 March 1968 is not followed.

(a) (Earlier decisions elsewhere are in agreement.)[2]

(b) There are convincing reasons for approving the appellate decision. That certain provisions of the Regulations, especially those for the protection of neighbours, can be treated as protective enactments for the purposes of § 823 II BGB does not stand in the way. For no such purpose can be detected in favour of electricity users.

(aa) The provision of the Regulations here in question is not an enactment for the protection of the plaintiff. Although admittedly most rules of a public law character operate in a general way to protect and further the interests of individual citizens, it does not follow that that *general* operation also specifies the cases where a protective enactment in question affords *him* an *individual protection*. That is not difficult to establish if the protective function of a rule can be detected in the statement of its purpose; but if, as often happens with recent enactments, the *travaux préparatoires* give only an imperfect indication or none at all, it is of no use to consider legislative purpose in the abstract: nor has this been done so far by the Federal High Court, despite some ambiguous formulations. In the last resort the question must be attacked directly, whether the creation of an individual claim for compensation appears meaningful, sensible, and tolerable in the light of the whole system of liability. Only by so doing can a development, rightly feared by the appellate court, be avoided, namely that the increasing tendency to base claims on § 823 II BGB might undermine Parliament's ruling *against* a general liability for pure economic loss. In this connexion it may be useful to ask whether in such cases an individual claim for an injunction would be sensible and tolerable.

(c) There is no need to go further into these aspects of the decision; for it appears from what has been said that the appellate court properly decided that the Regulations afforded no individual protection to users of electricity against possible economic damage.

(aa) According to the basic principle of liability laid down by federal law, there is, as a rule, no liability for indirect damage (economic damage that a third party suffers by mere reflex operation through injury to another's property); and this includes damage to an electricity user resulting from damage to a cable owned by an electricity supplier. That the failure to afford compensation is not felt to be intolerable is shown *inter alia* by the fact that the responsibility of electricity suppliers even for vital failures is excluded by regular nationwide conditions of supply. Although the possibility cannot be absolutely excluded that this principle may be set aside by protective Land legislation, nevertheless, such legislation should be interpreted to extend protection only if the need for it arises from a state of affairs in the law of the Land which could not have been anticipated on a federal level. Since that is obviously not the case here, the constitutional distribution of powers makes it unlikely that the Land legislator wantonly intended to extend protection by action repugnant to the federal rule.

(bb) But even apart from this constitutional aspect, based on the concept of constitutional demarcation of authority, the appellate decision must be approved. There is nothing to be said for the view that the Regulations, when regulating building, intended to afford to electricity users an abnormal individual protection when a cable is damaged. The appellate court rightly points to the lack of any corresponding provision in § 1 II of the LBauO, where danger to cables is especially to be anticipated, that is to say, where works are conducted in places open to public traffic. In other fields also electricity users have no individual protection, for instance where cables are endangered in traffic, mining or agricultural accidents. The possibility that a building regulation intends to afford a protection so much out of line in this particular field is very remote. The official statement of motives leading to the Regulations here in question lends no assistance. Moreover, it is noticeable that the basic duty of care already existed in the general law and was not originally created by the Regulations as part of Land law. Its inclusion in § 18 III only serves to sum up precautions required to be taken in works regulated by statute, and to form a basis for prosecution. There is nothing to show that an arbitrary individual protection was aimed at, alien to federal law and as part of a generally inappropriate set of Regulations.

2. The appellate court also appropriately rejects any liability to compensate for an interference with the plaintiff's business. It finds itself in agreement with the Senate decision of 1959[3] which dealt with a case on all fours with this one. The Senate, on reconsideration, holds fast in principle to its decision in spite of some loudly expressed academic criticism. The need to relate to a trade, as established by the 1959 judgment, which is denied in cases such as the present one, is essential if the protection provided by the case law in the event of a violation of the right of an established and operating business is not to be enlarged into a general delictual rule for the protection of traders. The highest court has always taken this point into account although the boundaries of this 'residual right' which affords special protection to traders have never been fully defined and much could be said in favour of a restrictive application of this delictual rule. In any event, matters cannot be otherwise in the case of a power cut of this nature which affects everyone and which is liable to cause widespread financial loss to persons who do not exercise any trade and to whom the general law of delict affords no claim for damages.

The above cannot be countered with the argument that where

damage is caused by an electricity failure a distinction between physical and economic damage makes little sense. In fact the Senate has so far awarded damages for physical damage in business according to § 823 1 BGB. This, it must be admitted, somewhat surprising limitation – von Caemmerer calls it 'crude' – rests on a binding general decision of the delictual law in force. It is impossible to recognise any reason for departing from it in favour of businesses. In any event, might not the danger of less foreseeable and perhaps much greater physical damage involved in such accidents justify a partial exemption of the tortfeasor from a risk that the electricity supplier frees himself from with state approval? But the present case affords no occasion for such an examination, since physical damage is neither manifest nor even doubtful.[4]

Notes

1. Cf. *S.C.M. (U.K.) Ltd* v. *Whittal & Son Ltd* [1971] 1 Q.B. 337; *Spartan Steel & Alloys Ltd* v. *Martin & Co.* [1973] Q.B. 27.

   In this case the plaintiff pleaded his case in tort (§ 823 1. and III BGB) and lost. A year later, another plaintiff argued his case in contract and also lost (BGH *NJW* 1977, 2208.) The facts were as follows: the defendant firm of contractors made a contract with a local body (Zweckverband) to excavate a particular area within the latter's jurisdiction. After the contract was concluded, an inspection of the site took place in the presence of representatives of the local body and the plaintiff (a near-by factory owner) and one of the defendant's foremen was warned about the presence of cables. He promised that when the digging reached that part, no mechanical excavators would be used. Owing to the negligence of one of the defendant's workmen (who did, in fact, use a mechanical excavator), one of the cables was severed and there was a power cut which affected the plaintiff who suffered economic loss (*inter alia* the payment of wages without being able to use the services of his employees; cf. *McMillan Bloedel* v. *Foundation Co. of Canada Ltd* (1977) 75 D.L.R. (3rd) 294). The plaintiff's first argument was that this was a proper case for applying the concept of Drittschadensliquidation (see note 2 to the previous case, p. 97, above), for, in his opinion, the defendant was in breach of his contract with the local body but the loss had fallen on him, a third party. The plaintiff's second argument was to invoke the notion of Vertrag mit Schuzwirkung für Dritte (see note 4 to the previous case, p. 98, above). The BGH objected to this use of the contractual concepts, *inter alia*, on the ground 'that the extension of contractual obligations is prevented by the fact that defective workmanship or neglect of safety measures may damage any persons imaginable – householders, tenants, industrialists – so that contractual protection would be extended to an unlimited circle of persons which it would no longer be possible to encompass'. For the use of this kind of 'consequentialist' argument see the discussion in vol. 1, ch. 2.

2. The decision of the Supreme Court of 1968 (BGH *NJW* 1968, 1279), which had awarded damages for pure economic loss under § 823 II BGB, met with little approval in the various Courts of Appeal which took a firm, opposite, stand and, in a sense, forced the Supreme Court to recant in this judgment. See: Bavarian Court of

Appeal, *VersR* 1972, 667; Court of Appeal of Karlsruhe, *NJW* 1975, 221, and Court of Appeal of Hamm, *NJW* 1973, 760. This last decision is of particular interest since it dealt with the question what amounts to damage to 'property' (which is, undoubtedly, compensated under § 823 I BGB; *BGHZ* 41, 123). In the Hamm case, which is an exact contemporary of our *Spartan Steel* decision, molten material solidified as a result of the power cut but, unlike *Spartan Steel*, the metal could be restored to its molten state and used once the power supply was resumed. In the court's view, since the interference and alteration was only temporary, it should not be treated as damage to property and thus should not be compensated – a view which many commentators of the case have not shared. The case raises more questions than any judgment could possibly answer. How long must the interference be before the damage can be characterised as property damage? Indeed, should the answer to this problem depend upon any time element? Akin to this is another question: what if the defendant's act prevents the plaintiff from moving or otherwise making use of his property; this will, invariably, cause him financial loss, but an Australian judge has suggested that this might well be regarded as injury to property in that chattel (Jacobs J. in *Caltex Oil (Australia) Pty Ltd* v. *The Dredge 'Willemstad'* (1977) 11 A.L.R. 227 at p. 278); and an important decision of the BGH (*BGHZ* 55, 158) has taken a similar view (plaintiff's vessel trapped in a small canal as a result of the defendant's negligence). The case, however, has other, complicated, aspects which cannot be discussed here; and seven years later the Supreme Court itself (BGH *NJW* 1977, 2264) chose to take advantage of the different facts of the later case and back-pedal from its earlier ruling.

3. *BGHZ* 29, 65. The legal literature on this (new) 'right of an established and operating business' is enormous. H. Buchner's *Die Bedeutung des Rechts am eingerichteten und ausgeübten Gewerbebetrieb für den deliktsrechtlichen Unternehmensschutz* (1971) is an excellent monograph. See also his shorter but more recent study 'Konsolidierung des deliktsrechtlichen Unternehmensschutz' in *DB* 1979, 1069 *et seq*. For a summary in English see K. Lipstein, 'Protected interests in the law of torts', 22 *C.L.J.* 85 (1963).

4. See Addenda, p. 341

3. Decision of the 1st Civil Senate of 25 May 1954
(*BGHZ* 13, 334)[1]

Letters and other private notes may not, as a rule, be published without the agreement of a living author and then only in a way approved by him. That follows from the protection of personality guaranteed in arts. 1, 2 of the Basic Law (Constitution) and operates even if the notes do not display the individual form required for the protection of copyright.

Basic Law arts. 1, 2; BGB § 823 I; Copyright Law 1

1. Zivilsenat judgment of 25 May 1954 in Re: Dr M (Plaintiff) v. 'D.W.' Verlags GmbH (Defendant) 1 ZR 211/53
   I. Landgericht Hamburg
   II. Oberlandesgericht Hamburg

The D Company published on 29 June 1952 in its weekly Journal...an article by K.B. with the title 'Dr H.S. & Co.' and the sub-title 'Political considerations concerning the foundation of a new bank'. The article contained a comment concerning the new Bank for Foreign Trade founded by Dr S in H,[2] and expressed itself in that connexion in opposition to Dr S's political activity during the National Socialist regime and the years after the War.

On the instructions of Dr S the plaintiff, an attorney, sent to the defendant company a letter on 4 July 1952, saying, *inter alia*:

I represent the interests of Dr S. In terms of § 11 of the Press Act I hereby require the following correction of the above-mentioned article in your issue of Sunday the 6th instant:

    1. It is incorrect that...

    2. ...

This claim for correction is made under the Press Act, in combination with the BGB, and also the law of copyright.

I ask you to inform me by telephone or in writing on or before midday, Saturday 5 July 1952, of your confirmation of the unrestricted execution of the required correction, failing which legal proceedings will be taken.

The defendant company gave the plaintiff no answer. But in the issue of 6 July it published, along with sundry expressions of opinion by readers on K.B.'s article, the following under the heading 'Letters from Readers':

Dr H.S. & Co.

    To the...(name of journal)

    I represent the interests of Dr H.S.

    1. It is incorrect that...

    2. ...

                Dr M, Attorney

In the contents of para 1. there was no reproduction of or extracts from the appropriate Nuremberg judgment concerning Dr S which the plaintiff had introduced in his letter of 4 July 1952. Otherwise they were unaltered.

The plaintiff sees in this kind of publication an injury to his right of personality. The publication of his letter, written in his capacity of attorney for Dr S, under the heading 'Letters from Readers' and with its contents falsified by the omissions and the choice of title, constitutes a deliberate misleading of the public. The incorrect impression was thus created that this was a mere expression of opinion by a reader on the previous article on Dr S, as was the case with other readers' letters printed under the same rubric. The plaintiff, however, had kept clear of taking any political attitude and had acted only as an attorney within the scope of his instructions. From a professional standpoint alone the conduct of the defendant company was intolerable. An attorney must be able to ensure that demands for correction made in his client's name must not be circulated in a misleading manner.

The plaintiff demanded that the defendant company be ordered to recall in its next issue under 'Letters from Readers' its statement that the plaintiff had sent a reader's letter to the defendant company in the matter of Dr H.S. & Co.'.

The defendant company takes the view that it was not bound to agree to the plaintiff's demand for a correction, because his letter did not conform to the requirements set out in §11 of the Press Act. It lay therefore within its discretion whether and at what place in its journal to print the communication.

The Landgericht granted the claim under §823 II BGB, in combination with §§ 186, 187 StGB. The Oberlandesgericht rejected the claim. According to the Court of Appeal's opinion there was, in the abbreviated publication of the plaintiff's letter under the rubric 'Letters from Readers', no unlawful disparagement of the plaintiff. The method of this publication certainly contained an incorrect statement of fact. The incorrect statement that the plaintiff had sent a reader's letter to the defendant company was, however, not apt to injure his credit, nor to bring him into contempt or lower his dignity in public opinion.

The appeal led to a restoration of the Landgericht's judgment for these reasons:

The Court of Appeal was in error in failing to examine whether the plaintiff's claim was justified on the basis of a disparagement of his personality rights. It dismissed the action only because it did not consider as proved the objective presuppositions (elements) of a delict in the sense of §§823 II, 824, BGB in combination with §§186, 187 StGB. This objection is rightly made in the appeal.

It can be left undecided whether the plaintiff's letter of 4 July 1952 was a written work in the sense of §1 of the Copyright Act and hence fell within the protection of copyright. The Reichsgericht has, indeed, constantly made the protection of correspondence to depend on whether it showed the individual form required for the protection of copyright (*RGZ* 41, 43, 48; 69, 401, 403). On the other hand it has been rightly pointed out in the academic literature that a need for the recognition of a personality right in respect of the use of one's own notes equally exists even when that protection cannot be derived from the personality right of the author, on the ground that they do not possess the form given by an individual intellectual activity...The Reichsgericht believed that it must deny such a protection of personality independent of copyright to publications of correspondence because the German law then in force contained no positive statutory provisions on a general personality right (*RGZ* 79, 397, 398; 82, 333; 334; 94, 1; 102, 134; 107, 277, 281; 113, 414; 123, 312, 320). It has indeed, in many decisions on § 823 BGB, approved of the protection of personality rights (*RGZ* 72, 175; 85, 343; 115, 416; 162, 7), but in principle it has recognised personality rights with an absolute power of exclusion only for certain specified personality interests. In the literature Gierke and Kohler[3] have already pleaded for the recognition of a comprehensive personality right...

Moreover, now that the Basic Law (Constitution of 1949) has recognised the right of a human being to have his dignity respected (art. 1), and also the right to free development of his personality as a private right, to be universally respected in so far as it does not infringe another person's right or is not in conflict with the constitutional order or morality (art. 2),[4] the general personality right must be regarded as a constitutionally guaranteed fundamental right.

No further discussion is needed here of whether and how far the protection of this general personality right, the limitation of which requires a balancing of interests, is restricted in particular cases by justified private or public needs, which outweigh the interest in the inviolability of the exclusive sphere of personality; for in this present case it is not evident that the defendant company has any interests worth protecting, which it could use to justify the conduct objected to by the plaintiff. On the contrary, by the defendant company's choice of a way of publishing the request for correction, omitting essential parts of the letter, interests of the plaintiff in the nature of personality rights have been infringed.

Every verbal expression of a definite thought is an emanation from the author's personality, even when the protection of copyright cannot be attributed to its form. It follows that in principle only the author is entitled to decide whether and in what form his notes are communicated to the public; for every publication of the notes of a living person under his name is rightly regarded by the public as proceeding from a corresponding direction of his will. The nature of the notes and the method of their communication is subject to the criticism and valuation of public opinion, which draws conclusions from those circumstances about the author's personality. While an unauthorised publication of private notes constitutes – as a rule – an inadmissible attack on every human being's protected sphere of secrecy, a modified reproduction infringes the personality rights of the author because such unauthorised alterations can spread a false picture of his personality. In general, not only unauthorised omissions of essential parts of the author's notes are inadmissible, but also additions through which his notes presented for publication only for certain purposes acquire a different colour or tendency from what he expressed in the form chosen by him and the kind of publication he had allowed.

In so far as concerns works protected by copyright, those legal principles have long been inferred by the courts from the creator's enjoyment of the personality right of an author, which is only a particular phenomenon of the general personality right (*RGZ* 69, 242, 244; 79, 397, 399; 151, 50). As regards the protection of personality the interest of the author in notes which are protected by copyright is essentially the same.

In the present case the plaintiff had unambiguously sent to the defendant company only a demand for correction and, indeed, in his character as attorney for Dr S. Thereby the defendant company was only empowered by the plaintiff either to publish the text in unshortened form or, restricting itself to the required correction, to make clear that there had been a demand for correction. Since the plaintiff does not ask for his original desire for correction to be carried out, it is unnecessary for the purpose of this decision to consider whether his letter of 4 July 1952 conformed to the conditions of the Press Act. If, in agreement with Court of Appeal this had to be denied, the only consequence would be that the defendant company had a right to refuse altogether to publish the letter. But it was not entitled to publish it under the rubric 'Letters from Readers' and, moreover, with the omission of the passages that would clearly show that the plaintiff was not putting forward his personal opinion in favour of Dr S but wished to obtain a correction under the Press Law.

The Landgericht's decision is to be approved, that this mode of publication – and also the placing of the correction side by side with five other letters on the article on Dr S published by the defendant company – was bound to produce the impression on an impartial reader that the plaintiff's letter gave his personal attitude to the controversy about Dr S. That misleading impression was also not dispelled by the literal reproduction of the plaintiff's introductory sentence; for that sentence, in its generally accepted character, told the reader only that the sender was Dr S's attorney. It did not make sufficiently clear that the content also of the letter in question referred to his instructions as attorney and that it had been composed by him not as a private person but in the exercise of his profession.

Accordingly the Court of Appeal was not in error in holding that the publication of the letter of corrections in shortened form under the rubric 'Letters from Readers' contained an untrue statement of facts. This also means that, through the mode of publishing it, the letter acquired a meaning not in conformity with its original composition and that this form of publication did not correspond to what the plaintiff had alone given permission for, namely broadcasting to the public the letter of correction in the form he had chosen.

The Landgericht was right in regarding the publication complained of, which according to its findings had become known to an extraordinarily wide circle of persons, as a continuing disparagement and therefore that the demand for revocation was justified.[5]

Notes

1. An excellent English summary of the German law on 'privacy' represented here by this and the next two cases, can be found in Zweigert and Kötz, *Introduction to Comparative Law*, II, § 20, with many references, to which add: K. Larenz 'Das "allgemeine Persönlichkeitsrecht" im Recht der unerlaubten Handlungen', *NJW* 1955, 521 *et seq.*; Justice Report, *Privacy and the Law* (1970); D.Jan McQoid-Mason, *The Law of Privacy in South Africa* (1978), especially ch. 3.

2. The reference is to Dr H.H.G. Schacht, a distinguished German economist and financier who played an important role in a restoration of a stable currency after the devastating German inflation of 1923. From 1923 to 1930 he served as president of the Reichsbank and became a supporter of the Nazi party. When Hitler came to power, Schacht played a leading role in the rearmament programme, but from 1938–9, onwards he was urging Hitler to reduce expenditure for armaments as the only way to balance the budget and reduce inflation. In July 1944 he was confined to a concentration camp until the end of the war and then he was one of the principal accused at the first Nuremberg trial. He was acquitted at the trial only to be brought before the German people's court at Stuttgart under the 'denazification' laws. Sentenced to eight years' detention in a labour camp, Schacht successfully appealed against this sentence and, as the facts of the case show, resumed his successful career as a financier.

3. O.v. Gierke, *Deutsches Privatrecht*, I, 707; III, 887; Kohler, 'Das Recht an Briefen', *Archiv für bürgerliches Recht* VII, 94 *et seq.* See Also, R.v. Jhering, *Jahrbuch für Dogmatik* 23, 155: cf. H.C. Gutteridge, 'Comparative Law of the Right to Privacy', 47 *LQR*

(1931), 203, 204.

4. 'Art. 1(1). The dignity of man shall be inviolable. To respect and protect it shall be the duty of all state authority.'
   'Art. 2(1). Everyone shall have the right to the free development of his personality in so far as he does not infringe the rights of others or offend against the constitutional order or the moral code. (Translation from Justice Report, *Privacy*, 21, para. 97.) Cf. E.J. Cohn's observations (*Manual of German Law* (1968), I, p. 65): 'the "right of privacy" is derived from a somewhat strained interpretation of arts. 1 and 2 of the Basic Law'.

5. Soon after this case was decided, the BGH had the opportunity to reaffirm the principles it had laid down in the Schacht case in another interesting case brought as a result of the publication of Cosima Wagner's private letters and diaries: *BGHZ* 15, 249; and again, two years later in the Paul Dahlke case (*BGHZ* 20, 345; facts similar to *Tolley* v. *Fry*). A year later, the BGH was prepared to look at the problem in the light of § 823 I BGB and, by so doing, to make negligent as well as intentional interferences with one's privacy actionable (*BGHZ* 24, 12), but the next great landmark was the 'gentleman rider' case which is the next case translated in the text.

4. Decision of the 1st Civil Senate of 14 February 1958 (BGHZ 26, 349)

Since the right of free expression of one's personality was recognised by arts. 1, 2 of the Basic Law as a fundamental value of the legal order, it is justifiable to allow an equitable compensation in money for non-pecuniary damage caused by the unauthorised publication of one's portrait on the analogy of § 847 BGB.

Law of Artistic Creations (1907) § 22; Basic Law Arts. 1, 2; BGB § 487
I. Zivilsenat judgment of 14 February 1958 in Re: S.H.KG (Defendant) v. S. (Plaintiff) 1 ZR 151/56.

I. Landgericht Köln
II. Oberlandesgericht Köln

The plaintiff is co-owner of a brewery in K. He is active as a gentleman[1] show-jumper. The defendant Limited Partnership is the manufacturer of a pharmaceutical preparation which is widely reputed as being able to increase sexual potency. To advertise this preparation in the Federal Republic, and in particular in K, it disseminated a poster with the picture of a show-jumper. Its basis was an original photograph of the plaintiff, which had been taken by a press agency at a show-jumping competition. The plaintiff had not given permission for the use of his portrait.

The plaintiff claimed damages from the defendant for the damage which he suffered as a result of the dissemination of the poster. He alleged that in the given circumstances he could only claim as damages what he would have obtained if he had allowed the defendant to use his portrait. As his professional and social position did not allow him, and his financial means did not compel him, to dispose of his portrait for advertising purposes, and in particular for the defendant's preparation, he would have done this, if at all, only for a fair price, at a rough estimate 15,000 DM at the very least.

The plaintiff applied for an order that the defendant pay by way of damages a fair sum to be fixed by the court.

The defendant denied any fault and pleaded that, after touching up, the plaintiff's features were not recognisable in the poster; and that it had not itself designed or produced the poster nor obtained the portrait from S, but had ordered it from the H advertising agency, which it had trusted, as a respectable, competent, and reliable firm, not to injure the rights of third persons. The defendant could not have known that the poster had been designed on the basis of a photograph, or that the photograph showed a 'gentleman' rider. Only as the case developed did it discover that it really concerned a portrait of the plaintiff. Thereupon it prohibited without delay any further use of the advertisement.

The Landgericht ordered the defendant to pay 1,000 DM to the plaintiff by way of damages. The Oberlandesgericht ordered the defendant to pay 10,000 DM to the plaintiff. The defendant's further appeal was unsuccessful for these reasons:

1. The Court of Appeal, in agreement with the Landgericht, found that the depiction of the rider in the poster allowed the plaintiff's person to be recognised despite the retouching. It rightly concluded that the dissemination of the poster without the plaintiff's permission injured his personality rights, namely his right to deal with his portrait, and that the defendant must compensate him under § 823 II BGB in combination with § 2 of the Law of Artistic Creations, if it was found to blame (cf. *RG* in *JW* 1929, 2257; *BGHZ* 20, 345, 347, *et seq.*). The Court of Appeal came to that conclusion seeing that the defendant had not observed the care required in the circumstances, since it had obtained in the course of its business the poster prepared by the H advertising agency without making certain that the person depicted had agreed to the intended use of his portrait.

The appellant's attacks on these findings must fail [further discussion not reproduced].

II. In awarding compensation to the plaintiff the Court of Appeal had in mind the licence fee which he could have demanded if a suitable contract had been arrived at between the parties. It held that it was justified in applying a method of assessing damages developed for breaches of copyright, because it was hard for the plaintiff to show whether and to what degree there had been any pecuniary loss. In contrast to the Landgericht, which had thought 1,000 DM to be sufficient, the court of appeal decided that 10,000 DM was the more appropriate figure.

Although the appeal is unsuccessful in the result, it must be conceded that the Court of Appeal's reasoning is not entirely appropriate to the peculiar facts of the case.

1. The appellant does not dispute that, even where there is an injury to the personality right to one's portrait, the damage can be estimated according to the payment that would presumably have been arranged if there had been a contract. Nevertheless the appellant argued that this method of assessing damages, which the Senate in its judgment of 8 May 1956 (*BGHZ* 20, 345 *et seq.* – Dahlke) declared admissable for the unauthorised publication of a portrait, could not be used if it was established that the person portrayed would, for special reasons, never have allowed his portrait to be used for advertising purposes.

If in the case under appeal pecuniary damage had actually been in question, this attack would not have been well founded. For according to settled case-law and academic opinion, where a claim to an appropriate compensation is recognised, it is not a question of applying the *general* provisions of the law of damages but of its customary supplementation to make good injury to valuable exclusive rights, based on the equitable consideration that the defendant should not be better off than he would have been if his application for permission had been granted. The claim to an appropriate compensation is therefore granted in all cases of unpermitted invasion of exclusive rights where permission is usually made dependent on payment and where, having regard to the kind of the right which has been violated, the invasion is habitually allowed according to the customs of daily life only – if at all – against compensation (*BGHZ* 20, 345, 353 *et seq.*). It is not at all necessary for a contract to have actually come into existence if the invader's conduct was otherwise unobjectionable.

2. It must, however, be agreed that the Court of Appeal, by the method of assessment it chose, did not really try to work out the economic loss to the plaintiff, but rather to adjust the satisfaction due to him for his non-material disparagement. In particular the reasoning

by which it arrived at the amount of the damage to the plaintiff shows that according to its opinion also he did not suffer any tangible pecuniary loss. In truth he claims not compensation for a non-existent pecuniary loss but an appreciable satisfaction for an unlawful attack on his personality protected by § 22 of the Law of Artistic Creations and arts. 1 and 2 of the Basic Law. He demands satisfaction for the fact that a widely disseminated poster, by making him, one might almost say, 'ride' for the purpose of advertising the defendant's tonic–and a sexual one at that–humiliated him and made him an object of ridicule. In such a situation it is absurd to award damages on the basis of a fictitious licence agreement. This way of estimating damage is appropriate only if one can start with the doing of some kind of pecuniary damage and all that is left is to alleviate the often difficult task of proving its amount. It fails if no pecuniary prejudice at all is in question. It fails also in the present case because it would assume that the plaintiff had done something that not only he, but all others of the same professional and social standing, must consider harmful and as a continuing degradation of his personality. It must convey an imputation that the plaintiff would, after all, voluntarily and for a large sum of money place himself in the unworthy position against which he is now defending himself.

The plaintiff's claim therefore cannot be supported by the Court of Appeal's chosen method of assessment, helped out by the fiction of a loss licence fee.

3. Moreover, basing the claim on unjustified enrichment is precluded because the plaintiff did not experience any pecuniary disadvantage and there is thus no pecuniary shift of the kind envisaged by § 812 *et seq.* BGB.

4. If, therefore, the kind of assessment adopted by the Court of Appeal fails, and it is shown that the plaintiff in truth suffered no pecuniary damage, the decisive question comes to be whether he can demand compensation for the immaterial damage which he has suffered as a result of the invasion of his personality following the appearance of his picture in the advertisement. On the facts before it the Senate answers that question in the affirmative.

This Senate has already said in its decision in *BGHZ* 13, 334, 338 that the sacredness of human dignity and the right to free development of the personality protected by art. 1 of the Basic Law are also to be recognised as a civil right to be respected by everyone in daily life, in so far as that right does not impinge upon the rights of others and is not repugnant to constitutional order or the moral law. This so-called general right to one's personality also possesses legal validity within the framework of the civil law and enjoys the protection of § 823 1 BGB under the designation of 'other right' (cf. also *BGHZ* 24, 12 *et seq.*).

Arts. 1 and 2 of the Basic Law protect–and indeed must be applied by the courts in the administration of justice–what is called the concept of human personality; they recognise in it one of the supra-legal basic values of the law. Thereby they are directly concerned with the protection of the inner realm of the personality which, in principle, only affords a basis for the free and responsible self-determination of the individual and an infringement of which produces primarily so-called immaterial damage, damage expressed in a degradation of the personality. To respect this inner realm and to refrain from invading it without authorisation is a legal command issuing from the Basic Law itself. And it follows from the Basic Law that in cases of invasion of this sphere protection must be given against damage characteristic of such an invasion.

On the limited field of portrait protection this was established in 1907 by the special rules contained in §§ 22 *et seq.* of the Law of Artistic Creations,[2] long before the Basic Law came into force and at a time when the civil law did not as yet protect a general personality right. For the protection afforded by § 22, according to which portraits may be distributed or shown publicly only with the subject's consent, rests in essence on the fundamental principle of a person's freedom in his highly personal private life, in which the outward appearance of a human being plays an essential part. The unauthorised publication of a portrait constitutes, as has long been recognised in legal literature, an attack on the freedom of self-determination and the free expression of the personality. The reason why a third person's arbitrary publication of a portrait is not allowed is that the person portrayed is thereby deprived of his freedom to dispose by his own decision of this interest in his individual sphere.

Once the violation of the right to one's picture is seen as affecting one's personality it is possible to seek an answer to the question how to compensate immaterial damage in § 847 BGB. This allows an equitable compensation in money for non-pecuniary loss in cases of 'deprivation of liberty'. It is true that deprivation of liberty is here understood to mean deprivation of freedom of bodily movement, as well as compulsion to act, by means of force or threats, whereas § 22 of the Law of Artistic Creations deals with deprivation of the free and responsible exercise of will. Already, however, before the Basic Law came into force, the opinion was often expressed that any attack on the undisturbed exercise of the will was to be regarded as an injury to freedom in the sense of § 847 BGB. Now that the Basic Law guarantees a comprehensive protection to the personality and recognises human dignity and the right to free development of the personality as a fundamental value, it has done away with the dogma held by the original draftsman of the BGB that there can be no civil law protection of a general personality right; and since a protection of 'inner freedom' without a right to compensation for immaterial damage would be in great part illusory, it would be intolerable to refuse compensation for that immaterial damage. Moreover, there is no obvious reason why § 847 BGB should not be extended by analogy to such attacks as injure the right to free exercise of the will, especially where that deprivation of intellectual liberty, just like deprivation of bodily freedom, renders natural restitution impossible. Where such blameworthy depreciations of the personality right are in question, the effective legal protection offered by the Basic Law can, in the absence of any special legal provision, be attained only through its inclusion in the injuries mentioned in § 847 BGB, since their injurious consequences are of necessity primarily immaterial.

This view is not at variance with the sense of § 35 of the Law of Artistic Creations. Of course the injured party can claim under it a penalty for the injury to his right to his portrait, and with it to have his immaterial loss made good, only in criminal proceedings and on condition that the injury was intended; but that special provision shows only that as early as 1907 the legislator regarded an infringement of § 22 as so far-reaching and threatening that it was considered necessary to grant expressly to the injured party a claim to compensation for the disparagement. The restriction of the criminal law claim for a penalty to intentional injuries accords with the legislator's limitation of the threat of punishment for an infringement of § 22 to intentional interference. That however does not mean that the same must apply to the civil law claims to compensation that are not regulated in the Law of Artistic Creations. On the contrary, since the Basic Law now recognises the general personality right as significant for civil law and has afforded a general civil law protection appreciably exceeding the narrow regulation of § 35 of the Law of Artistic Creations, the special provision of § 35 can no longer be cited in opposition to a more extensive civil law protection of the right to one's portrait. The general provisions of the BGB concerning delicts come into operation instead. That means that, at any rate since the Basic Law came into force, by an analogous application of § 847 BGB, any blameworthy injury to the right to one's own portrait involves a duty to make good immaterial damage also.

In so far as the Senate, following the case-law of the Reichsgericht, decided in the Dahlke case (*BGHZ* 20, 345, 352 *et seq.*) that immaterial damage cannot give rise to a money claim in the absence of express legal provision, its opinion cannot be upheld in the light of the foregoing discussions. The statement was *obiter*, since the facts disclosed pecuniary damage, which could be estimated on the basis of the usual licence fee.

III. The compensation to be paid to the plaintiff was fixed by the Court of Appeal at 10,000 DM. Although starting from a possible assessment according to the satisfaction that might have been paid in a case of contract on the usual terms, the court's arguments fully apply also to fixing the amount of an **equitable** compensation under § 847 BGB. They also show that the court really awarded the plaintiff compensation for the immaterial damage that had resulted.

As the Great Civil Senate explained in its decision of 6 July 1955 (*BGHZ* 18, 149), the claim for damages for pain and suffering offers the injured party an appropriate compensation for the depreciation of life (or personality) which is not of a pecuniary kind. But it also takes account of the notion that the doer of damage owes the injured party satisfaction for what he has done to him. It was emphasised in the decision that 'satisfaction', which forms an integral part of the award of compensation for immaterial damage, must take into account all the relevant circumstances. This Senate adheres to this view in this present case. If one therefore moves on from that position, it follows that the Court of Appeal was not in error in taking all the relevant circumstances into account in fixing the amount of damages. In particular that court explained that the fact the plaintiff had never been ready to take part in any advertising must be a factor in deciding the amount to be paid. It considered it especially serious that the advertisement was for an aphrodisiac, and so was not to be compared with advertisements for other products. The court was right in taking the view that people would be unlikely to allow their likeness to be used on a poster for this purpose and so run a risk of being recognised by a wider or narrower public, exposing themselves to the innuendos to which the defendant's preparation would give rise. The Court of Appeal also took the plaintiff's social and business position into account, pointing to the fact that he moved in a social circle the members of which were for the most part known to each other and where the risk of making oneself an object of ridicule was especially great. When, after considering and giving weight to all these special circumstances relevant to the amount of damages for pain and suffering, the Court of Appeal regarded the sum of 10,000 DM as appropriate compensation (§ 287 ZPO), it cannot be found to have acted contrary to law.

Note

1. This is a literal translation of the German text but it should be understood as referring to an 'amateur' rider. Note that in *Tolley* v. *J.S. Fry* [1930] 1 K.B. 467 the plaintiff's status as an 'amateur golfer' proved decisive in the success of his claim, for it enabled him to plead an innuendo that the public could make the defamatory inference that, although an amateur, he had prostituted his amateur status for money. On closer observation therefore this is a successful 'privacy' action disguised as an action for defamation.

2. What probably triggered of the passing of this act was the photographing of Bismarck's corpse by photographers who unlawfully broke into the room where he had died. The court took the view that they were guilty of trespass to property and were obliged to destroy the negatives under the rules of unjust enrichment (*RGZ* 45, 170).

5. Decision of the 6th Civil Senate of 19 September 1961 (*BGHZ* 35, 363)

Whoever is affected by an unlawful and blameworthy infringement of his personality right can claim compensation for immaterial damage if the circumstances, and in particular the seriousness of the injury or blameworthiness, require such satisfaction.

BGB §§ 253, 823, 847; Basic Law arts. 1, 2 1
vi. Zivilsenat judgment of 19 September 1961 in Re:
S.F. KG (Defendant) v. B. (Plaintiff) vi ZR 259/60
i. Landgericht Düsseldorf
ii. Oberlandesgericht Düsseldorf

The plaintiff is a professor in the law faculty of the University of G at which he holds a chair of International and Ecclesiastical Law. From a stay in Korea he had brought with him a ginseng root, which he placed at the disposal of his friend Professor H, a pharmacologist, for research. The latter mentioned in a scientific article on ginseng roots that he had come into possession 'of genuine Korean ginseng roots 'through the kind assistance' of the plaintiff. This led to the plaintiff being described in a popular scientific article, which appeared in the year 1957 in the *H and W* Journal, along with Professor H and other scientists, as one of the best known gineng researchers of Europe.

The defendant company dealt in a tonic containing ginseng. In its advertisement for this tonic the plaintiff was referred to as an important scientist expressing an opinion on its value, and in a editorial note, printed in immediate connexion with an advertisement in another journal, allusion was made to its use as an aphrodisiac. Both the advertisement and the journal were very widely distributed.

The plaintiff claimed that he had suffered an unauthorised attack on his personality right; and that the advertisement gave rise to the impression that he had, for payment, issued an opinion on a controversial topic in a department of knowledge not his own, and unprofessionally lent his name to advertising a doubtful product. He had suffered damage to his reputation as a learned man and been made an object of ridicule to the public and above all to his students. In reliance on *BGHZ* 26, 249 (the 'gentleman rider' case, pp. 111–18 above) he claimed 10,000 DM as satisfaction for the harm done to him.

The Landgericht awarded him 8,000 DM as damages for pain and suffering. The appeals to both the Court of Appeal and the Bundesgerichtshof were unsuccessful for these reasons:[1]

1. By invoking the plaintiff's scientific authority in its advertising to encourage belief in the effectiveness of its preparation for the mentioned purposes, the defendant company unlawfully disparaged his personality right (§ 823 I BGB). The reference to researches by the plaintiff, which lacked any objective foundation, was under the circumstances calculated to make him an object of ridicule in society and lessen his scholarly reputation. Moreover, he was bound to feel outraged by the way his name was used in advertising a preparation recommended as a sexual stimulant. The defendant company's conduct was also blameworthy. Before using the plaintiff's name for its advertisement it ought to have sought his agreement or at least to have ascertained whether and where he had stated what was asserted in its advertisement. The information in a popular science article in the *H and W* Journal ought in no way to have been adopted unseen; it was moreover substantially altered. The Court of Appeal rightly characte-

rised the defendant's conduct as irresponsible. Likewise approval must also be given to the Court of Appeal's finding that the defendant company was also responsible for the note in the *M* Journal which adopted in somewhat modified form the contents of the advertisement. Even if it was the advertising agency employed by the defendant company that caused the note to appear, the information contained in it depended on material supplied by the defendant company. At the very least, the defendant company had not supervised the advertising agency as was necessary.

2. The Senate also agrees with the Court of Appeal's view that the plaintiff has a claim to compensation for immaterial damage. The case is, in its main lines, very similar to those decided by the Bundesgerichtshof and reported in *BGHZ* 26, 349 (the 'gentleman rider' case) and 30, 7. In both cases the way a product was advertised attacked the protected sphere of the personality right of persons who claimed compensation for the unlawful injury. In both the conditions for compensation for material damage were absent or at any rate not proved. If, in the circumstances, no permission to use a name or portrait for advertising purposes is in question, it is not possible to estimate pecuniary compensation on the lines of a licence fee according to the principles governing so-called unilateral acquisition without permission. The first Civil Senate awarded damages for pain and suffering to the plaintiff in the case decided by it and reported in *BGHZ* 26, 349 and also regarded an award of so-called 'immaterial damages', with its function of satisfaction, as the adequate compensation that the law must afford to a plaintiff for the violation of his personality right. From the decision reported in *BGHZ* 30, 7 it must be taken that the standpoint of the fourth Civil Senate is at least not at variance with that of the first Civil Senate.

This Senate agrees with the first Civil Senate that satisfaction may be awarded to a person affected by the blameworthy infringement of his personality right. It is indeed stated in § 253 BGB that money compensation can be claimed for non-pecuniary damage only in cases expressly designated by the law. When the BGB established that enumeration principle, the high value of the protection of human personality and its special sphere had not received the recognition that it enjoys according to art. 1 and art. 2 1 of the Basic Law. From the standpoint of the BGB the protection of property interests always stood in the foreground, whereas the personal worth of a human being received only insufficient and fragmentary protection. In recognising a general personality right of mankind and granting it the protection of § 823 1 BGB, the courts drew for civil law purposes the conclusions resulting from the rank the Basic Law assigned to the worth of human personality and the protection of its free development. That protection however would be incomplete and full of loopholes if an infringement of the personality right did not give rise to a sanction adequate to the violation. Just as the restriction of protection by the law of delict to specific legal interests of a human being has proved too narrow to afford the protection of personality required by the Basic Law, so a narrowing of immaterial damages for immaterial loss, to cover only injury to specifically mentioned legal interests, no longer conforms to the value system of the Basic Law. For art. 1 declares it to be an urgent obligation on the public power to protect the sacred dignity of the human being. Art. 2 1 puts the right of a human being to free development of his personality at the head of the fundamental rights. If the law of delict, in protecting the personality right in the non-material realm, retreated completely to a position where it merely protected the particular personality interests mentioned in art. 2 II, which are emanations from the personality right, the civil law would not be paying attention to the value decision of the Basic Law. The elimination of damages for immaterial loss from the protection of personality would mean that injury to the dignity and honour of a human being would remain without any sanction of the civil law, which deals with the disturbance of essential values and makes the doer of injury owe satisfaction to the victim for the wrong done to him. The law would then renounce the strongest and often the only instrument calculated to ensure respect for the personal worth of the individual.

3. That does not mean that the legal consequences of injuries to body, health and freedom on the one hand and the violation of the personality sphere on the other must be exactly the same or at least largely correspond to each other. A need for differentiation is already indicated by the fact that the factual aspect of an injury to a general personality right is much less specific than where body, health or freedom is injured. That means that there are many marginal cases where the question is whether the case is one included in the generalised description of violation of the personality and whether, if it is, the unlawfulness is not excluded by the competing rights of the 'offender', among which the right to free expression of opinion deserves particular attention. It is precisely where a so-called balancing

of interest must take place that the limits of what is allowed are not always easy to fix. If for every overstepping of the limits, however petty, compensation for immaterial loss were to be awarded to the person affected, there would be a danger that unimportant injuries would be used inappropriately to make a gain. The purpose of awarding satisfaction would then be stultified. It must further be observed that it is more difficult to apply the general criterion of monetary value to measure immaterial injuries to the personality right than the consequences of bodily injuries. In injuries to the general personality right the satisfaction function of damages for pain and suffering advances into the foreground as that of compensation recedes. Hence it will always be necessary to look at the kind of injury to the personality right to see if the person affected, whose injury cannot otherwise be redressed, should be granted satisfaction for the wrong he has suffered. That will in general only be the case when the doer of damage is blamed for a serious fault or when an injury to a personality right is objectively significant. Only when such disturbances are serious may the civil law, taking seriously the protection of personality and its value as such, react against the injury by granting satisfaction to the person affected. Insignificant injuries do not call for satisfaction. Having regard to the special character of an injury to a personality right, Swiss law, which has devoted greater attention than the BGB to legal protection of the personality (cf. art. 49 I of the Swiss Code of Obligations), also restricts damages for immaterial loss to serious cases.

4. The conditions for an award of immaterial damages especially occur when – as in the present case – there is a wanton attack on the personality right of another person out of a desire to increase the force of one's commercial publicity. Such an unfair attempt to succeed can be effectively countered only if it is burdened with the risk of an appreciable material loss,[2] and on the other hand, anyone who seeks to make money out of an unfair invasion of the sphere of another's personality must not feel hurt if he is forced to pay a money compensation. For the plaintiff the outrage inflicted – in particular since the object was recommended for specific purposes – was not at all insignificant, the more so because he ran the risk of readers assuming that he had lent his name for a money consideration. The award of a money compensation by way of satisfaction was justified by the seriousness of the attack as well as by the seriousness of the fault.

The amount of the satisfaction to be given was for the judge of fact to assess. It could be attacked on appeal only if it rested on an incorrect finding of the applicable law or if the judge of fact overlooked essential points of view. No such defects, however, are here apparent. The Court of Appeal did right in attaching importance to the spread of publicity, which extended to Austria and Switzerland. It was also an essential factor in fixing the amount of the satisfaction that the defendant company continued the advertising complained of even *after* being warned by the plaintiff, thus displaying an especially reckless attitude. On the other hand the Court of Appeal observed in the defendant company's favour that the mention of the name in the advertisement was not especially prominent, so that it might have been noticed by the cursory reader.

Notes

1. The case is reproduced here for the light it throws on the legal basis of awards of damages for pain and suffering unaccompanied by material (or pecuniary) damage.
2. Cf. Lord Devlin's remarks in *Rookes* v. *Barnard* [1964] A.C. 1229, 1227: 'it is necessary to teach a wrongdoer that tort does not pay'.

6. Decision of the 6th Civil Senate of 22 June 1931 (RGZ 133, 12)

BGB § 254; Automobile Act 9
vi. Zivilsenat judgment of 22 June 1931 in Re:
K.u. Gen. (Defendant) v. M (Plaintiff) vi ZR 46/31.
i. Landgericht Gladbach – Rheydt.
ii. Oberlandesgericht Düsseldorf.

The facts appear in the reasons:

The only point in dispute in the appeal is whether the fault of the plaintiff contributed as a cause to the automobile accident of 9 November 1928 (§ 3 Automobile Act, § 254 BGB). The Court of Appeal, which decided in the plaintiff's favour, denied this for the following reasons. Admittedly he acted carelessly, in that as a pedestrian he failed, before crossing the road, to ascertain whether an automobile was approaching. The co-defendant driver, however, was not prevented from avoiding the accident, which he could easily have done, and which was his duty. No adequate causal connexion, therefore, existed between the plaintiff's conduct and the accident.

The complaint that in these explanations the concept of adequate causal connexion was misunderstood is well founded. There can be no doubt that a natural causal connexion existed betwen the plaintiff's conduct and the accident; for if he had not crossed the street at the very moment that the defendant's automobile overtook J's cart, he could not have been struck by it. That was apparently the view of the judge of first instance. But the facts also must also be regarded as showing an adequate causal connexion. Such a connexion exists where an act or omission, generally, not only under especial and quite improbable circumstances which are not to be anticipated in the regular course of things, is capable of producing the result that occurred.[1] But in view of present traffic conditions it cannot be accepted as inconceivable that at the moment a pedestrian crosses a road an automobile will pass over the same spot. The appellate judge seems to have been of the same mind; for he found a lack of foresight in the plaintiff's not looking round for any approaching automobiles, and therefore held him to have been at fault (§ 276 BGB).

Accordingly the causation and fault of both parties must be balanced against each other according to § 9 of the Automobile Act and § 254 BGB. This balancing essentially belongs to the finding of facts, and therefore to the Court of Appeal.

Note
1. See Addenda p. 341

7. Decision of the 3rd Civil Senate of 25 September 1952 (BGHZ 7, 198)

1. The causality of a blameworthy omission for a consequent damage cannot be denied on the ground that other not remote circumstances might have prevented the result. The denial is possible only if the damage could not have occurred in the normal course of events, but only through such special circumstances.

2. If by fault a danger to life is produced, the death that ensues is an adequate consequence of that danger even if there might have been a more or less great possibility of avoiding it.

3. Anyone who undertakes a prohibited abortion cannot plead in defence against his liability for the consequent damage caused by him that the consequences were not due to his fault. The express wish of the pregnant woman that the operation should be undertaken can lead neither to an exclusion of liability nor a plea of fraud, but can only be treated as a contributory fault of the pregnant woman.

BGB §§ 823, 242, 254; StGB § 218
III. Zivilsenat judgment of 25 September 1952 in Re:
SS (Plaintiffs) v. Dr B (Defendant)
III ZR 322/51

I. Landgericht Lübeck
II. Oberlandesgericht Schleswig

The orphan plaintiffs claim compensation from the defendant for the damage they suffered from their mother's death as the consequence of an abortion carried out by the defendant. She felt herself pregnant in May 1949 as a result of intercourse with Sp. The defendant, who practises as a doctor, was, at her request ready to perform an abortion in consideration of a fee. For that purpose he visited Frau S at Sp's home and with his help operated on her. He felt but misunderstood a peculiar structure in her womb and thought he noticed the remains of an afterbirth. After douching the womb, with Sp's help he placed the patient on a sofa, and ordered her to rest in bed for three days and to see him in his surgery in fourteen days. He left the house a few minutes before 4 p.m. Some twenty to twenty-five minutes later the patient complained of severe pains in her abdomen. At her request, Sp hurried to the defendant's surgery, reported that Frau S was in pain and obtained from him a pain-killer. When, after about an hour's absence, he came home, he found that her condition had deteriorated further. When a gynaecologist was eventually called in and arrived about 6 p.m., he found a severe internal haemorrhage, so he arranged for an immediate transfer to a hospital; and after about three-quarters of an hour he operated on the woman and found a rent in the womb and ascertained that the womb artery had been torn. Although he bandaged the source of blood and made a blood transfusion, the plaintiffs' mother died before the operation was complete.

The plaintiffs claimed compensation from the defendant in contract and delict[1] for medical and hospital expenses together with payment of an annuity and also a declaration that they were entitled to be compensated for all further damage.

Both instances rejected the claim; the appellants demanded the case be sent back for reconsideration.

Reasons:

1. The Court of Appeal agreed with the Landgericht that the defendant caused the death of Frau S from loss of blood by piercing the wall of her womb and thus damaging the womb artery. It came however to the conclusion that he was not at fault in causing the injury.

The experts were unanimously of the opinion that an injury such as happened here could have been inflicted by even the most conscientious and experienced medical man in the course of an abortion; in following it the Court of Appeal made no mistake of law. Thus, such an injury *could*, but *need not*, have resulted from a careless and improper use of the instruments. The Court of Appeal acted consistently in examining whether such a careless act of the defendant in the present case was to be inferred either according to the *prima facie* evidence or by way of circumstantial evidence. It said no to both questions.

(a) Whether this was a typical course of events affording sufficient *prima facie* evidence required, in the first place, a formulation of the results of experience and then its application to the present situation. Such a formulation is a conclusion of fact inferred from general circumstances and can, in these proceedings, be checked for correctness only in so far as it is drawn from established facts. The facts themselves cannot be checked; they must be proved by the person who seeks to found on them a *prima facie* case. The burden of proof is thus on the plaintiffs just as the other party must prove the possibility of a deviation from the typical course of events. When therefore the Court of Appeal reached the result, on the basis of expert opinions, that 'no formulation from the results of experience can be established that the piercing of a womb in an abortion can as a rule be traced to a careless use of instruments by a doctor', the unassailable finding of fact followed, that according to medical experience the injury in question was 'possible even with a careful use of instruments' and could 'find its explanation in the peculiar characteristics, not visible to the doctor, of the womb'. That under these circumstances experience afforded no *prima facie* evidence was based on no error of law.

(b) The Court of Appeal considered that the defendant was at fault in not affording the required medical care after finishing the operation. But it declined to attribute fault to the general conduct of the defendant, which would also provide, as the plaintiffs contend, *prima facie* evidence of a faulty use of the instruments and therefore of his being to blame for the injury.

The court took into account various surprising and irregular circumstancs such as the use of a camphor injection before the operation; the suspicion that a miscarriage was beginning; the failure to recognise the rupture of the artery; the leaving of an alleged afterbirth in the womb; and finally the omission, still to be discussed, of an immediate reference to a hospital. While it adhered to the opinion that they did not constitute errors in medical practice, it saw in both of the last circumstances two blameworthy omissions; yet it considered that they did not disclose a general prolonged lack of medical conscientiousness or care, and that there was, as a whole, no typical conduct justifying a *prima facie* presumption that the defendant did the injury to the wall of the womb and the opening of the artery through a careless use of the instruments.

Here also no objection can be taken on legal grounds to the Court of Appeal's decision....

(c) It is on the other hand possible to treat fault in such a situation as an indication that the doctor was not careful in the operation itself. That point also was not missed by the Court of Appeal. But it considered that evidence insufficient to afford it the necessary certainty. It considered that the proved omissions predominantly disclosed a lack of conscientiousness in the *after-care* of the patient, whereas a fault in the abortion itself would consist in lack of care in the use of the instruments. The basis of the fault in the two cases would be too different to enable secure enough conclusions to be drawn from the one to the other. The court was entitled to value the indication as a means of information, and that valuation could not be checked in these proceedings, so that no legal error can be found to exist in its judgment.

II. The Court of Appeal, however, rightly found that the defendant was at fault in his neglectful conduct after finishing the actual operation. He ought not to have left a doubtful situation without getting rid of the afterbirth, and he ought, by that time, to have had the patient sent at once to a hospital. That he did not do so was described by the expert, Professor Ph, as 'unintelligible', and the court of appeal rightly agreed with him. Complications had ensued which required further treatment in hospital, in relation to which it was irrelevant whether the defendant was to blame for them or not.

The Court of Appeal likewise declined to infer liability for the consequences because it denied causality. It inferred indeed from the opinions of the experts that an immediate transfer to the hospital would have improved the patient's chances of survival, but it held that death might have occurred even if there had been immediate transfer after the abortion and an operation without delay.[2] It could 'not decide beyond reasonable doubt that if the defendant had done his duty immediately after the operation or even when informed by Sp that the patient was in pain, her life would have been saved'.

These considerations do not make it quite clear whether the Court of Appeal had sufficiently in mind what was needed to prove causation. According to long-standing case-law it is not the strict rule of evidence in § 286 ZPO but that in § 287 that applies here...Under § 287 ZPO the court is not prevented from being convinced by the evidence and the circumstances that there is an adequate causal connexion, even if the possibility cannot without reasonable doubt be excluded that the damage could have occurred without the defendant's fault. If, as here, the blameworthy conduct consisted in an omission, the question of adequate causation ought to be formulated as 'whether that omission was in the ordinary way capable of producing a result, and not only under peculiar, quite improbable circumstances, not to be contemplated in the normal course of events'. It is not, therefore, a question of whether other, not remote circumstances could have produced the result, but whether the injurious consequence could not have occurred in the normal course, or rather would have been produced only by special circumstances of that kind. Here the Court of Appeal had merely found that a dutiful conduct would not certainly have prevented the result, and that finding cannot be regarded as sufficient to exclude the omission as the cause of the result. The Court of Appeal ought to have considered in accordance with § 287 ZPO – if need be after further questioning the experts – whether it could have produced such a result.

III. The Court of Appeal started from the position that the operation was an unlawful attack on the mother's bodily integrity, and therefore an infringement of the protective enactments §§ 223, 218 StGB.[3] Yet it was unwilling to infer any liability from them because it did not see any causal connexion between the operation and its fatal outcome. It explained that the defendant undertook the abortion as a doctor and carried it out according to the rules of medical art and science. Permitted abortions with the object of saving the life or health of the patient would be conducted in the same way. According to the expert, Professor Ph, injuries could occur outside the actual purpose of treatment. The doctor need not, however, as a rule take account of them when he started. In particular, complications dangerous to life were conditional on the intervention of peculiar or unfortunate circumstances, such as an opening of the womb artery through an injury to or spontaneous cleavage of the wall of the womb, which must in the normal course be disregarded. Even when such dangerous circumstances occur, the doctor would have means at his disposal to prevent a fatal outcome with some, though not an absolutely sure, prospect of success. Thus, the possibility that an abortion undertaken by a doctor would lead to a patient's death was too remote for the assumption of a causal connexion, giving rise to liability, between the operation and its fatal outcome.

1. These explanations exaggerate the requirements for adequate causation...It need not be decided whether there are medical operations in which complications dangerous to life can be produced only through the intervention of quite unique, quite improbable circumstances which can be disregarded according to the regular course of things. For an operation such as an abortion this was evidently assumed by neither the expert nor the Court of Appeal, for both reckoned with the possibility of such dangers and omitted to consider them only because in this case the doctor had appropriate means at his disposal, to which however the Court of Appeal accords only 'some, though not an absolutely sure prospect of success'.

If one starts from the position – as one must – that the entry of the aforementioned dangerous circumstances falls within the adequate consequences of an abortion, the further adequate causal connexion cannot be denied on the ground that there was some possibility of preventing the fatal outcome. This denial of a causal connexion is based on a fallacy similar to that which appeared in relation to the causality of the delayed transfer to the hospital. Once a danger to the patient's life appeared in any way, no peculiar and quite improbable circumstances were needed to lead to death, but, on the contrary, medical skill was needed to prevent it. Whether the prospects of success in those attempts to avert it were more or less great cannot alter the fact that a failure is the adequate consequence of a danger to life.

2. Moreover, the liability of the defendant cannot be denied on the ground that there was no causal connexion between the illegal operation and its fatal outcome. That connexion would be unimportant only if the operation was not illegal on the ground that the deceased not only agreed to but expressly wished it. The Court of Appeal was able to refuse to go more deeply into the question of what significance that wish had. It confined itself to the statement that consent to an abortion is forbidden and therefore legally inoperative... A consent is inoperative not only when influenced by a defect of the will, but also when it is repugnant to a legal prohibition or good morals and is therefore invalid (§§ 134, 138 BGB).[4] That presupposition is here affirmed by the Court of Appeal on the ground that an

infringement of § 218 StGB makes both the doctor and the patient punishable.

It is also not a defence to a claim that a plaintiff is acting deceitfully and in bad faith if he claims damages from a person whom he asked to afford a particular kind of medical assistance, so long as he keeps within what he was asked for. This invocation of good faith must also be denied to one who so severely infringes a prohibition of the Criminal Code. The legal position is not altered by the fact that a portion of the public, for various reasons, demands an abolition of the prohibition.

3. By undertaking the operation the defendant not only deliberately injured the body of Frau S, but also infringed the protective enactments contained in §§ 223, 218 StGB. Although the second paragraph aims in the first place at protecting the living embryo, it serves also to protect the pregnant woman; and that is enough to satisfy the conditions of § 823 II BGB. If, however, they are satisfied, it follows, as the Reichsgericht has pertinently said..., that the defendant is liable for all the injuries caused by his operation, even if they are not his fault. That, contrary to the Court of Appeal's opinion, there was a causal connexion between the death of Frau S and the operation is shown above at 1.

For these reasons also the legal dispute is not yet ripe for decision, since the defendant can rely on the consent and wish of the deceased in so far as that too implied fault in the undertaking of the operation. As matters stood, if she had not energetically desired the operation, the defendant would not have done it... That fault will have to be balanced against the defendant in respect of causality (§ 254 BGB), and the defence arising from it must affect the plaintiffs also in accordance with § 846 BGB.

Notes

1. From this and other cases reproduced below it will be noticed that German law, unlike French law, has never denied the possibility of concurrence of claims. Indeed, as the Reichsgericht said long ago (*RGZ* 88, 433, 434–5), 'The case law of the Imperial Court is fundamentally committed to the view that liability in contract and in tort may co-exist... The general legal duty not to inflict bodily injuries on another exists at all times and is owed to all persons, whether or not it was by virtue of a contract that he entered the defendant's sphere of activity. This general duty laid down by the law cannot be put aside by the fact that it was a contract which made the injury to the plaintiff possible. The contractor no less than the stranger remains under the protection of § 823; that protection, indeed, becomes even stronger when the contract especially obliges the defendant to take care, that is, in accordance with the contract. The general prohibition of unlawfully injuring another is only

individualised and strengthened by the fact that the contract gives the plaintiff a right by convention to have care taken, that is, the opposite of bodily injury. To say otherwise would be to deny the wrongfulness, in the sense of § 823, of causing bodily injury, on the mere ground that the plaintiff had an additional special claim to be kept uninjured – a result whose absurdity is obviously intolerable.' (Translation by Weir, *Encyclopedia*, p. 31.)

2. Cf. *Barnett* v. *Chelsea and Kensington Hospital Management Committee* [1969] 1 Q.B. 428.

3. In Germany abortion was, and in some circumstances still is, a crime. By the early 1970s the whole issue had become a highly contentious moral, religious *and* political issue with the coalition government's enactment of a Bill which legalised abortion during the first three months of the pregnancy. One of the Länder, dominated by the Christian Democratic party (then the official opposition in the Federal Parliament), obtained an injunction from the Constitutional Court preventing the implementation of the Act until the Court had ruled on its constitutionality. The Court was eventually seized of the dispute and ruled that the Act was unconstitutional since it violated article 2 of the Constitution of Bonn which, in para. 2, proclaims that 'everyone shall have the right to life and to inviolability of his person'. Soon afterwards a new Bill, influenced by some dicta in the decision, became law, and relaxed somewhat the severity of the criminal law by allowing abortion in certain medical and social circumstances. (Cf. *Roe* v. *Wade* [1973] 410 U.S. 113, holding that every woman has a constitutional right to decide whether to terminate her pregnancy up to the moment when the foetus becomes viable.)

4. § 134 BGB: 'A legal transaction which runs counter to a statutory prohibition is void unless otherwise stated by that statute.'
§ 138 BGB: 'A legal transaction which runs counter to public policy is void.'
'Also void is a legal transaction by means of which a person, exploiting the need, carelessness, or inexperience of another, causes to be promised or granted to him or to a third party a pecuniary benefit which exceeds the value of his performance to such an extent as to stand in obvious disproportion to it.'

8. Decision of the Court of Appeal of Stuttgart of 24 November 1964 (*NJW* 1965, 112)

A person who lends help in a traffic accident can, if he is injured in effecting a rescue, claim from the person who negligently caused the accident compensation in delict for the damage and in particular for his pain and suffering.

Oberlandesgericht Stuttgart judgment of 24 November 1964.

5 U 91/64

The defendant drove his car, in which were two workmates, down a street in Heilbronn. Unfit to drive because he had a blood–alcohol proportion of 1.8%, he drove into a stationary lorry. In the collision his car caught fire. The plaintiff, who saw the accident from his parents' petrol station, hurried with an extinguisher and, together with a passer-by, rescued the defendant and his two passengers from the burning car... He suffered severe burns and was unable to work for two weeks.

The defendant's insurer paid compensation for the pecuniary damage, but denied liability to pay for pain and suffering. The Landgericht rejected that claim, but the plaintiff succeeded on appeal for the following reasons:

In so far as compensation was awarded to the plaintiff for his material damage, the judgment was not attacked by the defendant. The plaintiff has appealed against the rejection of his claim to be compensated for his pain and suffering.

Contrary to the view of the Landgericht, the plaintiff is also entitled to be paid for his pain and suffering in delict under §§ 823 I and II, 847 BGB. The finding that the defendant's driving while unfit to drive did not afford an adequate cause for the plaintiff's injury, cannot be accepted. Admittedly, it is not every *conditio sine qua non* that constitutes an adequate cause, but only such a one as, generally and in accordance with an objective judgment or experience, is apt to produce such a consequence, or one that in general appreciably enhances the possibility of its occurrence; and therefore adequate causes do not include conditions which according to general human experience are completely irrelevant to its occurrence or are so remote from the possibility of its occurrence that according to common opinion they cannot reasonably be taken into account. All the same, the finding cannot be accepted that in the present case the bodily injuries to the plaintiff lay outside what was to be normally and objectively expected as a consequence of the accident. It is of course true that it occurred here only because of a further act, due to the free decision of the plaintiff, namely his intervention in order to rescue the defendant and his passengers. That does not however exclude an adequate causal connexion between the unlawful act and the consequence. It is not correct that where there is an independent and voluntary intervention by a third party an adequate causal connexion can only be recognised to exist if the intervention served to ward off an especial danger to the public and therefore was in performance of a legal or moral obligation. Admittedly in *RGZ* 29, 121 and 50, 223, where an adequate connexion was held to exist between the insufficient securing of a team of horses drawing a vehicle and the injuries to a person who tried to hold them up, attention was directed to the fact that the rescuer had acted in performance of a legal or moral duty. In *RGZ* 50, 223 attention was also expressly directed to the fact that the injured party had intervened to avoid a threatened accident to persons in the village street, and especially children coming out of school precisely at that moment. Nevertheless the Bundesgerichtshof in *NJW* 64, 1363, when holding that an adequate causal connexion existed between the conduct of a hit and run driver and an accident to a pursuing driver caused by an increase of speed, expressly said that the recurrent allusion in those decisions of the Reichsgericht to the fact that the rescuer's intervention had been in accord with a legal or moral duty should not be understood to limit liability to such cases, but only to show that in such cases the intervention of the self-sacrificing third person is nearly always automatic,[1] so that the injuries suffered in doing so were undoubtedly adequate consequences of the wrongful act. In the above-mentioned decision the Court drew the conclusion that in less threatening situations it turns on the circumstances whether the situation produced by the wrongdoer is generally to be considered apt to produce rescues by third persons and, if so, in the present form. In the case then decided the Court went on to say that after a sufficiently serious traffic accident it is not at all unusual for other drivers to take up the pursuit of a hit and run driver independently, and that such traffic camaraderie, even if it may not reach the level of moral duty, is a fact which prevents us from regarding such a pursuit of the escaping driver as the quite improbable and gratuitous intervention of a third party in the causal continuity. Thus, one may start from the position that even where such an intervention is the immediate cause, an adequate connexion may be held to exist between the damage and the event that was the initial occurrence, if the conduct of the third person was justifiable. It is therefore irrelevant that in the present case the plaintiff was not expected to assist and, therefore, under no legal duty to help. It can also be left undecided whether there was a moral duty to rescue. In any case there was a justification. Indeed morally his conduct was of a high standard. Although in the circumstances his intervention required considerable courage and intrepidity, one cannot agree with the Landgericht that the possibility of it must have appeared to an observer so remote that it could not reasonably have been taken into account...[2]

Moreover, one cannot agree with the judgment under appeal in regarding the injury to the plaintiff as not an imputable consequence of the defendant's unlawful act... It shows a misunderstanding of Larenz's position in invoking his opinion that even where there is an adequate causal connexion between the rescue by the plaintiff and the defendant's unlawful act, that act must be regarded as a meaningless condition of the rescue and the ensuing injury to the plaintiff, which must no longer be imputable as a consequence of the unlawful act, since although the defendant could in any case be blamed for negligence in relation to the plaintiff's injuries, the latter bears the full responsibility for his deliberate conduct and therefore a quite predominant share of responsibility falls on him. As the plaintiff in his grounds for appeal aptly says, Larenz was merely upholding the view that even where several persons caused, because they one after another provided conditions for the eventual consequence, one of them can be regarded as its author because he intended the act as his own and thereby reduced the condition that the others provided to the status of an indifferent and legally meaningless condition; side by side therefore with the responsibility of the one who deliberately produced the consequence by his unlawful act, that of another person who merely provided an adequate condition, even though he acted negligently, appears meaningless, so that the consequence cannot be imputed to him as his act. Thus, the Landgericht failed to see that the plaintiff, who, as has already been explained, had a justification for his deliberate intervention, and whose conduct was of a high moral order, acted neither contrary to law nor in blameworthy fashion. Moreover, if failed to see that Larenz, when referring to the above-mentioned decision of the Reichsgericht in RGZ 164, 125, expressly said that the free but faultless act of a third party did not exclude the imputation to the one who had provided an adequate condition... Further, the defendant was also to blame for the damage to the plaintiff through his negligence, because it was foreseeable not only objectively, as has already been said, but subjectively, and here also, just as objective foreseeability is required for an adequate causal connexion, infrequent and exceptional consequences are to be taken into account and only quite remote possibilities are to be left out of account. Such a remote possibility, however, as has already been discussed in connexion with the intervention of the plaintiff, was, neither objectively nor, from the defendant's point of view, subjectively, in question.

The defendant, therefore, is liable for the damage suffered by the plaintiff under § 823 I and II BGB. The plaintiff, therefore, is entitled to damages for pain and suffering under § 847 BGB. Admittedly, in the cases decided by the Bundesgerichtshof (*NJW* 64, 1363) only compensation for material damage was dealt with and not pain and suffering. There was there no question at all of personal injury to the driver pursuing the hit and run driver, but only damage to his car. This, however, seems immaterial. What is essential is that the Court affirmed liability for a delict.

It follows that where a person suffers personal injuries he can claim damages for pain and suffering. Moreover, the Reichsgericht in the case already mentioned of the rescue of passengers from a burning vehicle (RGZ 164, 125), expressly awarded damages for pain and suffering to the injured rescuer against the objection of the defendant.

Since the plaintiff's claim for damages for pain and suffering is based on an unlawful act, there is no need to go more deeply into whether a claim for damages for pain and suffering also lies under the head of *negotiorum gestio*. [Discussion followed about the amount of damages for pain and suffering.]

Notes

1. Cf. Cardozo CJ in *Wagner* v. *International Ry Co.*, 1921, 232 N.Y. 176, 133 N.E. 437: 'Danger invites rescue. The cry of distress is the summons of relief. The law does not ignore these reactions of the mind in tracing conduct to its consequences. It recognizes them as normal. It places their effects within the range of the natural and probable. The wrong that imperils life is a wrong to the imperiled victim; it is a wrong also to his rescuer.'
2. The German solution is clearly conceived in 'causal' terms. Common lawyers have also approached these problems in terms of 'proximate cause' – see Magruder J's decision in *Socony Vacuum Oil Co.* v *Marshall* 222 F. 2d. 604 (1st Cir. 1955) – but the more 'orthodox' approach is nowadays through 'policy' and 'duty'. See Cardozo's judgment in *Wagner* v *International Ry*, (quoted in 1, above) and, for English law, *Haynes* v. *Harwood* [1935] 1 K.B. 146 and *Baker* v. *Hopkins & Son* [1959] 3 All E.R. 225.

9. *Decision of the 6th Civil Senate of 22 April* 1958 (*BGHZ* 27, 137)[1]

1. Even where damages are claimed under § 823 I BGB, it must first be inquired whether the consequences for which compensation is demanded fall within the protection of the enactment, in other words, whether the damage proved arose from the breach of a legal interest which the enactment was passed to protect.
2. A person involved in a traffic accident who was acquitted in

criminal proceedings arising out of the accident cannot recover the defence costs of the criminal proceedings under § 823 1 BGB from the person whose fault caused the accident.

BGB § 823 1

VI. Zivilsenat judgment of 22 April 1958 in Re:

S.B. (Plaintiff) v R (Defendant)

VI ZR 65/57

I. Landgericht Memmingen

II. Oberlandesgericht Munchen

The plaintiff's motor cycle collided on a main road passing through a village with a motor car coming in the opposite direction which belonged to the defendant's husband, since deceased, as the latter turned left to enter a side street. The plaintiff was injured. Both vehicles were damaged.

Criminal proceedings were instituted against both drivers. The defendant's husband was convicted of causing bodily harm in a negligent manner but then died.[2] The death was not connected with the accident and occurred before the order of the court could be served upon him. The plaintiff was also sentenced by the Amtsgericht to pay 30 DM for speeding. On appeal the Bavarian Oberlandesgericht quashed this judgment and remitted the case to the court of first instance for rehearing. The plaintiff was then acquitted for lack of evidence.

He claimed from the defendant, as heir of her husband, compensation for the costs he had incurred in defending himself in the criminal proceedings.

The Landgericht declared his claim justified as to four-fifths and rejected any further claim. On appeal by the defendant, the Oberlandesgericht rejected the claim for the costs. The plaintiff lost his appeal against that decision for the following reasons:

The parties are still in dispute only over the question whether the defendant must also pay the plaintiff four-fifths of the costs which he had to pay to defend himself in the criminal proceedings. The Court of Appeal gave a negative reply on the ground that no causal connexion existed between the bad driving of the defendant's husband and the incurring of the defence costs. Whether the attacks against this decision of the Court of Appeal are justified may be left undecided since in any case the view of the court of appeal that this claim for compensation of the plaintiff is to be rejected must in the result be approved.

A finding of adequate causation is not decisive for the decision of the dispute. The current mode of thought which looks at the question of limiting liability only from the point of view of adequate causation is not always capable of providing a proper solution... In previous judgments the Bundesgerichtshof has already made clear its view that the formula of adequate causation does not suffice to solve the problem of limiting liability (cf. *BGHZ* 8, 325, 329; 10, 107, 108; 20, 137, 142, 143). In a search for other means, von Caemmerer has justly focused on the question whether the facts for which compensation is demanded lie within the area of the protection of the rule that has been broken. This formulation of the question is commonly applied and recognised in determining liability for breach of a protective statute (§ 823 II BGB). Here, as this senate also declared in its judgments reported at *BGHZ* 12, 213, 217 and 19, 114, 126, following the case-law of the Reichsgericht, it is a condition of liability that the damage lies within the scope of the interests protected by the protective enactment, that is to say that the damage arises from the injury to a legal interest for the protection of which the rule was made. This limitation applies no less if, as here, claims are raised under § 823 I BGB. Here, too, it must first be asked whether the damage in question lies within the protective purpose, in other words, whether it concerns dangers which fall within the scope of the risks for which the rule was made. For this reason the sense and scope of the rule violated by the defendant must first be inquired into...

The plaintiff, in demanding compensation for his defence costs, is claiming that damage be made good that he suffered in his estate, that is to say, economic damage. It is generally accepted that in § 823 I BGB, under which he primarily makes his claims, the estate as such is not protected. The only question therefore is whether the damage falls within another aspect of the field of dangers dealt with in § 823 I BGB, namely the integrity of the body, health and property. Its intention is to protect against all risks that arise from an infringement of those rights. Only the consequences of that infringement are imputed to the wrongdoer and only within that scope are the interests of the injured party protected by it.

If anyone, like the plaintiff, is injured in an accident and his motor vehicle is damaged, the costs of restoring his health and repairing his vehicle are undoubtedly within the protective purpose of § 823 I BGB. That applies also to his loss of earnings, because his injury makes him unable to continue his calling, and also to the loss of the use he makes of the vehicle in his business. All of these are consequences of the accident which are connected with the personal injury and the damage to the vehicle. Although to some extent economic damage is involved, they fall within the protection of § 823 I BGB. It is quite different with the expenditure the criminal proceedings brought upon the plaintiff. So far none of the mischiefs which the law was meant to protect against has materialised through the accident. This had nothing to do with the personal injury and property damage suffered by him through the accident, for it arose from his being suspected of committing a criminal offence and from the decision of the prosecuting authority to institute proceedings against him. The risk of becoming involved in criminal proceedings is a general risk that affects every citizen. It is independent of the personal injury and property damage suffered in an accident, for it occurs even where an accident produces neither of them, and even when the driving complained of leads to no accident at all. The risk of having to spend money in defending oneself against a criminal charge is not one that the law intends to avert when casting the protection of § 823 I BGB over the integrity of health and property. Thus that provision disappears as a foundation for a claim to have that damage made good, irrespective of whether there is an adequate causal connexion between the conduct of the wrongdoer and the damage done by him.

Moreover, the plaintiff cannot claim compensation for his defence costs under § 823 II BGB, in combination with § 13 StVG. For § 13 StVG...apart from protecting the orderly movement of traffic, also protects only the health and property of those engaged in it, but not their economic interests. The only damage that is still in dispute, the defence costs, touches neither the health nor the property of the plaintiff, but interests that are not protected by it...

None of the legal considerations that have been adduced support the plaintiff's claim to have his defence costs made good.

Notes

1. Professor von Caemmerer, amongst others, has criticised the ability of the adequate cause theory to set proper limits to the bounds of delictual liability (see, inter alia, 'Das Problem des Kausalzusammenhangs im Privatrecht', in *Gesammelte Schriften*, I, 395 *et seq.*). Put differently, this means that the plaintiff's claim will rarely if ever fail if adequate causation is the only 'corrective' device in the hands of the judge. This can, and often does, lead to excessive liability, and the courts have had, whenever possible, increasing recourse to more normative theories of causation, notably the 'scope of the rule' approach. This theory (or cluster of theories, since it appears in a number of slight variations), and some of its limitations, are discussed more fully in

chapter 3 of the first volume, but in the case reproduced in the text above, as well as in the one that follows it, one finds, perhaps, its clearest formulation.

2. In the case of certain minor offences it is possible for the court to impose a penalty – usually a fine – without a proper hearing though the person 'penalised' can object to this once the court's order is served on him. A proper hearing will then follow.

10. Decision of the 6th Civil Senate of 16 February 1972 (BGHZ 58, 162)

A person who is answerable for a traffic accident is not also liable for the damage that following drivers do by driving on to the pavement of the blocked highway in order to go round the scene of an accident.

BGB § 823; StVG § 7

VI. Zivilsenat judgment of 16 February 1972

in Re: S. Bundesrepublik (Defendant) v. Stadt B (Plaintiff)

VI ZR 128/70

I Landgericht Bremen

II. Oberlandesgericht Bremen

On 21 June 1968 there was a traffic accident on the L Street in B. A lorry of the Dutch armed forces, in an attempt to overtake an automobile which was in course of parking, collided with an oncoming car. Both drivers left their vehicles in the narrow passage made by the parking vehicle, waiting for the arrival of the police. In consequence the highway was, for the time, blocked for the following car drivers. Thereupon several drivers, who could not make headway because of the lorry in front of them, drove round on to the pavement to the right of the scene of the accident. About fifteen minutes later, when the police arrived, substantial damage had been done to the pavement. The City of B, as owner of the highway, had to spend 1,736.58 DM to clear it up.

The drivers who drove on the Pavement have not been identified.

The Bundesrepublik, under the provisions of the NATO Armed Forces Statute, compensated the owner of the car struck by the army lorry. The plaintiff city contended that the Bundesrepublik must also make good the damage done by those drivers who drove on the pavement.

Whereas the Landgericht rejected the claim, the Oberlandesgericht allowed it.

On appeal, by leave of the Oberlandesgericht, the Bundesgerichtshof restored the judgment of the Landgericht for the following reasons:

The Federal Republic, as is agreed between the parties, has, under the provisions of the NATO Armed Forces Statute, assumed liability for damage done by the lorry of the Dutch armed forces as if it had been done by a lorry of the German forces. The claim is based on § 839 BGB, in combination with art. 34 of the Basic Law, so that liability under §§ 831, 823 BGB combined with the provisions of the Road Traffic Ordinance is excluded. According to sect. 2 of § 839 I BGB the plaintiff city would have had to show that it could not have obtained compensation in any other way for the damage – in particular, not from the drivers who had actually caused the damage and who, if they had been ascertained, would doubtless have had to make it good....

There is no dispute between the parties that the conditions for this liability are satisfied. For, as the judgment under attack establishes, the driver of the lorry was even at fault, since the strict liability is not excluded by unavoidable circumstances (§ 7 II StVG). The only question is whether the damage that the drivers who were forced to halt behind the lorry did in driving round on the pavement could be traced back to a conduct giving rise to liability, in this case the occupational hazard of this lorry, for which the operator is responsible. The Court of Appeal said yes.

II. This standpoint cannot be accepted.

1. Admittedly, approval must be given to the Court of Appeal's holding that the causal connexion between the conduct of the lorry driver and the damage to the pavement was even in this case adequate (the decision of the District Court of Düsseldorf in the 'Greenbelt' case, is, to this extent, sound). It is well known that in cases like this drivers constantly – no doubt in breach of traffic regulations and subject to punishment for malicious damage (§ 303 BGB) – do not wait long enough for passage to be possible or for a diversion to be allowed by the traffic police. In view of the experience that the conduct of such drivers will always recur, it may also be assumed that a driver must foresee that an accident caused by him in the flow of traffic may lead to such reactions on the part of following drivers, with ensuing damage to the public streets, private front gardens, fences and so on. Nevertheless, in the present case, there is no absolute need to discuss fault as a ground for liability, because the plaintiff city can base its claim on § 7 StVG.

The appeal wrongly casts doubt on the view of the Court of Appeal that the lorry was 'in operation' when such drivers passed over the pavement. The lorry had not been taken out of circulation when it came to a stop and prevented other vehicles from going forward. For the purposes of § 7 StVG the operation of an automobile lasts as long as the driver leaves it in circulation and the danger involved by it persists (*BGHZ* 29, 163, 166). Moreover, the diversion made by the impatient drivers is still in close connexion, in both time and place, with the collision caused by the lorry (cf. *BGHZ* 37, 311, 318). If a following automobile, in an attempt to avoid striking the lorry in front of it, braked and skidded and so invaded the pavement, the damage caused would certainly fall within the operational hazard of the lorry. Nor would it be different if a following driver, in order not to collide or not to be overrun by subsequent participants in the traffic, had deliberately turned on to the pavement.

2. If, therefore, the adequate causal connexion and the connexion with the operational hazard of the lorry are admitted to exist, the decision of the dispute depends on whether such consequences also can be imputed to a causer of damage as rest upon the 'free' decision of a third party (so-called 'breach of the causal connexion' or 'no recourse'). That question does not depend, in cases of this kind, on whether the injured party bases his claim on § 823 II (in combination with the provisions of the StVG) or on § 823 I BGB or on § 839 BGB or, as here on the ground that the highway was blocked by an automobile, on §§ 7, 18 StVG.

(a) Despite the contention of the appellant this imputation is not to be rejected on the ground that such impatient drivers acted deliberately and unlawfully in driving on the pavement.

The imputation of damage is not automatically excluded by the intervention of a third party (*BGHZ* 12, 206, 211; 17, 153, 159; 24, 263, 266). Only when the causal nature of the first state of facts is completely irrelevant to the second event can it be said that the causal connexion is 'broken' (*BGHZ* 3, 261, 268, 17, 159). That is not the case here. That such drivers caused the damage unlawfully does not stand in the way of the imputation. Whether the intervention of the third party was lawful or unlawful is of no decisive importance for the question of imputation.

Just as irrelevant is it that a person is acquitted of liability for damage done by a third party on the ground that the latter acted wilfully. Accordingly, the driver and operator, whose automobile collided with a lorry so that its load fell on to the highway, must compensate not only for the goods that were damaged by the fall, or could not be put in safe keeping, but also the goods stolen from among those strewn on the highway. There the person liable for the fall cannot refer the injured party to his claim against the thieves: that damage also may be imputed to him, on the ground that he created the danger of their being stolen. That those consequences of his conduct causing liability (that is to say the operation of the damage-causing automobile, or the traffic blunder of his driver) no longer fell into the class of risks for the avoidance of which rules of liability are prescribed (§§7, 18 StVG; §§823 *et seq.* BGB, in combination with the provisions of the StVG), cannot be accepted (cf. *BGHZ* 27, 137, 140). Such duties to assume risks may also be established by statute. Thus, under certain circumstances, the duty of care of a person participating in traffic may extend so far that he must take care that he does not, by defective behaviour, induce third parties to contravene wilfully the rules of road traffic. Above all, the operator of an automobile is answerable for all damage that is connected with the operation of his vehicle, irrespective of the way its dangerous character had caused damage in a particular case; he is liable also for damage a joy-rider knowingly and deliberately causes by his vehicle, even for the reckless killing of a human being (*BGHZ* 37, 311, 316/317).

(b) On mature consideration however the case to be decided appears to be different. The drivers, once they came to a halt on the road, drove onto the pavement of their own free will. That was connected with the accident, and so with the manner of driving the lorry and the operational hazard involved in it, only so far as the accident and its blocking of the road provided an occasion for the behaviour of the drivers. This was, however, no more than an external circumstance which gave the motivation for wilful conduct, without regard for the public safety, of the drivers. It cannot, therefore, be regarded as a sufficient foundation for an imputable connexion (cf. also *BGHZ* 25, 86, 90; senate decision of 12 February 1963 – VI ZR 181/62). Above all, it cannot be said here that the conduct of the lorry driver and the blocking of the highway 'provoked' the conduct of the drivers (cf. *BGHZ* 57, 25, 28). The blocking of the highway did not constitute such situation compelling the intervention of the third parties. As regards the damage to the borderstrip the impatient drivers alone, and not the lorry driver, were 'masters' of their injurious conduct. Accordingly the present case affords no opportunity for examining whether, in discussing 'provocation' of the reckless conduct of a third party, effect should be attributed to the degree and importance of the danger caused to the property of others. The decision of the dispute follows from the principle that the activities which are important in deciding the imputation of a damage must always be made the subject of a valuation (*BGHZ* 18, 286, 288; 30, 154, 157; senate decision of 8 January 1963–VI ZR 80/62–and 12 February 1963–VI ZR 181/62–823 BGB).

In making the valuation there is no connexion sufficient to ground liability between the conduct of the lorry driver and the damage, even if, in the plaintiff's interest, attention is focused not only on § 7 StVG, but also on the fault of the lorry driver which led to the collision. Here the law, and above all the traffic ordinance, clearly distinguished the spheres of liability: the driver and operator of the lorry were liable for the collision and its consequences to others involved in the accident as well as for all objects thereby damaged. For the damage to the pavement on the other hand, only the drivers who drove on it are answerable. The current instructions and prohibitions applicable to the lorry driver protected the interests of those who, with their property, were near the highway only to the extent that the driver was not allowed to invade the pedestrian path with his lorry or to afford an occasion for other vehicles to swerve onto the ground next to the road in order to avoid a collision. But what happened after the accident, as a result of other vehicles driving over the pavement in order to get on quicker, does not fall within his sphere of duty. The lorry driver was not in a position either in fact or in law to hinder them. That the imputation made by the Court of Appeal goes too far is also plain because the plaintiff city, if it were correct, could claim also against the operator of the car with which the lorry collided, if he did not succeed in exonerating himself under § 7 II StVG; and in certain circumstances the concurrent liability of the automobile which was being parked on the right might have to be considered. It would also be going too far to hold an operator liable for the damage done by following drivers driving onto the pavement if, as a result of failure in its equipment, the lorry had slid across the road.

3. After all, it was not here the operational hazard of the lorry or the driver's way of driving that in any imputable way led to the damage of the pavement. That might, to be sure, have happened because the driver of the lorry left it standing until the police arrived in answer to their call. If the resulting hindrance to traffic (cf. 1 StVG) no longer had a reasonable justification, this conduct could have created a

liability for the damage done by the impatient drivers (§§ 823 I and II, 839 BGB), so that the operator also (according to § 831 BGB, here the defendant according to Art. 34 of the Basic Law) might be liable. But a liability on this ground must be legally distinguished from the liability due to the preceding conduct for the actual consequences of the accident. The liability could also affect anyone who blocked the highway not by a vehicle or had not been to blame for the accident.

Under what conditions such a liability should be allowed to exist needs no examination here. The plaintiff city has made no complaint against the driver on these lines.

III. The plaintiff city therefore can have recourse only to those drivers for the damage done by them. It runs the risk, if their identity can no longer be ascertained, of having ultimately to bear the damage. That is however a general loss that falls on anyone who has property adjoining a road used for traffic and one that it cannot shift off on to the defendant. In consequence the decision appealed from cannot stand.[1]

Note

1. See Addenda, p. 342.

11. *Decision of the 6th Civil Senate of 7 December 1911 (RGZ 78, 239)*[1]

Is the proprietor of a department store liable for the fault of his employee who does bodily injury to a customer in the display of goods?

BGB § 278

VI. Zivilsenat judgment of 7 December 1911 in Re:

S.J. & Co. (Defendant) v. W (Plaintiff)

VI ZR 240/11

I. Landgericht I Berlin

II. Kammergericht Berlin

For These Reasons:

According to the findings of the Court of Appeal the plaintiff, after making several purchases in the defendant company's department store, went to the linoleum department to buy linoleum floor-cover. She mentioned this to W, the sales assistant who served there, and looked through the patterns which he displayed for her to make a choice. W, in order to pull out the roll she pointed to, put two others aside. They fell, hit the plaintiff and her child, and struck both of them to the floor. The purchase of the linoleum was not completed because, in the plaintiff's words, she became seriously disturbed by the fall.

The Court of Appeal rightly attributed the plaintiff's accident to W's fault, on the ground that he had put the rolls, which were not stable enough because of their relatively small bulk, insecurely on one side, instead of furnishing them with lateral protection by leaning them against the wall, and this even though he could have foreseen that the plaintiff, as usually happens with the buying public, would approach the place where the goods she had asked to be displayed were stored. The Court of Appeal's view is comprised in the simple conclusion that the rolls would not have fallen if W had placed them carefully and regularly on one side.

The Court of Appeal's opinion that the defendant company is liable for W's fault under § 278 BGB cannot, in spite of the appellant's contention, be rightly objected to; and it conforms to the case-law of this Senate. W was acting for the defendant company (§ 164 BGB, § 54 HGB) when he entered into negotiation with the plaintiff. The plaintiff had asked for a piece of linoleum to be laid out for inspection and purchase. W had acceded to her request in order to make a sale. The proposal and its acceptance had for their purpose the conclusion of a sale, and therefore the production of a legal transaction. That was no mere factual proceeding, a mere act of courtesy, but a legal relationship came into existence between the parties in preparation for a purchase; it bore a character similar to a contract and produced legal obligations in so far as both seller and prospective buyer came under a duty to observe the necessary care for the health and property of the other party in displaying and inspecting the goods.

The judgments of this Senate have already proceeded on similar grounds, and it has been recognised in several decisions of the Reichsgericht that duties of care for the life and property of the other party can arise from bilateral or unilateral obligations, which have nothing to do with the legal nature of the relation in a narrower sense, but nevertheless follow from its factual character.

The defendant company made use of W's services for the fulfilment of the aforesaid obligation to the prospective purchaser, and is therefore answerable for his fault. This is in line with the thought expressed in § 278 BGB, that whoever himself owes a performance that he must carry out with the required amount of care must, when he makes use of an employee, answer for his careful performance, and that accordingly the other person to whom the performance is to be done must not be put in a worse position because he does not do it himself but commits it to an employee. It would be contrary to the general feeling of justice if, in cases where the person in charge of the business of displaying or laying out goods for exhibition, sampling, trial or the like carelessly injures a prospective purchaser, the proprietor of the business – with whom the prospector wished to make a purchase – should be answerable only under § 831 BGB and not unconditionally, so that the injured person should, if the proprietor succeeds in exonerating himself, be referred to the usually impecunious employee.

There is no need to go here into the legally questionable view of the Court of Appeal that the mere entry into a department store of a prospective purchaser or even a visitor without any intention of buying creates a contractual relation between him and the proprietor, including the widely discussed duties of care....

Note

1. This case, discussed in vol. I, chapter 4, represents a breakthrough in the effort to circumvent the basic provision on vicarious liability. For lack of space we have not included here any translated extracts of cases dealing with 831 BGB, but the interested reader can find a selection of translated texts in A. von. Mehren and J.R. Gordley, *The Civil Law System*, 2nd edn (1977), 714 *et seq.*

12. *Decision of the 8th Civil Senate of 28 January 1976 (BGB NJW 1976, 712)*[1]

If a child accompanies her mother shopping in a self-service store, she can, if she falls, have a claim for damages due to fault at the making of a contract under a contract with protective effects for third persons.

BGB §§ 328, 276
VIII. Zivilsenat judgment of 28 January 1976
VIII ZR 246/74 (Koblenz)

The plaintiff, who at the time of the accident was fourteen years of age, went with her mother to a branch of the defendant's, a small self-service store. Whilst her mother, after selecting her goods, still stood at the till, the plaintiff went round to the packing counter to help her mother pack the goods. In doing so she fell to the floor and suffered an injury which necessitated a lengthy treatment. Alleging that she had slipped on a vegetable leaf, she sued the defendant for breach of his duty to provide safe access. The Court of Appeal having dismissed as time-barred the claim for damages for pain and suffering, the parties are now in dispute only on the question whether the defendant is obliged to compensate the plaintiff for her economic loss as well as prospective damage.

The Landgericht rejected the claim as time-barred. The Court of Appeal granted it – after deducting one quarter for contributory fault. The defendant's further appeal was unsuccessful for these reasons:

I. The Court of Appeal found as proved that the plaintiff slipped on a vegetable leaf lying on the floor near the packing counter and suffered injuries which necessitated the expenditure in question and may possibly lead to future loss. These findings disclose no legal error; they are in fact undisputed on appeal.

II. According to the Court of Appeal's opinion the defendant had not furnished the proof incumbent on him that he had taken all necessary care for the safety of movement in his store and that the accident could only be attributed to the fact that another customer had shortly before let a vegetable leaf fall to the floor. These findings also cannot be faulted legally. They conform to the settled case-law of the BGH (*NJW* 1962, 31=LM 267 Fa BGB Nr. 13; cf. also *RGZ 78*, 239) both on the duty of a shopkeeper to ensure safety of movement and on the reversal of the burden of proof required by § 282 BGB in cases of claims for damages based on *culpa in contrahendo*. This point also is not contested on appeal.

III. The defendant therefore is liable – so continued the Court of Appeal – after taking the contributory fault of the plaintiff into account, for three-quarters of the existing and prospective loss, and that not only in delict, but also for fault in concluding the contract, since he infringed the contractual duty of protection and care which he had undertaken to the plaintiff on opening the self-service store. Moreover, the plaintiff also has a claim for damages under a contract with protective effects towards a third party because her mother was during the accident preparing to contract with the defendant and the plaintiff was being included as an assistant within the scope of that contract-like obligation. For claims, however, arising from fault in concluding a contract the limitation period is thirty years, so that the claim was brought in good time.

IV. These explanations stand up to examination – at least in result. Admittedly the main line of the Court of Appeal's reasoning, that the defendant is directly liable to the plaintiff for fault in concluding the contract, irrespective of whether a contract with protective effects towards a third party needs to be brought into the picture, gives rise to doubts. Liability for *culpa in contrahendo*, which, in cases like the present one, is more favourable to a plaintiff than the general liability in delict for breach of the duty to provide safe access – because of the increased liability for employees (§ 278 BGB in contrast to § 831 BGB), the longer limitation periods (§ 195 BGB in contrast to § 852 BGB) and the reversal of the burden of proof (§ 282 BGB) – rests on a legal obligation created by way of supplement to the written law. It arises from the process of bargaining for a contract and is largely independent of the actual conclusion or efficacy of a contract (*BGHZ* 6, 330, 333). The liability for a breach of the duties of protection and care arising from this obligation finds, in cases of the present kind, its justification in the fact that the injured party entered the other party's sphere of influence for the purpose of negotiating for a contract and can therefore rely on an enhanced carefulness in the other party to the negotiation (cf. also BGH *NJW* 1960, 720). This is borne out exactly by the present case in which the mother entered the slaes department of the defendant for the purpose of making a purchase and in doing so had to subject herself to a risk involved in the increased congestion, especially near the till, in a self-service store. It is, however, always a presupposition of liability for *culpa in contrahendo* in this type of contract of sale that the injured party enters the sales department with the purpose of contracting or of entering into 'business contacts' – and therefore at least as a possible customer, though perhaps without a fixed intention to purchase (cf. BGH, *NJW* 1962, 31). It need not be decided whether it is enough, in view of the peculiarities of sale in a self-service store, for a customer (when entering the sales department) to have intended at first only to have a look at the objects offered and be possibly stimulated to buy or only to make a preliminary comparison of prices with those in competing enterprises. In any case there is no sufficient justification for a contractual liability for *culpa in contrahendo* stretching beyond liability for delict when the person entering the store never intended to buy, perhaps because – leaving aside the shoplifter mentioned by the Court of Appeal – he is sheltering from a shower or using the store as a way through to another street or even only to meet other persons. The line may be difficult to draw in particular cases, above all because it depends on the difficult proof of unexpressed intention. In the present case, however, it is beyond dispute that the plaintiff from the start did not intend to make a contract herself but only to accompany her mother and help her in buying. A direct application of liability for fault in concluding a contract with the defendant is therefore excluded.

V. Nevertheless the appellate judgment is proved right in result, because it is supported by supplementary considerations.

1. If the plaintiff's mother had been injured in the same way as her daughter, there would have been no objection to making the defendant liable for *culpa in contrahendo* – as is also clearly stated in the appeal. In that case nothing need be said about the question, disputed in academic circles, whether in a self-service store the display of the goods constitutes an offer and the contract of sale is concluded by the buyer's accepting it in presenting the selected goods at the till – thus reserving a final decision until that moment – or whether the display of the goods constitutes only an invitation to make offers, which the customer for his part makes by showing them to the cashier and the latter accepts by registering it on behalf of the self-service store.[2] In any case the general run of the reasons for the judgment, even though it contained no express statement by the court of appeal, makes it obvious that at the moment of the accident the goods intended for the purchase had already been finally chosen and legal obligation already existed between the defendant and the plaintiff's mother justifying liability for *culpa in contrahendo*.

2. It is on the legal obligation that the plaintiff can rely to justify her contractual claim for damages. It accords with the long-standing case-law of this Senate in particular that in special circumstances even bystanders who do not themselves participate in a contract are included in the protection afforded by it, with the consequence that although they have no claim to have the primary contractual duty performed, they are entitled to the protection and care offered by the contract and can make good in their own name claims for damages arising from the breach of those subsidiary duties... It is not necessary to consider here the theoretical question whether such a contract with protective effects toward third parties, on which the courts have proceeded hitherto, is derived from the supplementary interpretation of a contract incomplete to that extent (§§ 133, 157 BGB), or whether, as is increasingly accepted in the literature, direct quasi-contractual claims arise on grounds independent of the hypothetical intention of the parties, perhaps from customary law, or on the basis of legal developments by the courts. In any case, according to both views it is essential that the contract, according to its sense of purpose and the requirements of good faith, demands an inclusion of third parties in its sphere of protection; and that one party to the contract can in honesty – and in a manner discernable by the other

party – expect that the care and protection owed to it will be equally extended to a third person. There is no good reason to exclude sales in general from this legally possible configuration as this is shown in particular by sales in shops to which buyers, in certain circumstances, must enter the sphere of influence of the seller. And that is also the view of the Sixth Senate in BGHZ 51, 91, 96.

3. Admittedly the inclusion of third persons in the sphere of protection of a contract – if the contrast between contractual and delictual liability established by the legislator is not to be destroyed or blurred – needs to be confined to narrowly defined cases. Whether the mere fact that the customer makes use of a third person in initiating and concluding a purchase in a self-service store is enough for the protected effect to be accepted as possible may be left undecided; for in the present case it must be added that the plaintiff's mother was responsible for her daughter 'for better or worse' (*BGHZ* 51, 91, 96), and therefore – and this should be known to the defendant also – for that reason alone it could reasonably be inferred that the daughter accompanying her should enjoy the same protection as herself. In such a close family relationship the courts have always seen themselves justified in extending contractual protection.

4. That in the present case the sale was not concluded at the moment of the accident is, in the result, unimportant. If one looks upon the duty of protection and care as the determining element of the legal obligation based on negotiating for a contract, and if one considers that the other party owes this duty of care both before and after the conclusion of the contract, the inclusion of third persons (who are equally worthy of protection) in the obligation follows. Moreover, there would be no rational ground for making the contractual liability depend on the chance of whether the negotiations had already led to a contract when the damage occurred; that is impressively shown by the present case, where the 'sale negotiations' had, in essence, been completed and the conclusion of the contract – possibly subject to a delay on the mother's part in completing it at the till, and for which the plaintiff's mother was not responsible – was in any case imminent. The appellant's contention, that a cumulation of liability for *culpa in contrahendo* and inclusion of a third party in the protective effect of a contract would lead to an unforeseeable widening of the risk on a seller, is directed in principle against the justification of both institutions in general. The danger of a flood of litigation, which cannot be dismissed out of hand, has, as has already been explained,

long been taken into account by the courts, which have imposed strict requirements on the inclusion of third parties in the protective sphere of a contract. As regards merely precontractual relations some reservation may be indicated. But in any case with so narrow a limitation there is no objection to an extension of protection if – as here – the person causing the damage could not reasonably have opposed any desire expressed by the mother, when negotiating for a contract, to have from the start the same protection expressly given to the child who was subsequently injured herself. Finally, in so far as the appellant contends that the long limitation period – combined with the reversal of the burden of proof – would intolerably worsen the evidentiary position of anyone sued for damages in such situations, the remedy must be found in Laches (Verwirkung) , of the existence of which there is no indication in this case.

Notes

1. Cf. *Ward* v. *Tesco Stores Ltd* [1976] 1 W.L.R. 810.
2. Cf. *Pharmaceutical Society of Great Britain* v. *Boots Cash Chemists (Southern) Ltd* 1952] 2 Q.B. 795 and contrast this with *Soc. des Eaux de Vittel c. Dehen Soc. Supermag-Rennes* GP 1962, 1, 135 and Note A. Tunc in *Rev.trim.dr.civ.* (1962) 305

13. *Decision of the 7th Civil Senate of 7 November 1960* (*BGHZ* 33, 247)

A contractor can plead by way of defence against the claim for damages of third party who has been brought under the protection of a contract that a fault of the customer contributed to the damage.

BGB §§ 254, 328, 334, 618

VII. Zivilsenat judgment of 7 November 1960 in Re: Sp. GmbH (Defendant) v. H & W Berufsgenossenschaft (Plaintiff)

VII ZR 148/59

I. Landgericht Bochum
II. Oberlandesgericht Köln

On 11 April 1953 two adjoining ferro-concrete plates became loose from the 16 to 18m high roof of the steelworks at W belonging to the Siemens-Martin-Stahlwerk and fell on two persons at work in the works, namely, the works engineer S and the steel worker L. S died at once, leaving a widow and two children. L was severely injured.

The roof had been erected by the defendant company between October 1952 and March 1953. In making use of the old roof

construction ferro-concrete plates developed by the defendant company were substituted for the former concrete layers (which formed
the ceiling).

The plaintiff association claims to be recouped for the payments
made as an accident insurer to the surviving relatives of the works
engineer S and to L.

It bases its claim on delict and on a 'positive breach of contract'
(positive Vertragsverletzung) (§§ 328, 618 BGB), in each case in
combination with § 1542 RVO (right of subrogation).

The defendant company denies that it did an unsatisfactory job in
performing the steelworks contract. It pleads in addition that the
steelworks were jointly at fault in defectively altering the roof. This
share of the fault must be imputed to the plaintiff. The defendant
company also pleads that the claim is time-barred.

The Landgericht dismissed the claim. On appeal, the Oberlandesgericht found the claim for payment justified in principle and
granted the declarations applied for.

The defendant company's appeal led to the decision being quashed
and the case being sent back for reconsideration for the following
reasons:

1.(a) The Court of Appeal left open the question whether the claim
in delict of the injured parties (and therefore of the plaintiff) was
time-barred. It granted them a direct claim against the defendant
company on a 'positive breach of contract' under §§ 328, 618 I and III,
844 BGB. The contract between the defendant company and the
steelworks included a subsidiary duty on the defendant company to
see that no damage should occur to the other party in doing the job
That obligation bound the defendant company under § 618 I BGB to
the customer's work force also; they had acquired direct claims for
damages through the breach of the obligation.

(b) That is in conformity with the opinion developed in the
case-law of the Reichsgericht and the Bundesgerichtshof. According to
it the basis of this liability is a contract for the benefit of third parties in
the sense that in its protection are included the persons to whom the
promisee on his part owes essential duties of care and protection.

(c) The Court of Appeal was not in error in including those injured
in the accident within the circle of those so benefited. That circle must
of course be limited and easily ascertainable. But it was so here. Both
the victims belonged to the work force and employees who were

regularly active in the shop roofed by the defendant company. It was a numerically limited and spatially confined group to which the employer owed a special duty of care in fitting out the workshop. It was only that circle that the Court of Appeal included in the protection afforded by the construction contract, not, as is said in the appeal, the several thousand employees of the steelworks' work force.

2. Nor was the Court of Appeal in error in affirming the transmission of the claims of the injured persons to the plaintiff under § 1542 RVO. That paragraph is, as the Senate has already decided (*BGHZ* 26, 365), applicable also to claims for contractual damages.

3. The Court of Appeal properly held that the defendant company contributed by its fault to the accident and was therefore bound to make good the damage on the ground of a 'positive breach of contract' (point discussed but not reported).

4. It left open the question whether the steelworks contributed at all by their fault to the accident, because in its opinion this was irrelevant.

That was rightly attacked in the appeal. The question whether in such a case the injured third party must have imputed to him under § 254 BGB a contributory fault of the other party to the contract with the person causing the damage has been answered in the affirmative by the Reichsgericht and the Bundesgerichtshof only where that party is the statutory representative or the employee of the injured party (*BGHZ*, 316; 24, 325; LM Nr. 2 to § 254 BGB (E) with further references).

The view is taken, moreover, in the legal literature that the person who owes compensation may quite generally, even when the other party to the contract – as here – is not the statutory representative or the employee of the injured third party, plead against the latter under § 254 BGB the contributory fault of that party to the contract.

That view must – contrary to the Court of Appeal's opinion – be accepted. As in every contract for the benefit of third parties, so also in a contract of the kind in question, the protected third party derives his rights against the doer of the damage only from the contractual relations between the immediate parties. That already follows from the legal principle underlying § 334 BGB, according to which defences under the contract available to the promisor can also be pleaded against the third party. The words in the decision of the Bundesgerichtshof in LM 2 of § 254 BGB (E) that 'the inclusion of the plaintiff in the contractual protection' implies that 'he must, along with the widening of his legal protection, take into account the legal disadvantages bound up with it' points in this direction and shows also that the solution found here conforms to equity.

It follows that the judgment under attack, in so far as it disregards any contributory fault of the steelworks, cannot be upheld.

5. It could of course stand if the plaintiff's claim could also be supported in delict, for to that extent the contributory fault of the steelworks might not affect the liability of the defendant company.

The Court of Appeal – consistently with its standpoint – did not examine that question. In particular it had left open the question whether this claim was time-barred. For want of the necessary findings, the Senate is itself not in a position to arrive at a decision.

The judgment under attack must therefore be set aside and the matter referred back to the Court of Appeal.

14. *Decision of the 6th Civil Senate of 10 February 1930* (RGZ 127, 218)[1]

Is a contractor liable in contract to pay compensation to a domestic servant of a customer for damage caused by the defective execution of a job? Contract for the benefit of a third party.

BGB §§ 133, 157, 278, 328, 618
VI. Zivilsenat judgment of 10 February 1930 in Re:
Firma B & R (Defendant) v. A (Plaintiff)
VI ZR 270/29

The plaintiff acted from the middle of April until the end of June 1926 as daily help to the widow M. On 10 and 11 August 1926 she was helping Frau M to move to a new dwelling; as from 15 August she had accepted a new post as a maid-servant. Frau M had employed the defendant firm to move the gas meter in the bathroom of her new dwelling. At the end of July the firm instructed their leading fitter B to do the job. On 11 August the plaintiff noticed a smell of gas in the dwelling, as she had done the day before. To discover the place of the leak she climbed a ladder in the bathroom and lit the gas burner with a match. The leaking gas was set alight and the plaintiff suffered appreciable damage to the upper part of her body. The gas escape was due to the looseness of an overflow screw on the meter. The screw had been installed by B. The Court of Appeal found that he had been grossly negligent in the unworkmanlike execution of the job.

The plaintiff first sued the widow M for damages in preliminary proceedings. At that stage the present defendant firm appeared as 'co-defendant' with Frau M. The action was dismissed on the ground that in any case the plaintiff was predominantly to blame (§ 254 BGB).

The plaintiff now sued the firm B & R and also B as co-defendants for damages and an annuity, and for a declaration of liability for further damage.

The Landgericht found the claim against both defendants justified as to two-thirds. The Oberlandesgericht reduced the award to one-half.

The appeal of the firm B & R (hereinafter called the defendant) was unsuccessful, apart from a determination of the duration of the annuity.

Reasons:

The essential grounds on which the Court of Appeal based its judgment were the following. The defendants were strictly liable without exoneration for damage caused by B under the contract made with Frau M. That contract bound the defendants to take the care normally required in carrying out the job; moreover, in performing that duty they made use of their employee B and must therefore take responsibility for him under § 278 BGB. Not only was Frau M entitled as a contracting party to have that care taken, and to be compensated for the damage caused by the neglect of it, but the plaintiff was also entitled in so far as the contract must be taken to have been a contract for the benefit of third parties.

Whether a contract was intended to bring § 328 I BGB into operation, so that the third party should acquire directly a right to claim the promised performance, must, under § 328 II BGB and in the absence of any special provision, be decided on the facts of each case, with particular reference to what can be recognised by both parties to have been the purpose of the contract.

The contractual purpose here signifies the objective means of determining the terms of the contract so that an agreement must be taken as covered by the contractual intention which the contracting parties could have arrived at if they had faced up to the elaboration of the details according to the purpose of the contract. Whether the extent of their agreement had actually been realised was beside the point. The application of these principles led to the conclusion that there was here a contract for the benefit of third parties. When a contract is made for the execution of a job in a customer's dwelling and danger is involved for anyone using it, the customer must be assumed to have intended – an intention capable of being observed by the contractor – that the interests of relatives living with him would be respected, and that they would for this purpose have the same rights as he himself has to be compensated for damage done to them through the doing of the job. For without such an extension of the contractual duties, injured dependants would be limited to non-contractual claims. Such a different treatment of the customer and his dependants would offend against a sound instinct for justice and be out of accord with the contractual intent of the customer, who, as the contractor must have been aware, would not wish to place his dependants in a worse position than himself as regards claims for compensation.

The position of the customer's domestic servants is the same. Here, too, the intention – capable of being recognised by the contractor – must be implied that he will respect the interests of the domestic staff, who must work on the premises where the contractor does the job and would have a claim to a safe system of work against the customer (§ 618 BGB). Where the customer contracts for a performace of a dangerous character, the contractor must know that he intends the performance to be carried out so as not to cause damage either to himself or to the members of his family or domestic staff, and that he is to stand in no better position than those belonging to his immediate household.

Now, the plaintiff was indeed not a domestic servant but only a daily help, and therefore, was not a member of the domestic community. But, when making the contract, the head of the household must have intended – and this intention must have been understood by the contractor – to ensure that, over and above the circle of her family dependants and domestic staff, all those persons to whom a master owes a duty of protection should enjoy the especial protection of a personal claim to have care taken of them under § 618 BGB. The daily help belongs to that class. This interpretation, however, must be subject to the limitation that only such persons must be regarded as benefiting from § 618 BGB as stand towards their employer in a relationship of some duration from which arises at least a moral duty on the employer to increase his protection. For a master must not be taken to intend to contract for the benefit of persons who serve only occasionally and temporarily on his premises and with whom he does not form any close attachment, such as arises from a longer use of their services and a more frequent contact, and even the creation of personal relations. The plaintiff stood in no passing relation to Frau M; for she was in regular service with her for about a quarter of a year and was also, as is stated more fully, in a long-standing relation with her.

But even if that no longer applied to 11 August 1926 – so says the appellate decision – a contract for the benefit of third parties would exist as regards the plaintiff. For during the removal and the putting in order of the new dwelling, the dangers involved in the furnishing were so much greater than in ordinary housekeeping that the occupier must be taken to have intended to provide special protection to all taking part in the removal. The contract for the benefit of third parties must be taken to have imposed a duty of care upon all taking part in it.

Against this the appeal contends that a contract for a job of work cannot be taken to include the protection of all those permanently or temporarily in a dwelling; for principles worked out for leases cannot be applied to contracts for a job of work.

This attack cannot succeed, in particular because the appellate judge's interpretation of the contract of work between the defendant and the widow M, to the effect that it was a contract of work for the benefit of the plaintiff, is free from legal error, above all in his application of §§ 133, 157, 328 BGB. Whether his definition of the circle of those benefited was entirely correct need not be discussed. In any case it includes persons who are entitled to damages from the customer under § 618 BGB.

The fundamental considerations on which the Court of Appeal proceeded are to the point, and are established by case-law of the Reichsgericht. It is in particular correct that the contract for the benefit of a third party can be an implied one, and that the decision whether a contract is to be regarded as having been made for the benefit of a third party also and whether the third party shall acquire rights immediately against the promisor depends essentially, in the absence of a special term, on a finding of the facts in each case. For that purpose regard must be had to the intention of the parties, the purpose of the transaction, and business usages. Especial attention must be paid to the supplementary interpretation of contracts. The business intention of the parties provides an objective indication; whether the parties were aware when contracting of the scope of their declarations is irrelevant. Finally, there is no requirement that the identity of the third party should be ascertained when the contract is made; it is enough for it to be ascertainable.

On this basis more recent judgments of the Reichsgericht have followed its earlier case-law in recognising more and more contracts for the benefit of third parties in cases where a third party has suffered damage [there follows an exposition of the slowly developing practice of the Court].

If, now, one comes to decide the present case, one arrives at the following conclusions. The plaintiff was a daily help in a long-term relationship with the widow M. Accordingly she was entitled and obliged, in the interest of her own health but also in the furtherance of her employer's business, to enter the bathroom from which the smell of gas semed to come. The gas escape rendered the premises in which she was bound to serve unfit to afford her protection against danger to life and limb. The unfitness was due to the grossly negligent way B, the defendant's 'employee', performed the job of fixing the gas meter (§ 278 BGB). Under § 618 BGB Frau M was subjected to obligations which the legislator considered so essential that their exclusion or limitation by contract was made illegal (§ 619 BGB). Under them Frau M was liable to compensate the plaintiff, although she was not herself to blame. For liability under § 618 BGB is contractual and hence § 278 BGB is applicable, so that Frau M had to answer to the plaintiff for the defendant's fault.

Now, Frau M's purpose, as the defendant could well realise, in making the contract, was to have the gas meter properly fixed, and in particular that the execution of the job should produce no danger to life and limb either to herself or to any persons to whom she might become liable under § 618 BGB. No objection in point of law can be taken to the further finding that the appellate judge made in interpreting the contract by way of supplementation, according to § 157 BGB, that Frau M and the defendant would have agreed to the direct liability of the latter for all damage for which Frau M might become liable to compensate persons through an improper fitting of the gas meter, if the parties, when making the contract, had contemplated such a possibility. For Frau M would have made the asssumption of such direct liability a term of the contract and the defendant would, in order to get the order, have accepted such a term, all the more so because he had in any case to do a perfect job and it made no essential difference to him whether he exposed himself to a direct claim for damages by the employee of Frau M or for an indemnity by the latter.

Note

1. Cf. *Green* v. *Fibreglass Ltd* [1958] 2 Q.B. 245.

15. *Decision of the Great Senate of 4 March 1957* (BGHZ 24, 21)[1]

Whoever, when employed in running a tramway or railway within the meaning of § 831 BGB, injures another person in life, body, health or property, acts unlawfully unless he acts in accordance with correct traffic practice. It is for the injured party to prove the act causing the injury and its consequences and for the management to prove that the conduct of the employee was in accordance with current traffic practice.

BGB §§ 831, 823
Great Senate for Civil Cases, decree of 4 March 1957
GSZ 1/56

Reasons:

1. The case submitted to the Great Senate for Civil Cases is based on the following facts:

The plaintiff took part in a family celebration and intended about 1.30 a.m. to return on the tramway run by the defendant enterprise from the 'Apotheke' stopping place. When he tried to mount the forward platform of the tramcar he fell: he was run over by the car and his right foot so severely injured that his leg had to be amputated below the knee. The plaintiff made the defendant, the driver, and the conductor of the vehicle responsible for the damage and put forward the following grounds for his claims:

The fall occurred because the tramcar started too soon. The conductor gave the departure signal and the driver started although both could have seen that the plaintiff was still just about to mount the forward platform. He had stood in front of the door when it started and had already grasped both the entrance handles. The driver did not stop immediately on getting the emergency signal from the conductor.

In his action the plaintiff demanded damages from the defendant, the driver, and the conductor of the tramcar.

The defendant, the driver, and conductor admitted his claims in part... Otherwise they claimed that the action should be dismissed and urged that:

The conductor gave the signal to start and the driver set the tramcar in motion only after the invitation to enter had been given and no one else was prepared to enter. The plaintiff had been standing by a group of persons who had not intended to ride, but had then hurried after the moving tramcar and tried to jump on. When the emergency signal was given the driver stopped at once. The plaintiff had been drunk and had only himself to blame for the fall.

The Landgericht allowed the claim, reduced to one-half. On appeal by the plaintiff and counter-appeal by the various defendants, the Oberlandesgericht dismissed the action against the driver and conductor and declared the defendant tramway company liable to pay compensation up to two-thirds.

On appeal the defendant company moved for a complete dismissal of the action.

2. It was disputed in the first place whether the defendant company also was liable under § 831 BGB for the damage caused by its employees. This question required examination because the plaintiff's claims were not completely supported by the Reichshaftpflicht-gesetz, in particular in so far as he demanded damages for pain and suffering.

The Court of Appeal found that the defendant company was responsible under § 831 BGB for the damage to the plaintiff, because the driver, and perhaps also the conductor, had caused the physical injury unlawfully and because the defendant company had not produced the proof necessary for exonerating itself under § 831 I 2 case 1 BGB from liability for its 'employees'. The Court of Appeal came to the conclusion that the way the fall occurred was not clear. It was possible that the plaintiff's allegations of fact were correct, but it was also possible that the accident happened in the way described by the defendant. In view of this negative result of the evidence, the Court of Appeal felt that the possibility could not be excluded that a causal connexion did exist between a presumable failure of choice and supervision on the defendant company's part, and the occurrence of the damage (§ 831 II 2 case 2 BGB).

3. The Sixth Civil Senate had doubts whether to follow the Court of Appeal's findings of law. The doubts were directed above all against the view that an 'employee' (for the purposes of § 831 BGB) engaged in tramway or railway traffic did damage unlawfully merely

by causing physical injury. It is a matter for discussion whether the basis of the unlawfulness must be further gone into in order to show whether the conduct of the employees is objectively contrary to good traffic practice. For that purpose reference is made to the traffic rules which regulate the conduct of participants in traffic in ever-greater detail. Recourse must also be had to the legal concept of social adequacy and to developments in modern criminal theory, more especially because according to it the concept of negligence includes essential requirements which relate to unlawfulness and not to fault. If a finding of unlawfulness in traffic accidents does not automatically follow from the resulting consequence but [is satisfied] only if a breach of the traffic regulations has occurred, then it seems probable, in view of the report laid before us, that the conception of the burden of proof hitherto followed in applying § 831 BGB can no longer be upheld. That must be true in particular of cases which resemble the one in question and are distinguished by the fact that, in view of the failure to clarify what happened on the occasion of the accident, no objectively irregular conduct on the part of the 'employees' can be established.

The Sixth Civil Senate attaches fundamental importance to the clarification of these questions of law. In accordance with § 137 GVG it submits them for decision to the Great Senate for Civil Cases and formulates them as follows:

'Does a person employed in tramway or railway traffic do damage unlawfully to another within the meaning of § 831 I BGB merely by injuring his life, body, health or property? Or is it a further condition of unlawfulness that the participant employed in the traffic conducted himself in an objectively irregular way? Is the employer who fails to exonerate himself from the charge of defective selection or supervision liable under § 831 BGB even if according to the evidence the possibility remains open that the "employee" observed the objective duties of care and, in particular, the rules governing highway or rail traffic?'

1. When § 831 BGB makes the employer's liability depend on whether his 'employee' did unlawful damage to another person in executing his task, this requirement connects it with the factual situations of the law of delict in which the unlawful acts involving a duty of compensation are described and delimited. Not every doing of damage products liability, but only such as falls within a liability situation of the law of delict, and, therefore, is an 'unlawful act' in the sense of §§ 823 *et seq.* BGB. Accordingly, for the purpose of traffic

accidents here in question, in the first place a reference is needed to § 823 BGB, especially 1. Claims for damages are constantly recurring from injuries to life, body, health or property in tramway and railway traffic. Now the wording of 823 1 BGB requires that the injury to the enumerated legal interests be unlawful, that is to say repugnant to the legal order. The legislator, however, when describing in legal terms the factual basis of illegality, indicates that he regards the breach of the legal interests listed in § 823 1 BGB as normally unlawful. By adding 'unlawful', however, he indicates that the mere breach does not, necessarily, involve unlawfulness, but that unlawfulness can for special reasons not exist. It may be questionable whether that indication was needed. It is certainly useful in applying the law, by making judges attentive to the fact that any factual description of unlawful conduct is bound to be incomplete and that therefore they are under a duty to examine whether a finding of unlawfulness based on a fulfilment of the factual conditions must be withdrawn on special grounds. Further, the BGB does not provide an exhaustive formulation for defining when there is a legal justification. The initial provision about consent as a justification was struck out in the discussion of the draft because it was desired to leave to practice the task of marking out the limits of justification. Moreover, the jurists and judges have also developed slowly those principles to which they may have resort for the purposes of excluding unlawfulness, such as on the basis of *negotiorum gestio*, the protection of vested rights, or the balancing of interests. There is, therefore, no exhaustive legal catalogue of justifications, no *numerus clausus* which would set limits to legal development. Accordingly, the matter must be gone into now that the report of the Sixth Civil Senate has submitted for discussion the question whether, in the special field of tramway and railway traffic, conduct fulfilling on its face the factual condition of § 823 1 BGB must no longer be adjudged unlawful if it was in harmony with the legal regulations laid down for the traffic.

The line of thought in that direction found in the report must in principle be approved. The draftsmen of the BGB may indeed not have recognised that these are matters for discussion which concern objective unlawfulness and not merely fault in the sense of personal blameworthiness. Only with the technical development of traffic and the increase in its dangers did modern mass traffic produce problems calling for regulatory legislation. The legislator was faced with the need to regulate by increasingly detailed provisions the duties of participants in traffic, so that the possibilities of danger should be reduced to a minimum. At the same time the legal provisions dealing with liability for risks were developed in order to apportion with social fairness in their economic effects the dangers and risks rendered inevitable by modern traffic. In the process it was more and more recognised that what was in question was not a liability for wrong but a duty on those in control of dangerous operations to assume responsibility for certain typical risks. With that legal development there is no longer any place in the law of delict for a doctrine that looks upon unavoidable injuries in tramway and railway traffic as unlawful injuries to persons or property and denies liability only for lack of fault. The legal order, in permitting dangerous traffic and prescribing in detail to its participants how to conduct themselves, declares that conduct conforming to those prescriptions is within the law. It is not right that conduct which takes full account of the orders and prohibitions in the traffic regulations should nevertheless be adjudged unlawful. The actual consequences afford no sufficient ground for it; for, in deciding whether conduct is unlawful within the meaning of the BGB provisions about delicts, one cannot leave unconsidered the act that produced the consequences. The rule must therefore be laid down that orderly conduct of a participant in tramway or railway traffic conforming to traffic regulations does not produce unlawful damage.

Whether this result implies a special application of the legal idea of so-called social adequacy may be left unanswered. Since the question here is restricted to the field of traffic law, there is also no need to go into whether the same result could equally be obtained by means of relying on modern criminal theory, which splits up the concept of negligence by treating the inquiry into the observance of objectively required care as appertaining to unlawfulness, and only the question whether the disapproved conduct should be imputed to *an individual doer* as an inquiry into fault. Doubt must in any case be expressed as to whether, if this complex concept of negligence in modern criminal theory were to be taken over into civil law, in the law of civil responsibility, also, under cover of a special inquiry into fault, a special standard of judgment should be imposed on the conduct of the doer of damage that took account of his personal characteristics. That might, indeed, appear to harmonise the legal concepts, but it would not allow for typical differences which arise from the specific characters and purposes of two different branches of the law. In particular, this view would not be in accord with the provision of § 276 1 2 BGB as it has always been understood in applying the law.

2. The question submitted to the Court now makes it necessary to inquire what are the consequences produced by the standpoint adopted for apportioning the burden of proof. Here it must be recalled that the legislator, by establishing separate factual bases for delicts, intended to lighten the judges' task of examining whether a wrongful act exists or not. Unlike the cases where delict is governed by a general clause, leaving a wide scope for judicial interpretation (§§ 823–25 BGB), in describing casuistically the wrongs giving rise to liability, the legislator affords a solid basis for applying the law, by suggesting, at least provisionally, the criterion of unlawfulness. Thus, an injury to one of the legal interests specially named in § 823 1 BGB to which the law affords a preferred protection, needs a special justification if it is not to be adjudged unlawful. That applies irrespective of whether the act was done intentionally. This relation of rule and exception established as part of the system of our law of delict and upheld in its application has, in accord with the recognised principles of the law of evidence, the consequence that the proof of a justification is for the person who infringes a protected legal interest. In this respect the justification afforded by conduct according to traffic rules in tramway and railway traffic can claim no separate status.

This apportionment of the burden of proof in applying § 823 1 BGB to traffic accidents means that the doer of damage can provide a basis for justification by proving that his conduct conformed to traffic rules. If the proof is supplied, proof of fault ceases to have any substance, because there is to start with no unlawful infliction of injury. If, on the other hand, the question whether his conduct in traffic was regular is not cleared up, one starts with an unlawful injurious act. The question of liability however is not yet decided; for § 823 1 also requires the injurious act to have been intentional or careless. The injured party must therefore prove that the doer acted intentionally or negligently, as defined by § 276 12 BGB, that is to say omitted to take the care required in daily intercourse. For that inquiry also it will of course be essential to know whether the provisions of the traffic regulations have been observed. That the question of conduct according to the traffic rules can be significant for unlawfulness and fault is due to the shape and legal classification of the concept of negligence. For the practical application of the law it remains that the injured party must prove in full the conditions of a claim for compensation under § 823 1

BGB and that accordingly–unless there is a *prima facie* case–an insufficient elucidation of the facts is to his disadvantage.

The apportionment of the burden of proof in applying § 831 BGB is different. There the legislator consciously made the employer's liability depend only on the 'employee's' acting unlawfully and not also on his doing the damage intentionally or negligently. In so far therefore as concerns the 'employee's' conduct, only those principles governing the burden of proof apply that affect the sphere of unlawfulness. Thus, the injured party must prove that the 'employee' by an adequately causal act injured one of the legal interests protected in § 823 I. It is on the other hand for the employer to prove that the 'employee's' conduct was regular, because it conformed to the legal rules for tramway or railway traffic. So far, doubt is to the disadvantage of the employer. On the other hand, if regular conduct of the 'employee' is proved, the conditions for a claim under § 831 BGB are unfulfilled, so that there is no longer any need to go into whether proof can be provided that there was no causal connexion between the prima facie presumption of faulty selection or supervision, and the damage. From that last-mentioned point of view the Reichsgericht had denied the employer's liability when the judge was convinced that even a carefully chosen and supervised 'employee' could not have acted differently in the given case. That the production of the exoneratory proof under § 831 I and II BGB makes it unnecessary to go into the question of unlawful injury is self-evident.

It is clear that as regards traffic accidents the course of which remains unelucidated, the regulation of the burden of proof set out above makes it better for the injured party if the 'employee' and not the employer himself has caused the accident. In the latter case the employer's liability is as a rule excluded, because no fault can be established, whereas where it is caused by the 'employee', the employer is liable if he cannot exonerate himself from the charge of imperfect choice and supervision. This preferential treatment was clearly intended by the legislator, for there is here a certain allowance for the fact that otherwise the injured party's legal position is quite unfavourable because exoneration is possible and usually successful. It is precisely for that reason that it would be wrong in applying the law to do away with the part favourable to an injured party in the regulation by the BGB of delictual liability for 'employees'. If one observes that emphasis is there placed – even though incompletely – on responsibility for enterprise risks, it is not unfair to impose on the one in whose sphere of influence the risk originated the burden of proof about the way the damage occurred, which he is usually, though not always, in a better position to satisfy than the one to whom it occurred. So far also as the provision of 'appliances and implements', which include the means of transport, is concerned, the law has for the same reason imposed on the employer within the framework of § 831 BGB an enhanced duty of elucidation and proof. If the evaluation of the employee's conduct is under discussion, attention must also be paid to the point of view that the employee – that is the meaning of the reversal of the burden of proof – must be considered to have been unfit for his task, until the employer proves that he showed the care described more fully in § 831 1 2 BGB.

Note

1. For further discussion of the meaning of unlawfulness, see vol. 1, chapter 2.

16. *Decision of the 3rd Civil Senate of 27 May 1963 (BGHZ 39, 358–65)*[1]

The plaintiff site-owner claimed damages from a local authority which had issued a building permit without adequately checking the architect's calculations regarding the load-bearing capacity of the foundations, as marked on the plan. Because of this error, the building collapsed while in process of construction, and both the builder and the architect were insolvent.

The plaintiff's claim was dismissed by the trial court and his appeal was also dismissed, for the following reasons:

1. The trial court rightly held that in checking and authorising the plans for the building the supervisory authorities are exercising a governmental function. In consequence, as the appeal court agrees, the plaintiff's claim against the defendant can only be based on the rules relating to the liability of officials (§ 839 BGB in connection with art. 34 Basic Law): it must be shown that one of the defendant local authority's officials in the exercise of the public function attributed to him was in breach of an official duty which he owed to the plaintiff...

2. In approaching the question whether, in giving building permission when it should not have done so, the local authority was in breach of official duties owed to the plaintiff the trial court correctly started by considering the purpose served by the official duty (see the references in BGB-RGRK to § 839 n. 40). In the first instance official

duties are imposed in the interest of the state and the public. If the sole function of an official duty is to promote public order, the general interest of the commonwealth in orderly and proper government, the satisfaction of exigencies within the service or the maintenance of a properly organised and functioning administration, then there is no question of any liability to third parties for its breach, even if its exercise has adversely affected them or their interest. Liability exists only where the official duty which was broken was owed by the official to the third parties themselves. Whether this is so and how wide the range of protected persons may be are questions which must be determined in accordance with the purpose served by the official duty. This purpose is to be inferred from the provisions on which the official duty is based and by which it is delimited, as well as from the particular nature of the official function in question. If, in addition to satisfying the general interest and public purposes, the official duty has the further purpose of safeguarding the interests of individuals, this is sufficient, even if the affected party had no legal claim that the official act in question be undertaken (*BGHZ* 35, 44, 46/47; BGH *VersR.* 1961, 944).

Before a building permit is issued the plans must be checked for conformity with all building regulations of public law (§2 II Provincial Building Ordinance). Such an investigation must encompass the structural safety of the building (§15 I e. §61 Provincial Building Ordinance); as the Court of Appeal was right to emphasise, with reference to Pfundtner – Neubert (*Das neue deutsche Reichsrecht* IV g 21 Intro.), concern for safety is one of its most important aims, since unsafe buildings pose a direct threat to life and health, the value of physical property and the safe conduct of business. The supervision of buildings thus permits the avoidance of dangers (*BGHZ* 8, 97, 104; see Baltz–Fischer, *Preussiches Baupolizeirecht* I *et seq.*). The provisions requiring the verification of the calculations concerning the load-bearing capacity of buildings are directed to the dangers which threaten the public from the collapse of unsafe constructions. While these provision and the official duties which they impose serve the protection of the public – the 'public interest' (Baltz–Fischer, ibid.) – they also protect every individual member of the public who might be threatened by its unsafe condition, that is, every person who comes into contact with the building as inhabitant, user, visitor (RG Recht 1929 no. 757; SeuffArch 83 no. 134; *JW* 1936, 803, *BGHZ* 8, 97, 104), neighbour (BGH *VersR.* 1956, 447), passer by (LM to BGB

§ 839 Fe no. 1) or workman, and who relies on its being safe. The owner or developer may also be a beneficiary of this protective function if he suffers damage to his body, health or property as a result of a collapse while he is visiting the building or inhabiting it, but only if the harm is a consequence of the danger from which it is the function of the official verification of the technical specifications to protect the public and hence the individual endangered. That is not the case here. True it is that the plaintiff has suffered damage as a result of the collapse of the building, but he is not a victim of the danger from which as a member of the public he was entitled to be protected by the official duties and the provisions which created them, since it was only the building itself and no other property of his which was damaged...

Note

1. We are grateful to Mr J.A. Weir for his kind permission to reproduce here his translation of this and the following decision.

17. *Decision of the 7th Civil Senate of 30 May 1963* (*BGHZ 39, 366*)

In 1951 the plaintiff contracted with the defendant builder to have a house built on his land and with the defendant architect to have the construction supervised. Cracks appeared in the ceilings because the concrete used was well below the requisite strength. The plaintiff claimed damages for the reconstruction of the ceilings which were in danger of collapse. Because he was out of time for a contract claim the plaintiff based his claim on the delict provisions § 823 I BGB and § 823 II BGB in connection with § 330 Criminal Code or § 367 no. 15 Criminal Code.

Reasons
The Court of Appeal rightly found that the facts disclosed no tort on which the plaintiff's claim for damages could be based.

1. There is no question of a claim for damages under § 823 I BGB on the basis that the plaintiff's property (Eigentum) has been damaged by fault. The land owned by the plaintiff, as compared with what it was, has suffered no harm through the defective method of construction. In so far as the land has been built on, as the Court of Appeal rightly stated, the plaintiff never owned it in an undefective condition. As the building proceeded, the plaintiff's ownership attached to each part of the building as it was constructed in the

condition in which it was constructed, with all the qualities and defects resulting from the incorporation of the building materials. To make someone the owner of a defective building is not to invade an already existing ownership (compare RG JW 1905, 367; Oberlandesgericht Karlsruhe *NJW* 1956, 913).

The decision of this senate in LM no. 4 to §830 BGB was a different case; there defective concrete balconies which had been built on to the top storey caused the collapse of the whole building.

2. The Court of Appeal also rightly rejected the claim for damages based on §823 BGB in connection with §330 Criminal Code. Under this last-named provision a person 'who in supervising or erecting a building in breach of generally recognised rules of building practice acts in such a way as to cause danger to others' is guilty of an offence. The trial court found that a danger existed within the meaning of this provision and this finding is not subject to review. But as the Appeal Court stated, §330 Criminal Code is solely designed to protect the lives and health of individuals (LK (edn. 8) §330 VII; Schönke/Schröder StGB (edn 10) §330 II 3 b; Oberlandesgericht Dresden OLG Rspr 18, 72; Kammergericht in Berliner Bauwirtschaft 1961, 544). It is only to this extent that the provision is a protective statute whose breach can give rise to a claim for damages under §823 II BGB. Damages can only be claimed under this text if the harm takes the form of the invasion of a legal interest for whose protection the rule of law was enacted (*BGHZ* 19, 114, 126; 28, 359, 365f.). The claim before us is for compensation for harm to an interest other than the legal interest protected by §330 Criminal Code.

Nor is the claim for those damages justified by the consideration that the replacement of the ceilings which are in danger of collapse is necessary to save the users of the rooms from imminent danger. It still remains the case that the cost of rendering the ceilings represents a harm which affects only the pecuniary interests of the plaintiff. This is evident if one imagines that a ceiling collapses and injures an individual: then certainly the harm attributable to the personal injuries must be compensated under §823 II BGB and §330 Criminal Code; but there would still remain the material harm requiring the replacement of the ceilings, and this would still affect only the economic interests of the plaintiff.[1]

3. The plaintiff finally relies on §823 II BGB in connection with §367 I no. 15 Criminal Code. This provision provides, inter alia, that it is an offence for a builder or building worker to construct a building

in deliberate deviation from the building plan approved by authority. According to the plaintiff, an offence was here committed because the approval of the plan was based on specific calculations, incorporated in the submission, relating to the load-bearing capacity of the construction, and these calculations were in turn based on the quality of the concrete to be used.

It is not necessary to decide whether the use of concrete inferior to that on which the stress calculations were based constitutes a deliberate deviation from the authorised plan. We agree with the Court of Appeal that § 367 I no. 15 Criminal Code is not designed to offer protection against harm of the sort for which the plaintiff claims damages.

It is true that in its decision reported in LM no. 1 to § 823 (BB) BGB the Bundesgerichtshof recognised that § 367 par. 1 no. 15 Criminal Code was a protective statute; that case, however, involved personal injuries suffered by a worker employed on the building site.

In the view of the Court of Appeal, § 367 I no. 15 Criminal Code is like § 330 Criminal Code in offering protection only to the human person.

This view is open to criticism. The final courts of appeal have accepted that the cognate provision of § 367 I no. 14 Criminal Code exists for the protection of property as well and that a breach of the provision may also give rise to claims for damages in respect of property damage under § 823 II BGB (*RGZ* 51, 177f., BGH 1 LM no. 2 to § 823 (BB) BGB). Both these decisions were concerned with harm caused to neighbouring buildings adjoining the building site and vested in third parties.

Thus it may be taken that the protective purpose of § 367 I no. 15 Criminal Code is also to be construed to guard against damage to property as well as damage to persons. In the present case, however, as has already been stated, there is no damage to property but a pecuniary loss attributable to the defective execution of the building work in breach of contract...[2]

Notes

1. See Addenda, p. 342.
2. See Addenda, p. 343.

18. *Extracts from BGB decision of 12 February 1979* *(WM 1979, 548)*[1]

The plaintiff claims damages from the defendants, an international bank, for loss suffered as a result of inaccurate information supplied to her by their German branch (and concerning the credit-worthiness of a third party).

Towards the end of 1970 the plaintiff was looking for a profitable way to invest some 130,000 DM and a finance broker, L, recommended the hotel P, built by U and opened to the public a few months earlier. U had financed his hotel by a number of loans including one for 2.5 million DM raised from the defendants and secured by a land charge. U, requiring a further 3.5 million marks, decided to raise this from private individuals with the help of advertisements and brokers offering 12% interest on all loans as well as a land charge for security. More precisely, he registered a land charge for 3.5 million DM in favour of the defendants which was divided into smaller parts each securing sums of 10,000 DM and 25,000 DM. The defendants, in consideration for the usual fee, were willing to assign these 'part land charges' to lenders and place the funds in a blocked account for U until the completion of all formalities. On 3 February L, the broker, gave the plaintiff the following information which was written on the defendants' paper but gave no date nor address:

Hotel P, George U.

This is a newly built luxury hotel with some 440 beds and conforming to international standards, which was officially opened in June 1970 in the presence of many dignitaries. So far as we know it has already entered into long-term arrangements with a number of international travel agencies. It is owned by U, whom we know as a client and as a competent business man. U also owns a hotel in Teneriffe and two sanatoria run by reputable persons. Owing to a great increase in building costs, U needs a further 3.5 million DM which is to be found on the open market. Any money advanced for this purpose will be credited to a blocked account with our bank and, after a notary has confirmed that the terms of the contract have been complied with, it will be credited to the hotel's current account. We, ourselves, have in the past made substantial payments to U against security but, due to an increase in building costs, U's liquidity is, at present, tight.

On 17 February, 1971 the plaintiff paid 130,000 DM which the defendants immediately credited to U's account. Three days earlier the defendants had asked U to repay their loans by 23 February and on 16 March they extended the repayment date to the end of May 1971. Meanwhile U was getting deeper and deeper into financial difficulties and on 23 December he applied for a composition with his creditors. Four months later bankruptcy proceedings followed. Both plaintiff and defendant withdrew from the auction of the hotel and the plaintiff will receive nothing from the bankrupt's estate.

The plaintiff brought an action claiming 65,000 DM since legal aid was granted to her only for this amount due to her contributory negligence. She argues that her loss is due to the defendants' letter which gave information which they knew to be false. The defendants deny that the information was wrong and also deny liability on the ground that they had not entered into any contract to supply her with information.

The court of first instance awarded the plaintiff 32,500, and ruled that she should bear the rest of the loss herself because of her contributory negligence. The defendants' appeal was rejected and their further appeal on points of law is also dismissed for these reasons:

I

The Court of Appeal accepted that the defendant is liable according to the law of contract. Their appeal on points of law fails.

1. The Court of Appeal found that the defendants knowingly and deliberately composed the notice (quoted above) and put it into circulation with a view to its being shown to potential private lenders to U.

(a) The Court of Appeal [also] found that the information it contained was both in form and content intended to reach a circle of private potential investors. Stripped to its essential the notice gives information which is intended to appeal to private individuals. This is true both of the description of U and of his other businesses. For instance, the reference to the official opening of the hotel in the presence of local dignitaries could only have aimed at making his business appear reliable in the eyes of private persons. Much of this material would clearly have been written in a different way if the document had been intended to be used solely for internal banking purposes. Its contents make sense only if they are seen as aiming from the outset to attract prospective private investors. And this is corroborated by the statement in the notice that the money lent would be transferred from the blocked account with the defendants to the hotel's account only after a notary had confirmed that the terms of the contract had been complied with. This method of concluding a contract is less important to a bank than the encumbrances which are not mentioned in the notice. But it is calculated to dispel doubts that may arise in the mind of an individual, inexperienced in money matters, reading the preceding passages which explain why the extra sums are required. The outward appearance of the notice also speaks in favour of this interpretation. Thus, it bears the business name and the description of the defendant but gives no indication of the person addressed, or the date or any other details that usually accompany letter-writing.

This interpretation is not only possible, but, indeed, necessary, the more so when one realises that the defendants, who were asked to handle the loan, were aware that only private individuals would be considered as lenders. The appeal is thus not able to reveal any error of law committed by the Court of Appeal when characterising the sense and purpose of the notice.

The argument that the Court of Appeal failed to take into account the fact that the defendants gave this kind of information in response to inquiries made by banks is also unsuccessful, for if this is taken to imply that the defendants supplied information to banks only, it runs clearly counter to the defendants' submissions before the lower court. There the defendants maintained that information concerning U was given only to individuals making specific enquiries. On the appellate level, therefore, one must assume that the defendants gave information not *only* but *also* to banks. This does not necessarily run counter to the Court of Appeal's interpretation. Since only private individuals would be considered as lenders, the banks must have inquired on their behalf and thus the information so acquired must have been destined only for their clients and not for themselves.

(b) Once it is accepted, as it must be, that the information supplied by the defendants was meant for potential investors, one must then also accept the further finding of the Court of Appeal, namely, that the defendants circulated this information so that it would be presented to a group of prospective investors. The assumption that the defendants intended to give the information to individual inquirers only, and had not agreed to its being passed on to other interested parties, is inconsistent with the purpose of preparing the information, namely to appeal to a group of individuals who might be interested in becoming lenders. Given that the defendants were themselves substantial creditors of U, and were anxious to relieve him of his financial difficulties, their intention was to bring the information to the notice of as many prospective lenders as possible. The assertion that the defendants supplied information concerning U only to individual inquirers does not rule out the possibility that the bank, in conformity with its purpose, approved of the information being passed on to other lenders. In any event, the defendants have failed to adduce any evidence to show that their notice had been brought to the attention of only a small group of individuals. The Court of Appeal was thus free to look at the objective contents of the notice.

2. The Court of Appeal was also not in error in finding that the defendants were fully aware that their information would be of great importance to the recipients and would be used as a basis of important investments. Since its prime purpose was to help attract finance for the hotel P, it is obvious that it was intended to help prospective investors to decide whether to lend money to U to the extent of at least 10,000 DM and was designed with that purpose in mind...

3. The Court of Appeal considered the information given to have been false in so far as it concealed facts which ought to have been disclosed. Thus, the reference to U's other properties created the impression that they also were available as additional security even though in actual fact they were already encumbered up to the hilt. The reference to the defendants' own substantial secured loans to U was also false since they had already called for their repayment at the time when the information [in the notice] reached the plaintiff... The inaccuracy of the notice is evident from a number of other undisputed facts, such as, for example, the concealment of the various charges on the sanatoria properties. To a lender such information is particularly important when making up his mind as to whether to make a loan or not... Contrary to the view advanced in this appeal, it must be said that it is customary to mention all substantial charges when information is given about land by a bank. According to the findings of the Court of Appeal, when the information was issued by the defendants, the entire hotel facilities as well as the sanatoria had not been paid for and U was no longer in a position to honour any bills drawn for them. These circumstances, which would normally point towards an extremely delicate economic situation, should have been made clear by the defendants at the time of issuing their notice since they would have had great bearing on the decision of the lenders. The defendants did not argue that they were unaware of the above; indeed this would have been unlikely for a bank like theirs, whose function it is to grant credit to borrowers. Nor did the defendants fulfil their duties by stating in their notice that U was faced with liquidity problems since this would not normally indicate to a private individual that bills had already been protested. All these findings are sufficient to characterise the information as false.

II

All the factual elements necessary to impose contractual liability for negligent advice are thus satisfied. According to the cases, where information is supplied by a bank a contractual or quasi-contractual relationship already tacitly exists between the bank and the inquiring party whenever the information supplied by the bank is of manifest significance to the inquiring party and it is clear that the latter will be relying on it in making substantial capital allocations (cf. decision of the Senate of 6 July 1970, *WM* 1970, 1021...). The situation in this present case is just that. In this case the bank addresses itself to a quite clearly defined group of prospective lenders who are interested in advancing money for a specific project. The information is aimed at this group, which the defendants wish to attract, and which they know will use this information to make vital economic decisions. This being clearly the purpose of the information, it can make little difference in law whether the seeker [of the information] directs himself to the bank or the bank to him. Given the purposes to be achieved by the information, the bank must realise that the persons likely to rely on it must understand it in the sense of a legally binding declaration (the distributor of the notice is a mere messenger). That is why in this case good faith causes a contractual relation to arise when a potential addressee has relied on it in making his decision. The appellant's argument, unsubstantiated by the facts of this case, that the information was only intended for banks, is immaterial since this does not preclude the fact that banks were then allowed to pass it on. The Court of Appeal is indeed wrong in treating this as a case of 'information to whom it may concern'. The Supreme Court has repeatedly insisted that it is, in principle, not possible to assume that a bank when giving information is willing to put itself under an obligation to an indeterminate and incalculable number of persons... However, this is not the case here, for, though the information is directed to persons still unknown to the bank, those persons can be determined by virtue of their interest and form part of a calculable group of persons.

III

1. Given that a contract to supply information was thus concluded by the parties, it became incumbent upon the defendants to supply

objectively correct information. This the defendants negligently failed to do (§§ 276$_1$ and 278 BGB) since as bankers they knew, or ought to have known, that the facts they failed to mention in their notice were important for the lenders in order to reach their decision.

2. The appeal before this court also claims unsuccessfully that the Court of Appeal erred on the aspect of causation... Practical experience however shows that the plaintiff would not have made U a loan if the defendants had given her adverse information by disclosing to her U's actual financial status.

IV

The argument raised in this appeal, that the defendants' negligence is overshadowed by the plaintiff's contributory fault in so far as she accepted the advice of the finance broker L against the advice of her bank and her tax accountant, cannot affect the judgment currently under appeal. For the Court of Appeal, in the exercise of its judicial functions, considered all legal and factual aspects of the case, and the appellants can point to no legal error prejudicial to them. Their argument that these facts should, from a point of view of law, be now differently appraised cannot thus be accepted.

Note

1. For a fuller discussion of this topic, see vol I, chapter 2.

PART IV
Extracts from French Cases
INTRODUCTORY COMMENTS[1]

The reader who studies a French case for the first time will find himself in a world that seems entirely different from that of English case-law. Hence a few words will not be out of place on the following topics:

1. The structure and procedure of the French courts;
2. The form of a French report;
3. The authority attaching to *jurisprudence*, as the French style their case-law.

1. The structure and procedure of the French courts

In matters of civil law, which alone is in question in the following pages, a case comes first before a Tribunal de grande instance of which there is usually one in each department, staffed entirely by professional judges. From this court an appeal lies on law or fact to the Cour d'appel. There are some thirty courts of this kind in metropolitan France, each of which has jurisdiction over a number of departments and a further three cours d'appel for the *départments d'outre-Mer*. From a Cour d'appel, or indeed from any court in the judicial hierarchy, a case may be taken on a point of law to the Cour de cassation, which sits in Paris. Technically speaking this is not an appeal but is known by the untranslatable word *pourvoi*.[2] Until just after the Second World War, the Cour de cassation was divided into four chambers, the Chambre des Requêtes, the Chambre Civile, the Chambre Sociale, and the Chambre Criminelle. Civil cases went first before the Chambre des Requêtes, whose function it was to decide whether there was a case fit to go on to the Chambre Civile. If the Chambre des Requêtes decided to reject the application it issued a reasoned judgment (*un arrêt motivé*). If, on the other hand, it decided that there was a case to go to the Chambre Civile, it sent the case on without any reasons. It was for the Chambre Civile to decide the *pourvoi*, and whether it regarded it as well or ill founded it always issued a reasoned judgment. The court had only two courses open to it – either to reject the application, or the quash (*casser*) the judgment of the court below. It could not substitute its own decision for the latter's decision. Accordingly if the decision was to quash, it had to be accompanied by a direction to a neighbouring Cour d'appel[3] to try the appeal afresh. It was then open to this second Cour d'appel to take its own view of the matter. It was not in any way bound by the decision of the Cour de cassation, but might, if it thought fit, accept the view of the Cour d'appel primarily concerned. If it did so, then the party aggrieved was at liberty to formulate a new application to the Cour de cassation, and steps were immediately taken to have the case decided by the full court (*toutes Chambres réunies*). If the full court adhered to the opinion of the Chambre Civile, it would then quash the decision of the second Cour d'appel, and send the case to a third neighbouring Cour d'appel with a compulsory direction to apply the law as the full court had determined it. As may well be imagined, the full procedure thus outlined would take a long time, and in fact in the case of *Connot c. Franck* (reproduced below) almost twelve years elapsed between the accident which gave rise to the proceedings and the final decision of the full court. It may also be a matter for some surprise that at any rate at the final stage the Cour de cassation did not simply give judgment for or against the applicant; but it must be remembered that the Cour de cassation cannot deal with questions of fact, and it is always possible that the third Cour d'appel might find the facts differently in the light of the law as finally stated by the full court, so that in theory at any rate it would be possible for the party who was successful before the full court to lose his case after all. Since the reforms of 1967 and 1978–9 (discussed below) the Court can now retain the case and decide it itself if it is satisfied that there is no dispute or uncertainty as to its facts.

The aforementioned organisation of the Cour de cassation, established in 1837, survived intact until 1947, when a number of reforms were introduced, the most important being the abolition of the Chambre des Requêtes and the Chambre Sociale and the creation, instead, of three Chambres Civiles. The number of Chambre Civiles was subsequently raised to four and, eventually, to five by the more important reforms of 1967 (loi 67.523 and loi organique 67.618 of 1967).

The abolition of the Chambre des Requêtes, prompted by the desire to avoid the double procedures it gave rise to, initially meant that the *pourvoi* came directly before one of the civil chambers which thus became seized of the dispute. However, it also meant the loss of a filtering device, which was felt strongly as the number of *pourvois* increased annually to some 14,500 in 1978 (of which more than 9,500 were on civil matters). The latest legislative reforms (lois of 12 juil. 1978 and 3 janv. 1979)[4] therefore introduced a new filtering device by ordaining that 'chacune des chambres comprend une *formation restreinte*, composée de trois magistrats au moins, qui examine les pourvois dès la remise de son mémoire par le demandeur; cette formation rejette les pourvois irrecevables ou *manifestement infondés*'. This method of filtering, unlike the one that existed until 1947, entrusts this task to a smaller section of that chamber which, if the *pourvoi* is *prima facie* acceptable, will be called upon to decide the dispute. This, apparently, saves time and also enables some members of the appropriate chamber to acquire an early familiarity with the facts of the case they may have to decide.

Another significant reform introduced by the 1967 laws and elaborated further in 1978 and 1979 was the institution of the post of Conseillers référendaires, of which there are now twenty-four. Initially, there was some doubt as to their status and proper functions, many arguing that their role should be merely to 'assist' the Conseillers. But the law of 1967 gave them the right to prepare reports and participate (without a vote) in the deliberations of their chamber on the cases they had worked on. The experience of this proved so successful that the latest reforms have further increased their status and functions by allowing them a vote in the cases in which they had drafted the report and also by allowing two of the most senior Conseillers référendaires to be part of the quorum of any of the chambers. The effect of both these changes is that it releases many Conseillers from these tasks and allows them to be used more profitably in other ways.

The original structure of the court, described at the beginning of this section, has been altered in other ways too. It is well known that the prime task of the Supreme Court is to ensure, as far as possible, the unity of the law in matters of principle, especially by solving disputes on matters of law between different Courts of Appeal or a Court of Appeal and the Supreme Court itself. This task, originally entrusted to the Chambres réunies, is now left to the Assemblée Plénière. But in addition to this task of 'external' harmonisation the court also has to ensure 'internal' harmonisation of its *jurisprudence*, a problem which has become more acute in recent years as the number of its chambers has increased. This unifying task was, after 1947, entrusted to a permanent body (called the Assemblée Plénière), which should not be confused with the present Assemblée Plénière, but its record proved dubious, partly because the various sections were not prepared to allow this apparently superior body to interfere with their own *jurisprudence.* So the law of 1967 replaced this body by what is now known as the Assemblée Mixte which had (and has) no permanent membership or existence but was, instead, composed by members of the two disputing chambers which could get together and try to work out some sort of reconciliation. In its early years this method of 'internal' harmonisation produced some important *revirements de la jurisprudence* (e.g. on the 'concubinage' and the question of the 'transport bénévole', discussed in volume 1). These meetings, however, became less frequent with the passage of time. It is difficult to explain this decline, but to the extent that this might have been due to difficulties in achieving a compromise between the two disputing sections, the law of 1979 may have improved matters by decreeing that that Chambre Mixte should henceforth include Conseillers from at least *three* sections of the entire court. Whether this inclusion of additional Conseillers, not directly involved in the dispute, will revitalise the Chambre Mixte and allow it to achieve its task, it is too early to say.

The student will find few points of procedure in the following pages, but it is worth mentioning that when an application comes before a chamber of the Cour de cassation it is first submitted to one of the judges (Conseillers) who presents a report explaining the facts and summarising the written arguments of the lawyers on both sides. Under the old procedure before the Chambre des Requêtes, the reporter gave the court a definite lead in one direction. The plaintiff's advocate then spoke in his favour, and finally the avocat général (in a case of the very greatest importance the Procureur Général de la République) gave his *conclusions*; then the chamber discussed the matter and gave its decision. Since the Chambre des Requêtes could not give a final decision against a respondent, the latter's advocate was not heard. Before the Chambre Civile or the full court the procedure was the same, except that the advocates of both parties had a hearing, and in proceedings before the full court the report was made by a Conseiller of the Chambre Criminelle,[5] who maintained a strict impartiality and did not give a lead to the court. The process is terminated with the decision which, in most cases, will either be an *arrêt de rejet du pourvoi* or an *arrêt de cassation*, the latter being from a legal point of view, invariably the most interesting in so far at least as it contains the reasons for quashing the decision of the lower court rather than merely affirming or repeating reasons already given by the inferior court.

2. The form of a French report[6]

The student who has studied the Chancery reports will recognise at once that an *arrêt* of the Cour de cassation resembles much more an English order than what we are accustomed to call a judgment; though it contains in skeleton form the reasons (*motifs*) which lie behind it. In the Cour de cassation the place of the English judgment with its full and even discursive discussion of the legal points involved is taken by the report and the *conclusions* mentioned above. The court itself in its *arrêt* tries to find one or more succinct formulas to express its meaning. These are often so laconic as to be almost unintelligible, or at least to give rise to interminable discussion among the jurists. The reason for this practice will be seen when the authority of French case-law is discussed. On the other hand, a Tribunal de grande instance will often give judgment at very considerable length, and but for the curious grammatical construction customarily adopted, this would often pass for an English judgment; but much of it is taken up with statements of the facts and arguments (known technically as *qualités*) which are drafted not by the court but by the parties. A Cour d'appel will usually be rather more terse in its style, but the full concision of which French judicial writing is capable will be found only in the Cour de cassation.

The grammar of a French judgment will cause only momentary difficulty; but it is perhaps worth mentioning that the judgment is framed as a single sentence, of which the subject and the verb occur at the very beginning and the very end respectively, and are divided by a number of 'whereases' (*attendu*, or in the lower courts *considérant*); these 'whereases', of course, contain the *motifs*. The actual decision will be found at the very end in the *dispositif* which starts with the words: 'Par ces motifs...'

Each *pourvoi* must be based on one or more *moyens* or grounds, each of which must refer to a particular article of the Code Civil or some other statute; and the court in its *arrêt* regularly announces that it has seen (*vu*) the enactments in question.

In the reports each case is preceded by a head-note indicating the points of law it contains. Since these usually reproduce, word for word, passages in the *arrêts* of the Cour de cassation, they do not, as a rule, make them easier to follow. They have therefore been omitted here, except in one instance.

Where cases are reported, or reprinted, after some delay, they have usually affixed to them a long note by an eminent judge or jurist. Different authors write for the two great and oldest series of reports, those of Dalloz, and the *Recueil Sirey* which since 1965 have merged and become the *Recueil Dalloz – Sirey*. The other two important reports are the *Semaine Juridique* founded in 1927 and the *Gazette du Palais* founded in 1881.[7] Extracts from some of these notes are reproduced below.

3. The authority attaching to French *jurisprudence*

The only source of law absolutely binding on a French court is the Code Civil or some other statute, but great persuasive authority attaches not only to the writings of jurists, but also to case-law (*jurisprudence*), particularly to the *jurisprudence la plus récente*. It is generally said that French law differs from English law in giving weight not to the individual decision but to the general run of decisions on a particular point (*jurisprudence constante*); and further that case-law does not enjoy substantially greater force than the writings of eminent jurists (*doctrine*). It seems clear that there has been a considerable development here. Certainly no one would attach great weight to a single decision of a Tribunal de grande instance, or perhaps of one of the more obscure Cours d'appel, unless it was approved by the jurists. But the Chambre Civile of the Cour de cassation rarely departs from its decisions, at any rate directly; and it seems that it adopted this practice not merely out of inertia, but also from a sense of the greater authority that will attach to its *jurisprudence* if it is known to be completely stable. On the other hand, the Assemblée Plénière is, of course, not bound by decisions of any of the Chambres Civiles, and it holds itself at liberty to change its mind. However, decisions of the full court are at all times extremely rare, and it is very unlikely that the full court will find itself in a position where it has to reverse one of its previous decisions. Indeed it is believed that it has never done so up to now. One therefore gets the impression that a decision of the Chambre Mixte or the Assemblée

Plénière has *almost* the authority of a decision of the House of Lords. The jurists may disagree with it, but they obviously feel that their best hope lies not in a frontal attack, but in a reasoned attempt to explain it away; and, as has already been said, the decisions tend to be laconic and obscure enough to make this possible. This very conciseness of the courts' judgments stems from a desire on the part of the judges not to bind themselves unduly for the future. They have nothing to learn from English judges in this respect; and if the French make no distinction between *ratio decidendi* and *obiter dictum* it is only because examples of the latter are not to be found in decisions of the highest courts. Indeed the Cour de cassation takes the utmost pains not even to appear to enunciate anything that could be taken to be a dogmatic construction. Like a good Common lawyer it keeps its secrets.

The immense importance of French case-law, most particularly in the area of delictual liability, can be seen from the most cursory inspection of any good French text-book, for the references to cases are as frequent as in any English book of the same kind. One must, however, always remember that one cannot speak of a point as not being covered by French law merely because there has been no decision upon the subject, for it is the business of a conscientious jurist to try to anticipate difficult problems, and suggest solutions; and the opinions of the jurists, at any rate if they are in agreement, make law, though like the decision of inferior courts, they may easily be overruled by reference to higher authority. In other words *doctrine* ought to, and commonly does, run ahead of *jurisprudence*, instead of, as is usually the case in England, behind, Thus the great change in French case-law from liability for fault to strict liability was largely prepared by the writings of Saleilles.

Case-law has been the decisive factor in developing the modern French law of civil responsibility; for, on the most important point, the boundary between strict liability and liability for fault, the Code Civil gave no unequivocal lead.

Notes

1. See generally M. Ancel, 'Case Law in France', *J.C.L.*, 3rd ser., XVI, p.1.
2. 'The nearest English equivalent is an appeal by case stated under ss. 83ff. of the Magistrates Courts Act, 1952, except that the Divisional Court can make a decision on the merits': Kahn-Freund, Rudden, Lévy, *A Source-Book on French Law,* 2nd edn (1979), 276.
3. Article 134–4 al. 1 of the Law of 3 janv. 1979 now allows the Cour de cassation to remit the case before the *same* (inferior) court which can, with a differently constituted membership, consider the case.

4. Discussion in detail by P. Hébraud in *D.Chron.* 1979, 205, *et seq.*; J.Boré, *D.Chron.* 1979, 247.
5. Since 1947, the proliferation of the *Chambres Civiles* has made it unnecessary to look (for reasons of added impartiality) to the Chambre Criminelle for a Conseiller/rapporteur. Otherwise, the procedure remains the same.
6. For a comparative discussion of the different styles see references given in note 6 at p. 198 of vol. 1 of this work.
7. for the history of these reports see: P. Rodière, *Travaux pratiques*, 1ère année, 2nd edn (1963), 1 *et seq.*

THE NOTION OF *FAUTE*

Faute does for French law what 'duty' and 'careless breach of duty' do for the English law: it determines, in other words, *both* whether a person can act without adverting to the consequences of his conduct *and* whether the standard of care, fixed by the judge, has been attained by the defendant in question. However, despite its crucial significance for article 1382 CC, the notion has received no official definition and academics have disagreed over its precise meaning in a manner which reminds one of the English controversy over a 'law of tort' or a 'law of torts' (see account in vol. 1, chapter 2). In the last resort, however, the question whether there is or is not *faute* is one of law and thus determined by the Cour de cassation – see case 7 (see also Cass. Civ. 15 janv. 1929, D.1929, 204; Cass. Civ. 16 juil. 1953, *J.C.P.* 1953, 2.7792).

Fault is usually divided into *faute par commission* and *faute par omission*. The most amorphous example of the former can be found in cases where the courts find that the defendant is liable because he did not behave as a *bon père de famille*, which, like our 'reasonable man' is nothing more than the anthropomorphic conception of justice. The objective standard adopted has often led to confusion between fault and error, with consequences which, though happy for the (innocent) plaintiff, can be most unfortunate for the (equally blameless) defendant (case 1). In such instances the desirable thing to do would be to indemnify the victim out of collective resources – hence the increased talk of bringing insurance and social security more and more into the area of the traditional law of tort (see vol. 1, chapter 4).

French law had never had any doubt that the victim of a crime should also have a claim in tort. But the commission of any act which is expressly prohibited by statute (whether criminal or not) will also amount to *faute*. Cases 2 and 3 offer a good illustration of the civil consequences that will flow from the violation of the right of privacy as set out in art. 9 CC. (For the German law on this see pp. 111–23 above; bibliographical references given in Zweigert and Kötz, vol. II, para. 20). The breach of regulations (for example laid down in accordance with the Road Traffic Code) will also be treated as *faute* (Cass. Civ. 22 nov. 1972, *G.P.* 1973, 1.72); and so will the violation of usages or customary rules. Thus, injury inflicted in the course of a sporting activity will not amount to *faute* unless it was done in clear contravention of the rules of the game (Cass. Civ. 15 mai 1972, D. 1972, 606; cf. *Wooldridge* v. *Sumner* [1962] 3 W.L.R. 616).

Faute par omission has caused greater difficulties but the English lawyer should have no problem in following the discussions once he has realised that French law is more willing than English law to impose liability for omissions. (See, in particular the important art. 63 of the Code Penal and its discussion in vol. 1, chapter 2). The way of imposing liability will also be familiar and, in the absence of a statutory enactment, it will depend upon the court's willingness to discover a pre-existing duty to act. Case 4 offers an extreme example which has had its supporters (Desbois) as well as its fierce critics (Carbonnier) (cf. Cass Civ. 17 juil. 1953, D. 1954, 533).

An abuse of an existing right may also amount to *faute*. Where the purpose of the exercise of a right is clearly to harm another person there will usually be little difficulty in condemning its exercise as antisocial and illicit. Case 5 is an oft-quoted decision, though its facts (briefly given in the decision of the court of Amiens and, it is submitted, inadequately considered) suggest that M. Coquerel might have been trying (as Mr Pickles was in *Mayor of Bradford* v. *Pickles*) to get the best possible price for his land rather than to hurt his neighbour. But French courts have gone further than this and have characterised as abusive any exercise of a right which the *bon père de famille* would not have made, thus integrating the notion *abus de droit* into the general discussion on *faute*. And in what we would call the law of nuisance they have gone even further, imposing strict liability, even for lawful use of one's land 'whenever the annoyance that results therefrom for others exceeds the reasonable limits of the ordinary forbearance expected of neighbours in their relations with each other' (see cases 6 and 7).

1. Cour de cassation Chambre Civile,
1 déc. 1965
Baier c. Serafinowski
(J.C.P. 1966, 2.14567)

La Cour; – Sur le premier moyen: – Attendu qu'il résulte de l'arrêt attaqué, partiellement infirmatif, que Michel Baier, âgé de neuf ans, et Bernard Serafinowski, âgé de onze ans, s'amusaient, dans un terrain vague, à donner des coups de pied dans une petite balle; qu'au cours du jeu, Michel Baier, manquant la balle, projeta en l'air une motte de terre qui vint frapper son camarade à l'oeil gauche et le blessa; que le père de la victime assigna Baier père en réparation du dommage causé à son fils; – Attendu que le pourvoi reproche à la Cour d'appel d'avoir admis que la maladresse du jeune Baier était constitutive d'une faute, sans examiner s'il ne devait pas être exonéré en tout ou en partie de la responsabilité mise à sa charge du fait que le jeu comportait des risques et qu'en y participant, la victime les aurait acceptés; – Mais attendu qu'ayant constaté que le jeune Baier avait, par suite d'un coup de pied mal dirige, frappé, non la balle mais une motte de terre et l'avait envoyée dans la direction de son camarade, la Cour d'appel en a justement déduit que la maladresse commise avait un caractère fautif; que, d'autre part, l'acceptation du risque n'étant pas une cause d'exonération de la responsabilité quasi-délictuelle, l'arrêt énonce justement qu'aucune faute ne peut être reprochée à la victime; – D'ou il suit que le moyen n'est pas fondé; – Sur le second moyen: – Attendu qu'il est fait grief à la décision d'avoir retenu la responsabilité du père de l'auteur du dommage, sur la base de l'article 1384, paragraphes 4 et 7 du Code civil, alors que 'le fait de jouer à la balle au pied dans un terrain vague constituerait une activité habituellement permise sans surveillance à des enfants de neuf à onze ans et que le danger n'était pas normalement prévisible'; – Mais attendu qu'ayant rappelé que le jeune Baier, âgé de neuf ans, s'amusait dans un terrain vague, hors de toute surveillance, à envoyer des coups de pied dans une petite balle, l'arrêt énonce que le père du mineur avait fait preuve d'une négligence fautive en ne surveillant pas son fils et que l'accident était prévisible; Que, de leurs constatations et énonciations, les juges du second degré ont pu, sans encourir les critiques du pourvoi, déduire que le père n'établissait pas qu'il n'avait pu empêcher le fait donnant lieu à sa responsabilité; D'où il suit que le moyen n'est pas fondé;

Par ces motifs: – Rejette le pourvoi formé contre l'arrêt rendu le 3 décembre 1963 par la Cour d'appel de Besançon.

2. Tribunal de grand instance, Paris, 11 juil. 1973
Dauphas c. Parti Communiste Français
(J.C.P. 1974, 2.17600)

Le Tribunal, – Attendu qu'au cours de la campagne électorale pour les élections législatives des 4 et 11 mars 1973, le Parti Communiste Français a fait apposer sur tout le territoire national une affiche destinée aux électeurs ruraux, qui représentait trois personnes occupées à lire ensemble, avec une évidente satisfaction, un document non identifié; que l'affiche portait les mentions suivantes: 'Pour la victoire du Programme commun, chance de l'agriculture familiale, faites confiance au Parti Communiste Français'; – Attendu que Dauphas, agriculteur à Malansac (Morbihan), s'étant reconnu sur cette affiche ainsi que sa fille et son fils mineurs, a introduit devant le juge des référés, le 16 février 1973, pour l'audience du 19 février, contre Georges Marchais pris tant en son nom personnel qu'en sa qualité de Secrétaire général du Parti Communiste Français, une demande tendant à la saisie et à l'enlèvement des affiches litigieuses; que, par ordonnance du 21 février 1973, le Juge des référés a donné acte au défendeur, sous les réserves par lui exprimées à l'audience, de ce que, bien qu'ayant agi, déclarait-il, d'entière bonne foi, il s'engageait à publier dans le quotidien *L'Humanité* du 22 février 1973, en première page, un avis encadré en caractères très apparents, conçu en ces termes: 'En exécution des engagements pris par lui devant le Tribunal de grande instance de Paris, le Parti Communiste Français demande à tous les responsables des fédérations et aux camarades intéressés d'arrêter immédiatement l'apposition de l'affiche "Chance de l'agriculture française" et de détruire toutes celles qu'ils détiennent; de plus, tous les exemplaires de cette affiche déjà apposés doivent être enlevés ou recouverts sur-le-champ ou, au plus tard dans la huitaine'; – Attendu que le Juge des référés a, en outre, désigné Zecri, administrateur judiciaire, avec la mission de veiller à l'exécution des engagements ci-dessus; – Attendu que l'avis ci-dessus a été publié en première page du journal *L'Humanité* du 22 février 1973; – Attendu que Dauphas, agissant tant en son nom personnel qu'en sa qualité de représentant légal de ses enfants mineurs, assigne le Parti Communiste Français devant le Tribunal en lui demandant de condamner celui-ci à lui payer la somme de 80,000 francs à titre de réparation du préjudice subi, d'ordonner l'arrachage sous astreinte des affiches et la publication de la décision à intervenir aux frais du défendeur dans le journal *Ouest France* et dans un autre quotidien, au choix du demandeur, le tout avec exécution provisoire; – Attendu que le Parti Communiste Français déclare à la barre renoncer au délai qu'il avait d'abord sollicité pour appeler en garantie l'agence Viva qui intervient volontairement aux débats; qu'au fond, il conclut au débouté, du demandeur et plus subsidiairement à une mesure d'instruction lui permettant de rapporter la preuve, par enquête et comparution personnelle, de ce que Dauphas aurait consenti à la publication de son image; – Attendu que la Société Viva conclut aussi au débouté de Dauphas et que le Parti Communiste Français demande de dire que si, contre toute hypothèse, une condamnation était prononcée contre lui, la Sociéte anonyme Viva serait tenue de le garantir contre cette condamnation.

I – Sur le fondement de la demande: – Attendu qu'à l'appui de sa demande, Dauphas invoque à la fois la jurisprudence relative à la publication sans autorisation du portrait photographique d'autrui, les dispositions de l'article 9 du Code civil relatives au respect de la vie privée et l'exécution incomplète par le défendeur des engagements pris devant le Juge des référés; qu'au soutien de ce dernier moyen, il verse aux débats des constats d'huissiers dressés dans plusieurs régions de France, y compris en Bretagne, et notamment deux constats émanant d'huissiers du département de la Dordogne d'où il résulte que dans 21 communes de ce département, visitées par les officiers ministériels, les affiches litigieuses subsistaient à l'expiration du délai de 8 jours mentionné dans l'engagement susvisé; – Attendu que le Parti Communiste Français soutient, comme l'Agence Viva, que Dauphas avait consenti sans réserve à la commercialisation de la photographie litigieuse, que l'affiche dont s'agit ne constitue pas une atteinte au respect dû à la vie privée et qu'il est allé, en ce qui le concerne, au-delà des engagements, pris devant le Juge des référés, qui se limitaient à la publication de l'avis susvisé; qu'il produit à cet égard des attestations de certains de ses membres domiciliés dans les départements du Morbihan, des Landes, de la Dordogne et du Tarn-et-Garonne, déclarant que les affiches litigieuses ont été enlevées ou recouvertes dans diverses localités, – Mais attendu que le défendeur verse aux débats l'attestation suivante du sieur Le Querrec, photographe; 'Je soussigné Guy Le Querrec, photographe à l'agence Viva, 8, rue Saint-Marc, Paris (75), précise que M. Dauphas a été informé, au moment de la réalisation du reportage photographique sur sa famille, que celui-ci s'inscrivait dans le cadre d'un travail d'agencer sur le thème 'Familles en France', pour être diffusé en exposition et déposé dans les archives de l'agence'; – Attendu que, sans qu'il soit nécessaire d'ordonner la mesure d'instruction sollicitée tant par le défendeur que par l'intervenante, il résulte de cette attestation elle-même que l'autorisation donnée par Dauphas de publier les diverses photographies prises de lui et des siens, au cours du reportage effectué à son domicile par Le Querrec, était limitée à des expositions organisées sur le thème 'Familles en France'; que le fait que Dauphas aurait su qu'après cette utilisation les clichés devaient rester en dépôt à l'agence n'implique nullement que celui-ci autorisait par là-même toute autre publication de son effigie, y compris celle destinée à la propagande d'un parti politique; – Attendu, dès lors, que, sans avoir à rechercher si l'affiche litigieuse a violé l'intimité de la vie privée de Dauphas, en l'obligeant à faire état publiquement de ses opinions politiques, et si le Parti Communiste a exécuté incomplètement les engagements pris devant le Juge des référés, qui impliquaient l'enlèvement des affiches litigieuses, il suffit de constater que, faute d'une autorisation dénuée d'ambiguïté, l'affiche litigieuse a constitué une atteinte au droit de toute personne sur son image;

II – Sur le montant du préjudice: – Attendu que le défendeur soutient que Dauphas n'a pu être lésé par l'association de son image à la propagande du Parti Communiste Français et qu'au surplus, si l'affiche litigieuse a pu le faire passer pour un sympathisant de ce parti 'aux yeux des rares personnes qui le connaissent', il a pu les convaincre du contraire par le retentissement qu'a eu dans la France entière la procédure de référé qu'il a introduite durant la campagne électorale; – Mais attendu que, quelle que soit la notoriété d'une personne, l'atteinte au droit qu'elle a sur son image lui cause un préjudice; que ce préjudice n'a pas été entièrement réparé par la connaissance que le public a pu avoir de la procédure de référé; que subsiste notamment le préjudice moral résultant, pour le demandeur, du fait que son image et celle de ses enfants ont contribué, contre son gré, à la propagande d'un parti politique; que, d'après les propres écritures du défendeur, le tirage de cette affiche ne s'est pas limité aux 4,500 exemplaires visés dans la facture versée aux débats; qu'il n'est pas contesté qu'elle ait été apposée dans la France entière; qu'il n'est pas allégué que le défendeur en ait fait enlever avant l'ordonnance de référé; qu'il en a subsisté, après cette ordonnance, dans certaines régions, y compris dans la région bretonne; qu'enfin, pour réduire le préjudice causé et pour en obtenir réparation, le demandeur a dû engager deux procédures dont le coût et les soucis de toute nature qu'elles lui ont occasionnés ne seront pas entièrement compensés par la condamnation du défendeur aux dépens; – Attendu, dans ces conditions, que le Tribunal dispose d'éléments suffisants pour dire qu'en réparation du préjudice subi tant par Dauphas que par ses enfants, le Parti Communiste Français devra verser au demandeur la somme de 20,000 F, les frais de constat étant par ailleurs compris dans les dépens; – Sur l'action en garantie: – Attendu que, tant devant le Judge des référés que devant le Tribunal, le Parti Communiste Français a toujours excipé de sa bonne foi, lors de l'acquisition du cliché litigieux; – Attendu qu'en acquérant ce cliché d'une agence commerciale spécialisée dans la vente de l'illustration photographique, le défendeur était, en effet, fondé à attendre que celle-ci cédât, en même temps que le consentement du photographe, celui des modèles eux-mêmes, aucune réserve n'ayant été formulée en ce qui les concerne; que l'action en garantie est d'autant plus justifiée qu'il résulte de la facture de l'agence Viva, versée aux débats, que celle-ci connaissait parfaitement la destination de la photographie litigieuse; – Sur la demande d'exécution provisoire: – Attendu que, faute par le demandeur d'établir d'urgence ou le péril en la demeure, il n'y a pas lieu d'ordonner l'exécution provisoire;

Par ces motifs: – Condamne le Parti Communiste Français à payer à Dauphas, ès nom et qualités, la somme de 20,000 F à titre de dommages-intérêts: – Dit que le présent jugement sera intégralement publié aux frais du défendeur dans le journal *Ouest France*, édition du Morbihan où figure la rubrique de la commune de Malansac; – Condamne en outre le défendeur aux dépens de l'instance principale dans lesquels sera compris le montant des constats effectués à la demande de Dauphas; – Dit que la Société Viva devra garantir le Parti Communiste Français du montant des condamnations ci-dessus prononcées et la condamne aux dépens de son intervention; – Dit qu'il n'y a pas lieu de statuer sur les autres demandes de dire et juger des parties principale et intervenante, auxquelles il a été suffisamment répondu dans les motifs qui précèdent.

3. Cour de cassation
2ᵉ Chambre Civile, 6 janv. 1971
Soc. Presse-Office c. *Sachs*
(D. 1971, 263)

Arrêt

La Cour; – Sur le moyen unique: – Attendu qu'il est fait grief à l'arrêt confirmatif attaqué (Paris, 5 mars 1969), d'avoir condamné la Société Presse-Office à payer des dommages et intérêts à Gunther Sachs, en réparation de l'atteinte portée aux droits de celui-ci, dans le périodique *Lui* qu'elle édite, alors, d'une part, que l'arrêt n'aurait pu, sans contradiction, admettre d'un côté que l'article incriminé n'était que la recollection de faits publiés antérieurement, avec l'autorisation expresse ou tacite de Sachs, et de l'autre qu'il portait atteinte à la vie privée de ce dernier, alors, d'autre part, que la publication de deux portraits de Sachs ne saurait constituer une atteinte aux droits de la personne sur son image, dès lors que celui-ci était un homme 'connu', que ces portraits n'avaient pas été pris au cours de sa vie privée et ne représentaient des scènes intimes et la caricature ne pouvant être sanctionnée sur le terrain de la vie privée, et alors, enfin, qu'il y aurait contradiction à reconnaître que les publications antérieures à celle de l'article incriminé qui n'avait fait que les compiler, limitaient l'étendue du préjudice subi par l'intéressé et qu'il y avait atteinte à la vie privée par l'effet de cette compilation, l'atteinte à la vie privée ne pouvant qu'avoir été ou ne pas avoir été;

Mais attendu qu'après avoir relevé que l'article incriminé relatait exclusivement des faits se rapportant à la vie privée de Gunther Sachs, l'arrêt énonce que cet étalage causait un préjudice à celui-ci, que sa tolérance et même sa complaisance passées à l'égard de la presse ne sauraient faire présumer qu'il ait permis définitivement et sans restriction à tout périodique de rassembler et de reproduire des affirmations parues dans d'autres journaux, qu'un tel comportement était seulement de nature à diminuer, le cas échéant, l'étendue du préjudice et à faire diminuer en conséquence le montant des dommages-intérêts, que l'article incriminé, en recueillant et rassemblant des renseignements fragmentaires, vrais ou faux, épars dans diverses publications, et en touchant de nouvelles catégories de lecteurs, a causé un préjudice à l'intimé, alors surtout que le choix des événements ou des 'potins' qui y sont relatés, faisait apparaître la personne privée de Gunther Sachs sous un jour déplaisant; que la publication non autorisée de deux portraits de l'intéressé, dont l'un s'apparente à une caricature, constituait une atteinte aux droits de la personne sur son image, que la tolérance traditionnelle commise à l'égard de ceux dont la profession ou l'activité permet de présumer de leur part une autorisation tacite n'existait pas en l'espèce; – Attendu qu'en l'état de ces constatations et énonciations, la Cour d'appel a pu, sans encourir les critiques du pourvoi, retenir la responsabilité de la Société Presse-Office, tant pour la publication de l'article que pour celle des portraits de l'intéressé; d'où il suit que le moyen n'est pas fondé;

Par ces motifs, rejette.

4. Cour de cassation
Chambre Civile, 27 fév. 1951
Cons. Branly c. Turpain
(D. 1951, 329)

Pourvoi en cassation contre l'arrêt de la Cour d'appel de Poitiers du 2 février 1943 (D.C. 1944.44, note de M. Deslois)

Arrêt

La Cour; – Sur le premier moyen: – Vu les art. 1382 et 1383 CC: – Attendu que la faute prévue par les art. 1382 et 1383 peut constituer aussi bien dans une abstention que dans un acte positif; que l'abstention, même non dictée par la malice et l'intention de nuire, engage la responsabilité de son auteur lorsque le fait omis devait être accompli soit en vertu d'une obligation légale, réglementaire ou conventionnelle, soit aussi, dans l'ordre professionnel, s'il s'agit notamment d'un historien, en vertu des exigences d'une information objective; – Attendu qu'il résulte des qualités et des motifs de l'arrêt attaqué que le professeur Turpain, après avoir, en 1931, contesté la valeur et la portée des travaux scientifiques d'Edouard Branly dans des articles publiés dans le journal *L'Antenne* et qui provoquèrent les plus vives controverses, écrivit pour *L'Almanach populaire 1939* un nouvel article intitulé 'Historique de la T.S.F.', où, exposant les travaux de Hertz et d'un certain nombre d'autres savants, dont lui-même, ayant joué, selon lui, un rôle dans la réalisation de la T.S.F., il préférait, cette fois, s'abstenir de prononcer le nom du professeur Branly et de faire la moindre allusion à ses travaux; que Branly, actuellement décédé et représenté par ses héritiers, reproche à Turpain d'avoir, dans l'article susvisé, manqué à son devoir de renseigner exactement les lecteurs et commis à son égard une faute de nature à engager sa responsabilité; – Attendu que l'arrêt infirmatif attaqué, tout en retenant des 'éléments de la cause' qu'Edouard Branly est reconnu comme étant l'auteur d'expériences déterminantes en la matière par de hautes personnalités scientifiques et par Marconi lui-même, a estimé néanmoins que Turpain n'a pas agi de mauvaise foi en omettant volontairement de citer l'oeuvre et le nom de Branly en ce qui concerne les origines de la télégraphie sans fil et qu'il n'a pas davantage agi par malice et avec l'intention de nuire; – Mais attendu que, sans qu'il y ait lieu de prendre en considération l'énonciation que l'attitude de Turpain n'avait pas été dictée par la malice ou le désir de nuire, cette énonciation étant inopérante à l'égard du quasi-délit, dont se prévalent les demandeurs et qui ne requiert pas cet élément intentionnel, il n'en reste pas moins que l'arrêt attaqué ne pouvait pas légalement dégager Turpain, en sa qualité d'historien, de l'obligation de réparer le préjudice résultant de l'omission incriminée, au seul motif que telle était 'son opinion, peut-être érronée, mais paraissant sincère'; – Attendu, en effet, que le juge, pour sainement apprécier la responsabilité imputable de ce chef à l'auteur du dommage, ne devait pas se borner à faire état exclusivement de l'opinion de Turpain, alors surtout que l'arrêt attaqué lui-même ajoute qu'il est 'possible qu'il ait cédé à cette opinion par ambition, dans le désir – que la Cour de Poitiers déclare à tort excusable – de surestimer ses propres expériences'; que la cour devait rechercher si, en écrivant une histoire de la T.S.F. dans laquelle les travaux et le nom d'Edouard Branly étaient volontairement omis, Turpain s'était comporté comme un écrivain ou un historien prudent, avisé et conscient des devoirs d'objectivité qui lui incombaient; que, pour ne l'avoir pas fait, les juges d'appel ont rendu une décision qui manque de base légale;

Par ces motifs, et sans qu'il y ait lieu d'examiner le second moyen, casse..., et renvoie devant la Cour d'appel de Bordeaux.

Note by
Henri Desbois

(1 à 4) Ĺ arrêt de la Chambre Civile du 27 fév. 1951 présente un double intérêt. Tout d'abord, il précise à quelles conditions un historien

engage sa responsabilité en commettant une omission volontaire, et par là même contribue à la défintion de la faute d'abstention dans l'action. Puis, à l'arrière-plan, apparaît une autre idée, qui vaut aussi bien pour l'abstention pure et simple que pour l'omission dans l'action, à cause des termes généraux en lesquels est rédigé le premier motif. En prêtant à cette important décision l'un et l'autre sens, nous ne croyons pas en déformer ni dépasser la portée.

1. – La responsabilité de l'historien au cas d'omission: L'abstention dans l'action. – Le tribunal civil de Poitiers, le 5 fév. 1941, puis la Cour d'appel, le 2 fév. 1943, tout en prenant sur les faits des partis opposés, avaient adopté en droit la même attitude: l'historien ne commet une faute, quand il s'est volontairement abstenu de citer, au cours du récit d'une invention, le nom d'un savant qui est génefalement considéré comme ayant joué un grand rôle, que si son omission a été inspirée par la mauvaise foi, par la partialité. Selon les premiers juges, le défendeur avait commis une faute intentionnelle, parce qu'il avait décidé d'ignorer l'oeuvre de Branly. Au contraire, la Cour d'appel décida qu'il n'avait été animé par aucune intention malicieuse, parce que ses travaux antérieurs révélaient de sa part la conviction que Branly n'avait pas apporté à l'invention de la T.S.F. la part que l'opinion commune, et même celle des spécialistes les plus qualifiés, s'accordent à lui reconnaître. Du moins, en droit, les deux juridictions limitaient la responsabilité de l'historien à l'omission de mauvaise foi.

La Chambre Civile condamne une définition aussi étroite de la responsabilité de l'historien au cas d'omission; les juges du fait n'ont pas seulement à s'assurer que l'écrivain a tenu compte d'un précepte élémentaire d'honnêteté: il ne lui faut pas seulement éviter d'attribuer à celui dont il narre la vie ou le rôle dans tel ou tel domaine de l'activité politique, militaire, scientifique, des actes ou des propos qu'il sait contraires à la vérité, ou, inversement, de taire, par parti pris politique ou jalousie professionnelle, des initiatives qui méritent d'être retenues. Les devoirs de sa profession lui imposent encore d'appliquer toute sa vigilance à un double objet: il doit, d'une part, exercer le contrôle de ses informations, afin de ne pas présenter comme véridiques des allégations erronées, sous peine d'engager sa responsabilité même s'il croit avoir dit la vérité; il lui faut, d'autre part, énoncer les opinions auxquelles, personnellement, il n'attache aucune autorité de la meilleure foi du monde, mais qui rencontrent l'adhésion de gens assez qualifiés et éclairés pour que le souci d'une exacte information lui interdise de les passer sous silence.

Pour l'historien, hormis la faute intentionnelle, la responsabilité peut donc relever de la négligence; celle-ci revêt deux formes: affirmer ou nier sans preuves suffisantes, – et c'est la faute de commission; ou bien, dans l'exposé d'une question déterminée, passer sous silence des faits auxquels une relation, non seulement honnête, mais sérieuse, devait faire allusion, – et c'est la faute d'abstention. Ces deux propositions sont complémentaires l'une de l'autre, car la négligence, ou l'imprudence, que frappe l'art. 1383 CC s'entend en un double sens: l'agent a accompli ce que la prudence lui interdisait de faire, ou bien il a omis ce que la diligence lui prescrivait d'accomplir. En un mot, celui qui a pris la décision d'agir est tenu, non seulement de s'abstenir de certains actes, mais aussi d'accomplir certains autres. Il existe deux manières de faillir dans l'action, abstraction faite de toute intention de nuire à autrui: la commission et l'omission, qui entraînent la responsabilité de l'agent à l'égal l'une de l'autre.

C'est donc à juste titre que la Chambre Civile a cassé l'arrêt de la Cour de Poitiers. Elle a fait abstraction d'une circonstance particulière, dans laquelle il aurait été possible de voir, sinon une manifestation de la volonté de nuire à la réputation de Branly, du moins une faute lourde, et comme telle assimilable à la faute intentionnelle: 'il est possible que l'historien ait cédé à cette opinion par ambition, dans le désir – que la Cour de Poitiers déclare à tort excusable – de surestimer ses propres expériences', L'arrêt ne retient que l'omission – 'non dictée par la malice et sans l'intention de nuire', c'est-à-dire un quasi-délit de même nature que celui qui consiste à affirmer ou à nier des faits sans une information et un contrôle suffisants. Peu importe que le professeur ait estimé en son âme et conscience que Branly bénéficiait d'une réputation injustifiée; il ne lui appartenait pas de traiter par prétérition ce renom, même après avoir, dans des publications antérieures, développé ses arguments et ses critiques: son silence était d'autant plus grave que l'article incriminé était destiné au grand public, qui risquait, ou bien de ne pas apprendre que le nom de Branly était, à tort ou à raison, lié par la tradition à l'invention de la T.S.F., ou bien d'être offusqué par une omission aussi étonnante. Et, quelle que fût l'ardeur de sa propre conviction, il ne pouvait ignorer qu' 'Edouard Branly est reconnu comme étant l'auteur d'expériences déterminantes en la matière par de hautes personnalités scientifiques et par Marconi lui-même'.

En présence de telles circonstances, la Chambre Civile aurait pu, croyons-nous, qualifier elle-même le comportement de l'historien, en déclarant qu'il avait commis une faute d'abstention dans l'action selon l'art. 1383; elle a laissé ce soin à la cour de renvoi, en se bornant à déclarer que les juges du fait 'devaient rechercher si, en écrivant une histoire de la T.S.F. dans laquelle les travaux et le nom d'Edouard Branly étaient volontairement omis, Turpain s'était comporté comme un écrivain ou un historien prudent, avisé et conscient des devoirs d'objectivité qui lui incombaient'. Ce motif rejoint celui qui prend place au seuil de son arrêt: l'abstention, même non dictée par la malice et l'intention de nuire, engage la responsabilité de son auteur, lorsque le fait omis devait être accompli... dans l'ordre professionnel, s'il s'agit notamment d'un historien, en vertu des exigences d'une information objective.

J. Carbonnier
Le silence et la gloire
(D. Chron. 1951, 119)

I

Il serait hors de saison de rouvrir de débat sur l'abstention fautive. Contre la négation, exagérément individualiste, du XIXe siècle, la réaction de notre époque a été légitime. Peu d'esprits refuseront, aujourd'hui, de souscrire aux motifs généraux que la section civile a placés en tête de son arrêt: que la faute prévue par les art. 1382 et 1383 peut consister aussi bien dans une abstention que dans un acte positif, que l'abstention peut engager la responsabilité de son auteur même quand elle n'a pas été dictée par la malice et l'intention de nuire. Mais de ces motifs généraux à l'application que suit, le passage n'est guère convaincant.

On a mentionné comme un précédent qu'une commune ait été rendue responsable d'un emprunt qui avait mal tourné, parce qu'elle n'avait pas opposé de démenti aux prospectus la présentant mensongèrement comme l'émettrice (Req. 10 avr. 1894, D.P. 94.1.340), et l'on aurait pu y ajouter toute la jurisprudence sur l'apparence, puisqu' elle sous-entend qu'il y a faute à laisser créer autour de soi, sans la démentir, une apparence contraire à la réalité (v. par ex. Req. 20 fév. 1922, D.P. 1922.1.201, note de M. Savatier. Comp. J.-Ch. Laurent, Note D.P. 1931.1.41). Mais, pour arriver à identifier ce silence-là avec celui de l'historien supprimant une célébrité qui lui déplaît, il ne faut rien de moins que la puissance d'abstraction des juristes, – même si nous considérons qu'ils sont, l'un et l'autre, la violation d'un devoir de renseigner autrui (Comp. Savatier, *Traité de la responsabilité civile,* 2ᵉ éd., t. 1, n° 46), car les renseignements destinés à l'enrichissement des connaissances ne ressemblent guère à ceux qui sont requis en vue de l'action. Dans un cas, si le silence attire l'attention du droit, c'est parce qu'il est dangereux, dangereux pour ceux qui auraient dû être renseignés et qui ne l'ont pas été; dans l'autre, c'est parce qu'il est offensant, offensant non pas pour le lecteur qui aurait dû être renseigné, mais pour un tiers. Jamais le sens commun ne confondra le silence-piège avec le silence-injure. De l'un à l'autre, il n'y a pas à conclure. Ce que l'on peut critiquer dans l'arrêt de la section civile, ce n'est pas qu'il ait fait du silence un délit, c'est qu'il en ait fait un délit de presse, un délit de la parole.

Notre système de responsabilité civile, fondé sur la *clausula generalis,* on ne peut plus *generalis,* de l'art. 1382, a un don d'ubiquité qui, à nos yeux prévenus, passe pour un incomparable avantage. L'inadaptation humaine qui en est la rançon pourrait bien, cependant, le compenser, et au delà. Un système de délits spéciaux, concrets, fragmentaires, comme en a connu le droit romain, comme en connaît encore le droit anglais, permet de traiter plus exactement les divers types sociologiques et psychologiques de fautes civiles, et se trouve ainsi, malgré son apparent archaïsme, plus proche des préoccupations scietifiques modernes. Il permet, du moins, de ne pas noyer dans une notion générale vague ces délits civils qui, transportés en droit pénal, prennent nom de délits de presse ou de la parole, d'atteintes à l'honneur et à la considération, et de construire pour eux une théorie particulière (*actio injuriarum, libel and slander*), où soit préservée leur originalité certaine, traditionnelle, postulée par la nature des choses. On pourrait se demander, du reste, si les rédacteurs du Code Napoléon ont réellement songé, en écrivant l'art. 1382, à faire disparaître le trésor de solutions équitables auquel l'ancien Droit était parvenu par l'étude des délits spéciaux, et notamment du délit d'injures (v. par ex. le *Traité des injures* de Dareau, 1775). Ce serait aussi une question que de savoir si les lois sur la liberté de la presse (en dernier lieu, la loi du 29 juillet 1881) n'avaient pas entendu instituer, pour toutes les manifestations de la pensée, un système juridique clos, se suffisant à lui-même, arbitrant une fois pour toutes tous les intérêts en présence, y compris les intérêts civils – et enlevant, du même coup, à l'art. 1382 une portion de sa compétence diffuse. Sans préjudice des indications de certains textes, comme l'ancien art. 58 de la loi de 1881, la considération du but poursuivi par le législateur suggérait cette interprétation: si la liberté de la presse doit être garantie, ne faut-il pas qu'elle le soit au regard des actions en dommages-intérêts autant que de la répression pénale? La question, pourtant, sans avoir été sérieusement examinée, à été tranchée en faveur du droit commun niveleur: la pratique admet que l'art. 1382 demeure partout sous-jacent à la loi du 29 juillet 1881, et des faits qui ne sont pas, à défaut d'un élément constitutif, pénalement répréhensibles comme diffamations ou injures, peuvent encore être saisis comme délits civils, en vertu des principes généraux de la responsabilité (v. par ex., en l'absence de l'élément de publicité, Req. 2 déc. 1946, D. 1947, 110). Ce qui ne veut pas dire que, dans l'appréciation de ces délits civils, la jurisprudence n'ait pas été fortement influencée par la théorie pénale (comp. Savatier, *op. cit.*, t. 1, n° 94). Comment aurait-il pu en être autrement? Dans la théorie pénale de la diffamation et de l'injure, elle trouvait une philosophie toute élaborée, le produit de réflexions séculaires sur les bienfaits et les méfaits de la langue des hommes, sur les aveuglements respectifs de l'envie et de l'amour-propre, etc., tandis que l'art. 1382 ne pouvait lui offrir qu'un schéma sec, dépouillé, visiblement conçu pour d'autres hypothèses, pour des blessures, des homicides, des dégâts matériels. Heureusement, il se rencontrait dans cet art. 1382 des parties assez plastiques – et, tout le premier, le concept même de faute – pour que, sans faire violence à légalité, les tribunaux pussent y accueillir quelques-unes des nuances venues du droit pénal.

Il nous semble que c'est précisément ce que, dans un style trop discret peut-être, la Cour de Poitiers avait voulu faire, en relevant que le professeur Turpain n'avait pas agi *de mauvaise foi*, n'avait pas agi *par malice et avec l'intention de nuire*. Certes, confrontées avec les seuls art. 1382 et 1383, de telles constations étaient inopérantes: partout oú la faute intentionnelle est concevable, il y a place pour la faute d'imprudence ou de négligence; le quasi-délit est l'ombre portée du délit. Mais référons-nous à la loi du 29 juillet 1881: une jurisprudence constante, et qui n'est pas toute pénale, décide que la diffamation et l'injure supposent essentiellement l'intention de nuire, la malice, la mauvaise foi (v. Req. 8 fév. 1909, D.P. 1909.1.535: 24 avr. 1914, D.P. 1918.1.96; Crim. 28 janv. 1916, D.P. 1920.1.95; 27 oct. 1938, D.P. 1939. 1.77, note de M. Mimin; 7 fév. 1945, D. 1945, 254; 1ᵉʳ juil. 1949, D. 1949, 447. Comp. la note de M. Nast sous Trib. civ. Seine, 29 mars 1926, D.P. 1928.2.68). C'étaient les propositions mêmes de la Cour de Poitiers.

Cette jurisprudence a été contestée (v.G. Le Poittevin, *Traité de la presse.* t. 2, n°s 729 et s.). Elle repose, cependant, sur une donnée très solide de l'expérience: c'est que, pour l'offenseur comme pour l'offensé, l'offense n'est pas dans la matérialité des gestes ou des mots, mais tout entière dans l'intention qui les anime. Le principe, qu'enseignaient nos vieux jurisconsultes, est qu' 'il n'y a d'injure qu'autant qu'il y a de l'affectation et un dessein marqué d'injurier' (Dareau, *op. cit.*, p. 94). 'Point d'injure sans esprit d'injure' répétait Portalis. L'intention coupable exigée en matière d'injure et de diffamation, ce n'est pas, d'ailleurs, exclusivement cet élément intentionnel par lequel le délit civil se définit, en contraste avec le quasi-délit. La notion est plus vaste, prend une coloration morale, qui explique que les tribunaux parlent également de mauvaise foi. On a pu leur reprocher, à cette occasion, de ne pas séparer intention et mobiles. Mais le vrai est qu'il s'agit toujours, pour eux, de rechercher si l'offense, physiquement réalisée, n'est pas psychologiquement vide de signification offensante, comme ils le font, sans que l'on s'en étonne, pour l'injure grave, cause de divorce. Cette appréciation morale dépend d'une foule de circonstances. Néanmoins, ainsi que le soulignait M. Mimin dans une pénétrante analyse (D.P. 1939.1.79), il est trois critères auxquels on peut tout ramener, trois critères de la mauvaise foi dans les délits de presse – ou, plutôt, de la bonne foi, car il sied d'inverser les termes et, puisque l'intention coupable se présume ici (v. Crim. 27 oct. 1938, 7 fév. 1945, 1er juil. 1949, précités), d'énoncer plutôt ce qui pourra justifier le défendeur: sa sincérité, la légitimité de son but, la correction de ses movens.

La Cour de cassation a voulu ignorer ce particularisme de la matière. Rien de plus caractéristique que sa surprise en voyant la Cour de Poitiers attacher des conséquences à la sincérité de l'historien. Surprise qui redouble, à constater que cette sincérité n'était même pas toute pure, puisqu'il pouvait bien s'y mêler un grain d'orgueil ou d'ambition. Il y a de quoi être surpris, en effet, au regard des principes généraux de la responsabilité: nos défauts ne sauraient justifier nos mauvaises actions (comp. H. et L. Mazeaud, *Rev.trim.dr.civ.*, 1943, p. 111). On conçoit, au contraire, dans l'atmosphère particulière des délits de presse, que la sincérité ne coïncide pas nécessairement avec l'impartialité, et qu'une dose de passion y soit excusable et excusante, que ce soit la passion partisane des luttes électorales (comp. Crim. 29 juil. 1899, D.P. 1902.1.118; Req. 24 avr. 1914, précité), ou celle des débats que l'on dit scientifiques.

Mais, pourrait-on objecter, cette question de sincérité n'a pas été décisive dans la cassation; ce qui a déterminé la section civile, c'est l'*incorrection des moyens* employés envers Branly, motif qui avait tout autant de poids dans le droit spécial de la presse que dans le droit commun de la responsabilité civile. De fait, tout l'arrêt suggère, s'il ne l'exprime formellement, cette idée que la faute a tenu, en l'espèce, à l'emploi du silence comme moyen de critique: l'historien pouvait contester que Branly fût l'inventeur de la T.S.F., mais à condition de s'en expliquer; il n'avait pas le droit de le laisser seulement entendre en se taisant. Nous voici de nouveau au silence-injure.

Remarquez que la théorie pénale admet qu'il puisse y avoir des silences injurieux ou diffamatoires. Mais ce sont des silences qualifiés, circonstanciés: des points de suspension habilement semés (comp. Le Poittevin, *op. cit.*, t. 2, n° 732), des réticences évocatrices ('X... ne fait plus partie de ma maison pour des raisons que je tairai'. Comp. Req. 16 janv. 1914, D.P. 1918.1.11. V. cep. Paris, 6 mars 1844, *Jur. gén.*, v° *Presse-outrage*, n° 822), ou encore, ainsi que les appelait l'ancien Droit, des injures obliques ('Moi, je ne suis pas un voleur'. Comp. *Jur. gén.*, *ibid.*, n° 820), – toutes insinuations que la théorie frappe au même titre que l'allégation directe (v. l'art. 29 de la loi de 1881, dans la rédaction de l'ordonnance du 6 mai 1944). Si ces silences sont jugés coupables, ce n'est point, – comme on serait tenté de l'imaginer, dans l'esprit des doctrines générales de la responsabilité, – parce qu'ils constituent des omissions dans l'action; c'est tout simplement qu'ils ne sont pas de véritables silences. La suspension, la réticence, la prétérition sont des figures classées de rhétorique. Ce sont des façons de parler; elles font partie du discours, comme, dans un tableau, les ombres font partie de la peinture aussi bien que les couleurs.

A côté de cela, il y a des silences absolus, des silences parfaits. Ils peuvent être éloquents, avoir un sens pour qui sait ou qui conjecture, parce qu'il est toujours possible, avec un minimum de pénétration, de deviner la pensée d'autrui. Mais rien ne les matérialise, et c'est pourquoi ils n'engagent pas la responsabilité. Peu importe qu'une abstention pure, en général, puisse l'engager. La question n'est pas la responsabilité en général, mais cette responsabilité spéciale que nous assumons pour nos paroles ou nos écrits, et le silence absolu n'est ni parole ni écrit, il est pensée pure. Nous nous faisons scrupule de reprendre contre la solution de la Cour de cassation ce que l'individualisme a trop dit, chaque fois qu'a été sanctionnée une responsabilité pour abstention fautive: que c'est mettre en péril la liberté. La liberté finira par devenir un vocable abusif. Il est beaucoup de libertés, et toutes ne sont pas également précieuses. Même la liberté de communiquer ses pensées ne peut être sans limite. Mais c'est la liberté de la pensée *intérieure* qui est ici en cause, et il n'est pas de valeur qui soit supérieure à celle-là.

Et puis, le silence a des vertus pratiques. La sociabilité est faite de silences. Le silence est respectueux, religieux, charitable. Il procède de la défiance de soi, du doute méthodique. Je suis, par intuition, persuadé qu'une assertion courante est fausse, sans être encore à même de le démontrer; serai-je forcé, en attendant, de faire semblant d'y croire? Le silence est l'issue honnête. Il est des mutismes officiels (on en entendra sur Verdun); il en est de laïques; certains interviennent *ad usum Delphini*, d'autres *brevitatis causa*. Apparemment, la Cour de cassation consentirait à admettre qu'il y eût ici des buts justificatifs. Mais le silence, par essence, est un vide, où tout, n'importe quel but, peut entrer; et quelle besogne inquisitoriale, peu digne de ce qu'il y a de positif, d'agnostique dans le droit, si les tribunaux doivent passer les silences au crible de l'art. 1382!

II

A quoi bon instruire plus avant le procès de tendance fait au silence? Il n'est pas sûr que l'historien se serait sauvé en parlant. Plus que de certaines armes, c'est peut-être de certaines cibles que la section civile a voulu lui interdire le choix. L'article incriminé n'aurait pas davantage trouvé grâce si, au lieu de se taire complètement sur Branly, il avait lapidairement déclaré: Branly n'a pas inventé la T.S.F. Il y aurait fallu des explications, et d'une ampleur suffisante, et, raisonnablement, pas n'importe lesquelles. De proche en proche, la Cour de cassation ne peut éviter d'instaurer un contrôle judiciaire de la manière d'écrire l'histoire.[1]

Ce contrôle serait encore relativement aisé si l'histoire n'était composée que de faits simples, dont l'existence pût se vérifier par oui ou par non. Mais l'histoire ne se contente plus d'enregistrer les événements; elle se préoccupe d'en découvrir les causes. Or, les causes sont complexes, enchevêtrées, obscures. Le consensus que l'on peut normalement espérer sur la description des événements ne se retrouve plus dans la reconstitution des causalités. Entre les deux, s'interpose un écran d'interprétation, donc de subjectivité. Ainsi en va-t-il pour la paternité des inventions, si souvent controversée, et pas seulement d'un pays à un autre: c'est qu'elle ne se déduit pas uniquement de la chronologie des expériences qui y ont conduit, point de fait, mais d'une appréciation du rôle respectivement joué par ces expériences dans le résultat final. Les civilistes devraient bien savoir à quoi s'en tenir: s'ils constatent tous que Bonaparte a participé aux travaux du Conseil d'Etat, ils ne sont point d'accord sur la part qu'il convient de lui attribuer dans l'œuvre de codification.

On entrevoit, dès lors, les réserves suscitées par les formules où la section civile, – combinant du reste, avec quelque éclectisme, deux doctrines différentes de la responsabilité, – s'est efforcée de définir la responsabilité de l'historien. Que l'on déclare qu'un historien est en faute pour avoir violé un devoir professionnel d'objectivité, ou pour ne s'être pas comporté comme un historien prudent, avisé et objectif, c'est toujours méconnaître l'existence de tout un secteur immense des sciences historiques où la subjectivité est légitime, parce qu'elle est inévitable. Avec la première formule, on raisonne comme s'il y avait une corporation des historiens, chargée de dresser pour eux un code de déontologie; avec la seconde, on paraît supposer un type abstrait, là où il serait souhaitable de ne trouver que des individualités irréductibles les unes aux autres. Observons-le, au risque de nous éloigner beaucoup de l'arrêt: plus un historien aura de génie, plus il tombera dans ce péché de subjectivité que la Cour de cassation tend sous ses pas. Michelet y aurait succombé à tous les coups. Veut-on le triomphe de l'histoire plate? C'est-à-dire de l'histoire conformiste. Car le signe le plus clair de l'objectivité pourrait bien être, aux yeux de la Cour de cassation, une certaine conformité aux opinions assises. L'historien ne serait pas obligé de discuter *toutes* les versions qui ont pu être proposées d'un même fait; du moins, il serait tenu de faire un sort à la version que l'on pourrait qualifier de principale, celle-ci se reconnais- sant à ce qu'elle a été adoptée par la *major et sanior pars* des historiens antérieurs. Les doctrines consacrées par le succès emporteraient ainsi avec elles une présomption de vérité. Pas irréfragable, il faut le concéder. Mais, même réfragables, les présomptions de vérité sont fort gênantes pour la libre recherche scientifique.

Que la recherche ait pour objet le grandeur d'un homme, l'importance de son rôle dans un événement, et le bénéfice de la présomption va fonctionner pour la conservation des gloires acquises. C'est peut-être la leçon la plus remarquable de l'arrêt *Branly* que cette invitation faite à l'histoire de se montrer circonspecte dans la discussion des grands hommes, à tout le moins tant que le temps ne les a pas fait sortir, eux et leurs héritiers, de la zone de protection de l'art. 1382. On peut ne pas éprouver beaucoup de sympathie pour cet exercice de virtuosité historique qu'est le 'déboulonnage' des statues. Mais, dans la réalité, ce ne sont pas les historiens qui réussissent à jeter à bas les statues, pas plus qu'à les ériger; c'est l'opinion publique. Par là jaillit une nouvelle objection contre l'intervention de l'art. 1382, non plus du côté de la faute, mais à l'autre bout, du côté du préjudice. L'art. 1382 protège incontestablement l'honneur et la considération des individus (Comp. L. 29 juil. 1881, art. 29). Seulement, affirmer, au rebours de la croyance commune, qu'un savant n'est pas l'auteur d'une invention déterminée, ce n'est s'attaquer ni à son honneur ni à sa considération. Certainement pas à son honneur: on ne prétend pas qu'il ait plagié, usurpé. Mais même pas à sa considération: ses talents professionnels ne sont pas déniés, ni ses qualités scientifiques. Ce qui est visé, c'est sa célébrité, sa gloire. Or, la gloire n'est pas un capital que les grands hommes se sont constitué une fois pour toutes et sur lequel ils ont désormais un droit acquis. Ce n'est pas davantage une parcelle de leur personnalité, qu'ils pourraient défendre *erga omnes*. Leur honneur, leur considération, ils pourraient les défendre ainsi. Ce sont des valeurs qui leur appartiennent, et que le sentiment coalisé de tous leurs semblables ne sauraient leur ravir, tandis que leur gloire, c'est entièrement dans ce sentiment des autres hommes qu'ils la trouvent. Ils en sont enveloppés, mais elle est en dehors d'eux. On a souvent parlé du soleil de la gloire. Cette image usée a au moins le mérite de faire sentir ce qu'il y a, dans la gloire, de commun, de public, d'inappropriable, et combien est juridiquement vaine la prétention de l'homme célèbre qui se plaint que sa gloire ait été lésée: c'est un préjudice impossible.

Un préjudice impossible, venu d'une faute impalpable: à cela se réduisait, sans doute, en termes de droit, cette trop fameuse affaire. Le droit ne gagne rien à s'annexer ces domaines chimériques, où l'opinion, autrefois, régnait seule, qui juge mieux et plus vite que lui, et plus délicatement, ayant à sa disposition le moyen subtil de l'oubli.

---

1. C'est ce que la cour de Paris avait refusé de faire, au sĩ̄cle dernier, dans un arrêt rendu au profit d'Alexandre Dumas père (Paris, 26 avr. 1865, *Rec. Sirey*, 65.2.289). Les motifs de cet arrêt contrastent vigoureusement avec ceux de l'arrêt *Branly: l'histoire n'est pas tenue*, lorsqu'elle rencontre un point obscur ou diversement raconte par les Relations du temps, *de rapporter les différentes versions* auxquelles il a donné lieu, mais seulement de choisir avec impartialité celle qui lui paraît la plus sûre, et si ce point vient à soulever une controverse, *ce n'est pas devant les tribunaux qu'elle peut trouver ses juges.*

5. Cour de cassation
Chambre des Requêtes, 3 août 1915
Coquerel c. *Clément-Bayard*
(D.P. 1917,1.79)

Arrêt de la Cour d'appel d'Amiens du 12 nov. 1913

La Cour, – Considérant que Jules Coquerel a acquis en 1910 une pièce de terre d'une longueur de 170 mètres environ, d'une largeur de 10 à 12 mètres, située sur le territoire de Trosly-Breuil, en face et à une distance de 90 mètres environ d'un hangar pour dirigeables construit par Adolphe Clément-Bayard; – Considérant que Coquerel, qui vit en mésintelligence avec Clément-Bayard, a établi sur la limite de sa propriété, et en face de la porte du hangar de Clément-Bayard, deux carcasses en bois d'une longueur de 15 mètres environ, d'une hauteur de 10 à 11 mètres surmontées de quatre piquets en fer de 2 à 3 mètres de hauteur, et séparées l'une de l'autre de quelques mètres; – Considérant que ces carcasses en bois ne sont ni closes ni couvertes; que Coquerel n'en retire et ne peut, dans l'état où elles se trouvent, en retirer aucun profit direct, qu'elles ne constituent même pas une clôture, puisqu' elles n'existent que sur une longueur de 25 à 30 mètres et sont séparées l'une de l'autre par un intervalle de plusieurs mètres; – Considérant qu'il est manifeste et ne saurait être méconnu qu'elles ne présentent aucun intérêt pour Coquerel et que Coquerel ne les a fait édifier que dans l'unique but de nuire à Clément-Bayard, en rendant plus difficiles, notamment en cas de vent violent, les manoeuvres de ses dirigeables à leur départ et à leur retour; qu'il s'ensuit que c'est à juste titre que les premiers juges ont estimé qu'il y avait là, de la part de Coquerel, un abus de son droit de propriété et l'ont condamné à supprimer les poteaux en fer surmontant les charpentes et dont l'un d'eux a causé, en 1912, des avaries à l'un des dirigeables de Clément-Bayard; – Considérant que Coquerel prétend, il est vrai, pour justifier ses agissements, qu'il n' a fait, en exécutant ces travaux et en augmentant ainsi l'intérêt de Clément-Bayard a se rendre acquéreur de sa pièce de terre, qu'un acte de spéculation; – Considér-ant que s'il est loisible au propriétaire d'un fonds de chercher à en tirer le meilleur parti possible, et si la spéculation est par elle-même et en elle-même un acte parfaitement licite, ce n'est qu'à la condition que les moyens employés pour la réaliser ne soient pas, comme en l'espèce, illégitimes et inspirés exclusivement par une intention malicieuse; –

Adoptant, en outre, sur ces divers points, les motifs du jugement non contraires aux présents;

Sur l'appel incident de Clément-Bayard: – Adoptant également les motifs du jugement: – Considérant que Clément-Bayard ne peut prétendre à la réparation d'un dommage éventuel et incertain; que rien ne démontre que les carcasses en bois, lorsqu'elles ne seront plus surmontées de poteaux en fer, lui causeront forcément un préjudice dont il soit fondé dès maintenant à se plaindre;

Par ces motifs, confirme.

Pouvoi en cassation par le sieur Coquerel – Arrêt

La Cour; – Sur le moyen du pourvoi pris de la violation des art. 544 et suiv., 552 et suiv. CC, des règles du droit de propriété et plus spécialement du droit de se clore, violation, par fausse application, des art. 1382 et suiv. CC, violation de l'art, 7 de la loi du 20 avr. 1810: – Attendu qu'il ressort de l'arrêt attaqué que Coquerel a installé sur son terrain, attenant à celui de Clément-Bayard, des carcasses en bois de 16 mètres de hauteur surmontées de tiges de fer pointues; que ce dispositif no présentait pour l'exploitation du terrain de Coquerel aucune utilité et n'avait été édifié que dans l'unique but de nuire à Clément-Bayard, sans d'ailleurs, à la hauteur à laquelle il avait été élevé, constituer, au sens de l'art. 647 CC, la clôture que le propriétaire est autorisé à construire pour la protection de ses intérêts légitimes; que, dans cette situation de fait, l'arrêt a pu apprécier qu'il y avait eu par Coquerel abus de son droit et, d'une part, le condamner à la réparation du dommage causé à un ballon dirigeable de Clément-Bayard, d'autre part, ordonner l'enlèvement des tiges de fer surmontant les carcasses en bois; – Attendu que, sans contradiction, l'arrêt a pu refuser la destruction du surplus du dispositif, dont la suppression était également réclamée, par le motif qu'il n'était pas démontré que ce dispositif eût jusqu'à présent causé du dommage à Clément-Bayard et dût nécessairement lui en causer dans l'avenir; – Attendu que l'arrêt trouve une base légale dans ces constatations; que, dûment motivé, il n' a point, en statuant ainsi qu'il l'a fait, violé ou faussement appliqué les règles du droit ou les textes visés au moyen.

Par ces motifs, rejette.

6. Cour de cassation
3ᵉ Chambre Civile, 4 fév. 1971
Epoux Vullion c. Sté immob. Vernet Saint-Christophe et autres
(*J.C.P.* 1971, 2.16781)

La Cour; – Sur le moyen unique:– Vu les articles 544 el 1382 du Code civil; – Attendu que le droit pour un propriétaire de jouir de sa chose de la manière la plus absolue, sauf usage prohibé par la loi ou les règlements, est limité par l'obligation qu'il a de ne causer à la propriété d'autrui aucun dommage dépassant les inconvénients normaux du voisinage; – Attendu que pour rejeter la demande en dommages-intérêts formée par les époux Vullion contre la Société Vernet Saint-Christophe, et déclarer par suite sans objet la demande en garantie formée par ladite société contre ses entrepreneurs, les Sociétés Paumelle et Bollard, à raison des désordres provoqués dans l'immeuble appartenant auxdits époux par la construction de bâtiments sur le terrain voisin, la Cour d'appel énonce qu'en l'absence de toute faute démontrée à l'encontre de la Société Vernet Saint-Christophe, maître de l'ouvrage, sa responsabilité ne pouvait être retenue: Qu'en statuant ainsi, alors qu'il résultait des propres constatations de l'arrêt que la Société Vernet Saint-Christophe avait enfreint l'obligation à laquelle elle était tenue de ne pas causer au voisin un trouble dépassant les inconvénients normaux du voisinage, la Cour d'appel a violé les textes susvisés;

Par ces motifs: – Casse et annule l'arrêt rendu le 13 mars 1969 entre les parties par la Cour d'appel de Paris, et renvoie devant la Cour d'appel de Reims.

2ᵉ espèce: Cour de cassation 3ᵉ Chambre Civile, 4 fév. 1971
Brun c. Sté civ. immob.

La Cour; – Sur le moyen unique:–Vu les articles 544 et 1382 du Code civil; – Attendu que si, aux termes du premier de ces textes, la propriété est le droit de jouir et disposer des choses de la manière la plus absolue, pourvu qu'on n'en fasse pas un usage prohibé par les lois ou par les règlements, le propriétaire voisin de celui qui construit légitimement sur son terrain est néanmoins tenu de subir les inconvénients normaux du voisinage; qu'en revanche, il est en droit d'exiger une réparation dès lors que ces inconvénients excèdent cette limite; – Attendu que, pour décider que la Société civile immobilière du 10, rue Joseph-Liouville à Paris, propriétaire d'un immeuble édifié en 1957, plus élevé que celui qui existait au n° 8 de la même rue, lequel a subi de ce fait des désordres dans le fonctionnement de ses cheminées et de ses conduits de ventilation, n'était tenue de supporter ni la charge des travaux d'exhaussement desdites cheminées prescrits par un arrêté préfectoral en date du 14 novembre 1958, ni celle d'une réparation pécuniaire qui était demandée, la Cour d'appel énonce 'que l'édification par la Société civile d'un immeuble constitue l'exercice normal du droit de propriété, exclusif de toute responsabilité quasi délictuelle ou délictuelle, à défaut d'imprudence, de négligence ou d'intention de nuire établies; que l'existence alléguée de troubles de jouissance excédant les inconvénients normaux du voisinage n'est pas caractérisée dès lors que l'article 8 de l'arrêté du 14 novembre 1958 fait obligation à chaque propriétaire d'immeuble d'élever les conduits extérieurs, dans tous les cas, même en l'absence de désordres affectant leur fonctionnement, à une hauteur déterminée au-dessus de toute construction distante de moins de huit mètres' . – Attendu qu'en rejetant, par ces motifs, la demande dont elle était saisie, sans rechercher si, antérieurement à la date d'application de l'arrêté susvisé, l'immeuble des demandeurs avait subi, du fait de la construction de celui de la Société civile, des désordres excédant la limte des inconvénients normaux de voisinage, la Cour d'appel n'a pas légalement justifié sa décision;

Par ces motifs: – Casse et annule l'arrêt rendu le 12 juin 1969 entre les parties, par la Cour d'appel d'Orléans, et renvoie devant la Cour d'appel de Reims.

7. Cour de cassation
Chambre Civile, 28 fév. 1910
Nourrigat c. Pech
(S. 1911,1.329)

Le 25 juin 1904, M. Nourrigat, ouvrier vigneron au service de M. Pech, en Algérie, conduisait une machine à soufrer les vignes, lorsque, le gérant de la ferme étant venu l'aborder, M. Nourrigat s'est arrêté pour donner des explications. Pendant qu'il parlait, l'indigène qui conduisait la machine mit l'attelage en marche. M. Nourrigat, en essayant de ressaisir les guides qu'il avait laissé échapper, eut la main droite prise par un engrenage, qui lui coupa trois doigts. M. Nourrigat a assigné son patron, M. Pech, devant le tribunal civil de Blidah, en paiement d'une somme de 30,000 fr., à titre de dommages-intérêts. Il a offert de prouver par enquête: 1° l'imprudence du conducteur, qui avait fait brusquement partir l'attelage pendant sa conversation avec le gérant; 2° une modification apportée à la machine après l'accident, indiquant sa mauvaise disposition antérieure. Par jugement en date du 10 mai 1905, le tribunal de Blidah a rejeté la demande de M. Nourrigat en ces termes: – 'Le Tribunal; – Attendu que la demande de Nourrigat est basée sur ce que le défendeur a commis une faute de nature à engagér sa responsabilité, quand il a négligé de faire recouvrir l'engrenage de la machine à soufrer, de manière à rendre impossible l'accident dont ledit Nourrigat a été victime le 25 juin 1904; Mais attendu que cette prétention ne saurait être accueillie; – Attendu, en effet, qu'il résulte des propres déclarations du demandeur que l'accident dont ce dernier a été l'objet s'est produit dans les circonstances suivantes: Nourrigat conduisait une machine à soufrer, lorsque, à un moment donné, le gérant de la ferme est venu lui parler; Nourrigat s'est arrêté; et il était occupé à donner au gérant des explications quand l'indigène qui conduisait l'attelage fit subitement partir les bêtes qui traînaient la soufreuse; Nourrigat voulut rattraper vivement les guides qui étaient tombées; mais il eut malheureusement la main droite prise dans l'engrenage, qui lui coupa trois doigts; – Attendu qu'il ressort de cet exposé que l'accident dont s'agit est dû uniquement à la propre imprudence du demandeur; – Attendu, en effet, que, si celui-ci a tout d'abord laissé tomber les guides qu'il avait à la main, c'est par suite d'un manque d'attention ou d'une distraction dont il est seul responsable; – Attendu qu'étant donnée l'obligation dans laquelle Nourrigat se trouvait par sa faute de ramasser les guides, il appartenait à ce demandeur de prendre les précautions nécessaires pour se mettre à l'abri de l'événement fâcheux qui s'est produit, soit en invitant l'indigène qui se tenait devant les bêtes à faire arrêter l'attelage, si les guides se trouvaient engagées dans l'engrenage de la soufreuse, de telle façon qu'elles ne pouvaient en être commodément retirées pendant la marche de l'appareil, soit en usant avec prudence des moyens utiles pour saisir les guides, de facon à éviter tout danger, dans le cas où cette opération aurait été possible même pendant le fonctionnement de la machine; – Attendu que le fait que la soufreuse n'était pas construite d'une manière irréprochable, c'est-à-dire rendant impossible tout accident, ne saurait par lui seul engager la responsabilité de Pech; – Attendu, en effet, qu'il suffit que l'appareil dont s'agit fût construit de telle sorte qu'il pût fonctionner et en réalité fonctionnat habituellement sans causer d'accident, pour que Pech échappe à toute responsabilité; – Attendu, en effet, que celui-ci ne saurait être tenu de réparer les consequences d'un fait résultant uniquement de la propre imprudence de l'ouvrier à son service; – Attendu qu'il n'est pas d'appareil, si simple qu'il soit ou si perfectionné qu'on puisse le supposer, qui ne soit susceptible de causer des accidents, quand celui qui l'emploie n'use pas des précautions nécessaires; – Attendu qu'il appartenait à Nourrigat, personne expérimentée et capable de conduire la soufreuse dont s'agit, de voir le danger qu'il pouvait causer en mettant sa main dans l'engrenage de cette machine, et d'agir en conséquence; – Attendu que l'on ne saurait légitimement faire grief au défendeur, ainsi que l'a fait Nourrigat, et tirer argument contre lui de ce que, postérieurement à l'accident du 25 juin 1904, ledit Pech a fait recouvrir l'engrenage dont s'agit de manière à empêcher le retour d'un fait du même genre; – Attendu que cette précaution dénote uniquement le souci de la part de Pech de mettre désormais son personnel à l'abri de tout risque, et de le prémunir contre les actes d'imprudence que ce personnel pouvait être amené à commettre; mais qu'on ne saurait en déduire que le fait de n'avoir pas pris dès l'origine cette précaution constitue une faute susceptible d'engager la responsabilité du défendeur, rien dans la loi actuellement applicable en Algérie ne faisant au patron une obligation de garantir l'ouvrier contra sa propre faute ou son imprudence; – Par ces motifs; – Déclare Nourrigat mal fondé en toutes ses demandes.'

M. Nourrigat a interjeté appel; mais un arrêt de la Cour d'Alger a, le 10 mai 1906, confirmé le jugement par adoption de motifs.

Pourvoi en cassation par M. Nourrigat. – 1er Moyen, Violation des arts. 1382 à 1385, CC, et 7 de la loi du 20 avril 1810, en ce que la Cour a rejeté la demande en dommages-intérêts d'un ouvrier agricole contre un patron, à raison d'un accident survenu dans son travail, sous prétexte que l'accident était imputable à la seule imprudence de l'ouvrier, alors qu'il était allégué par le demandeur, et qu'il n'a pas été dénié par l'arrêt, que l'accident avait eu également pour cause l'imprudence d'un préposé du patron, conduisant l'attelage d'une machine à soufrer les vignes.

2e Moyen. Violation des mêmes textes, en ce que la Cour a considéré que le fait de n'avoir pas couvert l'engrenage d'une machine agricole ne constituait pas une imprudence à la charge du propriétaire de ladite machine, alors qu'il est constant, en fait, que l'engrenage a été couvert aussitôt après l'accident litigieux, et que le propriétaire a ainsi reconnu la nécessité de la précaution qu'il n'avait pas prise.

Arrêt

La Cour; – Sur les deux moyens réunis; – Vu les arts. 1382 et 1384, CC; – Attendu que, si les tribunaux constatent souverainement les faits, il appartient à la Cour de cassation d'apprécier si les faits constatés présentent les caractères juridiques de la faute prévue par la loi et engagent la responsabilité de leurs auteurs; – Attendu que l'arrêt attaqué déclare, en fait, que Nourrigat, ouvrier agricole au service de Pech, conduisait une machine à soufrer les vignes, dont l'engrenage n'était pas recouvert par un appareil protecteur; qu'il s'arrêta pour donner des explications au gérant de la ferme, et que l'indigène, chargé de diriger l'attelage, fit partir subitement les bêtes qui traînaient la machine; que Nourrigat voulut alors ressaisir les guides qu'il avait laissé échapper, et qu'il eut la main droite prise dans l'engrenage, qui lui coupa trois doigts; – Attendu que la Cour d'appel a rejeté la demande en dommages-intérêts, par le motif que Nourrigat avait été victime de sa propre imprudence; – Mais attendu que les constatations ci-dessus énoncées impliquent, à la charge de Pech, l'existence d'une faute, qui a contribué à occasionner l'accident; que l'imprudence de la victime n'a donc pu exonérer Pech de toute responsabilité; – Attendu, dès lors, qu'en statuant comme il l'a fait, l'arrêt attaqué a méconnu les conséquences légales des faits par lui constatés, et a, par suite, violé les textes ci-dessus visés; – Casse, etc.

Extract from note by G. Appert

§ 1er

Quoi qu'il en soit, la Cour de cassation s'est bien gardée de poser une règle absolue. On sait avec quelle prudence extrême elle évite de jamais engager l'avenir par des formules générales. Dans l'espèce, en déclarant que le propriétaire de la soufreuse était en faute, elle n'a point posé en principe que tout propriétaire de machine est tenu d'y adapter les perfectionnements de protection qu'elle comporte. Il est permis de penser, par conséquent, que la faute tient aux circonstances spéciales de l'espèce....

§ 2

Il ne suffit pas qu'une personne soit en faute pour être tenue de réparations civiles. Il faut encore que le dommage soit la conséquence et même la conséquence directe de la faute commise. C'est là un point de jurisprudence bien établi...

Quoi qu'il en soit de cette explication, l'analogie avec l'arrêt ci-dessus recueilli frappera tous les yeux. 'L'accident, dit la Cour d'Alger, est *uniquement* dû à la propre imprudence du demandeur (c'est-à-dire de la victime).' La chambre civile affirme, au contraire, que la négligence du patron 'a contribué à occasionner l'accident'. Ici encore, on peut être tenté de dire que la Chambre Civile a trouvé une contradiction évidente entre les faits relevés par les juges du fond et la solution adoptée. Mais il importe d'examiner si cette contradiction n'est pas plus apparente que réelle.

Un accident n'est presque jamais le résultat d'une cause unique. Il a fallu, pour qu'il se produisît, un enchaînement de circonstances malheureuses, dont chacune, prise séparément, manque de gravité, bien que leur réunion ait entraîné de fatales conséquences. Une voiture, traversant un passage à niveau, est renversée par un train. On peut imaginer que le garde-barrière ait négligé de fermer les barrières, que l'heure du passage du train se trouve modifiée par suite de la négligence d'un chef de gare, ou par le mauvais état de la voie dû à l'absence de réparations nécessaires, que la marche de la voiture ait été retardée par la faute d'un domestique, que son conducteur ait été imprudent, etc. Les juges vont-ils partager la responsabilité, avec ses conséquences pécuniaires, entre tous ceux qui, de près ou de loin, ont contribué à causer l'accident? C'est une solution qui se conçoit théoriquement. Mais il ne semble pas que ce soit celle de la jurisprudence. Parmi les circonstances qui précèdent l'accident, certaines l'ont rendu inévitable. Il semble qu'il y ait tendance parmi les tribunaux à ne retenir que ces dernières; les premières, c'est-à-dire les causes occasionnelles, ne compteraient pas à leurs yeux. V. Cass. 31 mars 1909 (S. et P. 1910.1.188; *Pand. pér.*, 1910.1.188). Sans prétendre que l'art. 1151, CC, impose cette solution pour les fautes délictuelles, on peut soutenir qu'il lui est favorable. Si le législateur s'est refusé à tenir compte des dommages indirects, c'est que la faute commise n'en a été que la cause occasionnelle, et qu'il a fallu, pour qu'ils se pussent produire, un concours de circonstances fortuit. Telles ont été sans doute les idées qui ont prévalu près des juges de Blidah et de la Cour. d'Alger. Et c'est pourquoi ils ont pu, même après avoir reconnu que la machine n'était pas construite d'une façon irréprochable, affirmer que cet accident était 'uniquement dû à la propre imprudence de l'ouvrier'.

§ 3

Après avoir admis, contrairement à l'avis des juges du fond: 1° qu'il y avait eu faute du propriétaire de la machine; 2° que cette faute était la cause ou du moins une des causes de l'accident, la Chambre Civile décide que l'imprudence de la victime, imprudence qu'elle semble d'ailleurs reconnaître, ne peut faire retomber entièrement à sa charge les conséquences du préjudice qu'elle a subi. Il y a longtemps que cette doctrine passe pour une sorte d'axiome en jurisprudence, et très nombreux sont les arrêts d'appel cassés pour l'avoir méconnue... Pourtant, il est bon de savoir que la Cour suprême ne s'est pas toujours crue autorisée à intervenir en pareil cas. Quelques exemples feront foi de notre assertion.

Un courtier maritime avait omis de signaler, dans une police d'assurance, un fait important, si bien que la Comp. d'assurances, invoquant cette réticence, se considérait comme dégagée vis-à-vis de l'assuré. La Cour de Rennes, jugeant que l'assuré 'avait commis lui-même une faute bien plus grave, en ne prescrivant pas à son mandataire de mentionner dans la police ce point essentiel', déclara que les torts du mandant 'avaient affranchi le mandataire de toute responsabilité'; et la Chambre des Requêtes, qui alors tenait pour constant[1] que 'l'appréciation des actes ou des faits qui engagent la responsabilité de l'homme appartient au juge de fond', rejeta le pourvoi. V. Cass.Req. 6 fév. 1865 (*S.* 1865.1.167 – P. 1865.393). Un mari, dont la femme était née de relations adultérines (ce qui la privait de tous droits à la succession de ses parents), avait attaqué en dommages-intérêts sa belle-mère pour lui avoir caché le vice de la naissance de sa fille. La Cour de Caen repoussa la demande, parce que 'le mari avait à se reprocher de n'avoir pas pris de renseignements', et la Chambre des Requêtes rejeta le pourvoi, parce que, 'quand il y a faute réciproque, la question de responsabilité est abandonnée au pouvoir discrétionnaire des tribunaux'. V. Cass. Req. 12 déc. 1854 (*S.* 1855.1.593 – P. 1855.1.387). *Adde*, Cass. Req. 18 avril 1866 (*S.* 1866.1.430 – P. 1866.1175). Qu'est-ce à dire, sinon que les Cours de Rennes et de Caen estimaient que la négligence du demandeur avait été la seule cause du dommage dont il se plaignait? Si la conduite du défendeur n'était pas exempte de tout reproche, encore n'était-elle que l'occasion, ou, si on le préfère, une cause éloignée du préjudice: il n'en fallait pas tenir compte. La Chambre des Requêtes, qui alors s'en remettait au juge du fait le soin d'apprécier qui était en faute et qui était responsable, avait rejeté et devait rejeter les pourvois formés contre ses décisions.

§4

En somme, le pouvoir de contrôle que s'attribue la Cour de cassation en ces matières a singulièrement grandi depuis cinquante ans. Elle confiait alors aux Cours d'appel la mission de décider: 1° quelles précautions il convenait de prendre dans les circonstances diverses de la vie, c'est-à-dire ce qui constituait l'imprudence ou la négligence; 2° quelle était la cause directe et immédiate de chaque accident. Elle estime, au contraire, aujourd'hui qu'il lui appartient: 1° d'apprécier les faits au point de vue du caractère fautif qu'ils peuvent présenter; 2° de dire, au moins dans les cas de faute réciproque, quelle a été la cause du dommage.

L'exercice de ce contrôle permet à la Cour suprême de faire respecter le principe d'après lequel l'imprudence de la victime ne saurait décharger de toute responsabilité le tiers auteur de l'accident. Ledit principe resterait sans lui lettre morte, ou demeurerait à la discrétion des juges du fond, puisqu'ils pourraient s'y soustraire en affirmant que la victime s'est seule attiré, par sa maladresse, le préjudice dont elle demande réparation. Il n'en est pas moins vrai que la Cour de cassation en vient insensiblement à examiner les circonstances de chaque espèce, glissant ainsi sur un terrain qui devrait lui être fermé. On peut se demander si ces empiétements ne sont pas sans danger. V. d'ailleurs, la note précitée de M. Appert sous Cass. 13 janv. 1908.[2]

Notes

1. i.e. *jurisprudence constante*, settled case-law.
2. The law relating to *Accidents du Travail* (Workmen's Compensation Act) did not at that time apply to Algeria.

DAMAGE

'Damages' is the sum of money awarded by the court to the successful plaintiff of a tort action; 'damage', on the other hand, 'means the actual harm to an interest whether or not protected by law'. This latter definition, given by the American Restatement (Tort § 902, comment a(1939)), is one of the few one can find of the notion of damage in the Common law, and the lack of any detailed consideration of the concept must be due to at least two factors. The first is that in the Common law (unlike the Civil law) damage is not always a necessary ingredient of the cause of action (we know of torts actionable *per se*; the civilians do not); the second is the fact that in England until very recently the award of damages used to be wholly within the province of the jury (and in American jurisdictions they still are) and thus the 'purposes which the civilian lawyer was able to effectuate by means of the concept of damage had to be satisfied in England by other concepts over which the judge did have control such as duty and remoteness' (Tony Weir, 38 *Tul.L.Rev.* (1964), 665).

The opposite is true of French law where damage is an *important* and (like causation but unlike *faute*) *constant* element of liability. Moreover, the notion is conceived in a very general manner and includes equally patrimonial loss and 'dommage morale' (see case 8), being the product of a long process of generalisation and abstraction which, rather than make up a list of the kinds of harm worthy of compensation, chose instead to identify the general and permanent characteristics of reparable harm. The limits of reparability – and limits, of course, there must be – are thus set by three requirements, namely, that the harm in question is *direct, certain* and that it affects an *intérêt légitime*.

The requirement of directness is really connected with remoteness and as such is part of the wider problem of causation (see vol. 1, chapter 3). On the other hand, the requirement that the afflicted interest is legitimate has been highlighted in the many 'concubinage' cases represented here by the early harsh one (case 9) and the more recent one of 1970 (case 10) in which the Chambre Mixte put an end to

215

the 'internal conflict' between the Chambres Civiles and the Chambre Criminelle of the Cour de cassation (see note to French cases, above, pp. 179–80). Finally, the requirement that the damage be certain. This, naturally, includes *actual* damage, though even 'future' damage will do so long as it is not entirely 'hypothetical'. The French courts have performed wonders with this superbly flexible notion, the *perte d'une chance* line of cases offering instructive and often entertaining material. For lack of space we reproduce here one case only – a fatal accident case – which makes use of the requirement and achieves a result which English law, because of the limitations of its Fatal Accidents Acts, could never attain (case 11). The skilful use of the notion, however, has also ensured that this result is not automatically achieved. (See, for example, Cass. Soc. 27 nov. 1964, *G.P.* 1965, 1.133. In another amusing case the plaintiff, a well-known impresario, sued for the loss of the services of his leading tenor, who was injured by the defendant's negligence. The claim was rejected, *inter alia*, on the ground that the fall in takings '... peut dépendre de multiples circonstances ou incidents autre que la défaillance d'un interprète de talent'. Similarly Bruxelles, 22 janv. 1955,9 *Rev. crit.jur.Belge* (1955), 185 – an almost identical case involving the same singer and the same defendant.) Thus the more clear and meritorious cases seem to succeed while the more obviously frivolous claims are discouraged. The case-law, however, is very rich, and not all the decisions are always easily reconcilable with one another.

8. Cour de cassation
Chambre Civile, 13 fév. 1923
Lejars c. Consorts Templier
(D.P. 1923,1.52)

Arrêt

La Cour:–Sur la première branche du moyen unique: – Attendu que Templier ayant été blessé mortellement par un cheval qui appartenait à Lejars, L'arrêt attaqué (Paris, 21 janv. 1914) a condamné celui-ci, par confirmation du jugement, à payer aux trois fils et à la fille de Templier une indemnité comprenant, en outre du préjudice matériel, le dommage moral résultant de la douleur qu'éprouvent les enfants par la mort de leur père; qu'en statuant ainsi il n'a point violé l'art. 1382 CC visé au moyen; qu'en effet, cet article, d'après lequel quiconque par sa faute cause à autrui un dommage est obligé de le réparer, s'applique, par la généralité de ses termes, aussi bien au dommage moral qu'au dommage matériel; que, dès lors, la première branche du moyen n'est pas fondée;

Sur la seconde branche: – Attendu que l'arrêt attaqué déclare que les enfants de Templier ont été atteints dans leurs plus légitimes et plus chères affections et que les éléments de la cause permettent de déterminer l'importance de l'indemnité; que ces déclarations sont souveraines;

Par ces motifs, rejette.

9. Cour de cassation
Chambre Civile, 27 juil. 1937
Métenier c. Epoux Luce
(D.P. 1938,1.5)

La Cour: – Sur le premier moyen pris dans sa première branche: – Vu l'art. 1382 CC; – Attendu que le demandeur d'une indemnité délictuelle ou quasi-délictuelle doit justifier, non d'un dommage quelconque, mais de la lésion certaine d'un intérêt légitime, juridiquement protégé; – Attendu que, le sieur Sailly ayant été renversé et tué par un taxi-automobile que conduisait François Métenier, le tribunal de commerce de la Seine accorda deux indemnités, l'une de 15,000 fr. à la demoiselle Roussin, avec laquelle la victime vivait maritalement, l'autre de 10,000 fr. aux époux Luce, dont la femme était la fille naturelle reconnue de Sailly et de sa concubine, ces deux indemnités étaient mises à la charge de Métenier père, civilement responsable, en tant que commettant, du dommage causé par son fils; que, sur appel principal formé par Métenier père et sur appel incident des époux Luce, reprenant l'instance engagée par leur mère et belle-mère, décédée dans l'intervalle, la Cour de Paris (arrêt du 9 nov. 1932), confirmant la décision des premiers juges en ce qui concerne tant la responsabilité de Métenier que l'indemnité allouée aux époux Luce, mais la réformant pour le surplus, condamna Métenier père à payer: 1° la somme de 10,000 fr. aux époux Luce, pour réparation du dommage moral à eux causé personnellement par la mort de leur père et beau-père naturel, ainsi que pour remboursement des frais funéraires; 2° la somme de 20,000 fr. aux mêmes époux Luce, la dame Luce étant prise ici en qualité d'héritière de sa mère naturelle, la demoiselle Roussin, et cela en réparation du préjudice matériel causé à celle-ci par la mort de Sailly; que cette décision est fondée, d'abord sur la durée et la continuité des relations des concubins, puis sur l'existence d'une fille naturelle, par eux reconnue, élevée et entretenue à frais communs jusqu'à l'époque de son mariage, enfin sur la contribution apportée par Sailly aux besoins de la vie commune, auxquels il affectait la majeure partie de ses salaires; – Attendu que le pourvoi, se référant uniquement à la seconde de ces condamnations, reproche à l'arrêt attaqué d'avoir alloué une indemnité à la demoiselle Roussin à raison de l'accident causé à son concubin, le sieur Sailly, alors qu'il n'existait entre eux aucun lien de droit, de parenté ou d'alliance, et que les relations qui les unissaient avaient un caractère immoral, et d'avoir ainsi violé les art. 1382 et 1384 CC et 7 de la loi du 20 avr. 1810; – Attendu que le concubinage demeure, en toute occurrence, quelles que soient ses modalités et sa durée, une situation de fait qui ne saurait être génératrice de droits au profit des concubins et vis-à-vis des tiers; – Attendu, en effet, que les relations établies par le concubinage ne peuvent, à raison de leur irrégularité même, présenter la valeur d'intérêts légitimes, juridiquement protégés; que, susceptibles de créer des obligations à la charge des concubins, elles sont impuissantes à leur conférer des droits à l'encontre d'autrui, et notamment contre l'auteur responsable de l'accident survenu à l'un d'eux; que, spécialement, la créance d'aliments de la concubine, qui, du vivant du concubin, n'était que naturelle, ne saurait servir de base, au jour de l'accident et du décès, à une créance civile, s'affirmant par l'exercice, contre l'auteur du dommage, d'une action en responsabilité; d'où il suit qu'en statuant comme il l'a fait, l'arrêt attaqué a violé le texte susvisé;

Par ces motifs, et sans qu'il y ait lieu d'examiner ni la seconde branche du premier moyen, ni le deuxième moyen, casse... mais seulement en ce qui concerne l'indemnité de 20,000 fr. allouée aux époux Luce, du chef de la demoiselle Roussin, la dame Luce étant prise en qualité d'héritière de sa mère...; renvoie devant la Cour d'appel d'Amiens.

10. **Cour de cassation**
Chambre Mixte, 27 fév. 1970
Veuve Gaudras c. *Dangereux*
(D. 1970,201)

Arrêt

La Cour; – Sur le moyen unique; – Vu l'art. 1382 CC; – Attendu que
ce texte ordonnant que l'auteur de tout fait ayant causé un dommage à
autrui sera tenu de le réparer, n'exige pas, en cas de décès, l'existence
d'un lien de droit entre le défunt et le demandeur en indemnisation; –
Attendu que l'arrêt attaqué, statuant sur la demande de la dame
Gaudras en réparation du préjudice résultant pour elle de la mort de
son concubin Paillette, tué dans un accident de la circulation dont
Dangereux avait été jugé responsable, a infirmé le jugement de
première instance qui avait fait droit à cette demande en retenant que
ce concubinage offrait des garanties de stabilité et ne présentait pas de
caractère délictueux, et a débouté ladite dame Gaudras de son action,
au seul motif que le concubinage ne crée pas de droit entre les
concubins ni à leur profit vis-à-vis des tiers ; qu'en subordonnant ainsi
l'application de l'art. 1382 à une condition qu'il ne contient pas, la Cour
d'appel a violé le texte susvisé;

Par ces motifs, casse…, renvoie devant la Cour d'appel de Reims.

Note by M. le conseiller R. Combaldieu

(1 et 2) Enfin, voici la solution tant désirée par les juristes, les
praticiens, les plaideurs, les sociologues, voire les simples obser-
vateurs: la Cour de cassation, fidèle à sa mission, vient d'unifier sa
jurisprudence, restée longtemps divisée, relativement aux droits de la
concubine, à la suite du décès accidentel de son compagnon.

Souligner la portée pratique considérable de cet arrêt semble bien
inutile, comme semble inutile également le rappel des deux thèses
apparemment irréductibles qui s'affrontaient dans tous nos prétoires, à
quelque niveau que l'on se plaçât. Au sein de la Cour de cassation
elle-même, une profonde divergence de vues – une des plus graves
qu'elle ait connue – s'était fait jour entre la jurisprudence de la
deuxième Chambre Civile, appelée à juger les affaires de responsabilité civile et celle de la Chambre Criminelle, appelée quant à elle, à
statuer sur les demandes d'indemnisation formées par voie de

constitution de partie civiles par les victimes d'infractions. Alors que la concubine se voyait inexorablement repoussée par la première, elle se voyait, au contraire – sous réserve de certaines restrictions – accueillie par la seconde. De telle sorte que c'était, en définitive, de la nature – civile ou répressive – de la juridiction saisie que dépendait l'issue du procès. Plaideurs et praticiens comprenaient mal un résultat aussi déroutant, qui était determiné essentiellement par une manoeuvre d'aiguillage.

Les juges du fond eux-mêmes étaient – on le conçoit – dans l'embarras le plus grand. Non certes, qu'ils n'aient eu sur ce problème leur propre opinion, qu'ils s'efforçaient naturellement de faire triompher dans leurs décisions. Il n'en demeure pas moins que leur perplexité était grande, s'ils avaient le désir – légitime en soi – que leur décision subisse avec succès l'épreuve des voies de recours. Et dans maint petit tribunal de province, ne comportant qu'une seule chambre, composée de trois magistrats, inconfortable – il faut bien en convenir – était la position de ces derniers, obligés qu'ils étaient de juger alternativement affaires civiles et affaires pénales: devaient-ils brûler le lendemain au pénal ce qu'ils avaient adoré la veille au civil, ce qui était évidemment illogique, mais efficace quant à l'issue définitive du procès, ou, au contraire, devaient-ils persévérer dans leur opinion, quelle qu'elle fût, ce qui était la seule solution logique et psychologiquement valable, mais, par contre, une solution frappée d'inefficacité et sans portée pratique?

Bien sûr, des arguments étaient avancés de part et d'autre pour tenter de justifier des courants de jurisprudence aussi divergents: la Chambre Civile exigeait, on le sait, pour accorder une indemnité à la victime, qu'il y ait eu 'atteinte à un intérêt légitime juridiquement protégé', formule qui sonne bien certe, mais reste, au fond, assez creuse, équivoque et plutôt ésotérique et contre laquelle une partie de la doctrine s'est élevée parfois en termes assez vifs. La Chambre Criminelle, de son côté, a tenté de justifier son libéralisme par des arguments marginaux: l' autonomie et la spécificité du droit pénal, l'exercice de l'action civile tel que le réglementent les arts. 2 et 3 du code de procédure pénale; mais ces arguments ne paraissent pas décisifs et ne semblent avoir véritablement convaincu personne. Par contre, la Chambre Criminelle avait pris un solide appui sur le sempiternel art. 1382 CC, dont la merveilleuse concision n'est plus à vanter: elle faisait valoir que les termes généraux de l'art. 1382 ne font aucune distinction, pour accorder réparation, quant au lien qui unissait la victime décédée dans l'accident et la personne sollicitant la réparation.

Subordonner l'application de l'art. 1382 à une condition qu'il n'exprime pas, à savoir l'existence d'un lien de droit entre le défunt et le demandeur en indemnisation, c'est ajouter au texte de loi et formuler une exigence qui ne repose sur aucune base légale; pourquoi vouloir distinguer, en effet, là où la loi elle-même ne distingue pas? Telle était la motivation essentielle de cette jurisprudence répressive: on la trouve dans de nombreux arrêts de la Chambre Criminelle et spécialement dans celui du 20 janv. 1966 (D. 1966,184, et notre rapport); ce dernier arrêt, d'ailleurs, qui statuait dans un cas où le concubinage se doublait d'un adultére, en dressant une barrière et en manœuvrant un frein envers ce qui eût constitué l'outrance d'une jurisprudence, a rassuré les timides et les a ralliés à sa doctrine; cet effort, même modeste, de rapprochement entre deux points de vue apparemment irréductibles, a contribué, semble-t-il, à l'unification de la jurisprudence, en ce domaine.

Toutes ces incertitudes, tous ces flottements vont disparaître désormais – du moins, il faut l'espérer – à la suite de l'arrêt que vient de rendre la Chambre Mixte. Il y a lieu de s'en félieiter: car, la certitude de la règle de droit est au moins aussi importante que le fond même de la règle. Certains ont pu même soutenir sans paradoxe qu'une jurisprudence constante – fût-elle erronée – offre moins de dangers qu'une jurisprudence flottante et incertaine.

11. Cour d'appel de Colmar
Chambre détachée à Metz, 20 avril 1955
Football Club de Metz c. Wiroth
(D. 1956,723)

Arrêt

La Cour; – Attendu que le Football Club de Metz (F.C.M.) est régulièrement appelant d'un jugement en date du 22 févr. 1951 du tribunal de première instance de Metz, qui a rejeté sa demande en dommages-intérèts contre Wiroth, auteur responsable du décès, survenu le 13 avr. 1948 au cours d'un accident de la circulation, du joueur professionnel Kemp, lié par contrat au F.C.M., aux motifs que le préjudice allégué n'était pas certain en ce qui concerne la perte, par le

club, de l'indemnité de transfert de ce joueur ainsi que l'obligation de
pourvoir à son remplacement en exposant des frais élevés: qu'aucun
lien de causalité directe n'était prouvé entre la perte du joueur et la
diminution des recettes du club; qu'il expose que par jugement du
tribunal correctionnel de Thionville du 3 déc. 1948, confirmé par arrêt
de cette cour du 30 juin 1949, Wiroth a été déclaré responsable des
conséquences de l'accident ayant entraîné la mort de Kemp dans la
proportion de trois quarts, un quart restant à la charge de la victime;
que Kemp, joueur professionnel de football, était lié au F.C.M. par
contrat du 25 oct. 1945, souscrit par les parties pour la durée de la
saison sportive, mais renouvelé et enregistré chaque année auprès de la
Fédération française de football selon les règles strictes du statut
professionnel organisé et contrôlé par elle; que la perte d'un joueur,
engagé *intuitu personae*, et surtout d'un professionnel de la valeur de
Kemp, a occasionné au club appelant un préjudice direct dans
l'organisation de sa saison sportive ainsi que dans les résultats
techniques et financiers qu'il pouvait attendre de la collaboration de ce
joueur; que selon les statuts de la Fédération un joueur professionnel
ne peut changer de club que dans des conditions strictement
réglementées, que notamment le nouveau club est tenu de verser à
l'ancien une indemnité de transfert; que divers clubs (Reims et Stade
français) s'étaient intéressés à Kemp et avaient offert au F.C.M., en cas
d'accord pour le transfert, une indemnité de 2 millions de fr.; que
cependant le F.C.M. avait estimé ces offres insuffisantes en raison de la
valeur technique de Kemp, qui était ailier gauche naturel, et de sa
notoriété de vedette tant en France qu'au Luxembourg, dont il était
originaire; qu'à la suite de la perte de Kemp, qui marquait d'habitude
une grande proportion de buts, les résultats sportifs du club s'en
ressentirent, ainsi que les recettes des matchs; que lors du décès de
Kemp, le F.C.M. était classé 10ᵉ sur 18 en division nationale, qu'à la
fin de la saison 1948–49 il était tombé à la 16ᵉ place, puis à la 18ᵉ place
à la fin de la saison 1949–50, et fut expulsé de la division nationale
pour être relégué en deuxième division; que pour s'adjoindre de
nouveaux joueurs de la classe de Kemp, le F.C.M., qui perdait déjà
l'indemnité de transfert pour cette vedette, devait décaisser une forte
somme pour obtenir un remplaçant; qu'ainsi la preuve de son
préjudice étant rapportée, le F.C.M. peut prétendre à en obtenir
réparation; qu'il conclut: 'recevoir l'appel en la forme; au fond, y
faisant droit, infirmer le jugement entrepris: déclarer le F.C.M. non
seulement recevable mais encore bien fondé en sa demande quant au

principe: dire que Wiroth doit réparer le préjudice personnel, direct et certain subi par le F.C.M. en conséquence de l'accident du 13 avr. 1948 et en tout cas jusqu'à concurrence des trois quarts'; Attendu que Wiroth réplique que l'autorité de la chose jugée au pénal entre les parties s'oppose à une nouvelle demande du F.C.M. ayant le même objet et la même cause, le tribunal correctionnel ayant déclaré irrecevable la demande basée sur le délit d'homicide involontaire de Wiroth, faute de lien direct entre l'infraction et le préjudice allégué qui résulte de la rupture du contrat de travail qui liait le F.C.M. à son joueur Kemp; qu'il plaide subsidiairement que le F.C.M. ne justifie d'un préjudice ni direct ni certain éprouvé par lui du fait de la mort accidentelle de Kemp, auquel il était lié par un contrat de travail de durée indéterminée qui, conformément à la loi, pouvait être résilié à tout moment par Kemp sans indemnité; que le préjudice allégué par le F.C.M. en raison de la perte de la valeur de transfert du joueur Kemp et de sa valeur de remplacement est en tout cas purement eventuel et ne saurait donner lieu à réparation: que le préjudice invoqué du chef d'une diminution de recettes des matchs à la suite de la disparition de Kemp n'est pas établi, en l'absence de toute relation de cause à effet certaine et directe entre le décès de Kemp et les pertes alléguées: que très subsidiairement il y aurait toujours lieu de tenir compte, en ce qui concerne le principe de responsabilité de Wiroth, si le préjudice direct et certain subi par le F.C.M. était établi, de ce que la victime Kemp a concouru pour une part an moins égale à un quart à la réalisation du dommage causé par l'accident du 13 avr. 1948; qu'il conclut: 'déclarer le Football Club de Metz mal fondé en son appel, l'en débouter, confirmer le jugement entrepris, mais, l'émondant, déclarer le Football Club de Metz irrecevable en sa demande: subsidiairement, le déclarer en tout cas mal fondé dans toutes ses demande, fins et conclusions, l'en débouter':

Vu les pièces de la procédure, ensemble le jugement déféré et les mémoires des parties auxquels la cour se réfère expressément pour plus ample exposé des faits et moyens;

Attendu que toute personne, même morale, victime d'un dommage, quelle qu'en soit la nature, a droit à en obtenir réparation de celui qui l'a causé par sa faute ou par le fait de la chose dont il avait la garde; – Attendu que l'employeur de la victime, déclaré irrecevable en sa constitution de partie civile dans l'instance pénale dirigée contre le tiers responsable, du fait que son préjudice trouve sa source non dans le délit, fondement de l'action correctionnelle, mais dans le contrat qu'il avait passé avec la victime, est recevable à faire valoir son préjudice dans une instance civile séparée; qu'en effet, le jugement d'irrecevabilité de la constitution de partie civile ne s'applique qu'à la voie de procédure suivie, mais ne statue pas sur le fond du droit; que le moyen opposé de ce chef à la présente action est donc à écarter; – Attendu que pour rejeter la demande de dommages-intérêts du F.C.M. les premiers juges ont estimé qu'aucun lien de causalité entre la perte de son joueur et le préjudice allégué n'était établi; – Attendu, en effet, que le F.C.M. n'a été tenu à aucune prestation aux ayants droit de son employé en raison du contrat de travail liant les parties; – Attendu que le contrat de joueur professionnel du 25 oct. 1945, signé pour la durée de la saison de jeu 1945 – 46 par référence expresse aux statuts et règlements de la Ligue de football et de la Fédération francaise de football, a été renouvelé chaque année jusqu'au décès de Kemp; qu'il est certain qu'à l'expiration de chaque période saisonnière les deux parties pouvaient reprendre leur liberté; – Attendu que le footbal étant un jeu d'équipe, chaque joueur a un rôle fonctionnel à remplir; que la cohésion du travail en équipe exige une longue mise au point par un entraînement régulier et progressif des joueurs sous l'égide d'entraîneurs appointés par le club; que la pratique de ce sport, nécessitant des terrains de jeu, du matériel et du personnel, le financement de ces dépenses, notamment celles de fonctionnement des neuf équipes de joueurs amateurs du F.C.M., est réalisé par les recettes encaissées lors des matchs de l'équipe professionnelle; – Attendu que Kemp fut engagé en 1945 comme joueur professionnel par le F.C.M. en raison de sa valeur, de sa notoriété, de sa vigueur physique et de ses qualités techniques déjà affirmées; qu'en 1948, par son entraînement au sein de l'equipe, il en était devenu une vedette; que son jeu d'ailier gauche était facilité par ses dispositions de gaucher naturel; qu'il était ainsi un élément particulièrement efficace de l'équipe, assurant une place difficile de la ligne des avants; – Attendu que sa disparition a occasionné un trouble certain dans l'organisation technique de l'équipe, privée d'un joueur de qualité exceptionnelle; que tous les efforts déployés par le club au point de vue de sa formation et de son entraînement, ainsi que les dépenses y afférentes, se sont perdus avec le décès de ce joueur; que la désorganisation de l'équipe, conséquence directe de la mort de Kemp, est une source de préjudice certain, dont le F.C.M. est en droit de demander réparation; – Attendu qu'en outre, l'équipe professionnelle d'un club de football, en raison de la réglementation stricte de la Fédération nationale relative aux indemnités de transfert qu'un club cessionnaire doit verser au club cédant selon une procédure déterminée aux statuts, représente une valeur patrimoniale; qu'en cédant un de ses joueurs à une autre association, le club encaisse un capital parfois élevé; qu'en engageant de même un joueur professionnel d'une autre équipe, il est obligé de débourser des sommes importantes; que s'il est vrai qu'à la tin de la saison, à l'expiration de son contrat à durée indéterminée, le joueur peut se dégager de son engagement, il n'en demeure pas moins que normalement le joueur professionnel, surtout s'il est arrivé à une place de vedette, sollicite on bien le renouvellement de son contrat, ou bien son transfert à un autre club; que le décès d'un joueur professionnel à la suite d'un accident, dans l'hypothèse de la prorogation du contrat, prive le club d'un elément technique qu'il entend conserver pour maintenir la valeur de son équipe, et. dans le cas d'un transfert envisagé, de l'encaissement d'une indemnité substantielle; que l'impossibilité de réaliser, par suite du décès du joueur, la perception de l'indemnité de transfert, constitue une perte de chance entraînant également un préjudice certain; qu'en l'espèce, Kemp, joueur d'une grande notoriété et faisant figure de vedette de l'équipe, n'avait prévisiblement, compte tenu de son âge et de sa vigueur physique, aucun motif d'abandonner sa carrière de joueur professionnel; que l'éventualité d'une résiliation pure et simple de son contrat n'est établie d'aucune façon; que le F.C.M. justifie d'offres reçues d'autres clubs pour ce joueur en 1948; que quelle que soit la solution choisie par le club et par Kemp, – renouvellement du contrat ou transfert, – la perte de cette dernière possibilité prive le club d'une valeur patrimoniale certaine à la suite de l'accident dont l'intimé doit répondre; que l'évaluation de ce préjudice ne saurait évidemment être la contre-valeur de l'indemnité de transfert dont la réalisation restait cependant soumise à des aléas; que néanmoins ce chef de préjudice devra être chiffré en lui-même; – Attendu, par contre, que le F.C.M. n'établit pas qu'il a dû pourvoir au remplacement de Kemp, ni le préjudice, distinct des chefs de préjudice admis ci-dessus, qui en serait résulté pour lui; que la baisse des recettes du club n'est pas davantage prouvée et, le serait-elle, le lien de causalité avec le décès de Kemp ferait défaut; – Attendu que le partage de responsabilité opéré dans l'instance pénale entre Kemp et Wiroth dans la proportion de un quart à la victime et trois quarts à l'intimé, est *res inter alios acta* à l'égard de l'appelant et reste sans influence sur l'évaluation du préjudice direct et personnel causé à l'employeur de la victime par le tiers responsable de l'accident mortel; qu'à défaut d'éléments d'exonération intrinsèques qui ne sont ni allégués ni prouvés, aucun partage de responsabilité ne saurait jouer en la présente instance;

Par ces motifs, déclare le Football Club de Metz recevable et bien fondé quant au principe de son appel; infirme le jugement entrepris; dit que Wiroth est tenu de réparer le préjudice subi par l'appelant en conséquence de l'accident du 13 avr. 1948 en suite de la mort de Kemp; renvoie la procédure en première instance pour être statué sur le montant; condamne l'intimé aux dépens d'appel.

CAUSATION

With the exception of a few authors, the French have, on the whole, refused to adopt the clear distinction between cause in fact and cause in law which is so prevalent in German and Anglo-American law. Case 12 however, offers a good illustration of the proposition that even in French law the defendant's conduct must be a condition of the plaintiff's hurt before it can rank as one of its (legal) causes.

The next two cases (cases 13 and 14) deal with the problem of plurality of causes, which, invariably, takes up most of the section that French books devote to problems of causation. The plaintiff's hurt may thus be due to the conduct of more than one person; to his own conduct, coupled with the defendant's fault or, finally, to a 'force majeure' coupled with the conduct (fait fautif ou non) of the defendant. Some older cases, of which the *Lamoricière* (case 13) is, perhaps, the best known example, took the view that liability for the result should somehow be apportioned between the two (or more) causes (see also, Cass. civ. 13 mars, 1957, *J.C.P.* 1957,2.10084). The Gueffier case, on the other hand (case 14) is more characteristic of the present-day tendency to hold each cause responsible for the entire harm. The whole problem is too difficult to summarise in so short a space, and the reader would do well to consult vol. I, chapter 3, for a brief account in English; and Professor Starck's treatise (*Droit Civil: obligations* (1972), pp. 272 et seq.) for an excellent account in French.

The next set of cases (15–19) deal with the problem of mutually exclusive but equally possible causes which in France (but not in England) has occupied the courts with some measure of frequency in the context of hunting accidents. Most of these cases are fully annotated by French commentators and there is a brief but good discussion of them in English by Professor Catala (in 39 *Tul.L.Rev.* 747 et seq.), so little need be added at this stage. (For a comparative sketch, see vol. I, chapter 4) Suffice it to note: (a) how the courts managed through a series of fictions (common garde; common fault etc.) to avoid the harsh result they used to reach in days gone by; and (b) how the emergence of modern insurance practice has affected the development of the law. The decision of the Court of Grenoble (case 18) (and Professor Azard's note which, for lack of space, we have not managed to reproduce here) deserve special attention. Case 19 marks the end of this development.

The last two cases (cases 20 and 21) deal with particular aspects of causation.

12. Cour de cassation
Chambre Sociale, 7 mai 1943
Léo c. *Etablissements Milliat frères*
(S. 1943,1.106)

Arrêt

La Cour; – Sur le moyen, pris de la violation des art. 1382, 1383, CC, 7 de la loi du 20 avril 1810, 64, liv. 2, tit. 2, C. trav., défaut et contradiction de motifs; – Attendu que Léo, Anna, âgée de 13 ans 1/2, de nationalité italienne, ayant été victime, le 20 juil. 1936, d'un accident, générateur d'incapacité permanente de travail, en manipulant de lourdes caisses aux Etablissements Milliat, où elle était employée, son père, Léo, Gennaro, agissant ès qualité d'administrateur légal de sa fille, a introduit contre ces établissements une action en dommages-intérêts, fondée, au sens des art. 1382 et 1383, CC, sur la faute commise en imposant à cette fillette un tel travail et sur celle consistant dans le fait de l'avoir embauchée en violation des dispositions d'ordre public, relatives à la carte d'identité que doit posséder tout travailleur étranger: – Attendu que la Cour d'appel, ayant écarté cette dernière prétention pour se borner, avant dire droit, à voir déterminer par expertise ordonnée, si le travail imposé dépassait les forces de l'enfant et était effectué dans des conditions si défectueuses que l'employeur dût être constitué en faute, le pourvoi reproche à l'arrêt attaqué de décider que la faute commise par un employeur, en embauchant un travailleur étranger, non muni de la carte d'identité d'étranger, malgre l'interdiction édictée par l'art. 64, C. trav., précité, ne pouvait, contrairement à l'opinion des premiers juges, justifier à elle seule l'application de l'art. 1382, CC, motif pris de ce que cette faute n'avait pas été la cause du dommage éprouvé, alors que, sans ladite faute, l'accident, survenu à la victime, n'aurait pu avoir lieu: – Mais attendu que la présence de la jeune Léo dans les

Etablissements Milliat, en vertu d'un contrat illégal, ne saurait en la cause constituer une faute de la part de ceux-ci qu' autant que cette présence aurait été génératrice de l'accident, alors qu'elle n'en a été que l'occasion; qu'en effet, ce n'est pas parce que cette enfant, qui avait l'âge légal, était étrangère et se trouvait dans une situation irrégulière au point de vue de la protection du travail national, qu'elle courait plus de risques qu'un autre ouvrier ou était fatalement exposée par son entrée même à l'usine à y accomplir des travaux au-dessus de ses forces; d'où il suit qu'en statuant comme elle l'a fait, la Cour d'appel, par son arrêt qui est motivé et ne contient aucune contradiction, a légalement justifié sa décision, sans violer aucun des textes visés au moyen; – Rejette le pourvoi formé contre l'arrêt de la Cour de Lyon du 19 juin 1910, etc.

13. Cour de cassation
Chambre Civile, 19 juin 1951 (2 arrêts)
(D. 1951,717)

1er Arrêt

La Cour; – Attendu que l'appel formé par les Transports maritimes de l'Etat contre le jugement du tribunal de commerce de Marseille du 11 juil. 1947 était exclusivement dirigé contre les consorts Brossette; que, devant la cour, ils n'ont pris aucune conclusion contre la Compagnie générale transatlantique, qui a conclu elle-même à la confirmation du jugement; qu'en tant qu'il est dirigé contre ladite compagnie le pourvoi doit être déclaré irrecevable; – Déclare irrecevable le pourvoi formé par les Transports maritimes de l'Etat à l'égard de la Compagnie générale transatlantique; Sur le premier moyen: – Attendu que le paquebot *Lamoricière*, qui se rendait d'Alger à Marseille, a été, le 9 janv. 1942, assailli par une très violente tempête au large des îles Baléares, et a péri corps et biens; que la dame Brossette, veuve d'un passager disparu au cours du naufrage, agissant tant en son nom personnel que comme tutrice légale de son fils mineur, et Bastard, agissant en qualité de subrogé, tuteur des enfants d'un premier lit du défunt, ont sur le fondement des art. 1382 et 1384, § 1er, CC, assigné la Compagnie générale transatlantique et les Transports maritimes de l'Etat à l'effet d'obtenir la réparation du dommage par eux éprouvé; que, par jugement du 11 juil. 1947, le tribunal de commerce de Marseille a écarté l'application de l'art. 1384, a mis hors de cause la

Compagnie générale transatlantique, et, par application de l'art. 1382, a condamné les Transports maritimes de l'Etat à réparer l'intégralité du préjudice subi par les consorts Brossette: que, sur appel, la Cour d'Aix, a, par arrêt du 5 janv. 1949, confirmé le jugement en ce qu'il avait mis l'armateur hors de cause décidé que les Transports maritimes de l'Etat n'avaient commis aucune faute de nature à engager leur responsabilité sur le terrain de l'art. 1382, admis qu'ils étaient par contre tenus en principe, en vertu de l'art. 1384, § 1er, de réparer le préjudice causé, mais les a exonérés à · concurrence des quatre cinquièmes de ce préjudice, à raison de ce que le sinistre était dû principalement à des causes étrangères qui ne leur étaient pas imputables; – Attendu qu'il est reproché à l'arrêt attaqué d'avoir retenu la compétence des tribunaux de l'ordre judiciaire pour condamner l'Etat français, en tant que gardien du navire, à réparer, au moins partiellement, le dommage subi par les ayants cause de la victime; – Mais attendu que si les contrats de charte-partie et de gérance conclus en application de l'art. 21 de la loi du 11 juil. 1938 ont eu pour effet de transférer à l'Etat, avec ses profits et ses risques, l'exploitation de la flotte marchande, et de créer un véritable service public, tous les litiges nés entre l'Etat affréteur et les tiers ne ressortissent pas pour autant à la compétence de la juridiction administrative; qu'à bon droit l'arrêt attaqué a admis que le contrat de transport passé entre le sieur Brossette et l'armateur-gérant ne différait pas de celui que le premier aurait passé avec un armateur ordinaire et que, vis-à-vis· des tiers, l'exploitation du navire par les Transports maritimes de l'Etat était soumise aux règles du droit privé et de la compétence judiciaire; – D'où il suit que le moyen n'est pas fondé.

Sur le deuxième moyen: – Attendu que le pourvoi fait encore grief à l'arrêt d'avoir admis que la responsabilité du fait des choses existait en droit maritime, et que les Transports maritimes de l'Etat devaient, en qualité de gardiens·du navire, réparer le dommage causé aux ayants cause d'un passager disparu; – Mais attendu que l'art. 1384, § 1er, formule une règle générale qui s'applique à la navigation maritime toutes les fois qu'une disposition spéciale de la loi ne l'a pas, explicitement ou implicitement écartée; que la Cour d'appel a légitimement décidé que les Transports maritimes de l'Etat, qui avaient conservé l'usage et le contrôle du *Lamoricière* en étaient les gardiens au sens de l'art. 1384; que, malgré le pouvoir de direction dont il dispose à bord, le capitaine reste le préposé de l'armateur, et que cette qualité est incompatible avec celle de gardien du navire; que vainement le pourvoi relève que l'action propre des ayants causes de la victime ne saurait aboutir, par le jeu de l'art. 1384, § 1er, à une réparation plus étendue que celle à laquelle la victime elle-même aurait eu droit en vertu de son contrat; qu'il est en effet loisible aux intéressés de renoncer à la stipulation faite en leur faveur par le défunt au moment de la conclusion du contrat de passage, et de se placer sur le terrain de la responsabilité délictuelle; qu'il suit de là que le moyen n'est pas fondé;

Sur le troisième moyen: – Attendu, enfin, que le pourvoi reproche à l'arrêt attaqué d'avoir, tout en relevant dans les circonstances de la cause les éléments de la force majeure et du fait du prince, refusé d'exonérer de toute responsabilité les Transports maritimes de l'Etat, considérés comme gardiens du navire; – Mais attendu que des constatations souveraines de l'arrêt il résulte que le sinistre était dû principalement à 'une tempête d'une extrême violence à caractère de cyclone' et à l'attribution au navire, par voie d'autorité, d'un charbon défectueux et peut-être insuffisant; que cependant le dommage subi par les consorts Brossette ne procède pas exclusivement de causes étrangères au fait de la chose que les Transports maritimes avaient sous leur garde; que, par suite, la Cour d'appel a pu déduire de ses constatations que la réparation dudit dommage devait être mise pour un cinquième à la charge des Transports maritimes de l'Etat; qu'il s'ensuit que le moyen n'est pas fondé.

Par ces motifs, rejette.

2° Arrêt

La Cour; – Sur le premier moyen: – Attendu que devant la Cour d'Aix, saisie de l'appel du jugement qui avait mis à la charge des Transports maritimes de l'Etat la réparation intégrale du dommage qui leur était causé par la mort de leur mari et père, disparu le 9 janv. 1942 à bord du *Lamoricière*, les consorts Brossette ont conelu en premier lieu à l'application de l'art. 1384, § 1er CC contre les Transports maritimes de l'Etat et la Compagnie génerale transatlantique, pris en qualité de gardiens du navire, et, en second lieu, à la condamnation des mêmes, en vertu de l'art. 1382 CC pour diverses lautes relevées à leur charge; que la cour (Aix, 5 janv. 1949) a confirmé la mise hors de cause de la Compagnie générale transatlantique et a réformé le jugement au motif qu'aucune faute caractérisée ne pouvait être retenue à la charge du capitaine, mais que les Transports maritimes de l'Etat devaient répondre en principe, comme gardiens du navire, du dommage causé aux consorts Brossette; que l'arrêt a cependant admis que le sinistre était dû avant tout à 'une tempête d'une extrême violence à caractère de cyclone', ainsi qu' à l'attribution au navire, par voie d'autorité, d'un charbon défectueux et peut-être insuffisant; – Attendu qu'il est reproché à l'arrêt attaqué d'avoir écarté l'application de l'art. 1382 sans répondre à divers chefs de conclusions par lesquels les consorts Brossette invoquaient une réparation défectueuse des portes de soute du navire, ainsi que la réception et l'utilisation d'un combustible de mauvaise qualité et de quantité insuffisante; – Mais attendu que l'arrêt, qui faisait droit aux conclusions principales des consorts Brossette en retenant la responsabilité de l'affréteur, pris en sa qualité de gardien du navire, n'était pas tenu d'examiner le moyen tendant à établir des fautes à la charge du transporteur ou de ses préposés; que, d'ailleurs, en adoptant les motifs non contraires du jugement, qui s'était placé sur le terrain de l'art. 1382, et en relevant 'qu'il n'apparait pas qu'en l'état des circonstances de l'heure et des servitudes alors imposées á la navigation France-Afrique du Nord, une faute caractérisée au sens de l'art. 1382, soit personnelle et directe, soit procédant du fait du capitaine, leur préposé, ait été démontrée à l'encontre des Transports de l'Etat', l'arrêt attaqué a, en tant que de besoin, répondu aux conclusions prises par les intimés;

Sur le deuxième moyen: – Attendu que le pourvoi fait grief à l'arrêt d'avoir, tout en reconnaissant fondée l'action des consorts Brossette sur la base de l'art. 1384, § 1er, CC, limité néanmoins la responsabilité de l'Etat au cinquième du préjudice causé, motifs pris de ce que la tempête était constitutive d'un cas de force majeure et de ce que la mauvaise fourniture de charbon constituait le fait du prince: – Mais attendu qu'il ressort des énonciations de l'arrêt que la tempête au cours de laquelle le *Lamoricière* a sombré était d'une exceptionnelle violence, et que, de ce caractère, la Cour d'appel a pu déduire l'existence d'une cause étrangère au fait du navire; que, ni le fait qu'au cours d'un précédent voyage le *Lamoricière* avait affronté victorieusement une autre tempête sur la violence de laquelle aucune précision n'est donnée, ni le fait que le 9 janv. 1942, d'autres bâtiments de même classe ont résisté à la fureur des flots, ne sauraient détruire la valeur des constatations et appréciations des juges du fond: qu'enfin, ceux-ci ont pu voir dans l'obligation imposée aux Transpórts maritimes de l'Etat d'accepter et d'utiliser un charbon de mauvaise qualité à peine d'interrompre tout trafic maritime, une autre cause étrangère de nature à faire céder la présomption de responsabilité qui pesait sur eux; qu'ainsi le moyen n'est pas fondé;

Sur le troisième moyen: – Attendu qu'il est enfin reproché à l'arrêt d'avoir exonéré les Transports maritimes de l'Etat des quatre cinquièmes de la responsabilité par eux encourue, au motif que diverses causes étrangères seraient intervenues dans la réalisation du sinistre, alors que, dès l'instant où cette responsabilité ne pouvait être écartée, il était impossible de ne mettre à leur charge qu'une partie de la réparation du dommage; – Mais attendu que la Cour d'appel, qui avait constaté que le dommage subi par les consorts Brossette était dû principalement à des causes étrangères au fait de la chose que les Transports maritimes de l'Etat avaient sous leur garde et qui n'étaient pas imputables à ceux-ci, a pu déduire de ses constatations que la responsabilité dudit dommage devait, à concurrence d'un cinquième seulement, être mise à la charge du transporteur; que, dès lors, en statuant comme il l'a fait, l'arrêt attaqué n'a pas violé les textes visés au moyen et a donné une base légale à sa décision;

Par ces motifs, rejette.

14. Cour de cassation
2ᵉ Chambre Civile, 2 juil. 1969
Gueffier c. Ponthieu
(*G.P.* 1969,2. 311)

Pourvoi en cassation contre un arrêt de la Cour d'appel de Douai du 26 mai 1965.

Arrêt

La Cour, – Sur le moyen unique: – Attendu que, selon l'arrêt confirmatif attaqué, une collision se produisit sur une voie urbaine, entre l'automobile appartenant à Flévet, conduite par le préposé de celui-ci, Copin, et dans laquelle avait pris place Ponthieu, autre préposé de Flévet, et l'automobile qui la croisait, et qui était conduite par Gueffier, son propriétaire; que Ponthieu, blessé, a assigné Gueffier, sur le fondement des art. 1382 et 1384, al. 1ᵉʳ, CC, en réparation du préjudice par lui subi, et a mis en cause la caisse primaire de Sécurité sociale d'Avesnes; – Attendu que Gueffier fait grief à l'arrêt de l'avoir déclaré, en application de l'art. 1384, seul responsable de l'accident, alors que, la cause de l'accident ayant été jugée inconnue, les deux véhicules auraient dû être présumés avoir concouru l'un et l'autre à la réalisation du dommage, et que la collision ayant eu lieu au cours du travail de Ponthieu, ce dernier aurait été privé de la possibilité d'invoquer, contre son chef d'entreprise Flévet, la responsabilité de l'art. 1384, al. 1er, CC, ce qui aurait privé Gueffier du tout recours contre le coauteur de l'accident, et aurait mis Ponthieu dans l'impossibilité d'obtenir une réparation totale de son préjudice, Gueffier étant tenu seulement de sa part virile; – Mais attendu, d'une part, que l'arrêt relève que les circonstances de l'accident étaient indéterminées, et que Gueffier n'avait pas rapporté la preuve d'une cause exonératoire de sa responsabilité; – Attendu, d'autre part, que, dans le cas de concours de responsabilités, chacun des responsables d'un dommage ayant concouru à le causer en entier, doit être condamné, envers la victime, à en assurer l'entière réparation, sans qu'il y ait lieu d'envisager l'eventualité d'un recours à l'égard d'un autre coauteur; que par ce motif de pur droit, substitué à ceux de l'arrêt attaqué, celul-ci se trouve légalement justifié:

Par ces motifs, rejette.

15. Cour de cassation
Chambre Civile, 29 sept. 1941
Dame Bruneau et autres c. *Epoux Bruneau et autres*
(G.P. 1941,437)

La Cour, – Sur le moyen unique: vu l'art. 1382 CC;

Attendu que cet article exige pour son application qu'une faute ait été commise, un dommage éprouvé et que la faute ait été la cause du dommage;

Attendu qu'il résulte des motifs et des qualités de l'arrêt attaqué que la dame Bruneau a été blessée par un plomb de chasse provenant d'un coup de feu parti d'une ligne formée par 3 chasseurs marchant en tirailleurs, battant les haies sous le même alignement, deux d'entre eux étant séparés du troisième par une haie, sans qu'il ait été possible d'établir lequel des trois a tiré: qu'une information ouverte contre eux a été, par ce motif, close par une ordonnance de non-lieu;

Attendu que l'arrêt attaqué les a déclarés tous les trois solidairement responsables des conséquences de cet accident, motif pris de ce qu'en chassant dans les conditions susénoncées, exposés à tirer sans savoir ce qu'il y avait derrière les rideaux de verdure, 'ils avaient créé une zone dangereuse qui leur etait commune', et que 'cette faute était génératrice de leur responsabilité'; qu'au rèste, ils avaient ainsi implicitement accepté le risque des accidents inhérents au mode de chasse auquel ils se livraient;

Mais attendu que seule la faute du chasseur qui a tiré, sans s'assurer qu'il pouvait le faire sans danger, le coup de fusil dont un plomb a atteint la dame Bruneau, a été la cause de l'accident; que la faute retenue comme génératrice de la responsabilité des trois chasseurs et qui aurait consisté à créer une zone dangereuse en chassant en ligne sur un terrain coupé de haies, est sans relation avec le dommage: qu'il suit de là qu'en les déclarant tous les trois solidairement responsables du préjudice subi par la dame Bruneau. la Cour d'appel a condamné deux d'entre eux à réparer un dommage qu'ils n'ont pas causé; qu'elle a ainsi violé le texte de loi susvisé:

Par ces motifs, casse.

16. Cour de cassation
Chambre Civile, 5 juin 1957
Litzinger et autres c. Kintzler, et Thiriet c. Kintzler et autres
(D. 1957,493)

Arrêt

La Cour; – Joint, en raison de leur connexité, les pourvois n°s 1036 Civ. 54 et 1143 Civ. 54;

Sur le moyen unique pris en toutes ses branches de chacun des deux pourvois: – Attend qu'il résulte de l'arrêt confirmatif attaqué (Dijon, 3 mars 1954) que Nicolas, Roger, Cudel, Litzinger, Chauffaut Paul, Chauffaut Jean et Thiriet avaient, le 6 janv. 1952, chassé le chevreuil avec Kintzler; que, vers 16 heures, l'action de chasse était terminée et ce dernier venait de se retirer pour regagner son domicile, lorsque, les sept autres chasseurs ayant convenu de tirer une salve de coups de fusil pour célébrer la clôture de la chasse, il fut atteint, à proximité, par un plomb à l'oeil droit, entrainant une blessure qui lui fit perdre presque entièrement l'usage de cet organe; qu'il est précisé que, selon l'un d'entre eux, les sept chasseurs avaient tiré simultanément. et, suivant un autre, que les coups de fusil étaient partis 'comme une rafale de mitrailleuse'; – Attendu que, saisie de l'action, en responsabilité engagée par la victime, sur la double base des art. 1382 et 1384, al. 1er, CC, contre lesdits chasseurs, la Cour d'appel relève, pour les condamner solidairement entre eux, que 'la cause réelle de l'accident résidait dans l'action concertée des sept défendeurs qui ont participé à un tir qui ne constituait pas un acte normal de chasse, dans des conditions d'imprudence et de maladresse qui leur étaient imputables à tous': – Attendu que la responsabilité personnelle conjointe desdits défendeurs a été ainsi suffisamment et à bon droit déterminée, sans qu'il fût, par suite, aucunement nécessaire, ainsi que le soutient le moyen, d'identifier parmi eux l'auteur du coup de feu ayant occasionné la blessure; qu'en effet, plusieurs individus peuvent par une action concertée, ou même spontanément sous l'effet d'une excitation mutuelle, se livrer à une manifestation dont chacun doit partager la responsabilité des conséquences dommageables, en tant qu'elles procèdent, soit d'un acte unique, auquel tous ont participé, soit d'une pluralité d'actes connexes, que la cohérence dans leur conception et leur exécution ne permet pas de séparer; – Et attendu dès lors qu'il n'importe, en raison de leur caractère surabondant, que par les autres motifs erroniés, tirés de la responsabilité de plein droit du gardien de la chose, l'arrêt déféré, dont la décision est, d'autre part, légalement justifiée, so soit justement exposé aux critiques du pourvoi;

Par ces motifs, rejette les pourvois.

17. Cour d'appel de l'Afrique Equatoriale Française, 5 avr. 1957
Drouin et Gillet c. Mangala
(*J.C.P.* 1957,2.10308)

La Cour; – En la forme; – Attendu que l'appel interjeté par les sieurs Drouin Robert, Agent commercial à Dolisie, et Gillet Henri, fonctionnaire à Brazzaville, suivant requête du 9 novembre 1956 est régulier; – Qu'il y a lieu de le recevoir; – Le reçoit; – Au fond: – En fait: – Attendu que les faits se présentent comme suit: Au mois de juillet 1954, les sieurs Dutey, Gillet et Drouin convinrent d'une partie de chasse à l'éléphant dans la région de Loudima Sibiti. Partis le 10 juillet, les chasseurs, accompagnés de quelques pisteurs dont le nommé Mangala, ne rencontrèrent aucun gibier jusqu'au 12 juillet. Ce jour-là, vers 7 h. 30, ils aperçurent de la route Loudima Sibiti, où ils étaient engagés, un éléphant mâle solitaire à environ 250 mètres de leur groupe à main gauche. Cet animal broutait à ce moment sur le sommet d'une petite colline. Accompagnés de leurs pisteurs, les chasseurs pénétraient dans la brousse et empruntaient la piste 'avec le vent'. Les sieurs Dutey et Gillet ouvraient la marche, suivis de leur personnel. Drouin restait en arrière de la colonne, 'muni de son appareil photographique'. Il était entendu que le sieur Gillet devait avoir le privilège du premier coup de fusil. Au bout de 20 minutes de marche sous les hautes herbes, les chasseurs trouvaient l'éléphant, ils s'approchaient de lui à vingt mètres, la bête était parfaitement visible, Gillet et Dutey se portaient sur son flanc droit pendant que, derrière eux, Drouin essayait de prendre une photo. L'éléphant à ce moment se trouvait dans la partie non brûlée des herbes, alors que la progression des chasseurs s'était effectuée dans la partie brûlée de la brousse; le fusil de Drouin était porté par le pisteur Mangala. Alors que Drouin prenait une photographie, Dutey et Gillet tiraient à peu près simultanément; Gillet tirait sans doute le premier; l'animal touché à la tête accusait le coup et tombait en poussant des barissements. Peu après, il se relevait et dévalait une pente en direction d'un marigot situé à environ 40 mètres du coup de fusil. A ce moment, Drouin reprenait son fusil et, sur les conseils de Dutey, attendait environ une demi-heure, non sans avoir au préalable tiré plusieurs coups de feu sur la bête qui remontait la colline voisine et qui accusait chaque coup de fusil. Les chasseurs à ce moment se trouvaient à une cinquantaine de mètres, dans les grandes herbes. Une demi-heure après l'attente, ils reprenaient la piste fraîche. L'éléphant fut retrouvé un quart d'heure après. Il se trouvant alors à une quarantaine de mètres, à flanc de colline et entièrement visible. Dutey et Drouin tiraient chacun un coup de fusil et atteignaient la bête au flanc droit probablement à hauteur de la tête. C'est alors que, fortement touchée, celle-ci se mettait à tourner en rond. Dutey disait alors: 'allons-y'. Mangala faisait remarquer aux chasseurs le danger de se mettre à la poursuite d'un éléphant blessé; néanmoins ceux-ci prenaient la trace derrière les pisteurs. Ils franchissaient les deux petits marigots qui les séparaient de l'animal. Tout à coup, les deux pisteurs qui les précédaient se jetaient sur le côté en criant: 'Voilà l'éléphant'. L'éléphant se précipitait en effet sur Dutey qui tentait de s'échapper dans la direction opposée, alors que le pisteur Mangala revenait à vive allure sur les deux autres chasseurs en les prévenant à haute voix de la charge de l'animal furieux qui venait dans leur direction; Drouin tirait sans pouvoir l'arrêter; celui-ci se précipitait sur lui qui se jetait sur le côté. Dutey, à ce moment, se trouvant à 5 mètres derrière Drouin: il jetait un cri d'effroi. Drouin, Gillet et peut-être aussi Dutey tiraient plusieurs coups de feu ensemble; l'un de ces coups de fusil atteignait Mangala. L'éléphant abattu, Drouin appelait ses amis, seul Gillet répondait en lui signalant la blessure de Mangala. L'un d'eux portait le pisteur blessé près d'un buisson et revenait près de Dutey qui se plaignait, souffrait et demandait du secours, après avoir été bousculé par la bête furieuse. Il mourait quelques jours plus tard de ses blessures. Selon les déclarations de Mangala, Dutey était son employeur, les blancs qui l'accompagnaient étaient des invités de celui-ci. Drouin et Gillet étaient armés chacun d'une carabine 10,75 tirant à balles blindées. Il est impossible de déterminer quel est le fusil qui a provoqué la blessure de Mangala. – Procédure: – Poursuivis pour coups et blessures involontaires, Drouin et Gillet bénéficiaient, le 25 octobre 1956, d'une ordonnance de non-lieu; – Mangala s'adressa au Tribunal de Brazzaville pour demander à Gillet et Drouin la réparation du préjudice subi par lui; – Le Tribunal de première instance, par jugement du 13 octobre 1956 a dit qu'il était établi à la charge de ceux-ci une faute d'imprudence en relation de cause à effet avec l'accident survenu à Mangala Benoit le 12 juillet 1954; déclaré Drouin et Gillet solidairement responsables de cet accident; – Commis un expert avec mission d'examiner Mangala; donné acte à celui-ci de ce qu'il chiffrera définitivement sa demande au vu du rapport d'expert; condamné Gillet et Drouin à payer une somme de 30,000 francs à titre de provision; réservé les dépens; – Attendu que Drouin et Gillet demandent à la Cour de modifier cette décision au motif que le premier juge a à tort retenu leur responsabilité en l'espèce; qu'ils ne sont en aucune manière responsables de l'accident survenu au sieur Mangala; qu'il échet en conséquence de le débouter de toutes ses demandes, fins et conclusions; – Attendu que pour sa part, Mangala sollicita la confirmation pure et simple de la décision entreprise; – En droit; – Attendu que contrairement à l'opinion du premier juge qui a retenu à tort la faute des appelants, il apparaît que ceux-ci, en se défendant contre la charge de l'éléphant furieux, ont agi dans des conditions nécessaires et normales, et que rien, dans la cause, ne permet d'affirmer qu'ils aient, dans l'emploi de leurs armes, commis une imprudence caractérisée; – Attendu d'autre part que des faits ci-dessus exposés il résulte: 1° que les sieurs Gillet et Drouin avaient convenu de faire ensemble, en compagnie du sieur Dutey, une partie de chasse particulièrement périlleuse; 2° qu'ils avaient tacitement accepté de prendre en commun les risques de cette partie de chasse et de l'emploi d'armes dangereuses par leur nature même; 3° que les carabines, dont ils avaient la garde commune, étaient destinées à la destruction du fauve, qu'ils pouvaient rencontrer, et en cas de danger à la défense commune des chasseurs; – Attendu que l'accident survenu au pisteur Mangala, le 12 juillet 1954, est dû à la réalisation des risques précités; – Attendu que dans l'impossibilité de savoir quelle est l'arme qui a causé le dommage subi par Mangala, il suffit, pour justifier l'application de l'article 1384, § 1er, du Code civil, de constater que le préjudice éprouvé par celui-ci est la conséquence inéluctable de la garde commune des armes utilisées, garde qui comportait des risques acceptés en commun, et qui se sont malheureusement réalisés; – Attendu en conséquence que Mangala est fondé à demander que la responsabilité du préjudice qu'il a subi soit imputable aux sieurs Gillet et Drouin, par application des dispositions de l'article 1384, § 1er du Code civil précité; qu'il échet, d'autre part, confirmer la mesure d'examen médical prononcée par le premier juge et d'allocation d'une provision de 30,000 francs audit Mangala.

Par ces motifs; – Dit et juge que les sieurs Drouin et Gillet sont responsables de l'accident survenu le 12 juillet 1954 au sieur Mangala, par application de l'article 1384, § 1er du Code civil: – Confirme la mesure d'examen médical à subir par Mangala pour déterminer le degré réel de son invalidité définitive; – Accorde à celui-ci, par provision, une somme de 30,000 francs exigible dès la signification du présent arrêt; – Condamne Gillet et Drouin aux dépens.

18. Cour d'appel de Grenoble, 16 mai 1962
Cie d'assur. 'Le Continent' c. *Clavel, Garnier et Paul*
(D. 1963,137 and Note A. Tunc)

La Cour; – Attendu que Paul, Garnier et la Compagnie d'assurances *Le Continent*, qui les assure l'un et l'autre pour les accidents de chasse, ont réguliérement interjeté appel d'un jugement du tribunal de grande instance de Gap du 13 juil. 1961, qui a déclaré Paul et Garnier solidairement responsables, tant par application des art. 1382 et 1383 que de l'art. 1384, al. 1er CC, d'un accident de chasse dont a été victime Clavel, et les a condamnés, ainsi que la Compagnie *Le Continent*, à verser à Clavel une provision de 2,000 NF, une expertise médicale étant ordonnée; – Attendu que de la procédure d'information versée aux débats par les parties, il résulte que Clavel a reçu dans l'œil gauche un plomb de chasse, ce qui a nécessité son énucléation, que ce plomb provenait d'un coup de fusil tiré soit par Paul, soit par Garnier, lesquels, se trouvant à quelques mètres l'un de l'autre, avaient tiré l'un après l'autre sur un lièvre situé à une trentaine de mètres d'eux dans une direction peu différente de celle où se trouvait Clavel, qu'ils avaient aperçu avant de tirer; – Attendu qu'au vu des déclarations faites par les deux chasseurs aux gendarmes après l'accident, il paraît probable que c'est le coup de fusil de Garnier qui a causé la blessure de Clavel, car d'une part celui-ci ne s'est affaissé qu'après le coup de fusil de Garnier, tiré après celui de Paul, et d'autre part, la ligne de visée de Garnier était plus proche que celle de Paul de la direction de Clavel; – Attendu pourtant qu'il ne s'agit là que d'une probabilité car, d'une part, l'intervalle de temps entre les deux coups a été assez court pour que Clavel ait pu ne s'affaisser qu'après le deuxième coup de fusil, même s'il avait été blessé par le premier et, d'autre part, la dispersion assez grande des deux armes, relevée en cours d'informa-tion, ainsi que la possibilité d'un ricochet, ne permettent pas d'exclure l'hypothèse que Clavel ait été blessé par un plomb provenant du fusil de Paul; – Attendu que cet élément d'incertitude, qui a motivé l'or-donnance de non-lieu rendue par le juge d'instruction, ne permet pas de retenir la responsabilité personnelle de l'un ou l'autre des deux chasseurs; – Attendu que c'est à tort que le tribunal a retenu la responsabilité collective des deux chasseurs sur le fondement de l'art. 1382; qu'en effet il n'y a pas eu de leur part une faute commune dans leur façon de chasser; qu'ils ont commis une faute en tirant dans une direction trop proche de celle de Clavel, ce qui exclut que le ricochet, d'ailleurs non certain, puisse être considéré comme un cas fortuit, mais qu'il s'agit là de deux fautes individuelles distinctes et au surplus d'une gravité plus grande pour Garnier que pour Paul; que Clavel n'ayant été touché que par un seul plomb, une seule des deux fautes est en relation de cause à effet avec la blessure, sans qu'il soit possible de déterminer laquelle; – Attendu qu'à tort également le tribunal a retenu la responsabilité collective de Paul et Garnier sur le fondement de l'art. 1384 car, contrairement à ce qu'il retient sans motif, les deux coups de feu ne se sont pas confondus en une même gerbe de plombs puisque Garnier n'a tiré qu'après avoir vu que le coup de fusil de Paul n'avait pas tué le lièvre, et qu'il a tiré d'un emplacement et dans une direction différents; – Attendu que, s'il n'est pas possible de retenir la responsabilité de Paul ou celle de Garnier, il est certain que si ce n'est l'un c'est l'autre qui est responsable, tant comme gardien du plomb que comme ayant commis la faute de tirer dans une direction trop proche de celle de la victime; que, par ailleurs, la Compagnie *Le Continent* assure l'un et l'autre; que la victime ayant une action directe contre la Compagnie *Le Continent*, cette action est bien fondée, quel que soit celui des deux chasseurs qui est responsable, puisqu'il est constant que c'est nécessairement l'un ou l'autre; – Attenda qu'il échet en conséquence de dire l'action de Clavel mal fondée à l'égard de Paul et de Garnier, mais bien fondée à l'égard de la Compagnie *Le Continent*, et de déclarer celle-ci responsable des conséquences dommageables pour Clavel de l'accident litigieux, dans la limite du moins onéreux pour elle des deux contrats passés avec Paul et Garnier;

Par ces motifs, déclare recevable l'appel de Paul, Garnier et la Compagnie *Le Continent*; y faisant droit pour partie et réformant le jugement du 13 juil. 1961, déboute Clavel de son action contre Paul et Garnier; déclare la Compagnie *Le Continent*, en tant qu'assureur tant de Paul que de Garnier, responsable des conséquences de l'accident de chasse dont Clavel a été victime le 12 sept. 1960 dans la limite du moins onéreux pour elle des contrats d'assurances couvrant Paul et Garnier; la condamne à payer à Clavel la somme de 2,000 NF à titre de provision; confirme le jugement en ce qu'il a ordonné une expertise médicale.

A. Tunc, *Rev. trim. dr. civ.* 1963, 555.

Pour le bonheur des juristes et l'exercice de leur ingéniosité, les tribunaux sont périodiquement saisis de la réparation d'un dommage causé par un membre indéterminé d'un groupe de personnes.

Dans l'affaire sur laquelle statue la *Cour d'appel de Grenoble le 16 mai 1962* (D. 1963,137 et Note Pierre Azard), deux chasseurs avaient simultanément tiré sur un lièvre, commettant ainsi une imprudence à l'égard d'un tiers qu'ils avaient vu à peu près dans la même direction. Mais le tiers n'avait reçu qu'un plomb, ce qui établit qu'une seule des deux fautes avait causé le dommage. Réformant la décision de première instance et négligeant les efforts accomplis en France et à l'étranger dans des cas semblables pour justifier la responsabilité des deux tireurs (cf. cette *Revue* 1962. 644, n° 16, et la note fortement documentée de M.P. Azard sous l'arrêt, 1; cpr. cette *Revue* 1961. 142 n° 49), la Cour de Grenoble déclare que la victime, faute de pouvoir préciser le tireur dont le plomb l'a atteint, n'a d'action contre aucun des deux chasseurs.

L'arrêt irait-il à l'encontre du courant général d'indemnisation des victimes? Il n'en est rien. Considérant que les deux chasseurs sont assurés près de la même compagnie et que l'un d'eux est responsable, il condamne la compagnie 'dans la limite du moins onéreux pour elle des deux contrats passés' avec les chasseurs. Ce moyen n'est pas nouveau (v. les décisions citées par M. Azard, note sous l'arrêt, II, et par H. et L. Mazeaud et A. Tunc, *Traité*, 5° édit., t. III, n° 2718 et note 14). Il a déjà été discuté et l'est encore fort heureusement par M. Azard. Disons simplement qu'avec M. Rodière (note *J.C.P.* 1950,2.5736, II), nous pensons pouvoir l'approuver sans réserve (cf. H. et L. Mazeaud et A. Tunc, *op. et loc. cit.*). Quel qu'ait été le responsable, l'assureur devait garantie à la victime. Qu'importe alors l'incertitude sur l'agent qui déclenchait cette responsabilité? Tous les jours, les tribunaux prononcent des décisions qui ne sont pas justifiées de A. à Z. Quand ils déclarent qu'un certain résultat établit virtuellement la faute, c'est précisément qu'ils ignorent la faute qui a été commise. Et si les rédacteurs du Code eux-mêmes présument parfois la faute jusqu'à preuve d'une cause étrangère non imputable au débiteur (art. 1147, CC, c'est encore pour permettre aux tribunaux de prononcer une condamnation dans les cas où il y a tout lieu de penser qu'une faute a été commise, mais où la victime est dans l'impossibilité de la préciser. La solution donnée en l'espèce n'a donc rien qui puisse choquer au fond. Et les arguments de texte ou de pratique usuelle qu'on lui oppose ne semblent pas déterminants.

19. Cour d'appel de Rennes, 14 janv. 1971
Fonds de garantie automobile c. Hazevis et autres
(*J.C.P.* 1971,2.16733)

La Cour; – Considérant que le Fonds de garantie automobile, institué par l'article 15 de la loi du 31 décembre 1951, est appelant d'un jugement rendu le 23 juin 1970 par le Tribunal de grande instance de Vannes qui, statuant sur demande de Hazevis introduite contre Servoin et Allain, tendant à la réparation du préjudice corporel qu'il a subi lors d'un accident de chasse dont il a été victime le 22 décembre 1968, et sur intervention du Fonds de garantie, a jugé que l'auteur du coup de feu cause des blessures n'a pu être identifié et, faisant application de l'article 366 du Code rural, a décidé que le Fonds de garantie devait prendre en charge l'indemnisation du dommage, a commis expert pour déterminer celui-ci, a alloué à Hazevis une indemnité provisionnelle de 2,000 francs et l'a condamné aux dépens; – Considérant que Hazevis, intimé, a reporté appel sur Servoin et Allain et leurs assureurs qui concluent à la confirmation du jugement; que Hazevis, concluant à la réformation, demande à la Cour de juger que les chasseurs défendeurs sont tous deux responsables in solidum et, à titre subsidiaire conclut à la confirmation en ce que le Tribunal a décidé que le Fonds de garantie devait prendre en charge la réparation du dommage; que dans les deux cas il demande à être déchargé des dépens; – Considérant que les conclusions du Fonds de garantie tendent à condamnation in solidum de Allain et Servoin; que ceux-ci, intimés, concluent à la confirmation; – Considérant qu'il résulte des renseignements portés à la connaissance de la Cour par les parties qu'à la date sus-indiquée les sieurs Hazevis, Fablet, Servoin, Allain, Bertho et Maurice chassaient ensemble sur les terres de Saint-Dugast en Plumelec; qu'à un moment donné le groupe se scinda en deux: que pendant que Allain, Servoin, Maurice et Bertho remontaient ensemble un champ de choux, Fablet et Hazevis se tenaient de part et d'autre d'une haie bordant ce champ, le second dans un chemin de terre de l'autre côté de la haie à 3 mètres de Fablet et dans son prolongement par rapport à la position occupèe par l'ensemble des autres chasseurs remontant le champ et à 40 mètres environ de Servoin; qu' Allain se trouvait à 9 mètres de Servoin et en avant de lui par rapport à la direction qu'ils suivaient, c'est-à-dire vers Fablet qui était très visible pour eux alors que Hazevis était en partie masqué par la haie; – Considérant qu'une bécasse s'envola d'un point du champ situé entre Allain et Servoin en direction de Fablet et Hazevis; que Servoin la tira le premier, puis Allain, chacun d'un coup de feu; qu'il s'est écoulé environ 2 seconds entre ces deux coups; que la bécasse passant à proximité de Fablet fut également tirée par lui; que Hazevis reçut quelques plombs au visage entre le deuxième et le troisième coup de feu; – Considérant que le Tribunal, compte tenu des positions occupées par Allain et Servoin, de la succession des deux coups de feu antérieurs aux blessures, de l'existence de végétation assez dense en bordure du champ, s'est déclaré être dans l'impossibilité de déterminer l'origine des plombs ayant blessé Hazevis et de dire si ces projectiles ont suivi une trajectoire directe ou ont ricoché avant de l'atteindre; qu'il a écarté également la responsabilité conjointe susceptible d'entraîner une condamnation in solidum; – Considérant que toutes les parties sont d'accord pour admettre qu'il est impossible de déterminer l'arme, cause du dommage; – Considérant que pour demander à la

Cour de dire que Servoin et Allain encourent une responsabilité conjointe, le Fonds de garantie fait plaider que ces deux chasseurs ayant tiré simultanément dans la même direction. et alors qu'ils étaient proches l'un de l'autre, ont produit une trajectoire directe en gerbe unique de projectiles; que ce faisant, l'appelant suggère à la Cour d'appliquer la théorie émise par la Cour de cassation dans son arrêt du 11 février 1966; – Mais considérant que cette affirmation du Fonds de garantie relativement aux circonstances de fait de l'accident va à l'encontre des données certaines soumises à l'appréciation de la Cour; qu'il ne peut être question d'une gerbe unique dès lors qu'il est constant que Servoin et Allain, espacés de 9 mètres, ont tiré successivement un même oiseau se déplaçant rapidement et ayant effectué en cours de vol un crochet; que nécessairement les deux armes ont provoqué des gerbes distinctes; que, compte tenu de l'existence à proximité de la haie de pommiers sur les branches desquels des plombs ont pu ricocher, il est impossible de déterminer avec certitude de laquelle des armes provenaient les projectiles ayant blessé Hazevis; que dans ces conditions, la Cour ne peut que se rallier à la jurisprudence selon laquelle, pour retenir la responsabilité de tel ou tel chasseur, il est indispensable de prouver une relation de cause à effet entre le coup de feu qu'il a tiré et le dommage dont réparation est demandée ou de déterminer l'arme d'où est parti le projectile cause de ce dommage; qu'en conséquence la Cour ne pent que confirmer sur ce point le jugement qui a fait une exacte application de ce principe; – Considérant que l'auteur du dommage étant demeuré inconnu, il échet de faire application de l'article 366 *ter* du Code rural et de dire, après le Tribunal, que le Fonds de garantie devra prendre en charge la réparation du dommage subi par Hazevis; – Considérant qu'il n'est pas établi que Hazevis ait commis une faute en se séparant des autres chasseurs et en suivant un chemin derrière une haie dès lors qu'il est établi qu'il se trouvait a proximité immédiate de Fablet, lequel était parfaitement visible; – Considérant que le Tribunal a alloué à Hazevis une indemnité provisionnelle de 2,000 francs, qu'une majoration est demandée à la Cour; – Considérant que cette somme est suffisante pour permettre à Hazevis de couvrir les frais engagés pour soins; qu'il n'apparaît pas que l'incapacité de travail ait été totale pendant les trois mois qu'il indique; que dès lors il échet de maintenir le montant de l'indemnité provisionnelle allouée; – Sur les dépens: – Considérant que le Tribunal a mis les dépense de première instance à la charge de Hazevis, bien que son droit à réparation du préjudice ait été satisfait; – Considérant que l'intervention du Fonds de garantie automobile était nécessitée non pas pour couvrir l'insolvabilité de l'auteur désigné d'un dommage mais par substitution à l'auteur inconnu de ce dommage; qu'il doit alors supporter les frais afférents à la reconnaissance des droits de la victime; qu'au surplus il succombe dans son appel;

Par ces motifs, et ceux non contraires du Tribunal: – Ordonne la jonction des procédures enrôlées sous les numéros 72 et 218; – Reçoit le Fonds de garantie automobile et Hazevis en leurs appels; – Confirme le jugement entrepris; – Dit que les dépens de première instance et d'appel seront supportés par le Fonds de garantie automobile.

20. Cour d'appel de Paris, 8 janv. 1964
Cripia et Deverchin c. Veuve Desbordes
(D. 1964, comm. 70)

Considérant que au soutien de leur appel incident Cripia et Deverchin allèguent que le suicide de Desbordes est lié à un état pathologique antérieur qui a évolué normalement, et que cet état constitue un cas de force majeure qui les exonère de toute responsabilité dans le suicide de Desbordes; qu'ils proposent à la Cour de dire que les conclusions du rapport d'expertise médicale ne constituent pas, du point de vue scientifique une certitude, dire que la cause génératrice du suicide de Desbordes réside uniquement dans la prédisposition pathologique du sujet et non dans le traumatisme résultant de l'accident du 13 juillet 1953, que la responsabilité de Cripia et Deverchin dans ce suicide ne saurait être retenue; subsidiairement dire qu'en toute hypothèse l'incidence du traumatisme résultant de l'accident a donné lieu à l'allocation de dommages-intérêts qui ont satisfait entièrement les droits de la victime et de ses hériters; en conséquence débouter les consorts Desbordes de leurs prétentions;

Considérant qu'il a été définitivement jugé aux termes du jugement, plus haut visé du 11 avril 1956 que l'incapacité de 30% dont Desbordes demeurait atteint, était la conséquence de troubles mentaux dérivant de l'accident, qu'il a été de même reconnu aux termes du jegement du 7 juillet 1958, également passé en force de chose jugée, qu'il existait une relation de cause à effet entre l'accident du 13 juillet 1953 et les rechutes (dépressions nerveuses) d'octobre 1955 à mai 1957 et de juillet à septembre 1957;

Considérant qu'il résulte par ailleurs des termes plus haut reproduits du rapport d'expertise que le traumatisme subi dans l'accident a joué un rôle qui, bien que non exclusif, est certain dans la production de l'état mélancolique qui a entraîné le suicide de la victime;

Considérant qu'il n'est point établi que Desbordes ait présenté avant l'accident des troubles mentaux;

Considérant dans ces conditions que s'il convient de tenir pour acquis, comme l'a fait l'expert, que le suicide survenu le 24 septembre 1958 est dû à un état psychopathique lui-même imputable à la fois à l'accident du 13 juillet 1953 et à une prédisposition morbide de la victime, il échet également de reconnaître que cet accident a révélé l'état psychique latent de Desbordes et a été par suite la cause directe du dommage dont réparation est aujourd'hui demandée;

Considérant que ce dommage est né de l'aggravation survenue dans l'état de Desbordes postérieurement au mois de septembre 1957 et de son décès; qu'il est donc distinct du préjudice dont Desbordes a été indemnisé en exécution des jugements des 11 avril 1956 et 7 juillet 1958 lequel a eu à connaître des 'rechutes' survenues jusqu'au mois de septembre 1957; que dès lors la demande des consorts Desbordes est fondée dans son principe;

Considérant qu'à tort les premiers juges après avoir évalué le préjudice subi par les consorts Desbordes en suite du décès de leur auteur ont, au vu des conclusions du rapport d'expertise médicale, estimé que la responsabilité de Cripia et de Deverchin était en raison de l'état morbide de Desbordes, réduite à 40% et ont fait subir à cette évaluation un abattement correspondant;

Considérant en effet que les prédispositions morbides de Desbordes n'étaient pas de nature à exonérer même partiellement Cripia et Deverchin de la réparation du dommage, dès lors que l'accident, survenu par la faute de Cripia en a été la cause directe;

Considérant toutefois que ce dommage doit être apprécié en tenant compte de l'état morbide de Desbordes étranger à l'accident, état dont l'expert et les médecins représentant les parties ont été d'accord pour estimer qu'il réduisait en 1958 de 50% ses facultés de travail et dont il n'est pas douteux qu'il l'aurait à brève échéance amené à cesser toute activité;

Considérant que Desbordes était âgé de 53 ans à l'époque de son décès, qu'antérieurement il faisait valoir un petit domaine dont il était propriétaire dans la Marne à Brugny-Vaudancourt et qui couvrait 4 ha 8 a dont 1 ha 9 a planté en vigne;

Considérant qu'en l'état de ces divers renseignements comme des justifications produites il apparaît équitable de ramener de 5,805 92 francs à 3,500 francs le montant de l'indemnité compensatrice du dommage résultant de l'aggravation de l'état de Desbordes du mois d'octobre 1957 au jour de son décès, de porter de 5,400 à 12,000 francs, toutes causes de préjudice confondues, le taux des dommages-intérêts alloués à veuve Desbordes, de confirmer la décision déférée en ce qu'elle a fixé à 500 francs le montant des réparations dues à dame Didier et à dame Mignon;

Par ces motifs et ceux non contraires des premiers Juges,

Dit les appels recevables en la forme, dit partiellement fondé l'appel principal et mal fondé l'appel incident;

En conséquence confirme le jugement entrepris en ce qu'il a condamné Cripia et Deverchin à payer une somme de 500 francs à titre de dommages-intérêts à dame Desbordes-Didier ainsi qu'à dame Desbordes-Mignon, l'infirme pour le surplus et statuant à nouveau,

Condamne Cripia et Deverchin *in solidum* à payer à veuve Desbordes en réparation du préjudice subi par Desbordes du mois d'octobre 1957 au jour de son décès 3,500 francs, en réparation de son propre préjudice, toutes causes confondues, la somme de 12,000 francs;

Dit les parties mal fondées en toutes leurs autres demandes fins ou conclusions plus amples ou contraires non admises par le présent arrêt les en déboute.

21. Cour d'appel de Paris, 5 mai 1962
Dame Olejniczak c. Savin, Cie La Baloise Transports et Caisses Sécurité sociale
(G.P. 1962,2.172)

La Cour, – Statuant en audience publique sur l'appel principal interjeté par dame Vve Olejniczak, et sur l'appel incident de Savin et de la Cie La Baloise Transports, d'un jugement rendu par le Tribunal de commerce de la Seine le 12 janvier 1961, lequel, statuant d'office et contradictoirement à l'égard des caisses de Sécurité sociale, a condamné Savin et la Cie La Baloise Transports, conjointement et solidairement, à payer à dame Vve Olejniczak la somme de 18,716 NF, déclaré dame Vve Olejniczak mal fondée en le surplus de sa demande et l'en a déboutée;

Considérant que l'appelante demande à la cour de préciser que la somme de 18,716 NF, au paiement de laquelle Savin et la Cie La Baloise Transports ont été condamnés par ledit jugement, représente une indemnité complémentaire et doit lui être payée en sus des prestations qui lui seront versées par la Sécurité sociale à raison de l'accident dont son mari a été la victime le 18 juin 1957;

Considérant que Savin et la Cie La Baloise Transports intimés, demandent à la cour de dire et de juger que le préjudice subi du fait du décès d'Olejniczak a été justement évalué, toutes causes confondues, à 18,716 NF; que cette somme représente le préjudice total et non le préjudice complémentaire; que, par leur appel incident, ils demandent à la cour de dire et juger qu'aucune faute n'a été commise par Savin et, en conséquence, de la débouter de sa demande fondée sur l'art. 1382 CC; de dire et juger que la preuve que Savin, au moment des faits, était gardien du pain de glace n'est pas rapportée par dame Olejniczak et de la débouter en conséquence de son action fondée sur l'art. 1384 CC; de dire et juger qu'Olejniczak est décédé par suite de *delirium tremens* et qu'il n'y a aucun lien de causalité entre l'accident du 18 juin et le décès du 24 juin; de débouter dame Olejniczak de toutes ses demandes, fins et conclusions et de la condamner aux dépens de l^{re} instance et d'appel;

Considérant qu'il est constant qu'Olejniczak, cafetier de l'hôtel Lotti à Paris, a été victime, le 18 juin 1957, d'un accident du travail; que blessé il a été conduit à l'hôpital où il est décédé le 24 juin 1957; que dame Olejniczak a assigné, en avril 1960, Savin et son assureur, la Cie Baloise Transports, devant le Tribunal de commerce de la Seine, pour obtenir réparation du préjudice subi du fait de l'accident dont son mari avait été victime, et que c'est dans ces conditions qu'a été rendu le jugement déféré;

Considérant, en la forme, que les caisses de Sécurité sociale intimées ont été régulièrement assignées, mais n'ont pas constitué avoue; qu'il échet de statuer par arrêt contradictoire à l'égard de tous les intimés par application des art. 151 et 470 C. pr. civ., modifiés par le décret du 22 décembre 1958;

Considérant qu'il résulte des éléments de la cause, des renseignements et documents régulièrement produits et des débats, que Savin, glacier, accompagné d'un livreur a, le 18 juin 1957, à 6 h 30, livré à l'hôtel Lotti des pains de glace qu'il a placés lui-même après les avoir coupés comme il le faisait habituellement, dans la glacière; qu'au cours de cette opération, l'un des pains de glace qu'il avait mis sur la glacière pour le couper, a glissé pour une raison qui n'a pu être déterminée, et qu'il est tombé sur le pied d'un cafetier de l'hôtel, Olejniczak, venu boire un verre de vin près de la glacière; que celui-ci a été blessé; qu'aucune faute n'a pu être établie contre Savin, pas plus que contre le livreur qui l'aidait et que, par conséquent, sa responsabilité ne saurait être retenue par application de l'art. 1382 CC; que, par contre, il résulte de ce qui précede que Savin n'avait pas encore terminé sa livraison et que les pains de glace se trouvaient encore sous sa garde, ne passant sous celle de l'hôtel qu'a partir du moment ou il les avait déposés dans la glacière; qu'à défaut par lui de prouver un cas fortuit, la force majeure ou une cause étrangère qui lui soit imputable, il est donc tenu de la responsabilité de plein droit prévue à l'art. 1384 CC;

Considérant que Savin et la Cie La Baloise Transports soutiennent qu'Olejniczak étant décédé par suite d'une crise de *delirium tremens,* il n'y a pas de lien de causalité entre l'accident et le décès;

Mais considérant qu'il résulte aussi bien des pièces médicales régulièrement versées aux débats que du rapport d'autopsie que l'accident du 18 juin 1957 a déclenché la crise de *delirium tremens* et que la mort est donc en relation avec l'accident; que la complication qui se produit au cours du traitement forme, avec le traumatisme résultant de l'accident, un tout indivisible; que cet accident, sans être la cause directe et immédiate de la mort, n'en a pas moins précipité et accentué l'évolution de son état morbide; qu'il y a donc lien de causalité entre l'accident et la mort;

Considérant que dame Vve Olejniczak, tant dans ses conclusions que par son avocat à la barre, soutient que les 1ers juges, en fixant à 18,716 NF le préjudice qu'elle a subi par suite du décès accidentel de son mari, ont entendu lui allouer cette somme en plus de la rente qu'elle perçoit de la Sécurité sociale;

Mais considérant qu'ils ont pris la précaution de préciser que le montant de la condamnation était fixé toutes causes confondues; qu'il apparait à la cour qu'ils ont équitablement arbitré le préjudice total à 18,716 NF puisque, pour apprécier le dommage, il convient de tenir compte de l'état morbide de la victime antérieur à l'accident; qu'il résulte d'une lettre de la Caisse primaire de Sécurité sociale de la région parisienne, en date du 5 avril 1962, que le capital de la rente servie à dame Vve Olejniczak par ladite caisse s'élève au 1er mars 1961, époque de la dernière majoration légale, à 21,669,36 NF; qu'il n'y a pas conséquent de préjudice complémentaire;

Par ces motifs, et ceux non contraires des 1ers juges que la cour adopte, – Reçoit les appels tant principal qu'incident; – Dit l'appel principal de dame Vve Olejniczak mal fondé; l'en déboute;–Faisant partiellement droit à l'appel incident: confirme le jugement rendu par le Tribunal de commerce de la Seine le 12 janvier 1962; – Y ajoutant: dit et juge que la somme de 18,716 NF, montant de la condamnation, représente le préjudice total; la déboute de son action en tant que fondée sur l'art. 1382 CC; – Rejette toutes autres demandes, fins et conclusions contraires ou plus amples des parties.

LIABILITY WITHOUT FAULT:
ARTICLE 1384 CC

The next 19 cases all deal with stricter forms of liability, article 1384 CC taking up, for obvious reasons, most of the available space (cases 22–37). The decisions of the Cour de cassation of 16.6.1896 and the Chambre des Requêtes of 30.3.1897 represent the *fons et origo* of this development which, thirty years later, culminated with the *Jand'heur* decision which led Ripert to express the fear that article 1384.1 CC was about to devour article 1382 CC. Ripert's fears have not materialised. In 1971, for example, the Tribunaux de grande instance had to decide 9,907 actions based on article 1382 CC (of which 8,874 were successful) and 14,020 actions based on article 1384.1 CC (of which 12,414 were successful). Nevertheless, as these figures clearly show, the importance of article 1384 CC in the French system of *responsabilité civile* is enormous – hence the number of judgments reproduced in this sub-section. However, partly because of lack of space, and partly because the above-mentioned two decisions were rendered obsolete (in the context of industrial accidents) within a year of their publication, we have omitted them from this volume. But they are important decisions and, along with Saleilles' accompanying note, they will repay careful reading.

The collection of cases reproduced here deals with various aspects of liability under article 1384.1 CC and the reader will do well to study them *after* he has first read the relevant section of chapter 4 in volume 1. Here, little more need be added about them except to say that we felt it particularly useful to reproduce some of the *Conclusions* of the avocats généraux in some of the leading cases. These texts, often of excellent literary style, are particularly important not only because they offer a readable summary of prevailing court practice, but also because they give, often quite explicitly, the policy and technical arguments which lead the Cour de cassation to decide a case in a particular manner.

Most of the decisions are accompanied by 'notes' or 'observations' of varying lengths and the most important ones are commented upon in journals such as the *Revue trimestrielle de droit civil*. The serious student of French law must consult these notes with care and regularity if he wishes to understand fully the developing case-law. Given their importance our original aim was to reproduce some selected extracts. Once again, however, considerations of space have forced us to abandon this intention. Such space as we were allowed has thus been devoted to the judgments themselves.

The sub-section devoted to vicarious liability (cases 38–40) does little justice to this important subject. But something had to go and we felt this could without too much harm being done, given that the English student should be able to follow the French case-law on this subject – at least in its basic lines – without undue difficulty. We have, however, managed to include three cases; one dealing with the question of borrowed servants, the other two with the thorny and unresolved question of the master's liability in the event of an 'abus des fonctions' by his employee. Once again, however, this section will be better understood if the reader first consults our text in volume I, chapter 4, and the 'Introductory comments' to the French cases at pp. 177–84 of this volume.

22. Cour de cassation
Chambres Réunies 13 fév. 1930
Jand'heur c. Les Galeries belfortaises
(D.P. 1930.1.57)

Pourvoi en cassation contre l'arrêt de la Cour d'appel de Lyon du 7 juil. 1927 (D.H. 1927,423), – rendu sur renvoi de Civ. 21 févr. 1927 (D.P. 1927.1.97), – pour fausse application de l'art. 1382 CC, violation des art. 1384 du même code et 7 de la loi du 20 avr. 1810, en ce que l'arrêt attaqué a mis à la charge de la victime d'un accident causé par une automobile la preuve d'une faute imputable au conducteur, alors que la faute du conducteur devait être présumée.

Rapport de M. le conseiller Le Marc'hadour:

Le 22 avr. 1925, un camion automobile conduit par le nommé Steullet, chauffeur au service de la Société *Les Galeries belfortaises*, renversait, au moment où elle traversait une route, la jeune Lise Jand'heur, qui était grièvement blessée.

Saisi de l'action en 20,000 fr. de dommages-intérêts introduite contre la Société des *Galeries* par la veuve Jand'heur, tant en son nom personnel que comme tutrice légale de sa fille mineure, le tribunal de

Belfort, par jugement du 7 juil. 1925, déclarait applicable à la société défenderesse la disposition de l'art. 1384, §1er, CC, aux termes de laquelle l'on est responsable des choses qu'on a sous sa garde; mais, la présomption pouvant céder devant la preuve du fait, formellement articulé, que l'accident serait dû à la faute exclusive de la victime, le tribunal ordonnait qu'il serait de ce chef procédé à une enquête.[1]

Le 29 déc. 1925, cette décision était, sur l'appel des *Galeries belfortaises*, réformée par la Cour de Besançon: écartant l'application de l'art. 1384 par le motif que l'automobile était, lors de l'accident, actionnée par son conducteur, et que le dommage causé était, dans ces conditions, imputable au fait de l'homme et non au fait de la chose, l'arrêt admettait seulement la veuve Jand'heur à établir, dans les termes de ses conclusions subsidiaires, la faute du conducteur, l'art. 1382 étant, d'après lui, seul applicable en l'espèce.

Sur le pourvoi formé contre cette décision, votre chambre civile statuait, le 21 févr. 1927 (D.P. 1927.1.97), au rapport de M. le conseiller Ambroise Colin,[2] par un arrêt dont nous jugeons nécessaire de vous rappeler les termes: 'Sur le moyen unique pris de la fausse application de l'art. 1382, de la violation de l'art. 1384 CC, en ce que la Cour d'appel a mis à la charge de la victime d'un accident causé par une automobile la preuve d'une faute imputable au conducteur, alors que cette faute devait être présumée; – Vu l'art. 1384, alin 1er, CC; – Attendu. que la présomption de faute établie par cet article à l'encontre de celui qui a sous sa garde la chose mobilière inanimée qui a causé un dommage à autrui *ne peut être détruite que par la preuve d'un cas fortuit ou de force majeure ou d'une cause étrangère qui ne lui soit pas imputable*; qu'il ne suffit pas de prouver qu'il n'a commis aucune faute ou que la cause du fait dommageable est demeurée inconnue; – Attendu que... l'arrêt a refusé d'appliquer le texte susvisé sous le prétexte qu'au moment de l'accident le camion était actionné par Steullet, chauffeur au service du propriétaire, et que, dès lors, pour obtenir réparation du préjudice, la victime était tenue d'établir, à la charge du conducteur, une faute qui lui fût imputable dans les termes de l'art. 1382 CC; – Mais attendu que la loi, pour l'application de la présomption qu'elle édicte, *ne distingue pas suivant que la chose qui a causé le dommage était ou non actionnée par la main de l'homme; qu'il suffit qu'il s'agisse d'une chose soumise à la nécessité d'une garde en raison des dangers qu'elle peut faire courir à autrui...*; casse, renvoie devant la Cour d'appel de Lyon.'

Par son arrêt du 7 juil. 1927 (D.H. 1927,423), la Cour de Lyon, faisant sienne la thèse condamnée par votre chambre civile, réformait, comme l'avait fait la Cour de Besançon, le jugement du tribunal de Belfort. Le dispositif de l'arrêt résume ainsi le système qu'il adopte: 'Dit que l'accident imputé à une voiture automobile en mouvement, sous l'impulsion et la direction de l'homme, alors qu'aucune preuve n'existe qu'il soit dû à un vice propre de la voiture, ne constitue pas un dommage causé par une chose que l'on a sous sa garde dans les termes de l'art. 1384, § 1er, CC; déclare, en conséquence, que l'accident dont la mineure Jand'heur a été victime ne peut engager la responsabilité du conducteur ou de son commettant qu'autant qu'il est la suite d'une faute établie; que, partant, la charge de prouver une faute à l'encontre du conducteur incombe à la victime ou à ses représentants légaux.'

La veuve Jand'heur s'est pourvue contre cette décision, et, le 13 mai 1929, votre chambre civile, constatant que l'arrêt attaqué a statué comme l'avait fait l'arrêt cassé de la Cour de Besançon et se fonde en droit sur des motifs en opposition avec la doctrine de l'arrêt de cassation, a renvoyé la cause et les parties devant les chambres réunies.

Contre l'arrêt de la Cour de Lyon le mémoire ampliatif produit par Me Jaubert au nom de la demanderesse en cassation vous propose un moyen unique, celui-là même qui avait été invoqué, et admis par vous, sur le pourvoi formé contre l'arrêt cassé de la Cour de Besançon, et vous avez aujourd'hui à vous prononcer de façon définitive sur cette question, restée controversée, de l'application de l'art. 1384, § 1er, CC, aux choses inanimées et en particulier aux voitures automobiles.

Avant d'entrer dans l'examen du moyen et du mémoire en réponse, il importe, pensons-nous, de retracer devant vous l'évolution qu'a marquée en la matière la jurisprudence de vos chambres civiles jusqu'à l'arrêt du 21 fév. 1927, dont de nombreuses décisions, tant de la Chambre Civile que de la Chambre des Requêtes, ont depuis lors reproduit la doctrine.

La responsabilité civile est réglée dans notre code par les art. 1382 et suiv., et le principe général est posé dans l'art. 1382, aux termes duquel tout fait de l'homme qui cause à autrui un dommage oblige celui par la faute duquel il est arrivé à le réparer. La responsabilité est ainsi fondée sur la faute; l'idée de faute est le principe moral qui domine la matière. La faute d'ailleurs devra être prouvée: c'est l'application de la règle général posée dans l'art. 1315 CC. Dans certains cas, cependant, au lieu d'obliger la personne lésée à faire la preuve d'une faute commise par l'auteur du dommage, la loi établit une présomption qui la dispense de faire cette preuve. Tel est l'objet de l'art. 1384, dont le paragraphe 1er dispose: 'On est responsable non seulement du dommage que l'on cause par son propre fait, mais encore de celui qui est causé par le fait des personnes dont on doit répondre ou des choses qu'on a sous sa garde.' Et dans les paragraphes suivants de l'art. 1384, le code précise les conditions de la responsabilité résultant du fait d'autrui, l'art. 1385 réglant la responsabilité du fait des animaux et l'art. 1386 celle qui résulte de la ruine d'un bâtiment. Art. 1384, 1385, 1386, la responsabilité de plein droit qu'ils édictent repose dans tous les cas sur une idée de garde, sur la faute personnelle de celui qui s'est mal acquitté de sa charge de surveillant: en cas de dommage causé, le père ou l'instituteur est présumé avoir mal surveillé l'enfant; le maître, mal choisi ou mal surveillé son employé; une présomption semblable de négligence est à la base de la responsabilité du fait des choses dont on a la garde: la faute vient de ce qu'on a mal gardé.

C'est le principe que proclame votre jurisprudence pour la responsabilité du fait des animaux: 'Attendu, disent les arrêts de votre Chambre Civile des 27 oct. 1885 et 9 mars 1886 (D.P.86.1.207), que la responsabilité édictée repose sur une présomption de faute imputable au propriétaire de l'animal qui a causé le dommage ou à la personne qui en faisait usage au moment de l'accident.' L'art. 1385 crée donc à la charge de celui qui se sert de l'animal une présomption de responsabilité. Mais il fallait préciser la force et l'étendue de cette présomption: n'admettrait-elle pas la preuve contraire, et le gardien de l'animal ne s'exonérerait-il pas en prouvant qu'il n'a commis aucune faute? On observait à cet égard que l'art. 1384 *in fine*, en limitant la responsabilité des père, mère, instituteurs et artisans au cas où ils ne peuvent prouver qu'ils n'ont pu empêcher le fait dommageable, écarte toute possibilité d'excuse pour les maîtres et commettants, visés au même article; le silence gardé sur ce point par l'art. 1385, qui a été détaché de l'art. 1384, dont il n'est qu'une application, commande une solution semblable. 'Pour faire tomber, dit M. Larombière (*Théorie et pratique des obligations*, art. 1385, n° 9), la présomption qu'établit d'une façon si absolue l'art. 1385, il faut faire la preuve d'un cas de force majeure ou d'une faute imputable soit à la personne lésée, soit à un tiers dont le maître de l'animal n'est pas responsable' (v. également dans ce sens, Aubry et Rau, *Cours de droit civil français,* 5ᵉ edit., t. 6, § 448, note 10). Vos arrêts susvisés de 1885 et de 1886 consacrent cette thèse: 'Attendu, disent-ils, que la présomption ne peut céder que devant la preuve du cas fortuit ou d'une faute commise par la partie lésée.' Votre jurisprudence est depuis lors constante (Civ. 11 mars 1902, D.P.

1902.1.216; 17 juil. 1917, D.P. 1917.1.133; Req. 2 juil. 1902, D.P. 1902.1.431).

'L'on est responsable des choses dont on a la garde'; nous venons de définir le caractère et l'étendue de cette responsabilité en ce qui concerne les animaux. La chose dont on a la garde, c'est certainement l'animal, mais est-ce seulement l'animal? Ou, à côté de l'animal, qui est une chose animée, l'art. 1384, §1er, vise-t-il les choses proprement dites, c'est-à-dire les objets inanimés?

L'on a observé que le législateur de 1804 n'avait à aucun moment manifesté l'intention de régler la responsabilité résultant du fait des choses inanimées, l'animal seu apparaissant alors comme présentant des dangers pour les tiers, et l'on a dit; l'art. 1384, alin. 1, n'est dans sa partie finale qu'une disposition de renvoi à l'art. 1385, qui, dans le projet, n'était que le dernier paragraphe de l'art. 1384. Les choses dont on a la garde, ce sont les animaux seuls, une exception unique étant faite pour les bâtiments, qui font l'objet d'une disposition spéciale, celle de l'art. 1386.

Cette interprétation est, il faut le reconnaître, celle qui a long-temps prévalu: 'L'art. 1384, disait M. l'avocat général Sarrut dans ses conclusions du 16 juin 1896 (D.P. 97.1.433), n'a pas entendu formuler une règle générale, applicable à toutes les choses que le propriétaire aurait sous sa garde... Dans son 1er alinéa il annonce qu'il va être dérogé à la règle posée aux art. 1382 et 1383 dans certains cas, quant aux personnes et quant aux choses. Les exceptions concernant les personnes sont indiquées à l'art. 1384, dans les alinéas qui suivent; les exceptions concernant les choses le sont aux art. 1385 et 1386. Ces exceptions sont limitatives... Le code distingue nettement les choses animées, d'une part, les choses inanimées, d'autre part. Il n'etablit en thèse générale la responsabilité de plein droit du propriétaire qu'en ce qui concerne les choses animées (art. 1385); pour les choses inanimées, au contraire, le propriétaire n'est pas responsable en principe, sauf dans l'hypothèse de l'art. 1386, et encore à condition que la preuve soit faite que le bâtiment a péri par vice de construction ou défaut d'entretien.' Ainsi le dommage causé par une chose inanimée échappe aux prévisions de l'art. 1384 et ne peut donner lieu, le cas échéant, qu'à l'action de l'art. 1382. Telle était la solution admise par la jurisprudence et consacrée par l'arrêt, souvent rappelé, du 19 juil. 1870, rendu par votre chambre civile au rapport de M. le conseiller Larombière (D.P. 70.1.361). Il s'agissait en l'espèce de l'explosion d'une chaudière installée dans un lavoir, et le pourvoi soutenait que le propriétaire du lavoir devait être présumé en faute, dès lors que le fonctionnement de la machine avait été la cause d'un dommage. La Chambre Civile déclare qu'encore bien 'que l' explosion se rattache au fait actuel du propriétaire ou de ses agents', il appartient au demandeur d'établir, outre l'accident, la faute qu'il impute à ceux-ci, l'événement ayant pu être le résultat d'un cas fortuit et n'impliquant pas nécessairement la faute du défendeur; c'est, en somme, l'art. 1382 qui sera applicable.

Mais à l'encontre d'une interprétation qui, on ne manquait pas de l'observer, aboutissait à enlever toute portée à la disposition si générale et si formelle du paragraphe 1er de l'art. 1384, un mouvement doctrinal allait bientôt se produire, déterminé par le développement incessant du machinisme et la nécessité chaque jour plus impérieuse de protéger l'ouvrier contre les conséquences des accidents survenus au cours du travail. Déjà, à l'étranger, des lois spéciales avaient réglé la matière des accidents du travail; la jurisprudence française ne pouvait manquer d'être impressionnée par des tendances qui correspondaient à un souci évident de justice sociale, et, sans tenter encore de chercher en dehors de l'art. 1382 le fondement de ses décisions, elle allait s'efforcer d'en étendre autant que possible le champ d'application par une appréciation plus rigoureuse de la responsabilité du patron auquel sera imputée à faute l'omission des moyens préventifs de nature à empêcher l'accident ou des précautions considérées comme constituant une obligation du chef d'industrie.

Il n'en fallait pas moins pourtant rapporter la preuve de la faute conformément à l'art. 1382, et bien souvent l'accident apparaissait comme ayant sa cause immédiate, en dehors de toute faute du patron, dans l'outillage lui-même. L'explosion d'une chaudière, par example, pouvait se produire en dépit de la surveillance ou des précautions les plus attentives. Aucune faute ne pouvait être relevée contre le chef de l'industrie; c' était lui cependant qui avait fait installer la machine, cause de l'accident, lui qui en avait la direction, la surveillance et la garde; il était dès lors impossible qu'on ne fût pas tenté de rechercher si une responsabilité particulière ne résultait pas à sa charge d'une telle situation.

Dès le 21 juin 1895 (D.P. 96.3.65), le Conseil d'Etat entrait dans cette voie en accueillant l'action dirigée contre l'Etat par un ouvrier blessé dans un arsenal par un éclat métallique projeté par une machine, en dehors de toute faute d'un agent de l'Administration: 'La présomption, avait dit M. le commissaire du Gouvernement Romieu, qui, dans le travail manuel usité en 1804, était la faute de l'ouvrier, se trouve renversée aujourd'hui et doit, dans le travail mécanique moderne, être la faute de la machine.' L'ouvrier de l'industrie privée allait-il se trouver dans une situation moins favorisée que celui des ateliers de l'Etat?

L'art. 1384, § 1er, apparut alors comme fournissant la solution de la question ainsi posée: on est responsable, dit ce texte, des choses que l'on a sous sa garde, et ainsi se trouve créée une présomption de responsabilité à l'encontre du gardien de la chose, la garde impliquant la surveillance et le dommage causé faisant présumer une négligence dans cette surveillance. La formule est générale et absolue; elle ne distingue pas entre les choses susceptibles d'une garde et notamment entre les choses animées ou inanimées. Il est vrai que les art. 1385 et 1386 règlent l'application à la responsabilité résultant du fait des animaux ou de la ruine de l'immeuble, du principe posé dans l'art. 1384, § 1er, et qu'aucune disposition spéciale n'existe pour les choses inanimées. Faut-il en conclure que l'art. 1384 les a écartées de ses prévisions? A cet argument l'on a répondu que l'art. 1385 n'a pas pour seul objet de poser le principe de la responsabilité du fait des animaux; s'il en était ainsi il ferait double emploi avec l'art. 1384, § 1er, et serait, par suite, inutile; mais sa raison d'être essentielle est dans la disposition qui rend le gardien responsable, non seulement quand l'animal est sous sa garde, mais encore quand il est égaré ou s'est échappé. Rien de semblable n'était à prévoir pour les choses inanimées, et ainsi s'explique l'absence, en ce qui les concerne, d'un texte spécial ajouté à la disposition du paragraphe 1er de l'art. 1384.

Ce que l'on peut dire, c'est que le législateur de 1804 a été plus particulièrement occupé du dommage causé par les animaux, l'accident causé par les choses inanimées étant alors infiniment plus rare qu'aujourd'hui. Mais le texte de l'art. 1384, § 1er, est général, et les travaux préparatoires eux-mêmes n'apportent pas un argument décisif en faveur de la distinction proposée.

Telle est la thèse qui, le 16 juin 1896, a été consacrée par votre Chambre Civile (D.P. 97.1.433). Il s'agissait, en l'espèce, de l'explosion d'une machine d'une bateau à vapeur. 'Attendu, avez-vous dit, que l'explosion est due à un vice de construction; qu'aux termes de l'art. 1384 CC cette constatation, qui exclut le cas fortuit et la force majeure, établit vis-à-vis de la victime la responsabilité du propriétaire du remorqueur, sans qu'il puisse s'y soustraire en prouvant, soit la faute du constructeur de la machine, soit le caractère occulte du vice incriminé.' Ainsi était affirmée l'existence d'une présomption de responsabilité à la charge du propriétaire investi de la garde du bateau par lui confié à un préposé, la dite présomption ne cédant qu'à la preuve d'un cas fortuit ou de la force majeure, c'est-à-dire d'une cause étrangère non imputable au gardien de la chose.

Désormais, et bien que la loi du 9 avr. 1898 fût venue dans l'intervalle régler la question des accidents du travail, votre jurisprudence allait accepter et consacrer de façon constante l'applicabilité de l'art. 1384 aux choses inanimées. Qu'allait-il cependant falloir entendre par ce 'fait de la chose' qui engendre la responsabilité du gardien?

On conçoit, disait-on, le fait de l'animal qui a une activité propre et peut par lui-même causer un dommage; on conçoit moins aisément qu'il puisse y avoir un fait de la chose inanimée. Et l'on interpréta tout d'abord les mots 'fait de la chose' comme synonimes de 'vice de la chose': l'on appliquera donc l'art. 1384 lorsque la preuve sera faite de la défectuosité de la chose. La Chambre des Requêtes avait ainsi, le 30 mars 1897 (D.P. 97.1.439, 2ᵉ espèce), écarté la responsabilité du gardien, alors que l'on constatait le bon état d'entretien des chaudières qui avaient fait explosion, l'accident rentrant, disait-elle, dans la catégorie des cas fortuits. Le 3 juin 1904 (D.P. 1907.1.177), la même chambre, pour appliquer à un locataire la présomption à l'occasion d'une explosion de gaz, prend soin de relever que l'accident est dû à une détérioration de la canalisation. Le 29 avr. 1913, enfin, votre Chambre des Requêtes, au rapport de M. Michel-Jaffard (D.P. 1913.1.427), rejetait le pourvoi formé contre un arrêt écartant la responsabilité du gardien de la chose par le motif que le maillon de la chaîne d'un treuil qui s'était rompu, et avait causé l'accident, ne présentait aucun vice de construction et se trouvait dans des conditions normales eu égard à l'emploi auquel il était affecté. Ainsi se trouvait établi le cas fortuit exclusif de la responsabilité.

Mais le 21 janv. 1919 (D.P. 1922.1.25), votre Chambre Civile formulait une toute autre doctrine dans un arrêt que nous devons analyser. Une locomotive stationnant sur une voie de la gare Saint-Lazare avait fait explosion: la machine avait été vérifiée lors de sa construction et de ses réparations successives, elle avait résisté aux épreuves réglementaires, aucune faute ne pouvait être relevée à la charge de la compagnie ou de ses agents. La responsabilité de la compagnie n'en a pas moins été retenue: 'Attendu, avez-vous dit, que la présomption édictée par le paragraphe 1ᵉʳ de l'art. 1384 CC à l'encontre de celui qui a sous sa garde la chose inanimée qui a causé le dommage ne peut être détruite que par la preuve d'un cas fortuit ou de force majeure, ou d'une cause étrangère qui ne lui soit pas imputable; qu'il ne suffit pas de prouver qu'il n'a commis aucune faute, ni que la cause du dommage est demeurée inconnue; qu'*il n'est pas nécessaire que la chose ait un vice inhérent à sa nature, susceptible de causer le dommage, l'art. 1384 rattachant la responsabilité à la garde de la chose, non à la chose elle-même.*'

Voilà nettement affirmée, par une décision qui marque une étape importante dans l'évolution de la jurisprudence, l'existence de la présomption, et voilà précisé son caractère: le gardien de la chose inanimée est présumé responsable, et il ne s'exonérera pas en prouvant qu'il n'a pu empêcher le fait dommageable et n'a ainsi commis aucune faute. Cette solution, nous l'avons dit en analysant la jurisprudence relative à la responsabilité du fait des animaux, se déduit du texte même de l'art. 1384; elle est, au surplus, rationnelle: dans le cas prévu par l'art. 1384, §6, la personne lésée conserve, au défaut de la responsabilité des père, mère, instituteur ou artisan, un recours contre l'auteur de l'accident; il n'en est pas ainsi en cas de dommage causé par l'animal ou par la chose, et le gardien doit demeurer toujours responsable, à moins qu'il ne prouve l'existence d'une cause étrangère qui ne lui soit pas imputable, d'une responsabilité qui se substitue à celle qui, par la présomption, a été mise à sa charge.

L'arrêt précise, d'autre part, que le gardien ne saurait s'exonérer en prouvant que la cause du dommage est demeurée inconnue: la raison d'être de toute présomption n'est-elle pas de laisser à la charge de celui à l'encontre de qui elle est établie la responsabilité des accidents dont l'origine est restée mystérieuse?

Définissant enfin le fondement de la responsabilité, l'arrêt la rattache, non à la chose elle-même, mais à la garde de la chose. L'art. 1384 édicte une présomption de responsabilité personnelle: elle résulte, non pas d'un défaut de la chose, d'un vice inhérent à sa nature, mais d'un défaut de garde, d'un manquement présumé à l'obligation qui pèse sur le gardien.

La formule de votre arrêt de 1919 se retrouve dans l'arrêt de 1920 qui allait conduire le législateur à compléter le texte de l'art. 1384 et à apporter en même temps une consécration législative implicite à la jurisprudence nouvelle à laquelle avait donné lieu la disposition de son paragraphe Ier. Des fûts de résine entreposés dans la gare maritime de Bordeaux avaient pris feu et communiqué un incendie; vous avez, le 16 nov. 1920 (D.P. 1920.1.169) et le 15 mars 1921 (D.P. 1922.1.25), admis la responsabilité de la compagnie et dit qu'elle ne pouvait être exonérée par le fait que l'inflammation du brai ne résultait pas d'un vice inhérent à sa nature.

Bien qu'il s'agît d'un incendie résultant de l'inflammation d'objets mobiliers, les compagnies d'assurances s'émurent à la pensée que la jurisprudence allait peut-être s'étendre, dans le cas d'incendie d'un immeuble, au recours exercé par les voisins, et elles manifestèrent leur intention de majorer le taux des primes en prévision de ce nouveau risque. De là est née la loi du 7 nov. 1922 (D.P. 1923.4.89), qui, dans le but d'éviter à la propriété foncière un surcroît de charges, a ajouté à la suite du paragraphe 1er de l'art. 1384 cette disposition. 'Toutefois, celui qui détient à un titre quelconque tout ou partie de l'immeuble ou des biens mobiliers dans lesquels un incendie a pris naissance ne sera responsable, vis-à-vis des tiers, des dommages causés par l'incendie que s'il est prouvé qu'il doit être attribué à sa faute ou à la faute des personnes dont il est responsable.'

Il serait difficile de nier qu'il y ait là une consécration de l'interprétation donnée par vos arrêts du paragraphe 1er de l'art. 1384; en disposant pour le cas particulier de l'incendie et en exigeant dans ce cas la preuve de la faute du gardien de la chose, le législateur a manifestement entendu, et le mot 'toutefois' placé en tête de l'alinéa 2 souligne cette intention, apporter une exception au principe posé dans le paragraphe 1er, dont il justifie par là même l'application au dommage causé par les choses inanimées.

Votre jurisprudence était déjà fixée dans le sens de la responsabilité personnelle du gardien, l'accident étant présumé dû au défaut de garde, lorsque le développement incessant de la circulation automobile vous plaça en présence d'un nouveau problème.

La voiture automobile est évidemment une de ces choses inanimées qui, suivant l'interprétation donnée par la jurisprudence, rentrent dans le champ d'application de l'art. 1384, §1er. Sans difficulté, la jurisprudence a reconnu la responsabilité du gardien lorsque, la machine étant au repos ou abandonnée par le conducteur, un accident vient à se produire en dehors de toute participation actuelle de l'homme. On considérait que le dommage, en ce cas, était véritable-ment le fait de la chose; la présomption de l'art. 1384 devait jouer à l'encontre du gardien qui s'était mal acquitté de l'obligation de garde qui lui incombait.

Mais devait-il en être de même en cas de dommage causé par l'automobile actionnée et dirigée par son conducteur?

Aux termes de l'art. 1384, on est responsable du fait de la chose dont on a la garde. Quand pourra-t-on dire qu'il y a 'fait de la chose'? D'autre part, le fait de la conduite de l'automobile se concilie-t-il avec l'idée de garde?

Sur le premier point, on allait voir se reproduire au sujet de l'automobile la thèse que nous avons exposée et qui avait été soutenue en ce qui concerne les choses inanimées en général. Le fait de la chose, ce sera le vice propre de la chose, le vice de construction, le défaut d'entretien; ce sera même l'éclatement d'un pneumatique, la rupture de la direction ou des freins, tous événements provenant, en somme, de l'état de la voiture. Dans tous ces cas, l'accident sera causé par la chose en dehors de la participation de l'homme. Mais lorsque, le conducteur étant au volant, un accident se produira *sans que la preuve puisse être rapportée qu'il est dû à un vice des organes de la machine*, on se trouvera en présence du fait de l'homme dans la main duquel la voiture n'est, en somme, qu'un instrument qu'il dirige à sa volonté, et l'art. 1382 sera seul applicable.

D'autre part, peut-on dire que le conducteur d'une automobile en a la 'garde'? Le mot 'garde' implique l'idée de surveillance; on ne garde pas, on ne surveille pas l'automobile en marche, on la conduit, et à ce point de vue encore l'art. 1384 ne saurait s'appliquer.

Cette doctrine, consacrée par de nombreux arrêts de Cours d'appel, avait été, semble-t-il, admise par un arrêt de votre Chambre de Requêtes du 22 mars 1911 (D.P. 1911.1.354), qui, statuant dans une espèce où une personne avait été écrasée par une automobile alors qu'elle circulait sur une route, avait dit 'qu'il s'agit dans la cause, non de la responsabilité de la chose dans les termes de l'art. 1384, mais de la responsabilité résultant du fait du conducteur.'

Mais l'évolution marquée par vos arrêts déjà rappelés de 1919 et 1920 devait vous conduire en matière d'automobile à une autre solution, et le 29 juil. 1924 (D.P. 1925.1.5), votre Chambre Civile cassait un arrêt de la Cour de Paris écartant la responsabilité du propriétaire d'une automobile qui, dirigée par un de ses préposés, était, à la suite d'une embardée, montée sur un trottoir et avait pénétré dans une boutique où une personne avait été blessée; 'Attendu, avez-vous dit, que l'arrêt attaqué déclare que, l'accident *ne pouvant être attribué au mauvais état de l'automobile*, aucune faute ne peut être retenue à la charge de la Compagnie l'*Abeille*, qui détruit la présomption de faute pesant sur elle aux termes de l'art. 1384, § 1er CC; qu'en statuant ainsi il a violé l'article susvisé.'

On a beaucoup discuté en doctrine sur la portée de cet arrêt, où l'on a voulu voir une simple décision d'espèce. Il est certain qu'il n'a pas réussi à fixer la jurisprudence des cours et tribunaux; il semble cependant que la Chambre Civile, accueillant le moyen du pourvoi fondé sur la violation de l'art. 1384, reconnaît cet article applicable lors même que l'accident ne peut être attribué au vice de la machine, qu'aucune faute n'est imputable au conducteur et que le voiture est actuellement dirigée par ce conducteur. C'est l'application à l'automobile en marche de la doctrine consacrée de façon générale par votre jurisprudence pour les choses inanimées. Le 22 dec. 1924, le Conseil d'Etat (D.P. 1925.3.9) admettait à son tour la présomption à l'encontre d'un conducteur d'automobile, cette présomption ne pouvant être détruite que par les circonstances spécifiées par vos arrêts déjà cités.

Quoi qu'il en soit, l'affaire Jand'heur allait vous permettre de préciser votre pensée sur cette question toujours controversée de la responsabilité de l'automobiliste. La Cour de Besançon avait admis en l'espèce que l'accident causé par l'automobile en marche constituait, non le fait de la chose prévu par l'art. 1384, mais le fait de l'homme donnant lieu à la seule application de l'art. 1382.

Fait de la chose, fait de l'homme: on observait que la distinction ainsi posée aboutissait à ce résultat de faire peser la présomption de responsabilité sur le gardien dans le seul cas où, l'automobile étant au repos, son pouvoir dommageable est à peu pres nul, le droit commun de l'art. 1382 reprenant son empire au moment précis où la voiture, mise en marche, devient une source de dangers; résultat singulier si l'on considère que le législateur, en édictant la présomption de l'art. 1384, a eu évidemment en vue les personnes et les choses dont on a la surveillance ou la direction et qui peuvent être pour les tiers la source d'un dommage. La garde et les obligations qui en découlent ne survivraient donc pas au fait de l'embrayage?

Ce n'est pas dans le texte du code que l'on peut trouver la justification de la distinction proposée. L'on admet, au contraire, que les responsabilités des art. 1384 et 1385 sont gouvernées sur presque tous les points par les mêmes règles et sont issues de la même conception juridique: or, on ne distinguera pas, pour l'application de l'art. 1385, suivant que le cheval sera abandonné ou accompagné, suivant que le chien gardera une maison inoccupée ou chassera sous l'oeil et sous la direction de son maître.

La distinction, si elle était admise, devrait jouer pour toutes les choses inanimées comme pour l'automobile: l'explosion d'une locomotive donnerait lieu à l'application de l'art. 1384 quand l'accident se produirait en l'absence du mécanicien ou du chauffeur; dans le cas contraire et pour la machine en marche, l'art. 1382 pourrait seul être invoqué. Ce serait le renversement de toute votre jurisprudence en la matière.

Au surplus, il ne sera pas toujours facile de distinguer le fait de l'homme du fait de la chose: l'accident causé par l'automobile arrêtée pourra être dû au fait du chauffeur qui aura négligé de caler les roues ou de serrer les freins; d'autre part, l'accident survenu en cours de route peut avoir une cause d'ordre mécanique et imprévisible, tel qu'un vice de construction ou le défaut d'un bandage. L'application de l'art. 1384 dépendra-t-elle de preuves de cet ordre?

Enfin, il n'est point exact que l'automobile ne soit aux mains du conducteur qu'un instrument agissant à sa volonté. L'automobiliste n'est pas maître absolu de sa machine, pas plus que le conducteur n'est maître absolu du cheval qu'il mène: l'animal, être vivant, a, il est vrai, des initiatives imprévisibles; mais la machine porte dans ses flancs une force que l'homme crée, actionne et dirige, mais dont il ne peut prévoir et limiter les effets: c'est ce que l'on a appelé, assez improprement d'ailleurs, le 'dynamisme propre de la machine'; de cette force, de la vitesse qui en est l'effet, l'automobiliste n'est pas pleinement le maître. C'est, a-t-on pu dire, la force utilisée qui conditionne l'accident beaucoup plus que la personnalité du conducteur.

C'est dans ce sens qu'a statué l'arrêt du 21 fév. 1927 (D.P. 1927.1.97): 'Attendu, dit tout d'abord votre Chambre Civile, que la loi ne distingue pas suivant que la chose qui a causé le dommage était ou non actionnée par la main de l'homme'; et ainsi se trouve condamnée la thèse adoptée par la Cour de Besançon. L'art. 1384 s'appliquera sans distinction entre le fait de la chose et le fait de l'homme, la responsabilité se rattachant, ainsi que l'affirmaient déjà les arrêts de 1919 et de 1920, non à la chose elle-même, mais à la garde de la chose. Mais l'arrêt ne s'en tient pas à l'affirmation de ce principe. Dans la notion de garde, la Chambre Civile va trouver la limitation du champ d'application de la présomption édictée par le texte: l'obligation de garde qui est à la base de la présomption suppose que la chose avait besoin d'être gardée parce qu'elle était susceptible de causer un dommage à autrui. A la notion de garde s'associe donc la notion de chose dangereuse, et l'arrêt du 21 fév. 1927 ajoute au considérant dont nous avons donné lecture: 'Qu'il suffit qu'il s'agisse d'une chose soumise à la nécessité d'une garde à raison des dangers qu'elle peut faire courir à autrui.'

Cette fois, votre doctrine était clairement définie. La Cour de Lyon l'a écartée par l'arrêt suivant:... (v. D.H. 1927.423).

La thèse de l'arrêt peut se résumer ainsi. Si l'on a pu, par des motifs d'utilité pratique, dégager du texte de l'art. 1384, qui ne prévoit rien de tel, une présomption du fait des choses inanimées, elle ne peut s'appliquer qu'au cas où le dommage résulte *directement de la chose, d'un vice propre de la chose, abstraction faite de l'activité présente de l'homme.* Le gardien devait, en effet, se prémunir contre les périls auxquels la chose, arrêtée ou en marche, peut exposer les tiers: tel sera le cas d'un éclatement de pneu, d'une rupture de frein, de tout accident dû à un vice rendant dangereux l'usage de la machine. Il n'en peut être ainsi quand la machine est mue ou conduite par la main de l'homme: la direction imprimée comporte à tout instant de la part du conducteur les précautions nécessaires à la sécurité d'autrui; leur omission constitue la faute personnelle justiciable de l'art. 1382, en vertu du principe primordial que chacun répond, en dehors de l'exercice normal d'un droit, de son fait ou de son abstention préjudiciables. Il y a donc à distinguer suivant que le fait dommageable *se rattache par un rapport direct à l'homme ou à la machine*: l'auto dirigée est un instrument aux mains de l'homme et, en cas d'accident, un moyen de transmission d'un dommage subjectivement produit; elle ne sera dangereuse, en fait, qu'aux mains d'un conducteur imprudent ou malhabile. L'art. 1384 vise le cas où l'accident est survenu par le fait de la chose et a sa cause dans un défaut de garde ou de surveillance, non dans l'impéritie de la direction.

La Cour de Lyon rejette donc le système adopté par votre Chambre Civile et qui aboutit à substituer la présomption à l'application de l'art. 1382 chaque fois qu'au fait prépondérant de l'homme s'ajoute la détention intermédiaire d'une chose dont le juge reconnaît le caractère dangereux. Pas davantage la cour n'admet que le gardien ne soit pas autorisé à établir l'absence de faute, alors que, d'après l'art. 1352 CC, la preuve contraire est de droit contre les présomptions: il faut démontrer que le défendeur a fait de son droit un usage abusif, et il est injuste de condamner lorsque, la cause de l'accident étant inconnue, on ne sait pas s'il ne serait pas dû à la propre imprudence de la victime. Ce qui est logique, c'est d'imposer à la victime la preuve du manquement par elle allégué à la règle qui oblige le conducteur à agir avec prudence et vigilance.

En conséquence, la cour décide en principe que 'l'accident causé par une automobile en mouvement, sous l'impulsion et la direction de l'homme, alors qu'aucune preuve n'existe qu'il soit dû à un vice propre de la voiture, ne constitue pas un dommage causé par une chose qu'on a sous sa garde.' C'est le principe exactement contraire à celui qu'affirme votre arrêt de 1927, et que, dans le mémoire ampliatif joint au pourvoi de la dame veuve Jand'heur, Me Jaubert vous demande de consacrer à nouveau.

Le moyen est pris de la fausse application de l'art. 1382 CC, violation des art. 1384 du même code, 7 de la loi du 20 avr. 1810, en ce que l'arrêt attaqué a mis à la charge de la victime d'un accident causé par une automobile la preuve d'une faute imputable au conducteur, alors que la faute du conducteur devait être présumée.

L'exposé auquel nous avons procédé de l'évolution de votre jurisprudence en la matière nous dispensera, semble-t-il, d'analyser en détail un mémoire qui devait tout naturellement se référer à cette jurisprudence et vous en proposer le maintien.

On ne conteste plus guère, observe le pourvoi, que l'art. 1384, § 1er, crée une présomption de faute à la charge du gardien de la chose qui a causé un dommage; le fondement de cette présomption est dans l'obligation de garder la chose, et la garde s'impose logiquement pour les choses dangereuses, au nombre desquelles on ne peut nier qu'il faille classer l'automobile. Vainement prétend-on que, lorsque l'accident est causé par l'automobile en marche, il y a fait de l'homme et non fait de la chose. Il est vrai que, derrière toute manifestation de l'activité propre à certaines choses inanimées, on retrouve, en dernière analyse, le fait de l'homme: dans la grenade qui éclate, dans la chaudière qui explose, il y a, au fond, le fait du fabricant. Mais il ne suffit pas qu'il en soit ainsi pour que soit écartée l'application de l'art. 1384, qui, autrement, ne sera jamais applicable. On ne peut contester dans un grand nombre d'accidents l'existence du fait de la chose. L'arrêt attaqué reconnaît qu'il en sera ainsi de l'accident dû à un vice de la chose, tel qu'une rupture d'un organe de la machine échappant à toute prévision du conducteur. Mais la vitesse, raison d'être de l'automobile, est par elle-même une cause d'accident, car la machine possède, suivant l'expression admise, un dynamisme propre, et de cette vitesse il n'est pas vrai que le conducteur soit pleinement maître: l'auto en pleine action n'obéit pas instantanément à l'ordre de celui-ci, et l'accident causé par la machine en marche n'est pas exclusivement et en toute circonstance le fait de celui qui l'actionne et la dirige.

Faudra-t-il cependant rechercher dans chaque cas si l'accident provient du fait de la machine ou du fait du conducteur pour appliquer, suivant le cas, l'art. 1382 ou l'art. 1384? Le pourvoi observe que, s'il en était ainsi, on aboutirait à rendre le gardien responsable quand il ne conduit pas, la présomption cessant de s'appliquer lorsqu'il fait de la machine l'usage qui la rend dangereuse pour autrui. On aboutirait aussi à imposer à la victime l'obligation d'une preuve préalable dont la présomption instituée par l'art. 1384 a eu pour but de l'exonérer. Ce serait revenir à la doctrine qui impose à la victime la charge de la preuve du vice de construction, et que toute votre jurisprudence a condamnée.

L'automobiliste sera donc, sauf la preuve de l'existence d'une cause qui lui soit étrangère, responsable de plein droit du dommage causé par la machine, sans qu'il y ait à distinguer le fait de l'homme de celui de la chose.

La seule distinction à faire en la matière est celle que l'arrêt du 21 fév. 1927 établit entre les choses dangereuses et celles qui ne le sont pas. Il n'est pas exact de dire que cette distinction est purement arbitraire et étrangère au texte du code civil: l'art. 1384 n'institue la présomption qu'à l'occasion des choses qui nécessitent une garde, et seules les choses dangereuses pour autrui ont besoin d'être gardées.

La thèse ainsi formulée par le demandeur au pourvoi trouve son principal appui dans votre jurisprudence. Dans son mémoire en défense, Me Labbé observe, et avec raison, que cette jurisprudence ne s'impose pas aux chambres réunies, saisies pour la première fois de la question et chargées de poser définitivement les principes de la responsabilité du fait des choses inanimées.

Comme la Cour d'appel de Lyon, le défendeur au pourvoi estime qu'en déclarant applicable aux choses inanimées la disposition de l'art. 1384, § 1er, CC, la jurisprudence a outrepassé la pensée du législateur de 1804, l'idée de la faute aquilienne prouvée étant l'assise obligatoire de toute responsabilité et le texte susvisé, en instituant, par une disposition exceptionnelle, la responsabilité du fait des choses dont on a la garde, n'ayant eu en vue que les animaux et les immeubles, suivant les termes des art. 1385 et 1386. Mais, comme la Cour de Lyon aussi, c'est moins au principe même qu'il va s'attaquer qu'à l'application qui en a été faite par la jurisprudence.

L'art. 1385 déclare responsable le propriétaire de l'animal, et cela s'explique: l'animal agit indépendamment de son gardien, il peut échapper à sa surveillance; si cependant il cause un dommage, comme il ne peut être responsable, il est logique de s'adresser à celui qui aurait dû l'empêcher de nuire. Le gardien est ainsi présumé responsable du dommage causé *en dehors de lui*. Si l'on veut que l'art. 1384 s'applique aux choses inanimées, il faudra dire par analogie que le gardien ne sera non plus responsable que du dommage causé par la chose *en dehors de lui*. De même que l'animal a une activité indépendante susceptible de léser autrui, de même la chose ne peut engager la responsabilité du gardien que si elle a un dynamisme propre capable de causer un dommage *indépendamment de l'intervention de l'homme*. Le fait de la chose, c'est le vice proper de la chose. Il appartenait au gardien de la mettre hors d'état de nuire, et si le dommage se réalise il y a faute. Tel sera le cas d'une explosion de machine ou de munitions, mais non du dommage causé par un organisme mû ou conduit par l'homme. Il ne s'agit plus alors d'une chose soumise à garde et qui cause un dommage parce que mal gardée; la chose est un instrument aux mains de l'homme, un intermédiaire, le prolongement de l'activité humaine; le dommage est le fait de l'homme comme celui causé par l'arme ou le bâton qu'on tient à la main.

Envisageant le cas de l'automobile, on reconnaîtra donc que, si l'art. 1384 s'applique à la rupture du frein ou à l'éclatement d'un pneu, faits de la chose qui se conçoivent indépendamment de l'intervention de l'homme, on ne peut *a priori* déclarer l'automobiliste responsable des accidents causés par sa voiture *puisqu'il est toujours à même, à raison de la maîtrise qu'il a sur la chose, d'agir de façon que l'accident ne se réalise pas.* On est en présence du fait de l'homme; seul l'art. 1382 peut y être appliqué.

La situation s'analyse donc en ces termes: ou la victime *prouvera* le fait de la chose (rupture de frein, etc.), et alors la présomption de l'art. 1384 jouera contre le gardien, ou elle devra prouver la faute du conducteur.

C'est pour échapper, dit-on, à ce dilemme que l'arrêt de 1927 a introduit en la matière la notion de chose dangereuse, les choses dangereuses entraînant seules la responsabilité de plein droit de leur gardien. Or l'art. 1384, s'il parle des choses qu'on a sous sa garde, ne dit nullement que les choses qu'il vise sont seulement celles qui nécessitent une garde à raison des dangers qu'elles peuvent faire courir à autrui. D'ailleurs, la notion de garde est la même pour les animaux que pour les choses inanimées, les uns et les autres étant, d'après la jurisprudence, simultanément visés par l'art. 1384, §1er; or le critérium de danger est certainement étranger à l'art. 1385, qui ne distingue pas entre les animaux dangereux et les autres.

La vérité est que le code civil ne permettait pas de garantir aux victimes des accidents d'automobile la protection légale que tout le monde jugeait désirable; il en était tellement ainsi qu'un projet de loi avait été préparé en 1907 par la Société d'Etudes législatives sur le rapport de M. Ambroise Colin, et qu'en 1927 M. Ricolfi saisissait la Chambre des députés d'un projet spécial. Il n'appartient pas à la Cour de cassation de se substituer au législateur.

Au surplus, le système du pourvoi conduirait à des difficultés insurmontables d'application qui en sont la condamnation. Le critérium de danger étant admis pour l'application de l'art. 1384, comment classer les choses en deux catégories, dangereuses ou inoffensives? Y aura-t-il là une question de fait tranchée souverainement par le juge du fond, ou une question de droit relevant de votre contrôle?

Question de droit, dit M. Ripert (notes au *Dalloz* 1925, 1.5 et 1927 1.97), et il propose de distinguer trois catégories entre lesquelles la Cour de cassation pourra répartir les choses dangereuses: 1° celles qui sont mues par une force dont l'homme n'a pas la direction absolue; 2° celles qui, mises en mouvement par la force humaine, en amplifient l'effet; 3° celles que la pesanteur rend dangereuses, alors du moins qu'elles sont mises dans une position telle que cette force les entraîne. En réalité, on aboutit ainsi-à confondre la notion de chose dangereuse et celle de chose dommageable, le fait que la chose est devenue dommageable démontrant qu'elle recélait un danger; c'est l'extension indéfinie de l'art. 1384, toute chose pouvant, suivant les circonstances, être l'occasion d'un dommage.

Pour d'autres auteurs, comme M. Savatier (note au *Dalloz*, 1927, 2.169) ou M. Capitant (Chronique D.H. 1927, p. 52), il n'y a pas de distinction de principe à faire entre les choses dangereuses ou non, il n'y aura qu'une question de fait dont l'appréciation appartiendra aux juges du fond. Une même chose, en effet, est dangereuse ou non suivant les circonstances; l'automobile roulant en vitesse est dangereuse, elle ne l'est plus quand elle est arrêtée ou marche à petite allure. Mais alors on en viendra à distinguer les choses dangereuses par les circonstances dans lesquelles le gardien les aura placées; celui-ci aura dès lors la possibilité de prouver qu'il avait pris les précautions nécessaires pour que la chose fût inoffensive, et on reviendra par un détour à autoriser contre la présomption l'admission de la preuve contraire.

Ainsi, de deux choses l'une: ou bien on appréciera objectivement la notion de chose dangereuse, et alors on la confondra forcément avec la chose susceptible de causer un dommage, toute chose ayant causé un dommage se révélant par là même dangereuse, et l'art. 1382 se trouve éliminé au profit de l'art. 1384; ou bien on appréciera subjectivement, d'après les circonstances, et alors, le gardien étant admis à prouver qu'il avait fait le nécessaire pour que la chose ne fût pas dangereuse, on remène l'art. 1384 dans le sillage de l'art. 1382.

Telles étant, d'après le défendeur au pourvoi, les conséquences du critérium de danger, l'on observe, en outre, que ce critérium ne permettra pas de trancher toutes les difficultés. En cas de collision, par exemple, entre deux automobiles également dangereuses, y aura-t-il partage des responsabilités, ou en reviendra-t-on au principe de l'art. 1382 et à la preuve de la faute, que la présomption cependant devrait a voir pour effet d'écarter? La solution est encore plus douteuse lorsqu'il s'agira d'une collision entre deux choses inégalement dangereuses, comme une automobile et une bicyclette.

En réalité, le système de l'arrêt de la Chambre Civile tend, conclut le défendeur, en rendant la responsabilité presque irréfragable, à étendre dans notre droit la notion du risque créé, encore que la jurisprudence ait toujours paru l'écarter. Un tel système est choquant, car il place dans la même situation le chauffeur imprudent et le chauffeur soucieux des règlements; il est injuste, puisque le chauffeur qui n'a commis aucune faute sera responsable par cela seul qu'il n'aura pu prouver la faute de la victime, et alors même qu'en réalité c'est à cette faute que sera sû l'accident.

En se substituant au législateur et en créant un système légal de responsabilité des automobilistes, la jurisprudence issue de l'arrêt de 1927 aboutit à des conséquences devant lesquelles ont reculé les législations qui ont réglé cette question. C'est ainsi que la loi allemande du 3 mai 1909 et la loi autrichienne du 9 août 1908 laissent en dehors de leur champ d'application les automobiles dont la vitesse n'est pas supérieure à 20 ou 25 kilomètres à l'heure, et admettent les détenteurs à prouver que l'accident n'est pas dû au vice de la voiture et qu'ils avaient pris toutes les précautions nécessaires pour l'éviter. Cette dernière formule est celle de la loi italienne du 30 juin 1912. La loi anglaise du 14 août 1903 ne déclare responsable que celui qui conduit avec témérité ou imprudence eu égard à la nature de la route et au trafic qui s'y fait normalement au temps même de l'accident.

C'est par les motifs que nous venons de rappeler que le défendeur vous demande de rejeter le pourvoi.

Que vous soyez ainsi conviés à revenir sur la doctrine consacrée par une jurisprudence depuis longtemps établie, on ne le dissimule pas: l'on vous demande de dire que si l'art. 1384, § 1er, CC s'applique aux choses, inanimées, la présomption qu'il édicte vise seulement le fait de la chose, ces mots devant s'entendre du dommage résultant du vice propre de la chose, indépendamment de toute intervention, de tout fait de l'homme; or vous jugez depuis vos arrêts de 1919 et de 1920 que l'art. 1384 rattache la responsabilité à la garde de la chose, non à la chose elle-même; l'on vous demande de décider, par voie de conséquence, que l'accident n'est pas le fait de la chose lorsque la voiture automobile est sous l'impulsion et la direction de l'homme: vous avez jugé constamment le contraire depuis 1927. Cette jurisprudence ne lie pas les chambres réunies: entre les thèses opposées qui se partagent la doctrine et la jurisprudence des cours d'appel, vous aurez à choisir la solution qui désormais s'imposera.

Arrêt

La Cour; – Statuant toutes chambres réunies; – Sur le moyen du pourvoi; – Vu l'art. 1384, alin. 1er, CC: – Attendu que la présomption de responsabilité établie par cet article à l'encontre de celui qui a sous sa garde la chose inanimée qui a causé un dommage à autrui ne peut être détruite que par la preuve d'un cas fortuit ou de force majeure ou d'une cause étrangère qui ne lui soit pas imputable; qu'il ne suffit pas de prouver qu'il n'a commis aucune faute ou que la cause du fait dommageable est demeurée inconnue; – Attendu que, le 22 avr. 1925, un camion automobile appartenant à la Société *Aux Galeries belfortaises* a renversé et blessé la mineure Lise Jand'heur; que l'arrêt attaqué a refusé d'appliquer le texte susvisé par le motif que l'accident causé par une automobile en mouvement, sous l'impulsion et la direction de l'homme, ne constituait pas, alors qu'aucune preuve n'existe qu'il soit dû à un vice propre de la voiture, le fait de la chose que l'on a sous sa garde dans les termes de l'art. 1384, § 1er, et que, dès lors, la victime était tenue, pour obtenir réparation du préjudice, d'établir à la charge du conducteur une faute qui lui fût imputable; – Mais attendu que la loi, pour l'application de la présomption qu'elle édicte, ne distingue pas suivant que la chose qui a causé le dommage était ou non actionnée par la main de l'homme; qu'il n'est pas nécessaire qu'elle ait un vice inhérent à sa nature et susceptible de causer le dommage, l'art. 1384 rattachant la responsabilité à la garde de la chose, non à la chose elle-même; – D'où il suit qu'en statuant comme il l'a fait, l'arrêt attaqué a interverti l'ordre légal de la preuve et violé le texte de loi susvisé;

Par ces motifs, casse…, renvoie devant la Cour d'appel de Dijon.

Extracts from Articles and Notes on the Foregoing Case

Extract from article by Louis Josserand,
1930 D.H. Chronique, 28

Il nous paraît que la Cour de cassation, en substituant la présomption de responsabilité à la présomption de faute, a eu en vue et les solutions concrètes que nous venons de rappeler et l'idée dont elles procèdent; elle a fait un pas dans le sens de l'objectivation de la responsabilité du fait des choses inanimées, sur la voie de la substitution de la notion de risque au concept traditionnel de la faute, concept vieilli, qui, sans doute, est toujours indispensable, mais qui ne suffit plus à supporter, sur une base désormais trop étroite, l'édifice, devenu formidable et pesant, de la responsabilité.

S'il en est ainsi, si nous ne nous faisons pas illusion sur le sens et la portée de la formule utilisée par la Cour suprême, le processus suivi comporte les étapes suivantes: faute prouvée, présomption de faute, présomption de responsabilité, risque; la faute présumée, puis la responsabilité présumée n'auraient été que des procédés techniques permettant de ménager la transition entre la faute et le risque, ces deux pôles de la responsabilité.

Ainsi, de toute façon, l'arrêt des Chambres Réunies nous paraît digne d'être approuvé, il a ce grand mérite de restituer à la théorie de la responsabilité du fait des choses inanimées et sa véritable nature juridique et le vaste domaine qui lui est dévolu par la lettre de la loi comme par les nécessités de la vie moderne, si fertile en risques de toutes sortes; il faut y voir un arrêt de principe-type qui cristallisera autour de lui les données essentielles du problème et qui, en brisant les tentatives de refoulement de la thèse objective, contribuera à donner à l'homme, aux prises avec des choses toujours plus nombreuses et sans cesse plus redoutables, la sécurité juridique à laquelle il peut d'autant plus légitimement prétendre que sa sécurité matérielle se trouve de plus en plus menacée…

Extracts from article by Henri Capitant,
1930 D.H. Chronique, 30–2

Certes, il y a du vrai dans cette observation, et il faut reconnaître qu'en exigeant du gardien une preuve aussi difficile, souvent impossible, la Cour de cassation a inconsciemment glissé vers la théorie de la responsabilité objective. Mais ce n'est qu'un glissement, et si, comme on le prétend, elle substituait à la conception traditionnelle celle du risque, bien autrement redoutables seraient les conséquences de cette révolution. En effet, la conception nouvelle ferait tache d'huile et ne tarderait pas à envahir le terrain de l'art. 1382. Car, quelle raison y aurait-il de distinguer entre le dommage causé par le fait des choses et celui qui est causé par le fait de l'homme? On arriverait donc à effacer de l'art. 1382 le mot de faute et à affirmer que tout fait quelconque de l'homme qui cause dommage à autrui oblige son auteur à le réparer.

Ainsi, la faute serait rapidement éliminée de la responsabilité extracontractuelle, et, quoi qu'en pensent certains auteurs, cette évolution ne marquerait pas un progrès. Le risque ne peut être le fondement unique de la responsabilité. Qu'on l'applique, dans certains cas, par exemple en matière d'accidents du travail, même en matière d'accidents d'automobiles, cela peut se concevoir, mais l'étendre à tous les dommages que l'activité de l'homme peut causer à autrui serait fort dangereux. Ce serait faire peser sur les hommes une responsabilité écrasante; ce serait paralyser l'esprit d'initiative. Personne n'oserait plus rien faire, puisque la plus grande diligence ne mettrait pas à l'abri de la responsabilité. Aussi, aucune législation, à l'exception du code civil soviétique, n'a-t-elle adopté cette thèse; et encore, le code civil soviétique, lui-même, n'a-t-il pas pu proscrire cette notion de faute, laquelle reparaît fréquemment, soit dans les textes législatifs, soit dans les décisions de la jurisprudence. En effet, le risque exige un contrepoids, qui est l'assurance. Or, on peut bien s'assurer contre un risque déterminé, par exemple, l'accident du travail, l'accident d'automobile, mais on ne le peut pas contre toute espèce de risques...

Si, comme nous le croyons, l'arrêt du 13 février dernier ne modifie pas la base sur laquelle repose la responsabilité délictuelle, en revanche, il consacre implicitement deux innovations dans la jurisprudence de la Cour suprême. Il résulte, en effet, de son texte, et ici aucune divergence d'interprétation ne paraît possible, qu'il n'y a plus lieu, pour l'application de l'art. 1384, 1er alin., de distinguer entre les choses inertes ou dangereuses, mobilières ou immobilières. Rien n'obligeait la Cour à se prononcer sur ces deux questions, car elles dépassent le cadre de l'arrêt qu'elle avait à apprécier, et il n'est pas, on le sait, dans ses habitudes, de se lier pour l'avenir. Si donc elle a jugé bon de passer sous silence les prudentes restrictions que la Chambre Civile avait formulées en 1927, c'est que sa volonté bien formelle était d'élargir le domaine de l'art. 1384...

Cette nouvelle doctrine a pour résultat de déplacer le centre de la responsabilité délictuelle; elle le transporte de l'art. 1382 à l'art. 1384, 1er alin.; elle vide le premier au profit du second.

La fortune de ce lambeau d'article si longtemps ignoré est vraiment singulière; voilà qu'il devient le texte fondamental du chapitre des délits et des quasi-délits.

Cette évolution ne constitue pas, à notre avis, un progrès. L'équilibre, si sagement établi par le code civil est rompu; son système est vraiment bouleversé. En décidant que l'individu est responsable de plein droit de tout dommage qui paraît causé par le fait d'une chose inanimée, quelle qu'elle soit, la Cour de cassation fait peser sur l'homme un risque trop lourd, contre lequel il ne peut se prémunir par l'assurance. Il ne lui suffit plus de se comporter en homme très diligent, de prendre toutes les précautions qu'exige la prudence. Si attentivement qu'il veille sur ses choses, sa responsabilité peut être engagée et il lui sera presque impossible de s'en décharger. La juste mesure est dépassée. Au fond. M. Josserand a raison; la notion de faute n'est plus qu'une fiction. Sans bien s'en rendre compte, la jurisprudence lui substitue celle de risque. Nous ne serions pas étonné qu'un jour prochain le législateur dût intervenir pour remettre les choses au point.

Extracts from note by Georges Ripert,
  D.P. 1930.1.57

Le plus sage serait peut-être de ne retenir que la décision elle-même en se bornant à constater qu'elle confirme la jurisprudence antérieure. Il nous suffirait alors, puisque nous avons défendu cette jurisprudence, de renvoyer à la note publiée sous l'arrêt de la chambre civile. Mais nous ne pouvons pas ne pas remarquer que, si l'arrêt des Chambres Réunies accepte la décision de la Chambre Civile, il ne la reproduit pas littéralement. La Cour de cassation apporte trop de soin à la rédaction de ses arrêts pour que de nouveaux motifs ne soient pas dignes d'attention. Il se peut que ce soit attacher trop d'importance à des formules qui n'ont peut-être été adoptées que dans la lassitude d'un long délibéré. Un arrêt solennel mérite pourtant d'être étudié phrase par phrase...

D'ailleurs, il n'est plus temps de déclarer que cet arrêt n'apporte rien de nouveau, car déjà les commentateurs s'en sont emparés. Il a été accueilli par le cri de triomphe de M. Josserand (Chronique D.H. 1930, p. 25), la parole de regret de M. Capitant (Chronique D.H. 1930, p. 29), le doute discret de M. Maurice Picard (*Revue des assurances*, 1930, n° 2, p. 259), sans parler des commentaires anonymes naturellement moins réservés dans l'éloge et la critique. Chacun s'est déjà attribué le droit d'interpréter à sa façon une formule qui permet la discussion... Les divergences et les variations des annotateurs ne sont après tout que la rançon de l'indépendance de la pensée et de l'ardeur dans la recherche; les incertitudes de la jurisprudence ont cette plus grave conséquence de compromettre la sécurité juridique en faisant renaître des discussions que la fixité de la règle aurait arrêtées. La Cour de cassation ne peut voir du reste, dans les nombreux et audacieux commentaires de sa décision, que la preuve de l'attention avec laquelle les civilistes étudient les motifs de ses arrêts et les formules qui les expriment.

1. – Qu'y a-t-il de nouveau dans l'arrêt des Chambres Réunies? Peu de chose à la vérité, et cet arrêt est plus remarquable par ce qu'il ne dit pas que par ce qu'il dit.

...L'art. 1384, § 1er, n'est applicable que si le dommage est dû au fait d'une chose qui devait être gardée parce qu'elle était dangereuse. La seule preuve du dommage établit dans ce cas que le gardien de la chose a manqué à son obligation, et ce gardien est par suite présumé en faute, à moins qu'il ne parvienne à démontrer que le dommage ne provient pas en réalité du fait de la chose.

Cette formule heureuse trouvait son appui dans le texte même de l'art. 1384, § 1er, expliquait l'existence et la portée de la présomption de faute, et délimitait le domaine d'application de la responsabilité du fait des choses, en faisant une distinction raisonnable. Si cette distinction a été critiquée par certains auteurs, ... c'est peut-être qu'elle n'a pas toujours été bien comprise...

De telles critiques ont-elles touché la Cour de cassation? On pourrait le croire, puisque l'arrêt rapporté ne reproduit pas la formule qui figure dans l'arrêt de 1927. D'autre part, les mots *présomption de faute* ont disparu; ils ont été remplacés par les mots *présomption de responsabilité*.

Faut-il attacher une grande importance à cette formule de la présomption? Y a-t-il dans la pensée de la Cour une différence entre présomption de faute et présomption de responsabilité? Nous ne le croyons guère...

Une autre modification de la formule de l'arrêt mérite d'être remarquée. La Chambre Civile, dans son arrêt du 21 févr. 1927, citait l'art. 1384, § 1ᵉʳ, comme établissant une présomption de faute pour les *choses mobilières* inanimées, et rappelait par là sa jurisprudence qui écartait l'application de l'art. 1384 pour les dommages causés par les immeubles. La chambre des requêtes, par un arrêt du 6 mars 1928 (D.P. 1928.1.97, note de M. Josserand), statuant sur le cas d'un accident causé par un ascenseur, a décidé qu'il y avait lieu d'appliquer la présomption de faute. On a voulu voir dans la modification de la formule de l'arrêt de 1927 une approbation de cette jurisprudence... Il serait dangereux de vouloir déduire de cette suppression la preuve que la Cour de cassation est décidée à appliquer l'art. 1384, § 1ᵉʳ, à tous les dommages causés par le fait des immeubles. Disons simplement qu'elle a voulu réserver la question.

Chose qui peut paraître plus grave, l'arrêt ne parle plus de la nécessité de la garde *à raison des dangers que la chose peut faire courir à autrui.* Il n'était pas indispensable, pour casser l'arrêt attaqué, de se prononcer sur l'étendue d'application de la responsabilité du fait des choses, puisque la discussion portait uniquement sur la distinction du fait personnel et du fait de la chose. Nous croirions volontiers que la Cour de cassation, en supprimant cette formule, a voulu simplement éviter tout ce qui pouvait diviser inutilement les esprits...

Or quand on rattache la responsabilité à la garde de la chose, on est nécessairement conduit, pour admettre une présomption de responsabilité, à analyser cette idée de garde afin de déterminer l'étendue de l'obligation... La jurisprudence a généralisé cette obligation de garde parce qu'elle s'est aperçue que certaines choses, dangereuses pour les tiers, doivent être étroitement gardées pour éviter qu'elles ne causent un dommage: un moteur, une voiture par exemple. Mais elle sera bien obligée de reconnaître qu'il y a des choses que l'on n'a pas besoin de garder pour éviter des dommages, parce qu'elles sont par elles-mêmes inoffensives. S'il est constaté qu'une de ces choses a été l'instrument du dommage, il n'y a aucune raison pour présumer une faute dans la garde. La faute de la victime ou celle d'un tiers est beaucoup plus vraisemblable...

II. – Mais d'autres, se flattant également d'interpréter l'arrêt des

Chambres Réunies, estiment que la Cour de cassation a voulu abandonner la distinction présentée par sa Chambre Civile, qu'elle a voulu admettre la plénitude d'application de l'art. 1384, §^{er}, et que par là même, réalisant un progrès décisif en matière de responsabilité civile, elle s'est ralliée à la théorie du risque en la déguisant mal sous les mots de présomption de responsabilité...

Que l'on puisse ainsi interpréter sa décision, voilà qui est de nature à mettre la Cour de cassation en garde contre les formules trop larges. Il est bon que les défenseurs les plus qualifiés de la théorie du risque s'emparent de cet arrêt pour y voir un bulletin de victoire. Leur chant d'allégresse ne peut manquer d'effrayer la Cour de cassation, car elle ne saurait tout de même pas s'attribuer le droit de changer le fondement donné par le code civil à la responsabilité civile et, de sa propre autorité, substituer le risque à la faute, comme on l'incite à le faire.

Il est vrai que son procureur général s'est amusé à lui montrer dans de vieux usages de procès faits aux choses comme une préfiguration de la théorie de la responsabilité objective, et que, bon grammairien autant qu'érudit historien, il lui a dit que le mot 'choses' est le terme le plus général de la langue française et n'a pas été employé par hasard dans l'art. 1384, § 1er, CC. Il a dû reconnaître pourtant qu'il n'y a, en faveur de la théorie du risque, aucune tradition, aucune disposition légale expresse, et que la jurisprudence a eu depuis 1896 à forger la théorie de la responsabilité du fait des choses. Cherchant lui-même quel pouvait être le fondement d'une telle responsabilité, il a déclaré: 'Il y a toujours un fait personnel sous le dommage causé par la personne ou la chose dont on répond.'

Alors même que l'on serait partisan d'une évolution de la théorie de la responsabilité vers le principe du risque créé, il nous paraît impossible de soutenir qu'un tel principe puisse être introduit dans nos lois ou notre jurisprudence d'une façon aussi simple et brutale que celle qui consisterait à dire: chacun est responsable du risque qu'il a créé, ou des choses qui lui appartiennent et dont il a la garde. M. Capitant remarque avec infiniment de raison que, dans aucune législation du monde, une règle d'une application aussi rigide n'a été donnée pour déterminer la responsabilité, et il ajoute que, sous peine de paralyser l'esprit d'initiative et d'écraser l'activité, il est impossible d'adopter la théorie du risque sans en limiter l'application et sans la corriger par l'assurance (Chronique D.H. 1930, p. 31).

Ajoutons que, malgré son apparente simplicité, la théorie du risque conduit à une inextricable difficulté, puisqu'il s'agit de déterminer la responsabilité civile sur le seul examen de la causalité entre le fait et le dommage et que ce problème de causalité est par lui-même insoluble (v.G. Ripert, *La règle morale dans les obligations civiles*, 2ᵉ édit., 1927; Planiol, Ripert et P. Esmein, *Traité prat. de droit civil*, t. 6, n° 539). En particulier dans la responsabilité du fait des choses, il ne sert de rien de dire: on est responsable de la chose qui a causé le dommage, car encore faut-il savoir dans quels cas la chose est la *cause* du dommage, et il n'y a en pure logique aucune raison de rattacher le dommage au fait de la chose plutôt qu'au fait de la victime ou à un cas fortuit quelconque, tout dommage étant le résultat d'une infinité de causes.

Si la théorie de la responsabilité du fait des choses n'était qu'une manifestation de la théorie du risque, nous aurions, à côté du principe général de la responsabilité délictuelle, une règle particulière de responsabilité objective; la première puiserait sa source dans la faute, la seconde dans le risque créé (Josserand, Chronique D.H. 1930, p. 5 et 28; *Cours de droit civil positif français*, t. 2, nos. 553 à 555). Rien ne nous autorise à dire que nos lois civiles connaissent cette double règle. En tout cas, la Cour de cassation ne l'a pas dit, puisqu'elle a senti la nécessité d'appuyer sur un texte du code civil la règle qu'elle a donnée et de la justifier par la notion de présomption de faute. Notre système de responsabilité étant basé sur la faute, la responsabilité du fait des choses ne peut être expliquée et appliquée que si l'on trouve dans la matérialité de l'accident une raison de présumer la faute de celui qui a la garde de la chose.

III. – Reconnaître l'existence d'un double principe de responsabilité civile, en voyant dans l'art. 1384, § 1ᵉʳ, une règle de responsabilité objective, serait d'ailleurs en fait faire de cette règle la règle de droit commun, et réduire l'art. 1382 à une portée d'application restreinte. Suivant la remarque très juste de M. Capitant (Chronique D.H. 1930, p. 32), on viderait l'art. 1382 de son contenu en profit de l'art. 1384.

Il n'est pour ainsi dire pas d'accident matériel où le dommage ne soit causé par le fait d'une chose. Même si je frappe avec la main, la bague que je porte au doigt peut augmenter la rudesse du coup et entraîner l'application de l'art. 1384, § 1ᵉʳ. Il faudrait supposer une collision entre deux individus pratiquant le nudisme intégral pour qu'il y eût lieu à l'application de l'art. 1382! Encore se trouvera-t-il bien un juriste pour dire que le corps n'est qu'une chose sous la garde de la volonté, et qu'il faut par conséquent appliquer l'art. 1384 au dommage dû au fait corporel de l'homme!

Si l'on applique l'art. 1384, § 1ᵉʳ, sans aucune distinction, toutes les règles de notre droit civil sont déséquilibrées. Si cette règle est applicable à tous les immeubles et dans tous les cas, comme la suppression dans l'arrêt des mots 'chose mobilière' permet à quelques-uns de le croire, pourquoi exiger dans l'art. 1386 la preuve du défaut d'entretien ou du vice de la construction? Le fait matériel de la chute de l'immeuble devrait suffire, et il paraît impossible d'admettre que dans le cas le plus grave, la ruine de l'immeuble, la règle de protection des tiers soit la plus faible. Pourquoi admettre, avec la loi du 7 nov. 1922 (D.P. 1923.4.89), qu'il n'y a pas de présomption de responsabilité au cas d'incendie, puisque le dommage provient d'une chose inanimée? Mieux encore, les lois sur les accidents du travail deviennent absurdes: elles ont la prétention d'établir un régime favorable aux ouvriers, mais le risque professionnel n'est qu'une application du risque créé, et le caractère forfaitaire de la réparation est une restriction inadmissible de la réparation due!

... Il y a des cas où il suffit de constater la matérialité de l'accident et de connaître la chose qui en a été l'instrument pour présumer que le gardien de cette chose est en faute parce que, susceptible de causer un dommage à autrui, cette chose devait être gardée. On ne veut pas dire autre chose quand on soutient qu'il faut faire une distinction entre les choses dangereuses et celles qui ne le sont pas. On ne pourra prétendre que la Cour de cassation condamne cette distinction que lorsqu'elle aura cassé un arrêt qui aura refusé d'appliquer l'art. 1384, § 1er, en constatant que celui qui a l'usage d'une chose ne présentant aucun danger doit être cependant présumé en faute.

IV. – En tout cas, si cette notion de chose dangereuse paraît impossible à admettre parce qu'elle imposerait une distinction entre les choses qui n'est pas écrite dans la loi, attachons-nous fermement aujourd'hui à l'*idée de garde*, qui n'a pas été abandonnée dans l'arrêt des Chambres Réunies. L'interprète dira quel est le fondement et la portée de cette obligation de garde. Il nous suffit que la jurisprudence en reconnaisse l'existence. Elle peut se contenter d'affirmer, sans qu'elle ait besoin d'expliquer...

... S'il voulait prendre la première place et prétendait assurer la réparation de tous les dommages causés par les choses, sans limitation de l'indemnité, sans garantie de l'assurance, il apparaîtrait comme une règle intolérable et qui, loin de faire régner la justice, substituerait sans raison au hasard du dommage le hasard de la réparation.

Ou, s'il en était autrement, c'est qu'il y aurait eu dans les esprits une profonde évolution, que la propriété ou la possession des choses ne serait plus considérée comme une source de profits, mais comme une cause de risques, que l'initiative apparaîtrait toujours comme coupable et l'activité comme condamnable. Nous n'en sommes pas là. Le code civil des Républiques socialistes soviétiques lui-même ne condamne que les personnes et les entreprises 'dont l'activité cause une aggravation du danger pour l'entourage' (art. 404).[3] Il y a du moins dans cette idée d'aggravation du danger une restriction à l'idée abstraite du risque créé.

Extracts from note by Paul Esmein,
S. 1930.1.121

II. C'est sur une question d'ordre plus général qu'on attendait surtout de connaître le sentiment des Chambres Réunies: celle de savoir si la présomption de l'art. 1384 s'applique à toutes choses quelconques. En efet, depuis l'arrêt de la Chambre Civile du 21 fév. 1927 précité, cette Chambre, puis celle des Requêtes, déclarent la présomption applicable *aux choses soumises à la nécessité d'une garde en raison des dangers qu'elles peuvent faire courir à autrui.* V. Cass. Civ. 25 juil. et 26 oct. 1927 (*S.* 1928, 1.89), et la note de M.P. Esmein; Cass. Req. 1er mai 1929 (*Rec. Gaz. Pal.,* 1929, 1. 75). Les Chambres Réunies maintiendraient-elles cette distinction entre les choses dangereuses et non dangereuses, soumettant à la présomption les dommages causés par les premières seules, distinction approuvée par les uns, critiquée par les autres? V. notre note précitée, et Planiol et Ripert, *Traité pratique de dr. civil,* t. 6, *Les oblig.,* par P. Esmein, n° 615. Elles ont gardé le silence. Elles n'avaient pas à statuer sur ce point, mais seulement sur l'application de la présomption aux accidents causés par les choses actionnées par l'homme. Mais on ne manquera pas, du côté des partisans de l'extension de la responsablitité du fait des choses, d'invoquer ce silence même, ainsi que certaine expression employée, et la position très nettement prise par le procureur général, M. Paul Matter, dans ses conclusions (v. celles-ci au *Rec. Gaz. Pal.,* 1930, 1. 393). V. Josserand, *La Responsabilité du fait des automobiles devant les chambres réunies, Dalloz hebd.,* 1930, *Chronique,* p. 25.

Le fait même de ne pas reproduire la formule *choses soumises à la nécessité d'une garde en raison des dangers qu'elles peuveni faire courir à autrui,* est, dira-t-on, significatif. Il ne peut être involontaire.

On relèvera de même l'expression *présomption de responsabilité,* substituée à celle de présomption de faute, jusqu'ici employée par les arrêts comme par les auteurs. Et ceci conformément à une suggestion contenue dans les conclusions de M. Paul Matter.

Or celui-ci se rallie nettement à la thèorie qui fonde la responsabilité sur le risque créé et en charge celui qui a le profit de la chose, comme une contre-partie de ce profit. A plusieurs reprises, il cite des passages caractéristiques de Saleilles, auxquels il donne son entière approbation, et il affirme que l'art. 1384 s'applique au fait des choses sans aucune limitation. Il est vrai qu'ailleurs il déclare 'qu'il y a toujours un fait personnel sous le dommage causé par la personne ou la chose dont on répond', et il justifie une à une les responsabilités des art. 1384 à 1386 par l'idée d'une faute de surveillance, garde, choix ou éducation. Ses conclusions n'en constituent pas moins dans leur ensemble un plaidoyer en faveur de la responsabilité sans faute.

Il ya a plus: l'éminent magistrat prétend que cette responsabilité est consacrée par une tradition ininterrompue depuis les temps primitifs, ou, du moins, interrompue seulement pendant un siècle, le 19e (ce qui est bien peu de chose dans l'histoire de l'humanité)...

Comme, d'autre part, il est certain que les poursuites contre des choses, encore plus que celles contre des animaux, n'ont été sous la monarchie que des fait exceptionnels, on doit reconnaître qu'il n'y avait pas, en 1804, de tradition dans le sens d'un principe général de responsabilité du fait des choses.

iv. Il n'en résulte pas que la jurisprudence inaugurée en 1896 soit condamnable, si l'on admet, conformément à la doctrine formulée par M. le premier président Ballot-Beaupré dans son discours du *Centenaire du Code civil* (t. I, p. 27), rappelé par M. Paul Matter, que, lorsque le sens d'un texte pris en lui-même s'y prête, les juges peuvent l'interprétet conformément 'aux réalités et aux exigences de la vie moderne'. Or, l'art. 1384, alin. 1er, contient une formule visant en soi les choses en général. D'autre part, on ne voit pas de raison de ne pas rendre responsable de la même façon que le gardien d'un animal le gardien d'une chose lorsqu'elle est susceptible de nuire à autrui autant que peut l'être un animal. L'argument d'analogie est ici pressant. – Mais il ne s'ensuit pas que l'on doive appliquer l'art. 1384, alin. 1er à toutes choses sans distinction. La limitation aux choses dangereuses est conforme à la tradition: Si l'ancien droit n'avait, en définitive, établi de responsabilité spéciale que pour le fait des animaux, c'est parce qu'il n'a pas connu de choses assez constamment dangereuses, en dehors du fait de l'homme, pour qu'il fût utile d'en établir une. Les temps contemporains en ont connu au contraire avec les machines, puis les automobiles qui entraînent l'homme qui les conduit.

Les Chambre Réunies n'ont cependant pas reproduit la formule par laquelle les Chambres Civiles, depuis 1927, avaient manifesté l'intention de limiter le domaine de la présomption de faute. Mais cette suppression peut s'interpréter de deux façons. Ce peut être la volonté d'écarter toute distinction et de consacrer avec une portée générale la doctrine du risque. Ce peut être aussi la pensée que les choses dangereuses ne le sont que suivant les circonstances, que même toutes choses peuvent ou non, suivant les circonstances, justifier une responsabilité de plein droit. Cette pensée, énoncée par ceux qui ont critiqué la formule de 1927 (Capitant, *Dalloz hebd.*, 1927, *Chronique* 49; Savatier, *Semaine juridique*, 1927, 433, et *Dalloz*, 1927.2.169) conduit à abandonner celle-ci sans que son abandon implique l'adoption de la doctrine du risque. Peut-être encore, simplement, les Chambres Réunies n'ont-elles pas voulu s'engager sur une distinction dont la base reste encore obscure et sur laquelle l'expérience seule permettra de voir clair, comme le montrent les sérieuses discussions qu'elle a soulevées...

En admettant qu'on doive renoncer à distinguer suivant que les choses ont ou non besoin d'une surveillance particulièrement vigilante, les magistrats hostiles à une responsabilité des cas fortuits trouveront dans la notion de cas fortuit ou de force majeure un terrain éminemment favorable à la restriction.

Croit-on, par exemple, que les propriétaires de terrains qui par un glissement du sol, ont endommagé des fonds inférieurs ou des maisons, seront rendus responsables du chef de l'art. 1384? Il y a là pourtant un vice comparable au vice d'une machine inconnu de son gardien.

D'ailleurs l'adoption comme principe directeur de l'idée de risque attaché au profit n'aurait pas de tous points le résultat que ses promoteurs en attendent. Elle recèle en elle-même une source de limitation et même de réaction. Si, en effet, on s'attache au profit, la justice impose de tenir compte du profit que la victime a tiré de la chose au même titre que du profit du gardien. C'est l'idée qui a inspiré la jurisprudence et lui a fait écarter la présomption de faute au cas de dommage causé à une personne transportée gratuitement en auto-mobile (v. Cass. Civ. 7 janv. 1929, *S.* 1929, 1.249, et la note de M.P. Esmein). Elle est susceptible des applications les plus variées, d'autant plus que le profit peut consister dans un simple plaisir procuré: à la personne admise à visiter une habitation, un parc, des collections, etc.; au touriste qui se promène en forêt ou en montagne et est blessé par la chute d'un arbre ou d'un rocher; à celui qui, venu sur le bord d'une chaussée pour assister à une cavalcade ou à une course d'automobiles, est blessé par un cheval ou une voiture lancée à toute vitesse.

Inversement, la doctrine du profit fait obstacle à la solution qui semble justement prévaloir au cas de dommage causé, par la rencontre de deux choses ou d'une chose et d'un animal, à l'un des deux, et qui consiste à considérer les deux présomptions, chargeant respectivement les deux gardiens, comme s'annulant, et à exiger la preuve d'une faute (v. Planiol et Ripert, *op. cit.* t. 6, n. 621). La théorie du profit conduit à rendre les gardiens responsables en proportion du profit tiré par chacun d'eux, par exemple proportionnellement à la valeur respective des choses ou animaux.

Et pour conclure, enfin, nous estimons que même si l'on veut faire une certaine part à l'idée du risque, il serait aussi imprudent qu'inexact de lui donner la première, et d'abandonner la doctrine de la présomption de faute, qui s'est révélée capable de donner satisfaction aux désirs de développement de la responsabilité civile. L'examen de l'arrêt ci-dessus nous a conduit à penser que tel reste le sentiment de la Cour de cassation (rappr. Capitant, *Recueil Dalloz hebdomadaire*, 1929, *Chronique*, p. 29).

Notes:

1. An inquiry into the facts relating to this allegation. This would not be done in open court.

2. One of the joint authors of Colin et Capitant, *Cours élémentaire de Droit civil français*, and formerly a professor at the Paris Faculty of Law. It is the custom to appoint a law professor as a *conseiller* (judge) of the Cour de cassation; and in many instances, such as this, these professor-judges have exerted great influence on the development of the law.

3. This is not quite correct; it takes no account of art. 403.

23. Cour de cassation
Chambre Civile, 20 mars 1933
Dame Veuve Delcayre c. Messal
(D.P. 1933,1.57)

Pourvoi en cassation contre l'arrêt de la Cour d'appel de Montpellier du 2 déc. 1930 (D.P. 1931.2.129), pour violation de l'art. 1384 CC, de l'art. 7 de la loi du 20 avril 1810, défaut de motifs et manque de base légale, en ce que l'arrêt attaqué a décidé, pour refuser à Mme veuve Delcayre le bénéfice de l'art. 1384 précité, que les deux parties à la collision ayant subi des dommages, les présomptions résultant du dit article en faveur de chacune d'elles se neutralisaient et s'annulaient, – alors, d'une part, qu'aucune présomption résultant de l'art. 1384 ne pouvait jouer en faveur de M. Messal, lequel, n'ayant formulé aucune demande de dommages-intérêts, faisait valoir uniquement cet article par voie d'exception et pour éluder la réparation des dommages subis par Mme Delcayre, ce que l'art. 1384 n'autorise pas, – et d'autre part, qu'en admettant même que chacun des gardiens des véhicules tamponnés eût, pour la réparation du préjudice par lui subi, invoqué contre l'autre l'art. 1384, il n'en serait pas résulté, par une sorte de neutralisation des présomptions découlant de ce texte, l'impossibilité pour aucun de ces gardiens de s'en prévaloir, mais bien que chacun d'eux au contraire aurait été en droit, en l'invoquant, de réclamer à l'autre la totalité du préjudice subi par lui du fait de la collision.

Arrêt

La Cour; – Sur le moyen unique: – Vu l'art. 1384, alin. 1er CC; – Attendu que la présomption de responsabilité établie par cet article à l'encontre de celui qui a sous sa garde la chose inanimée qui a causé un dommage à autrui, ne peut être détruite que par la preuve d'un cas fortuit ou de force majeure ou d'une cause étrangère qui ne lui soit pas imputable; qu'il ne suffit pas de prouver que le gardien de la chose n'a commis aucune faute; – Attendu qu'une collision s'est produite le 29 juin 1928, sur la route de Béziers à Narbonne, entre une automobile dirigée par Messal et une bicyclette conduite par Delcayre, lequel a trouvé la mort dans cet accident; que, poursuivi, sous prévention d'homicide par imprudence, devant la juridiction répressive, Messal a été acquitté, mais que la veuve Delcayre l'a assigné en dommages-intérêts devant la juridiction civile en vertu de l'art. 1384 CC; – Attendu que l'arrêt attaqué constate que l'automobile a causé la mort de Delcayre et mis sa bicyclette hors d'usage, sans relever expressément une faute à la charge de la victime; que, néanmoins, il rejette la demande de la veuve pour le motif que la voiture a été détériorée par le choc de la bicyclette et que, les deux véhicules s'étant réciproquement causé des dommages, les présomptions de responsabilité qui pèsent sur les conducteurs des voitures se neutralisent; – Mais attendu que la présomption de responsabilité édictée par l'art. 1384 CC à l'encontre du gardien de la chose est subordonnée dans son application à la seule condition que le dommage ait été causé par le fait de celle-ci; qu'elle ne saurait être détruite en tout ou en partie du fait que les deux gardiens se sont réciproquement cause des dommages; – Attendu qu'il résulte des propres énonciations de l'arrêt attaqué que le dommage subi par la veuve Delcayre l'a été par le fait de l'automobile conduite par Messal, et qu'il résulte implicitement mais nécessairement des termes de l'arrêt que la cour ne s'est pas préoccupée de rechercher si l'accident était dû ou non à la faute de la victime; d'où il suit qu'en statuant comme il l'a fait l'arrêt attaqué a violé le texte ci-dessus visé;

Par ces motifs; – casse, renvoie devant la Cour d'appel de Nîmes.

24. Cour de cassation
Chambre Civile, 19 et 24 fév. 1941
(D. 1941,85)

1re *Espèce*: – *Epoux Cadé* c. *Ville de Colmar* – Arrêt
Pourvoi en cassation contre un arrêt de la Cour d'appel de Colmar
du 23 janv. 1937

La Cour; – Sur le moyen additionnel, lequel est préalable... – (Sans intérêt);

Et sur le premier moyen: – Attendu que la dame Cadé, prise d'un malaise dans une cabine de l'établissement de bains municipal de la ville de Colmar, s'est affaissée sur le sol et a été brûlée au bras par le contact prolongé d'un tuyau du chauffage central; que les époux Cadé ont assigné la ville de Colmar en se fondant notamment tant sur la faute de la surveillante des bains, préposée de la ville, qui, appelée par la malade, aurait eu le tort de ne pas demeurer un temps suffisant auprès d'elle, que sur l'art. 1384, § 1er, CC, en raison du dommage causé par la tuyauterie dont la ville avait la garde, ainsi que sur la responsabilité contractuelle de la ville; qu'ils ont été déboutés par la Cour d'appel de Colmar (arrêt du 23 janv. 1937), motif pris, d'une part, de ce que la préposée n'avait commis aucune faute, d'autre part, de ce que l'accident a eu pour cause le malaise de la dame Cadé, qui a provoqué sa chute au contact d'un tuyau du chauffage central, et non ce tuyau, qui n'a joué qu'un rôle purement inerte, et enfin de ce que, si le contrat intervenu entre l'établissement de bains et la dame Cadé comportait l'obligation de ne pas mettre en danger la santé ou la sécurité de sa cliente, il n'impliquait pas celle de la garantir contre un état de santé défectueux que l'établissement ignorait; – Attendu que le pourvoi, abandonnant le terrain de la responsabilité contractuelle, fait en premier lieu grief à cette décision d'avoir écarté la présomption de responsabilité qui, en vertu de l'art. 1384, § 1er, CC, pesait sur la ville de Colmar, sans établir soit la force majeure, soit la faute exclusive de la victime; – Mais attendu que, pour l'application de l'art. 1384, § 1er, CC, la chose incriminée doit être la cause du dommage; que si elle est présumée en être la cause génératrice dès lors qu'inerte ou non elle est intervenue dans sa réalisation, le gardien peut détruire cette présomption en prouvant que la chose n'a joué qu'un rôle purement passif, qu'elle a seulement subi l'action étrangère génératrice du dommage; qu'il résulte des constatations des juges de fond que tel a été le cas en l'espèce, la tuyauterie contre laquelle la dame Cadé s'est affaissée se trouvant installée dans des conditions normales et la cause génératrice du dommage résidant toute entière dans la syncope qui a fait tomber la dame Cadé de la chaise où elle était assise, et a permis qu'elle demeurât inanimée en contact avec un tube chaud assez longtemps pour être brûlée; – Attendu que les demandeurs reprochent encore à l'arrêt attaqué d'avoir méconnu le caractère fautif des agissements de la surveillante de l'établissement de bains, préposée de la ville, mais que cette critique n'est pas mieux fondée que la première; qu'en effet, l'absence de faute de la femme de service résulte des constatations mêmes de la Cour d'appel, qui relève qu'appelée par la dame Codé, elle lui est venue en aide dans la mesure ou cette, dernière le lui a demandé; – Attendu qu'il suit de là que, loin de violer les textes visés au moyen, l'arrêt attaqué, qui est suffisamment motivé, en a fait une exacte application;

Par ces motifs, rejette.

25

2ᵉ Espèce: – Pialet c. Veuve Guise – Arrêt
Pourvoi en cassation contre un arrêt de la Cour d'appel de Nîmes
du 7 juin 1934

La Cour; – Sur le moyen unique: – Attendu qu'alléguant que son fils mineur, en traversant le soir la terrasse du café tenu par Pialet pour entrer dans l'établissement, avait buté contre une chaise pliante gisant à plat sur le sol, était tombé, s'était grièvement blessé, et se fondant sur l'art. 1384, § 1er, CC, la dame Guise a assigné Pialet en payement de dommages-intérêts; qu'il est reproché à l'arrêt (Nîmes, 7 juin 1934) d'avoir, pour ordonner une enquête en vue d'établir la réalité des faits articulés, déclaré en principe l'art. 1384 applicable à l'espèce, alors que, la chaise étant une chose inerte, son gardien ne saurait être responsable d'un fait qu'elle n'a pas accompli; – Mais attendu qu'en établissant à la charge du gardien de la chose, dont le fait a causé un dommage, une présomption de responsabilité qui ne cède que si le gardien prouve que le fait n'a pu être par lui ni prévu ni empêché, l'art. 1384, § 1er, ne distingue pas suivant que la chose est inerte ou en mouvement; qu'il suffit, pour que la responsabilité du gardien soit encourue, qu'il soit établi que la chose est en quelque mesure la cause du dommage, qui, sans elle, ne se fût pas produit; qu'en statuant dès lors ainsi qu'il l'a fait, l'arrêt attaqué n'a pas violé le texte visé au moyen;

Par ces motifs, rejette.

In a note to these two decisions (at D.C. 1941, J.85) M. Jacques Flour, Professor at the Faculty of Law at Dijon, points out that they both turn on the question whether art. 1384, § 1er, is applicable to 'des choses inertes', and that they are easily reconciled in terms of the following principles:

'(*a*) L'art. 1384, § 1er, est applicable aux choses inertes, invocable par celui qui les heurte;

(*b*) Mais il n'en est ainsi qu'autant que la chose a véritablement causé le dommage;

(*c*) Le rôle de cause est présumé dès lors que la chose est intervenue dans la réalisation du dommage; c'est au gardien de "détruire cette présomption en prouvant que la chose n'a joué qu'un rôle purement passif" (1er espèce. Sur ce point, v. déjà dans le même sens: Civ. 9 juin 1939, 16 janv. 1940 et 21 janv. 1941, précités).

La différence d'une espèce à l'autre n'est donc qu'une différence de fait: la tuyauterie n'était pas cause de la brûlure, la chaise l'était de la chute.'

However, he calls attention to the eternal difficulty of detecting the true cause of an accident and, after agreeing that these decisions can only be explained by a theory of 'adequate' causation, opines that they might just as well have been decided on a basis of presence or absence of fault, 'adequate' meaning no other than 'foreseeable'. He points out, indeed, that it is often more difficult to apply a theory of causation than to recognise fault, and says:

'Tout ce qu'il peut y avoir de variable et de contingent dans l'appréciation de la faute est l'inévitable rançon d'un système de responsabilité subjective. Tout *jugement*, et c'en est un que de constater une faute, est, dans une large mesure, insusceptible de prédétermination. Au contraire, l'un des buts d'un système de responsabilité objective est précisément d'écarter ces incertitudes, de fournir une règle que les événements mêmes mettent en jeu et non le jugement de l'homme, une règle automatique requérant une simple *constatation*. Sinon, les avantages en sont illusoires. N'est-il pas alors paradoxal que l'art. 1384, § 1er, aboutisse à cette analyse, plus subtile que jamais, des circonstances de l'accident, alors que l'on a toujours enseigné que ce texte a précisément pour but d'assurer l'indemnisation de la victime *lorsque la cause du dommage reste inconnue?*'

26. Cour de cassation
Chambres Réunies, 2 déc. 1941
Cons. Connot c. Franck
(D.C. 1942, J.25)

Pourvoi en cassation contre l'arrêt de la Cour d'appel de Besançon du 25 févr. 1937 (D.H. 1937,182), statuant sur renvoi après cassation prononcé par arrêt de la chambre civile du 3 mars 1936 (D.P. 1936.1.81, note de M. Capitant), – pour 'violation des art. 1382 et 1384 CC et de l'art. 7 de la loi du 20 avr. 1810, en ce que l'arrêt, sans relever les circonstances qui caractérisent le vol et la conduite d'une voiture automobile par un tiers, a exonéré le propriétaire, gardien de celle-ci, des conséquences d'un accident causé par elle, pour le motif, d'une part, que le fait de la soustraction aurait transféré la garde au voleur, et, d'autre part, que l'accident ne serait pas la conséquence directe d'un abandon supposé fautif, au sens de l'art. 1382, alors que des faits constatés il résulte que le propriétaire n'avait pu se décharger de la garde juridique du véhicule en manquant précisément à son obligation de gardien, et que, d'ailleurs, ce manquement caractérise un quasi-délit'.

Arrêt

La Cour; – Sur le moyen unique pris en sa première branche: – Attendu qu'il résulte des énonciations de l'arrêt attaqué que, dans la nuit du 24 au 25 déc. 1929, une voiture automobile, appartenant au docteur Franck, et que celui-ci avait confiée à son fils Claude, alors mineur, a été soustraite frauduleusement par un individu demeuré inconnu, dans une rue de Nancy où Claude Franck l'avait laissée en stationnement; qu'au cours de la même nuit, cette voiture, sous la conduite du voleur, a, dans les environs de Nancy, renversé et blessé mortellement le facteur Connot; que les consorts Connot, se fondant sur les dispositions de l'art. 1384, alin. 1ᵉʳ, CC, ont demandé au docteur Franck réparation du préjudice résultant pour eux de la mort de Connot; – Attendu que, pour rejeter la demande des consorts Connot, l'arrêt déclare qu'au moment où l'accident s'est produit, Franck, dépossédé de sa voiture par l'effet du vol, se trouvait dans l'impossibilité d'exercer sur ladite voiture aucune surveillance; qu'en l'état de cette constatation, de laquelle il résulte que Franck, privé de l'usage, de la direction et du contrôle de sa voiture, n'en avait plus la garde et n'était plus dès lors soumis à la présomption de responsabilité édictée par l'art. 1384, alin. 1ᵉʳ, CC, la Cour d'appel, en statuant ainsi qu'elle l'a fait, n'a point violé le texte précité;

Sur le moyen pris en sa seconde branche: – Attendu que, dans leurs conclusions en cause d'appel, les consorts Connot soutenaient que Franck, en abandonnant sa voiture automobile sur la voie publique sans prendre aucune précaution en vue d'éviter un vol, avait commis une faute, au sens de l'art. 1382 CC, faute qui avait eu pour conséquence directe le dommage dont les demandeurs poursuivaient la réparation; que, pour rejeter ces conclusions, l'arrêt déclare qu'il n'y a lieu de rechercher si Franck a commis la faute qui lui est imputée, aucun lien de cause à effet ne pouvant exister entre la faute prétendue et l'accident dont Connot a été victime; que le pourvoi fait grief à l'arrêt d'avoir, en statuant ainsi, violé l'art. 1382 CC; – Mais attendu que ce grief n'a pas été examiné par la Chambre Civile à l'occasion du pourvoi formé contre l'arrêt rendu le 10 juil. 1931 par la Cour d'appel de Nancy; que l'arrêt de la Chambre Civile du 3 mars 1936, qui a cassé l'arrêt précité de la Cour de Nancy, est fondé exclusivement sur la violation de l'art. 1384, alin. 1ᵉʳ, CC; – Attendu, d'autre part, qu'aux termes de l'art. 1ᵉʳ de la loi du 1ᵉʳ avr. 1837, les chambres réunies de la Cour de cassation n'ont compétence pour statuer que lorsque le deuxième arrêt ou jugement rendu dans la même affaire, entre les mêmes parties, procédant en la même qualité, est attaqué par les mêmes moyens que le premier; qu'il échet, en conséquence, de renvoyer à la Chambre Civile la connaissance de la seconde branche du moyen;

Par ces motifs, déclare le moyen mal fondé dans sa première branche et, pour être statué sur la seconde branche dudit moyen, renvoie la cause et les parties devant la Chambre Civile.

M. le Président Lagarde a présenté, devant les Chambres Réunies; le rapport suivant:

I. – Les consorts Connot ont formé un pourvoi contre un arrêt rendu le 25 févr. 1937 par la Cour d'appel de Besançon (D.H. 1937,182), qui les a déboutés d'une action en dommages-intérêts par eux exercée contre le docteur Franck.

Le 24 déc. 1929, le docteur Franck, qui habite à Champigneulles, près de Nancy, confiait sa voiture automobile à son fils Claude, alors mineur, pour permettre à celui-ci d'aller passer la soirée à Nancy. Vers 23 h. 30, Claude Franck laissait la voiture de son père devant un bar de la rue des Dominicains et entrait dans cet établissement. A sa sortie, vers 1 h. du matin, il constatait que sa voiture avait disparu. Au moment même ou il faisait cette constatation, sa voiture, conduite par un individu qui est demeuré inconnu, renversait, sur la route de Frouard à Champigneulles, un passant, le facteur Connot, qui succombait presque immédiatement.

Les ayants droit de la victime introduisirent alors contre le docteur Franck, devant le tribunal civil de Nancy, une instance basée sur l'art. 1384 CC, et, subsidiairement, sur l'art. 1382 du même code. Leur demande était rejetée par jugement du 21.janv. 1931, confirmé le 10 juillet suivant par arrêt de la Cour d'appel de Nancy (D.P. 1936.1.83). Je détache quelques lignes de cet arrêt:

'Attendu que la responsabilité légale de l'art. 1384 porte non sur le propriétaire, mais sur le gardien de la chose...; qu'au moment de l'accident, le gardien de l'automobile n'était pas le docteur Franck, mais un malfaiteur inconnu...; – Attendu, d'autre part, que le fait d'avoir laissé sa voiture sans surveillance, dans une rue de Nancy, ne constitue pas, à la charge de Franck, une faute au sens de l'art. 1382...; – que, d'ailleurs, s'il y a eu faute, la mort de Connot n'en est pas la suite directe et immédiate et n'a qu'un rapport indirect et lointain avec l'abandon de la voiture et même avec le vol...'

Sur pourvoi des consorts Connot, est intervenu l'arrêt suivant, rendu le 3 mars 1936 par votre Chambre Civile:

'Vu l'art. 1384, § 1er, CC; – Attendu qu'aux termes de ce texte, le gardien de la chose est présumé responsable du dommage causé par celle-ci, à moins qu'il n'administre la preuve que ce dommage provient d'un fait qu'il n'a pu ni empêcher, ni prévoir; – Attendu que le vol d'une automobile abandonnée sur la voie publique ne saurait, à défaut d'autres circonstances, constituer un cas fortuit ou de force majeure exonérant des conséquences de l'accident causé par ce véhicule celui qui, légalement, n'a pas cessé d'en avoir la garde; – Attendu que, dans la nuit du 24 au 25 déc. 1929, le jeune Franck, à qui son père, le docteur Franck, avait confié sa voiture automobile, a mis celle-ci en stationnement sur la voie publique; que sa voiture lui fut volée par une personne dont l'identité n'a pu être établie; que, sous la conduite de cet individu, l'automobile, traversant, la même nuit, à toute vitesse, la commune de Champigneulles, renversa et tua sur le coup le facteur Connot; – Attendu que le docteur Franck ayant été actionné par la veuve de la victime, en vertu des dispositions des art. 1384 et 1382 CC, celle-ci a été, pr l'arrêt attaqué, déboutée de sa demande, pour le motif que le stationnement des automobiles dans les rues était non seulement toléré, mais réglementé par l'autorité administrative; qu'ainsi, il ne constituait pas une faute au sens de l'art. 1382; qu'en tous cas, y eût-il faute, elle était sans relation immédiate et directe avec l'accident, lequel était dû uniquement à la maladresse et à l'imprudence du conducteur; – Mais attendu que l'arrêt constate que le jeune Franck avait abandonné sa voiture sans surveillance sur la voie publique; que, dans ces conditions, la garde n'avait pas cessé de lui appartenir et, par suite, d'appartenir légalement à son père, propriétaire de la voiture en question, qui la lui avait confiée, et que ni l'usage ni la tolérance administrative ne sauraient soustraire le gardien de la chose, du fait de laquelle un dommage à été causé, à la présomption de responsabilité qui pèse sur lui en vertu de l'art. 1384 CC; – D'où il suit qu'en statuant ainsi qu'il l'a fait, l'arrêt attaqué a violé le texte ci-dessus visé; – Par ces motifs, casse..., renvoie devant la Cour d'appel de Besançon.'

La Cour de Besançon, saisie de l'affaire, a, par arrêt du 25 fév. 1937, jugé comme la Cour de Nancy. Elle a décidé: d'une part, que la garde, au sens de l'art. 1384, constituant un pouvoir de fait et non un pouvoir de droit, le vol avait eu pour conséquence de retirer au docteur Franck sa qualité de gardien et de transférer cette qualité au voleur; d'autre part, qu'à supposer que le docteur Franck et son fils aient commis une faute en abandonnant leur voiture sans surveillance sur la voie publique, aucune relation de cause à effet n'existe entre cette faute et l'accident dont le facteur Connot a été victime.

Les consorts Connot se sont pourvus contre l'arrêt de la Cour de

Besançon et l'affaire a été renvoyée devant les Chambres Réunies, par un arrêt de la Chambre Civile en date du 18 juil. 1938, dont voici le texte:

'Vu l'art. 1ᵉʳ de la loi du 1ᵉʳ avr. 1837; – Attendu que, par arrêt du 3 mars 1936, la Cour a cassé l'arrêt rendu par la Cour d'appel de Nancy le 10 juil. 1931, au préjudice de la dame veuve Connot..., et renvoyé la cause et les parties devant la Cour d'appel de Besançon; que ladite cour a statué le 25 fév. 1937, comme l'avait fait l'arrêt cassé et s'est fondée, en droit, sur des motifs qui sont en opposition avec la doctrine de l'arrêt de cassation; – Attendu que le second arrêt ainsi rendu dans la même affaire, entre les même parties procédant en la même qualité, est attaqué par le même moyen que le précédent; – Par ces motifs, renvoie devant les Chambres Réunies...'

II. – Le pourvoi propose un moyen unique qui est ainsi formulé: Ce moyen comporte une division en deux branches:

1ʳᵉ branche: violation de l'art. 1384, en ce que l'arrêt a déclaré que le vol de sa voiture automobile avait fait perdre au défendeur la qualité de gardien;

2ᵉ branche: violation de l'art. 1382, en ce que l'arrêt a exonéré le défendeur de toute responsabilité, alors que le vol et l'accident qui en a été la suite seraient les conséquences directes d'un quasi-délit commis per ledit défendeur.

Voici, en ce qui concerne la première branche du moyen, les motifs de l'arrêt attaqué:

'Attendu que, dans la nuit du 24 au 25 déc. 1929, le jeune Franck, fils alors mineur de l'intimé et habitant avec lui, étant venu de Champigneulles passer la soirée à Nancy avec la voiture automobile appartenant à son père et que celui-ci lui avait confiée, laissa ladite voiture en stationnement, rue des Dominicains, devant le "Bar Américain", où il pénétra; que cette voiture fut volée par un ou plusieurs individus demeurés inconnus; – Attendu que, dans la même nuit, vers 1 h. du matin, à Champigneulles, le facteur Connot fut renversé et tué sur le coup par une voiture automobile qui n'était autre que celle volée à Franck, rue des Dominicains, conduite à grande vitesse et maladroitement par le voleur où l'un de ses complices, lequel, après l'accident, continua la route en accélérant son allure et ne put jamais être retrouvé ou identifié dans la suite, alors que la voiture volée, et qui avait causé la mort de Connot, était découverte quelques heures après, abandonnée sur le territoire de Jarville, par le ou les voleurs, après l'accident...; – Attendu que les consorts Connot soutiennent que le vol de la voiture automobile de Franck n'avait pas privé celui-ci de la garde juridique de ladite voiture; qu'il doit donc être considéré comme en étant encore le gardien au moment où elle a causé le dommage dont ils poursuivent la réparation; que la présomption de responsabilité résultant des dispositions de l'art. 1384 doit, en conséquence, peser sur Franck, qui ne pourrait être exonéré qu'en rapportant, ce qu'il ne fait pas, la preuve que ce dommage provient d'une cause qui lui est étrangère et qu'il n'a pu ni prévoir ni empêcher; qu'ils font valoir encore que le vol, dans les conditions où il s'est produit, ne saurait constituer ce fait imprévisible, et qu'au surplus Franck doit d'autant plus être réputé avoir conservé après le vol la garde juridique de la voiture dérobée, que c'est par suite d'un défaut de surveillance de sa part et, par conséquent, d'une faute qui lui est imputable, que le vol a pu s'effectuer; – Attendu que, par définition, la garde d'une chose consiste dans le fait de la conserver et de la surveiller; que cesse donc d'avoir la qualité de gardien d'une chose celui pour lequel la surveillance de ladite chose est devenue une impossibilité absolue; que le qualificatif "juridique" que l'on adjoindrait au mot "garde" ne saurait en changer la signification; que la garde est, par essence, un fait matériel et ne peut être, par cette adjonction, transformée en une entité juridique sans violer sa définition même; qu'il en résulte que le propriétaire, le possesseur ou le détenteur d'une chose, dès lors qu'il a perdu le pouvoir de la surveiller, soit par lui-même, soit par un préposé, en a perdu par cela même la garde, qu'on la qualifie de matérielle ou de juridique, qualifications qui n'ont aucune influence sur le sens du mot "garde"; – Attendu que la doctrine est d'accord avec la jurisprudence que ce mot "garde" n'a pas une signification différente dans l'art. 1384 et dans l'art 1385; que si le législateur avait admis l'existence d'une garde juridique, avec les caractères invoqués par les appelants, il n'aurait pas été nécessaire de rendre le propriétaire ou celui qui se sert d'un animal, responsable du dommage causé par ledit animal, échappé ou égaré; qu'en opposant, dans cet article, le cas où l'animal qui a causé le dommage est sous la garde du propriétaire ou de l'usager au cas où il est égaré ou échappé, le législateur a implicitement, mais indiscutablement, décidé qu'une chose qui échappe à la surveillance de quelqu'un cesse, par ce fait même, de rester sous sa garde; – Attendu que lorsque, par l'effet du vol, Franck s'est trouvé, à partir de la voie de fait qui l'a dépossédé de sa voiture, dans l'ignorance du lieu où elle se trouvait et des circonstances dans lesquelles il en était usé par le ravisseur, par conséquent dans l'impossiblité d'en assurer la surveillance, il en avait, dès cet instant, perdu la garde, laquelle était passée au voleur, qui, entendant se comporter comme propriétaite, assumait par là-même le risque de la chose volée, dont il profitait seul; – Attendu, d'autre part, que les appelants soutiennent vainement que le vol de la voiture ne constituait ni un cas de force majeure, ni un fait imprévisible susceptible d'exonérer Franck de la présomption de responsabilité qui pèse sur lui comme gardien de ladite voiture; qu'en effet, si le vol, dans les circonstances de fait où il a été commis, ne présente le caractère ni d'un fait imprévisiblē, ni d'un cas fortuit ou de force majeure, cette considération est sans intérêt du moment que, par l'effet du vol, Franck avait perdu la garde de la voiture, laquelle garde était passée au voleur, qui l'exerçait à l'instant où s'est produit l'accident qui a causé la mort de Cannot; – Attendu enfin que l'argument tiré par les appelants de cette circonstance que le vol de la voiture aurait été, selon eux, la conséquence d'une négligence de Franck dans la surveillance qu'il devait exercer sur elle en sa qualité de gardien, et ne saurait être invoqué par lui pour se faire décharger de la présomption de responsabilité, n'a pas plus de valeur; que, même dans le cas où le vol n'aurait été rendu possible que par la négligence du gardien de la chose volée, celui-ci n'en aurait pas moins perdu la garde de ladite chose, dès l'instant que la surveillance lui en était devenue impossible; que, s'il était établi qu'il existât une relation suffisante de cause à effet entre cette négligence et un dommage consécutif au vol, l'auteur de ladite négligence pourrait encourir une responsabilité découlant, non de la présomption de l'art. 1384, mais de la faute relevée contre lui, et ce, par application des art. 1382 et 1383; que la recherche…d'une telle responsabilité…rentre dans le cadre de l'examen qui sera abordé ci-après…; – Mais qu'il résulte de ce qui vient d'être dit que la responsabilité de l'intimé ne peut être retenue par application de la présomption mise par l'art. 1384 à la charge du gardien de la chose qui a causé le dommage, puisqu'il n'avait plus cette qualité de gardien au moment de l'accident.'

Il n'est pas contesté que, jusqu'au moment du vol, le docteur Franck était demeuré gardien de la voiture qu'il avait confiée à son fils mineur. D'autre part, le docteur Franck ne prétend pas que le vol, dans les circonstances où il a été commis, doive être considéré comme un événement de force majeure, dans les termes de l'art. 1148 CC. Il soutient seulement que, lorsque l'accident s'est produit, il n'était plus gardien de sa voiture. Et la question que soulève la première branche du moyen se pose en ces termes: le gardien d'une voiture automobile, quand il est dépossédé de cette voiture par suite d'un vol, conserve-t-il cependant la garde de sa voiture et demeure-t-il soumis à la présomption de responsabilité qu' édicte l'art. 1384, ou bien la qualité de gardien passe-t-elle au voleur?

Voici la thèse du pourvoi. [The arguments summarised by the *rapporteur* are not reprinted.]

Extracts from note by G. Ripert,
D.C. 1942, J. 27

En réalité il y a présomption de faute, et la faute commise est une faute dans la garde. Le gardien a manqué à l'obligation légale de surveillance qui lui incombe et qui est une simple précision de la grande obligation de ne pas nuire à autrui par sa faute. Cette expression: *faute dans la garde* a déjà été employée par certains auteurs... Mais si on entend la garde dans le sens de garde juridique, la notion n'a aucun sens quant au problème de la responsabilité civile. Ce que l'on reproche à celui qui a la garde juridique, ce n'est pas d'avoir causé le dommage, c'est d'avoir perdu la garde matérielle (V.H. et L. Mazeaud, *Traité de la responsabilité civile*, t.2, n°s 1313 et suiv.). Par exemple, le propriétaire de l'automobile serait présumé en faute, alors que le dommage est causé par le voleur de la voiture, parce que sa faute consisterait à ne pas avoir empêché le vol. Avec la notion de garde matérielle, tout change. Le gardien est présumé en faute parce que le dommage est dû au fait de la chose, et que cette seule circonstance démontre qu'il n'a pas rempli son obligation de surveillance...

Est-ce à dire que nous revenions au point de départ, comme l'écrit M. Savatier? En aucune façon. Le grand travail qui a été fait sur la responsabilité du fait des choses ne semble pas inutile. Nous sommes sur la même route, mais plus loin.

L'analyse du fait de la chose permet de découvrir la faute là où échouerait la preuve directe. Le fait de la chose accuse et en quelque sorte maintient la faute. Il *matérialise le lien de causalité entre la faute et le dommage*. La chose n'est jamais par elle-même la cause du dommage; elle en est l'instrument. Mais l'usage de cet instrument dénonce la faute première de celui qui s'en sert. Quand la Cour de cassation exige que la chose soit la cause génératrice du dommage, elle sait bien que l'expression est un pléonasme..., et aussi qu'elle déforme l'idée de cause...;mais elle veut marquer par là que l'usage d'une chose ne peut faire présumer la faute de celui qui la grade que si le dommage résulte de cet usage. L'instrument du dommage révèle la faute dans la garde.

The case finally came up to the Chambre Civile for decision of the point whether the younger Franck had been negligent in leaving the car unprotected outside the café: see pp. 297–300

27. Cour de cassation
Chambre Civile, 22 déc. 1941
Parris c. *Frendzel et autres*
(*S.* 1942,1.49)

Arrêt

La Cour; – ... Au fond: – Sur le moyen uniqe, pris dans sa deuxième branche; – Vu l'art. 1384, alin. 1ᵉʳ, CC; – Attendu que, pour anéantir totalement la présomption de responsabilité édictée par cet article à l'encontre du gardien de la chose qui a lésé autrui dans sa personne ou ses biens, il ne suffit pas d'une faute commise par la victime elle-même, mais qu'il faut que cette faute, n'ayant pu être ni prévue, ni conjurée dans ses conséquences par le gardien de la chose, ait été l'unique cause du dommage; – Attendu qu'il résulte des constatations de l'arrêt attaqué que le 3 sept. 1936, à midi, au moment où il venait de quitter le trottoir pour faire 'un pas ou deux' sur la chaussée de la rue du Faubourg-Poissonnière, le sieur Parris a été heurté et renversé par l'arrière d'une voiture automobile que son conducteur Frendzel s'efforçait de garer contre ce même trottoir entre deux autres véhicules déjà en stationnement; – Attendu que, pour décharger entièrement Frendzel et son assureur des condamnations prononcées contre eux par les premiers juges à raison de ces faits, la Cour d'appel a considéré, d'une part, que Parris s'était rendu coupable d'une faute en descendant brusquement et 'à l'aveugle' de son trottoir pendant le cours des manœuvres d'avant en arrière et d'arrière en avant qu' exécutait, non sans bruit, la voiture de Frendzel et, d'autre part, qu' aucun reproche n'était à faire à Frendzel pour n'avoir pas fait fonctionner son appareil avertisseur, une telle précaution ne s'imposant pas pour la protection des piétons auxquels la descente sur la chaussée est interdite; – Mais attendu que le gardien d'une voiture à moteur, surtout quand il se livre à une manœuvre périlleuse comme celle dont s'agit, doit prévoir de la part des piétons, quelque manquement toujours possible et parfois involontaire, aux prescriptions des règlements sur la circulation; qu'il est, en conséquence, en faute s'il néglige de prévenir les passants du danger auquel ils sont exposés par la marche anormale de son véhicule; d'où il suit que, même si elle était certaine, la faute relevée à la charge de la victime ne serait pas la cause unique du dommage et qu'elle ne suffirait dès lors pas à justifier l'exonération totale de responsabilité dont l'arrêt a fait bénéficer les défendeurs; sans qu'il soit besoin de statuer sur la première branche du moyen, casse l'arrêt de la Cour de Paris du 23 janv. 1939...

28. Cour de cassation
Chambre Civile, 6 janv. 1943
Cons. Connot c. Franck
(D. 1945, J. 117)

Après cassation, par la Chambre Civile (3 mars 1936, D.P. 1936.1.81), d'un arrêt de la Cour d'appel de Nancy du 10 juil. 1931 qui, à la suite d'un accident causé par une automobile volée, écartait la responsabilité du propriétaire, la Cour de Besançon, statuant sur renvoi (25 fév. 1937, D.H. 1937.182), s'est prononcée dans le même sens que l'arrêt cassé. D'où un nouveau pourvoi, rejeté par les Chambres Réunies le 2 déc. 1941 (D.C. 1942, J. 25). Mais la Chambre Civile, saisie en 1936 d'un moyen unique tiré de la violation des art. 1382 et 1384 CC, ayant accueilli le pourvoi du chef de l'art. 1384 et n'ayant dès lors pas eu à se prononcer sur la violation prétendue de l'art. 1382, les Chambres Réunies se sont déclarées incompétentes, aux termes de l'art. 1er de la loi du 1er avr. 1837, pour statuer sur le second grief, repris dans le moyen du pourvoi formé contre l'arrêt de la Cour de Besançon, et elles en ont renvoyé l'examen à la Chambre Civile (v., sur ce point, le rapport de M. le président Lagarde, D.C. 1942 J. 33

(D.A. 1943, J. 17)

La Cour; – Sur la deuxième branche du moyen faisant l'object du renvoi des chambres réunies à la Chambre Civile; – Attendu qu'à la suite de la mort du sieur Connot, écrasé dans la nuit de Noël 1929 par une voiture automobile conduite par un individu resté inconnu qui l'avait soustraite, la même nuit, dans une rue de Nancy où le jeune Franck, alors encore mineur, l'avait abandonnée momentanément, la veuve et les enfants de la victime exerçaient contre Franck père, propriétaire du véhicule: 1° principalement, l'action de l'art. 1384, al.

1er, CC, rejetée définitivement en suite de l'arrêt des Chambres Réunies du 2 déc. 1941, et, 2°, à titre subsidiaire, l'action de l'art. 1382, au sujet de laquelle la Chambre Civile a à se prononcer actuellement; – Attendu que si le maître de la chose inanimée ayant causé un préjudice à autrui se trouve déchargé de la présomption de responsabilité de l'art. 1384, al. 1er, CC quand cette chose était déjà passée, lors de l'événement dommageable, sous la garde d'une autre personne, en particulier d'un voleur connu ou inconnu, la partie lésée n'en conserve pas moins le droit de réclamer à ce maître, par l'action de l'art. 1382, la réparation du préjudice résultant directement pour elle des fautes personnelles dont il se serait rendu coupable, notamment en négligeant les précautions commandées par les circonstances et la nature de la chose pour la sécurité des tiers; – Mais qu'en ce cas la victime demanderesse des dommages-intérêts a à sa charge la preuve de la réunion, en la circonstance, de toutes les conditions exigées pour l'application de l'art. 1382, soit la faute du défendeur, le préjudice et le lien direct de cause à effet entre cette faute et ce préjudice; – Attendu que les consorts Connot alléguaient bien, à l'encontre du mineur Franck, diverses particularités de fait susceptibles, à leur dire, de faire ressortir l'omission par celui-ci des mesures de prudence en rapport avec la nature de la chose abandonnée momentanément, qui lui étaient imposées par les principes du droit commun; – Attendu qu'il est vrai aussi que la cour d'appel s'est abstenue de vérifier l'exactitude matérielle et le mérite des prétentions des demandeurs à cet égard; – Mais attendu que les conclusions desdits demandeurs ne fournissaient aux juges du fond aucune précision de fait d'où l'on pût inférer que, dans cette espèce, le préjudice subi par les parties fût la conséquence directe des fautes imputées par elles au mineur Franck; qu'en cette situation, la cour d'appel a pu juger qu'en l'absence de toute circonstance particulière propre à faire preuve de l'existence de ce dernier élément de causalité indispensable pour l'application de l'art. 1382, la demande subsidiaire des consorts Cannot n'était pas justifiée;

Par ces motifs, et abstraction faite d'autres considérations erronées de l'arrêt qui peuvent être tenues pour surabondantes, rejette.

The Chambre Civile applied this reasoning in *Préfet de police* c. *Greene*, D. 1947, J. 41, to facts which sufficiently appear from the following extract:

'... que la cause directe de l'accident qui a occasionné le dommage réside dans le fait personnel de la maladresse ou de l'imprudence du conducteur, c'est-à-dire du voleur, et qu'on ne saurait dès lors découvrir un rapport direct de cause à effet entre la négligence du propriétaire ayant consisté dans le défaut de fermeture à clef des portes de l'automobile laissée en stationnement, d'ailleurs autorisé, sur la voie publique et du non-enlèvement de la clef de contact, et le préjudice dont il est demandé réparation...'

Extracts from note by M. André Tunc, D. 1945, J. 119

Le soin avec lequel l'arrêt a été préparé fait qu'il n'est pas hasardeux, pour en déterminer la portée, de rechercher au delà de la solution qu'il donne, la position qu'il implique sur les problèmes doctrinaux. L'adoption de cette solution nuancée marque le rejet des théories extrêmes selon lesquelles la faute obligerait à réparer, soit tout le préjudice conditionné par elle, soit le seul préjudice en résultant directement. C'est bien entre elles, d'ailleurs, que se situent la vérité et l'opportunité (b).

Parmi les multiples théories intermédiaires, celle de la 'causalité adéquate', adoptée d'ailleurs par M. le doyen Roubier, paraît à la fois réunir la plupart des suffrages (v. cependant Hébraud, note au *Rec. Sirey*, 1942,2.41) et rendre compte de notre jurisprudence (et même de notre jurisprudence en matière de responsabilité du fait des choses inanimées...). Elle consiste à rechercher si la faute était généralement propre, suivant le cours naturel des choses, à produire le dommage, ou si celui-ci ne s'est produit que par un concours de circonstances accidentel ou fortuit...Malgré la difficulté de la question, nous croyons qu'une formule plus précise – mais ayant approximativement la même signification – pourrait être proposée. On pourrait dire que *la faute oblige à réparer toutes ses conséquences directes, et toutes les conséquences nécessaires du fait ou de la situation qu'elle a directement créés* (c'est presque exactement la formule de Pothier, *Obligations*, n° 167, éd. Bugnet, t. 2, p. 67, et peut-être aussi celle qui rend compte du droit anglais: v. Marty, n°s 12 et 13. Comp. encore Ripert, notes au D.P. 1921.2.17 et D.P. 1928.2.41, et H. et L. Mazeaud, n° 1673)...

(b) M. Roubier, dans sa note aux *J.C.P.* 1942,2.1867, affirme bien que la faute n'oblige à réparer que le dommage 'direct', mais, avec certains auteurs, il donne au mot une signification particulière: un dommage pourrait être 'direct' sans être 'immédiat'; il en serait ainsi lorsqu'il viendrait après une suite d'événements à travers lesquels se retrouverait l'enchaînement logique de cause à effet. Parler dans ce cas

de caractère direct nous semble une subtilite de terminologie qu'il est préférable d'éviter.

29. Cour de cassation
Chambre Civile, 23 janv. 1945
Desbons c. Consorts Deyssieu
(D. 1945, J. 317)

Arrêt

La Cour; – Sur le moyen unique: – Vu l'art. 1384, § 1er, CC; – Attendu que, pour l'application de ce texte, la chose incriminée doit être la cause du dommage; que si elle est présumée en être la cause génératrice dès lors qu'elle est intervenue dans sa réalisation, cette présomption est détruite par la preuve que la chose, inerte ou non, n'a joué qu'un rôle passif et a seulement subi l'action étrangère génératrice du dommage; – Attendu qu'il résulte des énonciations de l'arrêt attaqué (Bordeaux, 19 mars 1940) que Deyssieu, débouchant à motocyclette d'un chemin joignant la route de Gradignan à Léorgnan, a, en tournant à droite pour se rendre à Gradignan, dérapé sur le sable et le gravier qui recouvraient le virage en déclivité à cet endroit et, après avoir parcouru ainsi une distance de 7 m., s'est mortellement blessé en venant se jeter sur l'aile gauche arrière de l'automobile de Desbons qui abordait les lieux en tenant régulièrement sa droite; que l'arrêt ajoute 'qu'une haie empêchait Deyssieu d'apercevoir les usagers venant de la direction de Gradignan; qu'habitué à effectuer ce parcours, dont il connaissait toutes les particularités, il devait se montrer particulièrement prudent, de façon à céder le passage à tout conducteur venant sur sa droite'; – Attendu qu'en l'état de ces constatations, d'où il résulte que l'automobile occupait sa place normale sur la route et n'a joué qu'un rôle passif dans l'accident, l'arrêt attaqué a néanmoins décidé, sans donner aucun motif de ce partage, que l'imprudence de la victime n'exonérait le conducteur, gardien de l'automobile, que dans la proportion de moitié de la présomption de responsabilité édictée par l'art. 1384, § 1er, CC; – D'où suit qu'en statuant ainsi, l'arrêt attaqué n'a pas légalement justifié sa décision;

Par ces motifs, casse.

Extract from Note by M. René Savatier,
 D. 1945, J. 319

Capendant, la résorption de la présomption de responsabilité de l'art. 1384 dans la simple responsabilité née de la faute serait un véritable recul. Et il y a tout un autre courant de jurisprudence qui continue à donner à l'art. 1384 un sens propre. En dépit de son équivoque, la formule de la Cour de cassation, que nous citions au début de la seconde partie de cette note, l'illustre clairement. Il ne suffit pas, pour exonérer le gardien d'une chose véritablement active dans l'accident, que celui-ci 'prouve qu'il n'a commis aucune faute'. La responsabilité attachée au risque de la chose existe donc *indépendamment de toute faute du gardien*, de toute recherche de caractère normal, adéquat, prévisible, de la causalité du dommage....

Et des arrêts fort récents continuent à attester l'inutilité de toute recherche de faute dans les véritables applications de l'art. 1384. C'est ainsi que la Chambre des Requêtes a encore affirmé le 22 janv. 1945 (*Rec. Gaz. Pal.* 1945, 1.84) que l'automobiliste n'était pas exonéré de la responsabilité d'un accident tenant à la rupture de sa direction, du fait du mauvais montage de cette direction par un ouvrier inconnu, lors de la fabrication de l'automobile. Il apparaissait pourtant, dans cette espèce, que le gardien de l'automobile était absolument exempt de faute. L'accident était pour lui aussi imprévisible et anormal que le fait, dans l'arrêt ci-dessus, pour l'automobiliste qui tenait sa droite et marchait à une allure normale, de voir un motocycliste se jeter sur lui après dérapage. Cependant, on comprend parfaitement que, dans le premier cas, l'automobiliste ne puisse pas s'exonérer du dommage qui résulte *directement et, activement du fait de la chose*, tandis que, dans le second cas, il soit irresponsable du dommage passivement causé par elle. Seulement, pour justifier cette différence, il faut restaurer les deux principes étouffés sous la frondaison trop touffue de la jurisprudence récente:

Le premier est que l'art. 1384, *principe d'une responsabilité seulement subsidiaire*, n'a pas à jouer quand l'examen des fautes désigne un responsable normal.

Le second est que, lorsqu'aucune faute n'est établie à l'origine du dommage, le gardien de la chose *active au moment de l'accident* doit, et doit seul, réparer ce dommage.

30. Cour de cassation
Chambre Civile, 20 oct. 1931
Cormery c. *Messire*
(D.H. 1931,538)

Sur le moyen unique.

Attendu que la présomption de responsabilité édictée par le premier alinéa de l'art. 1384 CC, à l'encontre de celui qui a sous sa garde la chose inanimée qui a causé un dommage à autrui, peut être détruite par la preuve d'un cas fortuit, de force majeure ou d'une cause étrangère qui ne lui soil pas imputable;

Attendu que la demoiselle Cormery qui circulait à bicyclette a été renversée et blessée par une voiture automobile conduite par Messire venant en sens inverse;

Attendu qu'il est fait grief à l'arrêt de n'avoir pas répondu aux motifs du jugement repris par l'intimé, lequel concluait à la confirmation dudit jugement;

Mais attendu que l'arrêt, d'une part, a infirmé le jugement, en disant que cette décision ne reposait que sur une hypothèse des juges, à savoir que Messire n'ayant pas de permis de conduire devait être réputé inhabile conducteur, et, d'autre part, constate que les enquête et contre-enquête ordonnées par la cour démontrent que l'accident dont a été victime la demoiselle Cormery a été occasionné par une faute personnelle de celle derniére: qu'il déduit de ce qui précède que Messire a été à tort déclaré responsable par les premiers juges, sa responsabilité ne pouvant résulter ni de l'art. 1382 CC, puisqu'aucune faute n'était établie à sa charge, ni de l'art. 1382 du même code, puisque la présomption légale édictée par ce texte se trouve détruite par la faute démontrée de la victime; d'où il suit que l'arrêt attaqué a répondu aux motifs du jugement; qu'il est dûment motivé et que, loin de violer les textes visés au moyen, il en fait une juste application;

Par ces motifs, rejette.

31. Cour de cassation
Chambre Civile, 5 janv. 1956
Bouloux et veuve Lathus c. *Soc. 'L'Oxygène liquide' et autres*
(D. 1957,261 and Note R. Rodière)

La Cour; – Sur les moyens uniques et identiques des deux pourvois: –
Vu l'art. 1384, al. 1er, CC, lequel est ainsi conçu: 'On est responsable

non seulement du dommage que l'on cause par son propre fait, mais encore de celui qui est causé par le fait des personnes dont on doit répondre, ou des choses que l'on a sous sa garde'; – Attendu que la responsabilité du dommage causé par le fait d'une chose inanimée est liée à l'usage ainsi qu'au pouvoir de surveillance et de contrôle qui caractérisent essentiellement la garde; qu'à ce titre, sauf l'effet de stipulations contraires valables entre les parties, le propriétaire de la chose ne cesse d'en être responsable que s'il est établi que celui à qui il l'a confiée a reçu corrélativement toute possibilité de prévenir lui-même le préjudice qu'elle peut causer; – Attendu qu'il résulte de l'arrêt confirmatif attaqué (Poitiers 29 oct. 1952) que la Société *L'Oxygène liquide* avait expédié, par voie ferrée, au 'Comptoir des carburants' un certain nombre de bouteilles métalliques remplies d'oxygène comprimé; qu'à l'arrivée en gare, ces bouteilles furent prises en charge par Bertrand, entrepreneur de transports; qu'au cours de leur livraison dans les locaux du comptoir destinataire, l'une d'elles éclata; que la cause de cette explosion, en l'état de l'expertise effectuée, serait restée inconnue, encore qu'il n'ait point été prouvé ni même allégué que l'accident fût la conséquence d'un acte ou d'une circonstance extérieurs à l'objet; que Lathus, préposé de Bertrand, ainsi que Bouloux, employé au service du 'Comptoir des carburantes', furent blessés par les éclats de la bouteille; – Attendu que, pour débouter lesdites victimes, ensemble les caisses de sécurité sociale intervenantes, de leurs actions en réparation dirigées, sur la base de l'art. 1384, al. 1er CC, contre la Société *L'Oxygène liquide*, la Cour d'appel appuie sa décision sur ce motif que 'seul, celui qui a la garde matérielle d'une chose inanimée peut être responsable de cette chose', ce qui n'était pas le cas pour la défenderesse; – Mais attendu qu'au lieu de se borner à caractériser la garde par la seule détention matérielle, les juges du fond devaient, à la lumière des faits de la cause et compte tenu de la nature particulière des récipients transportés et de leur conditionnement, rechercher si le détenteur auquel la garde aurait été transférée avait l'usage de l'objet qui a causé le préjudice ainsi que le pouvoir de surveiller et d'en contrôler tous les éléments; – Attendu qu'en refusant de se déterminer sur ce point, la Cour d'appel n'a pas mis la Cour de cassation à même d'apprécier quel était, en l'espèce, le gardien de la chose au sens de l'article visé au moyen; d'où il suit que l'arrêt attaqué manque de base légale;

Par ces motifs, casse...., renvoie devant la Cour d'appel d'Angers.

303

32. Cour de cassation
Chambre Civile, 18 déc. 1964
Trichard c. Piccino
(D. 1965,191 and Note P. Esmein)

Conclusions de l'avocat général Schmelck:

Sous le coup d'une crise d'épilepsie, un automobiliste (T) heurte un attelage et en blesse grièvement le conducteur. Poursuivi devant le tribunal correctionnel, l'automobiliste est relaxé, une expertise médicale ayant établi qu'il était en état de démence au moment de l'acte qui lui était reproché. Déboutée en tant que partie civile, la victime (P) s'adresse alors au tribunal civil et assigne l'auteur de l'accident en dommages-intérêts sur la base de l'art. 1384, al. 1er, CC. Le litige aboutit à un arrêt de la cour d'appel de Nîmes qui retient la responsabilité de T:... et le condamne à réparer l'intégralité du dommage. C'est cet arrêt qui est frappé de pourvoi et c'est dans ces conditions que la Cour de cassation est appelée à trancher à nouveau l'importante et délicate question de la responsabilité civile du dément. Elle s'était déjà prononcée à ce sujet en 1947, par un arrêt de principe qui a été excellemment défendu par M. le conseiller Lenoan, dans une note parue au Dalloz (D.1947,329B) mais qui, il faut bien le reconnaître, est loin d'avoir recueilli l'unanimité ds suffrages de la doctrine. Nous aurons l'occasion de revenir sur cette décision. Pour l'instant, rappelons que dans l'espèce dont vous êtes saisis, la question se pose sans ambiguïté puisque la démence du défendeur a été formellement constatée par un jugement du tribunal correctionnel, lequel a désormais autorité de chose jugée.

Précisons également que le débat se situe dans le cadre de l'art. 1384, al. 1er, et que, par conséquent, il importe peu de s'interroger sur le point de savoir si l'acte d'un dément peut ou ne peut pas être considéré comme fautif, au sens de l'art. 1382.

La responsabilité de l'auteur du dommage doit être appréciée uniquement sous l'angle de la responsabilité du fait des choses et, dès lors, les seules questions que la cour ait à résoudre sont les suivantes:
– Un dément peut-il être 'gardien' d'une chose?
– Dans l'affirmative, la démence peut-elle être considérée comme une cause étrangère de nature à exonérer le gardien de son obligation de réparer le dommage causé par sa chose?
– Enfin, d'une manière plus générale, la présomption de responsabilité

de l'art. 1384, al. 1er, implique-t-elle la faculté de discernement?

Dans l'arrêt critiqué, la Cour d'appel a répondu à ces trois questions. Elle l'a fait d'une façon explicite en ce qui concerne les deux premières, implicitement en ce qui concerne la dernière. Pour condamner T... à la réparation intégrale du dommage, l'arrêt fait état des considérations suivantes:

1° T était le propriétaire de la voiture, il était habilité à la conduire, la voiture était à son usage, il exerçait sur elle tous pouvoirs de direction et de contrôle. Il avait donc la garde de la voiture et en tant que gardien il est présumé responsable.

2° T ne pouvait se libérer de la présomption de responsabilité qui pèse sur lui qu'en prouvant que l'accident est dû à une cause étrangère, pour lui imprévisible et irrésistible. Il ne rapporte pas cette preuve car, d'une part, l'obnubilation passagère de ses facultés intellectuelles ne peut être considérée comme une cause étrangère parce qu'elle se rattache à son être même et que, d'autre part, la preuve n'est pas rapportée que la crise qu'il a subie était pour lui imprévisible donc inévitable.

Avant d'en venir aux critiques que le pourvoi dirige contre la décision, j'aimerais examiner de plus près les arguments de la Cour d'appel.

Qu'il me soit permis de les reprendre dans l'ordre inverse de celui dans lequel ils viennent d'être présentés, c'est-à-dire dans l'ordre croissant des difficultés.

Voyons d'abord le problème sous l'angle de l'exonération, ensuite seulement sous celui de la garde.

A. – Admettons pour l'instant que T puisse être considéré comme ayant conservé la qualité de gardien, en dépit de son état, et qu'il puisse légitimement invoquer l'absence de discernement pour tenter de se dégager de sa responsabilité. Dans cette hypothèse encore faut-il, pour qu'il puisse être exonéré, qu'il soit établi qu'il n'a pas connu son état, encore faut-il que les troubles qui l'ont affecté lorsqu'il conduisait sa voiture n'aient pas été pour lui imprévisibles.

Nous pouvons passer rapidement sur cet aspect de la question car il ne fait pas difficulté.

'Attendu', dit l'arrêt, 'que T ne démontre pas qu'il ignorait son état pathologique et que, par suite, les manifestations en étaient normale-ment imprévisibles pour lui, qu'en l'espèce l'imprévisibilité condition-ne l'irrésistibilité puisqu'il aurait été facile à T de se prémunir contre une perte de conscience prévisible en s'abstenant de rester seul dans sa voiture, ou d'une manière plus efficace encore en s'abstenant de la conduire.' Ces motifs apparaissent d'autant plus pertinents qu'il résultait de l'expertise médicale versée au dossier pénal que T avait des habitudes alcooliques anciennes et qu'il était sujet à des crises d'épilepsie qui le privaient momentanément de ses facultés.

Ainsi, il est hors de question que la cause étrangère invoquée par T ait été pour lui imprévisible. Ne serait-ce que pour cette raison, elle ne peut être libératoire?

Mais là n'est pas le point essentiel. La Cour d'appel est allée plus loin dans son raisonnement, Et c'est ce pas supplémentaire qu'elle franchit qui donne tout son intérêt à la discussion. L'arrêt ne se contente pas de se fonder sur le caractère prévisible de la crise qui a affecté le conducteur pour déclarer celui-ci responsable. Si la Cour d'appel se contentait de ce seul argument, elle serait conduite à exonérer T de sa responsabilité au cas où il ne serait pas habituellement sujet à de semblables crises, au cas où sa privation de conscience aurait été fortuite. C'est précisément cette conséquence que la Cour d'appel entend écarter en soutenant que, d'une manière générale, la démence n'exonère pas le gardien parce qu'elle ne peut pas être considérée comme une cause étrangère. Elle affirme en effet 'qu'une obnubilation passagère des facultés intellectuelles, qu'elle soit qualifiée de démence au sens de l'art. 64 c. pén. ou qu'elle procède d'un quelconque malaise physique, n'est pas un événement susceptible de constituer une cause du dommage extérieure ou étrangère au gardien puisqu'il est lié à ses fonctions vitales et se rattache à son être même'.

En somme, la Cour d'appel pose le principe que seul un événement extérieur, un événement qui ne se rattache pas à la personne même du gardien peut être considéré come une cause étrangère de nature à exonérer ce dernier de sa responsabilité.

Cette affirmation est-elle orthodoxe en l'état actuel de votre jurisprudence?

En d'autres termes, admettez-vous que la cause étrangère qui seule peut libérer le gardien soit nécessairement une cause extérieure. Il semble, Messieurs, que ce soit bien là votre doctrine. En effet, depuis que les Chambres Réunies ont, le 13 fév. 1930, affirmé le principe que 'la présomption de responsabilité ne peut être détruite que par la preuve d'un cas fortuit ou de force majeure, ou d'une cause étrangère qui ne soit pas imputable au gardien', vous avez eu maintes fois l'occasion de vous pencher sur cette notion de 'cause étrangère non imputable'.

Déjà, vous définissiez la force majeure comme l'événement extérieur au gardien, qu'il ne peut ni prévoir ni surmonter. Vous avez ensuite étendu les caractères de la force majeure aux autres causes d'exonération, à la faute de la victime et au fait du tiers et vous en êtes arrivés finalement à admettre que non seulement la cause étrangère doit être extérieure au gardien, mais qu'elle doit même être extérieure à la chose.

Cela vous a permis de rendre le gardien responsable des vices cachés de sa chose et d'affirmer qui ni l'éclatement d'un pneu, ni la rupture d'un organe de direction, même s'ils sont dus à un défaut de structure inconnu du gardien, ne peuvent libérer celui-ci de son obligation de réparer le dommage. Cela vous a permis également de considérer qu'aucune défaillance personnelle du gardien, ni une crise cardiaque, ni une syncope, le privant partiellement de ses moyens, ne sont des causes d'exonération.

Faut-il faire une exception pour la démence?

Certes, le dément n'a plus son discernement, il est privé de ses facultés intellectuelles. Mais l'homme qui est terrassé par une crise cardiaque ne l'est-il pas tout autant?

A la verité, ni la syncope, ni le malaise cardiaque, ni la démence partielle ou totale ne devraient être de nature à exonérer le gardien. Aucune privation des facultés intellectuelles ne devrait emporter cet effet parce qu'elle ne rompt pas le lien de causalité entre le gardien et le dommage, parce qu'elle n'établit pas que le dommage n'est pas dû au fait du gardien. Ce n'est que dans l'hypothèse où la perte de conscience serait elle-même provoquée par un fait extérieur, – par exemple la projection d'une pierre qui, blessant le conducteur, provoquerait son évanouissement – que la cause étrangère devrait pouvoir être utilement invoquée.

B. – Ces objections n'ont certainement pas échappé au demandeur au pourvoi. Aussi bien n'est-ce-pas au plan de la cause étrangère qu'il se place pour rejeter la demande de la victime. Il ne se pose pas la question de savoir si 'l'obnubilation passagère des facultés intellectuelles' de T peut être assimilée à une cause étrangère. Son approche du problème est plus subtile.

Remontant aux sources mêmes de la responsabilité telle qu'elle découle de l'art. 1381, al. 1er, il s'attache à démontrer que les conditions fondamentales de cette responsabilité ne sont pas réunies en l'espèce. En effet, dit-il, d'une part un dément ne peut pas être gardien et d'autre part un dément ne peut être déclaré responsable car l'imputation d'une responsabilité implique la faculté de discernement.

En cela le pourvoi reprend les arguments de cet arrêt de la Chambre Civile du 28 avr. 1947 (D. 1947,329, Concl. Lenoan, Note Lalou: S. 1947,1.115) auquel j'ai déjà fait allusion. Il s'agissait en l'espèce d'un dément qui, brandissant un revolver, avait tiré sur un tiers et l'avait mortellement blessé.

Voici les attendus de cet arrêt: 'La Cour: – Sur le moyen unique: – Attendu que l'arrêt attaqué déclare qu'il est constant que Girel était en état de démence au moment où la balle du revolver qu'il tenait à la main a atteint et blessé mortellement Escoffier et que cet état n'est pas la conséquence d'une faute antérieure de sa part; – Atendu que, de ces constatations souveraines, la Cour d'appel a pu déduire que la présomption de responsabilité édictée par l'art. 1384, al. 1er, CC dont se prévalaient les ayants droit d'Escoffier, ne saurait être retenue à l'encontre de Girel; – Attendu, en effet, que tant l'usage et les pouvoirs de direction et de contrôle, fondement de l'obligation de garde au sens de l'article précité, que l'imputation d'une responsabilité présumée, impliquent la faculté de discernement; d'où il suit que l'arrêt attaqué a légalement justifié sa décision – Rejette le pourvoi.'

Remarquons tout d'abord:

– Qu'il s'agit d'un arrêt de rejet, qu'il stipule que 'de ces constatations souveraines la cour a pu déduire'...

On serait donc tenté de n'attribuer à cette décision qu'une portée relative. Mais, aurait-elle entendu poser un principe, la question est de savoir si ce principe est encore valable, compte tenu de l'évolution générale de votre jurisprudence en matière de responsabilité du fait des choses.

L'argumentation de l'arrêt, qui est aussi celle du présent pourvoi, repose sur deux considérations:

1° Un fou n'a pas sur la chose les pouvoirs de direction et de contrôle qui sont les fondements de l'obligation de garde, parce que ces pouvoirs impliquent la faculté de discernement.

2° L'imputation d'une responsabilité présumée implique, elle aussi, la faculté de discernement.

Ces deux assertions sont-elles toujours vraies? Reprenons-les séparément.

1° Le pouvoir de commandement sur la chose implique-t-il la faculté de discernement?

Il faudrait assurément répondre par la négative si la garde se confondait avec la direction matérielle de la chose. Il faudrait admettre de même que la démence ne romprait pas le lien de garde si celui-ci s'analysait en un droit sur la chose, tel que le droit de propriété ou la possession, par exemple. Mais l'on sait que, d'une part, l'on peut être gardien d'une chose sans en avoir la détention matérielle et que, d'autre part, l'on peut être gardien sans en être titulaire d'un droit sur la chose.

La garde, en effet, telle que vous l'avez forgée, se présente comme un pouvoir relativement à la chose, le pouvoir d'en faire usage, par soi-même ou par autrui, de la diriger, de la contrôler. Ce pouvoir suppose-t-il que celui qui le détient soit conscient de ses actes?

Il est permis d'en douter non point seulement parce que le critère de la folie, de l'avis même des experts, n'est guère précis et que la distinction qu'établit la jurisprudence entre l'absence totale de la raison, qui exclut la responsabilité, et l'absence partielle de raison, qui la laisse subsister est bien aléatoire, mais encore parce que ce pouvoir de commandement, caractéristique de la garde, ne se rattache pas aux facultés intellectuelles de l'intéressé. Pour conforter cette idée, permettez-moi de faire appel aux savants auteurs que sont MM. Mazeaud et Tunc.

Faisant, dans la 4ᵉ édition de leur *Traité* sur la responsabilité civile, la critique de l'arrêt de 1947, ils s'insurgent en ces termes contre l'affirmation que le pouvoir de commandement sur la chose implique la faculté de discernement:

'Pareille affirmation paraît contestable, encore qu'il s'agisse d'un pouvoir intellectuel et non matériel car on peut avoir un pouvoir de commandement relativement à une chose sans être à même de l'exercer raisonnablement. Quoi qu'en dise la Cour de cassation, le fou qui brandit un revolver a bien la direction et le contrôle de son arme, de même que l'aliéné dont le chauffeur conduit la voiture.'

'De même que l'aliéné dont le chauffeur conduit la voiture'... N'est-ce point là que se trouve la clé du problème? Raisonnons, si vous le voulez bien, sur l'exemple de la voiture qui n'est pas conduite par son propriétaire, mais par le chauffeur de ce dernier. La jurisprudence et la doctrine sont unanimes pour reconnaître que, dans ce cas, c'est le propriétaire qui est gardien de la chose et non point le préposé. Imaginez alors que le propriétaire devienne fou et que, dans le même temps ou même après coup, le chauffeur provoque un accident.

Admettrez-vous que la victime reste sans recours sous le prétexte que le propriétaire, qui ne conduisait pas, était privé de raison? Nous pourrions 'corser' l'exemple en prenant le cas d'un entrepreneur de transports ayant de nombreux véhicules en circulation. Supposons qu'il meure en laissant pour unique héritier un enfant de quelques mois qui devient propriétaire de l'entreprise. Cet enfant n'a pas plus de discernement que le dément. Admettrez-vous que, bien que propriétaire des véhicules, il n'en soit pas le gardien?

L'on pourrait être tenté de soutenir que, dans les deux exemples pécités, la garde pourrait être censée transférée aux chauffeurs? Mais cette suggestion ne résiste pas à l'examen car, d'une part on voit mal sur quelle base juridique s'effectuerait le changement de garde et d'autre part, admettre que le chauffeur est gardien reviendrait à assimiler la garde à la direction matérielle de la chose, solution définitivement condamnée.

A la vérité, force est d'admettre que la garde est une notion juridique qui ne dépend pas de l'état de santé du gardien. Force est d'admettre que le pouvoir de commandement sur une chose n'est pas détruit par l'absence de discernement. Ce faisant, vous respecterez, me semble-t-il, et l'esprit et la lettre de l'art. 1385 qui définit légalement la garde, qu'il s'agisse de la garde des animaux ou de la garde des choses inanimées, en des termes que je me permets de rappeler: 'Le propriétaire d'un animal, ou celui qui s'en sert, pendant qu'il est à son usage, est responsable du dommage que l'animal a causé...'

2° Il nous reste à présent à examiner le dernier argument du demandeur au pourvoi.

L'imputation d'une responsabilité implique-t-elle, dans tous les cas, la faculté de discernement? Telle était bien la formule de l'arrêt de 1947. Sans doute, en s'exprimant ainsi, la Chambre Civile avait-elle voulu manifester qu'elle entendait écarter la théorie du risque et s'en tenir à la responsabilité basée sur la faute.

C'est bien sur ce terrain que nous entendons également nous placer. Nous admettrons nous aussi que le fondement de la responsabilité du fait des choses reste la faute, bien que la présomption que l'art. 1384, al. 1er, fait peser sur le gardien ne puisse pas être détruite par la preuve de l'absence de faute.

Cela étant, que veut dire la formule employée par la cour? Elle signifie, à n'en pas douter, que ne peut être présumé responsable celui qui n'a pas conscience de ses actes, autrement dit qui ne peut pas être 'responsable'. Ce qui revient à dire que ne peut être présumé responsable celui qui ne peut pas avoir commis de faute.

C'est bien d'ailleurs l'explication ingénieuse donnée par M. le conseiller Lenoan dans le commentaire de l'arrêt. Mais on a pu reprocher à cette explication de n'en être pas une, en réalité. Comme le font très justement remarquer MM. Mazeaud et Tunc 'la preuve de l'absence de faute consiste toujours à démontrer l'impossibilité de toute faute'. Or nous savons que la preuve de l'absence de faute ne libère pas le gardien. Il lui faut démontrer la cause étrangère.

Mais il est permis d'adresser un reproche plus profond à la formule précédemment rappelée. C'est que le raisonnement qu'elle traduit s'inspire d'une définition de la faute qui n'est pas celle généralement admise par la Cour de cassation. En faisant intervenir la notion de discernement, on fait de la faute civile, une faute morale, analogue à la faute pénale, et ce n'est pas ainsi que vous l'entendez d'habitude. Vous n'appréciez pas la faute *in concreto*, subjectivement par référence aux capacités intellectuelles de l'auteur du dommage, à sa personnalité psychique ou à son état d'âme. Vous l'appréciez *in abstracto* par comparaison au comportement d'une personne avisée placée dans les mêmes circonstances externes. Dès lors, il importe peu que l'auteur du dommage soit physiquement ou intellectuellement diminué, qu'il soit ou ne soit pas en possession de ses moyens, qu'il n'ait plus, totalement ou partiellement, conscience de ses actes. Seul importe le fait qu'il ne s'est pas conduit comme se serait conduit, à sa place, un homme normalement prudent et normalement diligent. C'est bien ainsi que la Cour de cassation raisonne quand elle retient la responsabilité des demi-fous, des monomanes, des personnes diminuées physiquement ou intellectuellement, dans le cadre de l'art. 1382. Pour revenir à notre espèce, il n'y a aucune raison logique d'établir des distinctions entre les différentes causes physiologiques qui peuvent amener un conducteur à ne plus être maître de son véhicule, Sa responsabilité doit être le même, que sa défaillance provienne du cerveau ou d'un autre organe du corps. Vouloir analyser les raisons de son comportement anormal, c'est se substituer au médecin, au psychologue, au psychiatre: ce n'est plus faire oeuvre de juriste.

Me faut-il ajouter qu'il est choquant de priver la victime de tout recours dans un cas, celui de l'absence totale de raison, et de l'admettre dans tous les autres cas d'altération de l'intelligence?

Je n'aurai garde d'insister davantage. Quel que soit le point de vue auquel on se place, que ce soit sur le plan de l'esprit juridique ou de l'esprit de justice tout court, il n'y a plus de motif sérieux à ne pas admettre la responsabilité civile de l'individu privé de raison en ce qui concerne les dommages causés par les choses dont il a la garde, et il ne semble pas que l'arrêt de 1947 puisse encore servir de précédent valable.

Dans la savante partition que la Cour de cassation a composée sur le thème de l'art. 1384, al. 1er, cette décision apparaît désormais comme une fausse note qu'il conviendrait d'effacer. Vous obtiendrez ce résultat en rejetant le pourvoi.

Trichard c. Piccino – Arrêt

La Cour; – Sur le moyen unique; – Attendu qu'il résulte de l'arrêt attaqué (Nîmes, 13 mars 1961), rendu après renvoi de cassation, le 11 fév. 1959, d'un arrêt de la Cour d'appel d'Aix du 20 nov. 1956, que Trichard, conduisant sa voiture automobile, heurta, en la dépassant, une charrette menée par Piccino: que projeté à terre et blessé, ce dernier assigna en réparation de son préjudice, sur le fondement de l'art. 1384, al. 1er, CC, Trichard qui, sur le plan pénal, avait bénéficié d'une decision de relaxe au motif que, victime d'une crise d'épilepsie, il se trouvait, au moment des faits, en état de démence au sens de l'art. 64 c. pén.; – Attendu que le pourvoi reproche à l'arrêt d'avoir retenu la responsabilité de Trichard en sa qualité de gardien du véhicule ayant causé l'accident, alors que le dément se trouverait exonéré de la présomption de responsabilité édictée par l'art. 1384, al. 1er, CC; – Mais attendu que pour décider que Trichard devrait, par application du texte susvisé, réparer l'intégralité du préjudice souffert par Piccino, l'arrêt relève, à bon droit, qu'une obnubilation passagère des facultés intellectuelles, qu'elle soit qualifiée de démence au sens de l'art. 64 c. pén., ou qu'elle procède d'un quelconque malaise physique, n'est pas un événement susceptible de constituer une cause de dommage extérieure ou étrangère au gardien; – Attendu que de ces constatations et énonciations, la Cour d'appel a justement déduit que l'absence épileptique au cours de laquelle s'était produit l'accident, n'avait pas pour effet d'exonérer Trichard de la responsabilité qui pesait sur lui en sa qualité de gardien; – d'où il suit que le moyen n'est pas fondé;

Par ces motifs, rejette.

33–5 Cour de cassation
Chambre Mixte, 20 décembre 1968
(3 Arrêts)
(D. 1969,37)

Conclusions de M. l'avocat général Schmelck:

Monsieur le Premier Président, Messieurs.

Après le brillant exposé que vous venez d'entendre, je regrette davantage encore que, dans cette importante affaire, qui met en jeu des principes fondamentaux, les débats n'alent pas été contradictoires et que personne ne soit venu à la barre défendre cet arrêt 'contestataire', que Me George a même qualifié de 'révolutionnaire', et contre lequel il a lancé tant de traits acérés.

Néanmoins, c'est en apparence seulement que l'équilibre de la discussion est rompu, car en réalité, la Cour d'appel de Paris ne se présente pas seule devant ses juges. Dans la position qu'elle a prise, elle ne manque pas d'alliés, et des plus qualifiés, qui, par avance, lui ont prêté leur voix pour défendre la thèse qu'elle soutient.

En effet, en n'exigeant plus de la personne transportée à titre gratuit la preuve d'une faute de son conducteur quand elle lui réclame réparation de son préjudice, en soumettant le transporteur bénévole aux règles habituelles de la responsabilité du fait des choses, la décision qui vous est déférée n'a fait que traduire le vœu formulé ces dernières années par la grande majorité de la doctrine.

Qu'il s'agisse des auteurs qui voient dans l'art. 1384. al. 1er, l'énoncé d'un principe autonome de responsabilité, détaché du concept de la faute, ou de ceux qui persistent dans la tradition classique, il ne s'en trouve plus guère pour défendre le régime de faveur dont la Chambre Civile a fait bénéficier le transporteur bénévole, en rendant au repport du conseiller Ambroise Colin, son arrêt bien connu du 27 mars 1928 (D.P. 1928.1.145, Note G. Ripert; S. 1928,1.353, note Gény).

Voilà donc. Messieurs, le problème du transport bénévole à nouveau posé devant vous et, cette fois, dans son principe même, et d'une manière qui ne laisse place à aucun détour. Vous aurez à dire s'il faut continuer d'imposer à la personne transportée à titre bénévole, qui a été victime d'un accident qu'elle impute à son transporteur, l'obligation de prouver la faute de ce dernier, ou bien si cette personne peut dorénavant bénéficier des mêmes facilités et de la même protection que toute autre victime d'un dommage causé par un véhicule.

Ce que vous demande ce pourvoi, c'est de ne pas revenir sur une décision de principe qui n'a certes pas été prise a la légère puisqu'elle a été rendue après délibération en chambre du conseil et qui, par la qualité de ceux qui l'ont inspirée, puisait aux meilleures sources de la science juridique. Ce à quoi vous invite la Cour d'appel de Paris, soutenue en cela par un mouvement doctrinal quasi unanime, c'est de ne pas attendre davantage pour adapter la règle de droit à l'évolution des choses.

1. – Car c'est bien de cela qu'il s'agit. Nul ne songe, en effet, à jeter l'anathème sur l'arrêt de 1928. Il venait à son heure. Au stade de développement alors atteint par le droit de la responsabilité quasi délictuelle, la solution consacrée ne heurtait aucun principe juridique et pouvait s'abriter derrière des considérations d'équité.

A. – Que l'on veuille bien se reporter aux temps où la décision fut rendue. Nous sommes en 1928. Ce n'est plus la 'belle époque', celle des calèches et des landaux, mais ce n'est pas encore l'ère du véhicule à moteur, moyen de locomotion universel et indispensable accessoire des loisirs comme de la vie quotidienne. L'usage de l'automobile est encore le privilège des gens fortunés. Cependant, il y a déjà plus d'un million de voitures en circulation (sur douze millions à l'heure actuelle) et les accidents se multiplient. Le problème de l'indemnisation des dommages ne se pose pas encore avec la même ampleur qu'aujourd'hui, mais déjà son acuité est telle qu'il devient une préoccupation majeure.

Aussi le droit de la responsabilité est-il en pleine gestation. Pour porter aide aux personnes accidentées, déjà l'on a admis qu'il serait peu équitable de leur imposer de prouver la faute de l'auteur du dommage: c'eût été, dans la plupart des cas, rendre impossible la réparation. Déjà, on leur permet de se prévaloir de l'art. 1384, al. 1er, CC, 'découvert' au siècle précédent pour secourir les accidentés du travail. Déjà l'on décide que le gardien d'une chose inanimée est présumé responsable du dommage causé par cette chose.

Mais les contours et le contenu de la nouvelle règle restent encore imprécis. L'on hésite encore sur le point de savoir si le domaine d'application de l'art. 1384, al. 1er, recouvre toutes les choses ou s'il convient de le limiter aux seules choses mobilières. On se damande également s'il ne faut pas faire une distinction entre les choses dangereuses en elles-mêmes et celles qui, a priori, paraissent inoffensives. De même l'on discute encore de la force qu'il convient de donner à la présomption que l'on fait peser sur le gardien; est-ce une simple présomption que l'intéressé peut combattre en prouvant qu'il n'a commis ni imprudence, ni négligence et qu'il n'a contrevenu à aucun règlement, ou bien est-ce une présomption plus rigoureuse qui ne tombe que devant la preuve de la force majeure et de la cause étrangère, mais alors, quel caractère lui donner? Enfin, la notion de garde elle-même n'est pas encore clarifiée: l'on s'attache encore à cette idée que le gardien est celui qui tire profit de la chose.

Toutes ces questions ne trouveront leur réponse que quelques années plus tard, devant les Chambres Réunies avec l'arrêt *Jand'heur* du 13 fév. 1930 (D.P. 1930.1.57, Note Ripert: S. 1930.1.121, note Esmein) et l'arrêt *Franck* du 2 déc. 1941 (S. 1941,1.217. Note H. Mazeaud; D.C. 1942, 25, Note Ripert: *J.C.P.* 1942.2.1766, Note Mihura). Elles la trouveront dans le sens d'une généralisation de l'art. 1384. al. 1er, et d'un affermissement de la responsabilité découlant de la garde.

C'était donc dans un climat où beaucoup de brume flottait encore sur les cimes que la Chambre Civile était appelée à décider des principes applicables en matière de transport bénévole.

Quelques années plus tôt elle avait dénié aux personnes transportées à titre gratuit la possibilité de se placer sur le terrain de la responsabilité contractuelle. Il restait à décider si ces personnes ne pouvaient pas, en revanche, fonder leur action sur les dispositions tout aussi favorables de l'art. 1384, al. 1er.

Compte tenu des incertitudes de la doctrine juridique, compte tenu également de ce que les appréhensions suscitées par le concept d'une responsabilité sans faute étaient loin d'être apaisées, on conçoit volontiers que la Cour de cassation, à juste titre prudente jusque dans ses audaces, ait eu scrupule à franchir ce pas dès l'abord.

La Chambre Civile était d'autant plus tentée de refuser à la personne transportée à titre gratuit les facilités qu'elle était prête à reconnaître à toute autre victime d'un accident de la circulation que cette restriction lui était inspirée par une de ces 'raisons du cœur' auxquelles le juge, si épris de système soit-il, ne reste pas insenible. Comme on l'a souvent souligné, l'assurance automobile n'était alors ni obligatoire, ni généralisée. S'il n'avait pas eu la sagesse de se garantir, le conducteur complaisant supportait seul tout le fardeau de la réparation. Dans ces conditions, n'eût-il pas été excessif, pour ne pas dire indécent, de permettre à la victime de ruiner la personne qui n'avait fait que lui rendre service et à qui elle ne pouvait rien reprocher de précis? (cf. Mazeaud et Tunc, *Traité de la responsabilité civile*, t. 2, 5ᵉ éd., n° 1282).

Un tel aboutissement pouvait paraître d'autant plus choquant que certaines victimes n'étaient pas tellement dignes de protection. Il y avait le cas de l'auto-stoppeur: à l'inverse de l'ami que vous transportez aujourd'hui alors qu'il vous a transporté hier. n'abuse-t-il pas quelque peu de votre complaisance? Alors, tant pis, si, ne pouvant établir de faute à votre encontre, il reste privé d'indemnité. A n'en point douter ce cas particulier n'a pas été sans influencer la Chambre Civile.

Mais ces seules considérations morales, quel que fût leur intérêt, ne lui fournissaient pas le fondement juridique de sa décision.

A la vérité, celle-ci était difficile à justifier en droit, car, à partir du moment où l'on accordait à l'art. 1384, al. 1ᵉʳ, une signfication et une portée particulières, cet article, par la généralité de ses termes ('on est responsable... du dommage causé par le fait... des choses que l'on a sous sa garde') n'autorisait apparemment aucune dérogation à la règle qu'il édictait.

Quels ont alors été les arguments mis en avant par la chambre civile?

Il est essentiel de les rappeler puisque la décision qui vous est déférée en conteste précisément le bien-fondé.

Que dit l'arrêt du 27 mars 1928?

Il s'exprime en termes vigoureux et frappés, qui dépassent le cas d'espèce.

La Chambre Civile commence par rappeler: 'que la présomption instituée par l'art. 1384, al. 1ᵉʳ, CC à l'encentre du gardien d'une chose mobilière inanimée soumise à la nécessité d'une "garde", en raison du danger qu'elle peut faire courir à autrui, a été établie pour protéger, en assurant, le cas échéant, leur indemnisation, les victimes du dommage causé par une chose à l'usage de laquelle elles n'ont point participé'.

Et elle ajoute: 'que cette présomption ne peut donc être invoquée contre le gardien d'une voiture automobile par ceux qui ont pris place dans cette voiture, soit en vertu d'un contrat, soit à la suite d'un acte de courtoisie purement bénévole: que les premiers trouvent leur protection dans les obligations imposées au transporteur par les stipulations expresses ou implicites du contrat; que, quant à ceux qui ont accepté ou sollicité de participer à titre gracieux à l'usage de la voiture, en pleine connaissance des dangers auxquels ils s'exposaient eux-mêmes, ils ne peuvent obtenir de dommages-intérêts du gardien de l'automobile que s'ils établissent, à sa charge ou à celle de son préposé, une faute qui leur soit imputable dans les termes des art. 1382 et 1383 CC'.

En somme, la Cour de cassation partait de cette idée que l'automobiliste était un être dangereux, créateur de risques pour les tiers, alors que lui-même tirait profit de l'utilisation de son véhicule. Dès lors, il lui semblait normal que le piéton fût digne d'une protection particulière, mais non point le passager qui, lui aussi, retirait avantage de l'usage de la voiture. Elle renforçait cette idée par la considération que 'les transportés bénévoles avaient accepté ou sollicité de participer à l'usage de la voiture en pleine reconnaissance des dangers auxquels ils s'exposaient eux-mêmes'.

Ainsi la Haute assemblée motivait la limitation qu'elle apportait à l'art. 1384, al. 1er, par deux considérations essentielles:
– la participation de la victime à l'usage gratuit de la chose;
– l'acceptation des risques.

B. – Messieurs, reconnaissons-le, cette double justification n'a pas résisté longtemps aux assauts de la doctrine. Reconnaissons également qu'elle s'accorde actuellement assez mal avec les principes de la responsabilité quasi délictuelle, tels qu'ils ont été dégagés au fil des ans par votre propre jurisprudence.

De savants auteurs, qu'une simple affirmation ne pouvait satisfaire, n'ont pas manqué de se demander *pourquoi* la participation à l'usage de la chose priverait la personne transportée du bénéfice de la présomption de responsabilité pesant sur le gardien?

Serait-ce parce que, en utilisant le véhicule, elle en partagerait la garde? Cela pourrait se concevoir si l'on confondait la garde avec l'usage de la chose, ou bien encore si l'on admettait que le gardien était la personne tirant profit de l'utilisation de cette chose. Ces idées avaient encore cours en 1928. Mais elles ne peuvent plus servir d'explication aujourd'hui que l'on définit la garde comme un pouvoir de direction, un pouvoir de commandement sur la chose. MM. Mazeaud et Tunc observent fort pertinemment dans leur traité (5e éd., t. 1. p. 286) que, sauf cas exceptionnel, 'le passager n'a pas d'ordre à donner, il n'est donc pas gardien'.

Serait-ce alors, parce que, comme l'a souligné la Chambre Civile, le transporté bénévole a 'pleine connaissance des dangers auxquels il s'expose lui-même'? Mais, a-t-on fait remarquer, à ce compte le piéton ne devrait pas être mieux traité que le passager, car, lui aussi, a pleine connaissance des dangers qu'il court en traversant la chaussée. Au demeurant, et d'une manière générale, l'acceptation des risques par la victime n'est pas considérée, à elle seule, comme une cause d'exonération du gardien. Vous ne lui reconnaissez cette vertu que lorsqu'elle revêt un caractère fautif, lorsque la chose utilisée présente un danger exceptionnel, lorsque la victime commet une imprudence en acceptant ou en sollicitant de participer à son usage. Il y a faute à prendre place dans une voiture dont le mauvais état est apparent, dont le conducteur est manifestement en état d'ébriété. Il peut y avoir faute à prendre place dans une voiture de course au moment d'une compétition (Civ. 2e, 24 janv. 1964, *Bull, civ.* 1964, 2, n° 90, p. 67; D. 1964, Somm. 101; 24 nov. 1966, *Bull. civ.* 1966, 2, n° 922, p. 644; 10 mars 1966, *ibid.* 1966, 2, n° 328, p. 235).

Mais vous n'admettez pas que monter dans une voiture normale, pour accomplir un trajet normal, avec un conducteur... en état... normal, soit le fait d'une légèreté coupable.

Serait-ce alors qu'il existerait – ou que l'on pourrait admettre qu'll existat – entre le passager et son transporteur bénévole, un accord préalable, au moins implicite, par lequel le premier aurait renoncé à se prévaloir de la présomption de responsabilité. Mais cet argument ne résiste pas davantage à l'examen. D'abord, a-t-on pu dire, une telle convention est purement 'divinatoire' (Mazeaud). En outre, voudrait-on la sous-entendre, qu'elle devrait s'analyser normalement en une renonciation à toute action en indemnité contre le transporteur – hors le cas d'une faute volontaire – et non point comme une simple renonciation à des facilités de preuve. Enfin – et l'objection n'est pas moins sérieuse – si une telle convention avait été réellement passée, eh bien, elle serait nulle, puisque nous nous trouvons dans le domaine de la responsabilité délictuelle ou quasi délictuelle, et qu'en telle matière, la jurisprudence refuse tout effet aux clauses de non-responsabilité (cf. notamment. Civ. 3 janv. 1933. D.H. 1933,113; 18 juil. 1934, D.P. 1935.1.38, Note Roger; Civ. 2ᵉ, 11 déc. 1952, D. 1953, 317, Note R. Savatier; 17 fév. 1955, D. 1956,17, Note Esmein; *J.C.P.* 1955,2.8951, Note Rodière).

De tout ceci, – qui est bien connu et qui est abondamment traité dans tous les manuels – il résulte qu'aucun des arguments juridiques proposés pour expliquer le sort exceptionnel réservé au transporteur bénévole, n'est vraiment satisfaisant.

Les commentateurs de l'arrêt de 1928 ne s'y sont pas trompés: la vraie raison, la seule, qui permettait de refuser au transporté à titre bénévole les mêmes facilités qu'aux autres victimes d'accidents de la circulation, c'était une certaine conception de l'équité qui préférait priver la victime de reparation plutôt que ruiner la personne qui lui avait rendu service. Mais, c'était là un mobile moral, ce n'était pas un motif juridique.

C. – Dans la mesure où elle pouvait paraître opportune dans le passé, la solution l'est-elle encore aujourd'hui?

Voilà qui peut être sérieusement mis en doute et qui l'est de tous côtés, nous l'avons déjà montré.

L'on ne saurait nier qu'en quarante ans les choses ont bien changé! Les données du problème ne sont plus les mêmes; de son côté, la conjoncture juridique s'est modifiée.

Que ce soit au plan de la prévention, de la répression ou de la réparation des dommages, les accidents de la route sont devenus la hantise des pouvoirs publics, à tel point que l'on a sérieusement songé à substituer à notre actuel système d'indemnisation, fondé sur la responsabilité, un système de garantie ou de sécurité collective d'où serait exclue toute appréciation de la responsabilité. C'est qu'en effet le chiffre des accidents ne manque pas d'être impressionnant. La route tue journellement plus de 50 personnes et en blesse gravement 300 autres. J'ignore quel est, dans cette hécatombe, le nombre des passagers retirés morts ou estropiés des décombres de la voiture où ils avaient pris place, mais on peut être assuré qu'il figure en bon rang dans la statistique. N'a-t-on pas appelé la place du passager à l'avant de la voiture la place du mort?

Dans la mesure de vos possibilités, sans doute plus larges dans ce domaine que dans d'autres, mais néanmoins limitées, vous avez su faire face à la situation. D'une part, vous avez étroitement délimité les causes d'exonération du gardien du véhicule. D'autre part, vous avez étendu le bénéfice de l'art. 1384. al. 1er, à toutes les victimes d'un dommage causé par véhicule, à celles qui ont subi directement ie dommage et à celles qui ne sont atteintes que par ricochet. Conjoint, enfants, parents, alliés – la concubine elle-même, selon la chambre criminelle – toutes les personnes lésées par l'accident peuvent désormais invoquer la présomption de responsabilité qui pèse sur le gardien du véhicule.

Toutes, … sauf une cependant: le passager de la voiture (ou son ayant droit), quand il demande réparation à son transporteur.

La survivance de cette exception paraîtrait moins surprenante si les mobiles d'équité qui l'avaient inspirée jadis, conservaient leur valeur. Mais sous ce rapport également la situation s'est transformée du tout au tout depuis que sont intervenus la loi du 27 janv. 1958 et les décrets pris pour son application. Instituant l'obligation de s'assurer pour la conduite des véhicules à moteur, ces textes ont singulièrement amélioré la condition du transporteur bénévole. Nous aurons l'occasion de préciser l'exacte portée de la protection qu'ils lui apportent.

Pour l'instant, bornons-nous à rappeler que, de nos jours, grâce à l'assurance obligatoire, le conducteur d'une automobile, qui est assigné en dommages-intérêts par l'ami qu'il transporte, ou l'auto-stoppeur qu'il a recueilli, ne répond plus sur son propre patrimoine du dommage qu'il a causé: la collectivité des assurés paie pour lui.

Quel est, dès lors, du transporteur bénévole auteur de l'accident, mais qui n'en supportera pas les conséquences pécuniaires, ou de l'occupant de la voiture, victime qui a droit à réparation, celui des deux qui est le plus digne d'intérêt et qui mérite le plus de sollicitude? Cette fois, 'la voix du cœur' plaide en faveur du transporté.

Au plan de l'équité, les rôles sont désormais inversés.

II. – Messieurs, je serais tenté d'arrêter là une démonstration qui n'a rien d'original et ne fait que reprendre un argument souvent développé: privé, à l'heure actuelle, de son support moral, le régime privilégié du transporteur bénévole, est, du même coup, privé de sa véritable raison d'être et de sa seule justification.

Voilà qui devrait suffire à le condamner.

Mais d'autres considérations encore, de caractère plus technique, commandent de ne pas persister dans les errements anciens.

C'est qu'en effet l'interdiction faite à la personne transportée à titre gratuit de fonder son action sur les dispositions de l'art. 1384, al. 1er, a fini par entraîner la Cour de cassation dans de telles 'impasses' (le mot est de M. le doyen Savatier) que certains commentateurs n'ont pas hésité à qualifier la situation 'd'imbroglio juridique'. Sans doute pareil jugement est-il excessif dans sa sévérité. Il n'en reste pas moins que les solutions vers lesquelles on s'est orienté prêtent le flanc à la critique sur le plan des principes, et, qu'à certains égards, elles peuvent heurter des esprits essentiellement épris de logique.

Voilà qui est particulièrement sensible dans deux domaines:
– celui de l'appréciation de la faute du transporteur;
– celui de la détermination des droits de la victime, transportée à titre gratuit, quand, dans le cas d'une collision, elle demande réparation au gardien du véhicule qui ne la transportait pas.

A. – Avant d'examiner le premier de ces points, j'aimerais apporter une précision qui sera en même temps un hommage rendu à la chambre à laquelle j'ai l'honneur d'appartenir. Elle n'a pas été la dernière à prendre conscience de ce qu'il n'était plus possible de traiter avec défaveur les personnes transportées gratuitement. Elle a eu à connaître de trop d'affaires où une telle attitude conduisait à l'injustice. Votre deuxième chambre s'est donc efforcée d'améliorer le sort des victimes tout en se maintenant dans la ligne de l'arrêt de 1928, qu'elle avait scrupule à désavouer directement et à elle seule. Son action s'est portée dans deux directions.

En premier lieu, elle a restreint au maximum la notion de transport gratuit. En second lieu, elle s'est attachée à faciliter au demandeur en réparation la preuve de la faute du conducteur.

(1) Le premier procédé n'appelle pas de remarque particulière du point de vue qui nous occupe. On a pu lui reprocher de conduire à des solutions manquant d'unité, mais il n'est guère critiquable au plan des principes. En décidant que la 'gratuité' doit être appréciée du côté du gardien, auquel en incombe par ailleurs la preuve (Civ. 2ᵉ, 14 mars 1958, D. 1958, 385, Note R. Savatier; S. 1958,239; J.C.P. 1958, 2,10674, Note P. Esmein), en décidant en outre qu'il doit s'agir d'un geste vraiment désintéressé, d'un véritable 'acte de courtoisie'; et en allant même très loin dans l'appréciation du caractère intéressé du transport, – n'a-t-on pas estimé à un moment donné que la participation aux frais d'essence, si minime soit-elle, ne permettait plus de considérer le transport comme bénévole (Cf. Civ. 2ᵉ, 2 juil. 1964, *Bull. civ.* 1964, 2, n° 535, p. 399. – *Contra:* 16 oct. 1964, *ibid.* 1964, 2, n° 622, p. 455; D. 1965, Somm. 42), – votre deuxième chambre n'encourt aucun reproche d'ordre général. Elle reste dans la logique du système établi et n'est en contradiction avec aucune idée reçue. Il en est de même lorsqu'elle limite l'application des règles propres au transport bénévole au cas où le dommage a eu lieu au cours même du transport et qu'elle l'écarte dans le cas où le dommage s'est produit immédiatement après (Civ. 2ᵉ, 11 janv. 1967, *Bull. civ.* 1967, 2, n° 15, p. 9; D. 1967, Somm. 82).

(2) En revanche, utilisant le second procédé consistant à donner à la victime, bien que son action soit fondée sur l'art. 1382, des facilités de preuve analogues à celles que procure l'art. 1384, al. 1ᵉʳ, votre deuxième chambre s'est placée dans une position inconfortable. Ce point est important, et mérite quelques explications.

C'est dans un arrêt du 5 avr. 1962 (*Bull, civ.* 1962, 2, n° 383, p. 273; D. 1963, 78; S. 1963, 34, Note Meurisse) que l'on trouve l'ébauche d'une théorie dans laquelle la deuxième Chambre Civile a persisté jusqu'à ce jour, Le cas qui lui était soumis était celui d'une personne transportée à titre gratuit, blessée dans un accident dont la cause précise n'était pas connue, et où aucune infraction aux règles de la circulation, aucune imprudence caractérisée ne pouvait être reprochée au conducteur.

Selon les constatations de la Cour d'appel, la voie était large, le sol sec et en très bon état, le véhicule se trouvait en bon état de marche. Néanmoins 'à la fin d'une légère courbe, la voiture avait heurté le trottoir de droite, puis parcouru 27 mètres sur celui-ci, éraflant un premier arbre avant de s'abîmer sur un second'. Se bornant à constater que le conducteur avait perdu le contrôle de son véhicule sans s'arrêter au fait que la cause exacte de cette perte de contrôle n'avait pu être déterminée, la Cour d'appel déclarait ce conducteur responsable de l'accident et le condamnait à indemniser le passager, blessé dans l'accident.

La deuxième Chambre Civile approuva cette décision dans les termes suivants:

'Attendu que le défaut de maîtrise dans la conduite d'un véhicule en marche par son conducteur constitue une faute, dès lors qu'il n'est pas démontré qu'il doit être imputé à une circonstance étrangère à ce conducteur;

'Attendu que, cette preuve n'étant pas rapportée en l'espèce, la constatation de cette faute suffit à justifier la décision.'

En prenant cette position, la Chambre revenait sur sa doctrine antérieure, qui lui faisait dire, le 2 juin 1961, encore 'qu'à défaut de certitude sur les circonstances de l'accident, aucun reproche ne pouvait être formulé contre le conducteur' (*Bull. civ.* 1961, 2, n° 412, p. 297). Elle renonçait désormais à exiger la preuve de l'élément précis caractérisant l'imprudence, la négligence ou l'inobservation des règlements. Elle en venait à affirmer que, lorsqu'un véhicule s'était comporté anormalement, il y avait lieu de présumer que ce comportement anormal était dû à un défaut de maîtrise du conducteur sur son véhicule et que ce défaut de maîtrise constituait une faute.

Depuis lors, une trentaine d'arrêts, aussi bien de rejet que de cassation, ont été rendus dans le même esprit, sinon exactement dans les mêmes termes.

Si bien qu'à présent, en fait, et bien que théoriquement l'on soit toujours sur le terrain de la faute, il n'est guère demandé davantage au transporté à titre bénévole qui introduit une action en dommages-intérêts contre son conducteur que ce qui est demandé au piéton qui réclame réparation au gardien du véhicule qui l'a blessé. Dans les deux cas, il suffit à la victime d'établir que le véhicule est à l'origine du dommage, par exemple qu'il s'est déporté sur la gauche (Civ. 2e, 7 juil. 1966, *Bull. civ.* 1966, 2, n° 753, p. 530), ou qu'il a quitté la chaussée (1er déc. 1966, *Bull. civ.* 1966, 2, n° 936, p. 655), pour qu'aussitôt la charge de la preuve soit inversée et qu'il appartienne au défendeur de démontrer qu'il n'est pour rien dans le dommage. Encore la jurisprudence s'est-elle montrée très exigeante dans l'admission de la cause étrangère. L'on est allé jusqu'à décider, dans un cas où l'embardée du véhicule avait été provoquée par l'éclatement d'un pneu, que le conducteur était responsable puisqu'il n'était pas arrivé à reprendre le contrôle de sa voiture (Civ. 2e, 18 mars 1966, *Bull. civ.* 1966, 2, n° 378, p. 267).

C'est, on le voit, une véritable responsabilité de plein droit 'au petit pied', qui a été instituée.

Les seules différences qui existent encore entre le sort réservé au transporteur bénévole, sur la base de l'art. 1382, et celui du gardien sur la base de l'art. 1384, al. 1er, se limitent à ceci:

En premier lieu, le transporteur bénévole peut se dégager de toute responsabilité en prouvant que l'accident est dû à un vice de la machine, ignoré de lui. En effet, la présomption qui pèse sur lui est une présomption de faute qui tombe devant la preuve de l'absence de faute. Au contraire, le vice inhérent à la chose laisse entière la responsabilité du gardien qui ne peut s'exonérer qu'en démontrant que le dommage est dû à une cause étrangère extérieure à la chose dont il a la garde.

En second lieu, le transporteur bénévole est dégagé de toute obligation de réparer s'il n'était pas en possession de ses facultés mentales au moment de l'accident; au contraire, le gardien est aujourd'hui tenu de réparer, même s'il était en état de démence (Civ. 2e, 18 déc. 1964, D. 1965,191. Note Esmein, Concl. Schmelck; *J.C.P.* 1965, 2.14304, Note Dejean de la Batie; 4 nov. 1965, D. 1966,394, Note Plancqueel; 21 janv. 1966, *Bull, civ.* 1966, 2, n° 102, p. 73; D. 1966, Somm. 91; 1er mars 1967, *Bull, civ.* 1967, 2, n° 96, p. 68).

En troisième lieu, le transporteur bénévole ne peut plus être déclaré responsable lorsqu'une juridiction répressive a reconnu qu'aucune faute pénale ne peut être retenue contre lui (soit que les faits reprochés ne constituent pas une infraction, soit que, constituant une infraction, ils sont couverts par la prescription); au contraire le gardien peut encore être condamné civilement, même s'il a bénéficié d'un jugement de relaxe.

Sous réserve de ces points particuliers, l'on peut dire que la responsabilité du transporteur bénévole est désormais – pratiquement – appréciée de la même manière que celle du gardien.

Heureux en lui-même, et répondant à sa manière au souhait souvent formulé d'unifier les règles de l'indemnisation, ce résultat n'est malheureusement atteint qu'au prix d'une sollicitation des principes et d'une véritable oblitération de la notion de faute. Et c'est bien là ce qui est fâcheux.

Ce que l'on a appelé la 'théorie de la faute virtuelle', ne peut, en effet, s'expliquer que de deux manières:
– ou bien elle signifie que le conducteur est présumé en faute dès lors que son véhicule se comporte anormalement;
– ou bien elle signifie que le fait de ne pas rester maître de son véhicule est une faute en soi.

Dans la première hypothèse, il a été reproché à la Cour de cassation d'avoir créé de toutes pièces une nouvelle présomption de faute qu'aucun texte ne prévoit (v. Boré, D. 1963, Chron., p. 21 *et s.* – v. également Rodière, obs. *Rev. trim. dr. civ.* 1964, 310, 311 et 375). Sans doute le grief n'est-il pas sans réplique, et peut-on rétorquer que, les règles de la responsabilité du fait des choses étant votre œuvre, vous disposez dans ce domaine d'une plus grande latitude que dans d'autres; faire peser une simple présomption de faute sur le transporteur bénévole, c'est, sans doute aussi, se montrer moins audacieux qu'on ne l'avait été en rendant le gardien d'une chose responsable de plein droit des dommages qu'elle cause. Mais il n'en reste pas moins que cette présomption de faute, mise à la charge du transporteur bénévole, ne peut se réclamer d'aucun texte, alors que la responsabilité du fait des choses a pu, elle, trouver appui dans les termes mêmes de l'art. 1384, al. 1er.

Dans la seconde hypothèse, c'est-à-dire si l'on interprète les décisions de la deuxième Chambre Civile comme érigeant en faute le seul fait de perdre le contrôle de la voiture, c'est alors – il faut bien l'avouer – donner de la faute une définition qui n'est pas généralement admise, et que la même chambre ne retient d'ailleurs pas, en dehors du cas du transport bénévole. C'est aussi rompre le principe de l'unité de la faute civile et de la faute pénale, qui est à la base de l'art. 1382, car – la Chambre Criminelle l'affirme bien souvent – le juge répressif ne peut induire l'existence d'une faute du conducteur du seul fait que le véhicule s'est comporté anormalement. Il ne peut le faire pour la simple raison que le doute doit bénéficier au prévenu.

La dualité dans l'interprétation du même texte et du même concept juridique, les contradictions auxquelles on aboutit, sont incontestablement les grandes faiblesses du système juridique construit par la deuxième Chambre Civile. Aussi bien la première chambre a-t-elle eu scrupule à suivre son homologue et ş'est-elle partagée sur la question, vous donnant ainsi l'occasion de la reprendre demain, sous l'éclairage nouveau que lui donnera éventuellement votre décision dans la présente affaire.

B. – Aussi discutable qu'il soit en droit, le système de la faute virtuelle a, au moins, le mérite de pallier les inconvénients découlant de l'application de l'art. 1382 au transporté à titre bénévole. Moins satisfaisante sous ce rapport, et tout aussi controversée sur le plan juridique, apparaît la position prise en ce qui concerne les droits de la personne transportée à titre gratuit, blessée dans une collision, lorsqu'elle se retourne non plus contre le conducteur de la voiture où elle avait pris place, mais contre le gardien de l'autre véhicule. Dans ce cas, il ne saurait être question d'exiger d'elle la preuve d'une faute. Elle bénéficie de la présomption de responsabilité qui pèse sur le gardien du véhicule en question.

On s'attendrait donc à ce que ce gardien fût tenu pour responsable de l'intégralité du dommage, sauf pour lui de s'exonérer en prouvant que l'accident est uniquement dû à une cause étrangère, tel le fait de l'autre conducteur. Ce n'est pourtant pas la solution actuellement retenue. Depuis l'arrêt *Pilastre* du 9 mars 1962 (S. 1963, 2, Note Meurisse), votre deuxième chambre décide que la personne transportée à titre gratuit ne peut demander au tiers coauteur la réparation intégrale de son préjudice sur la base de l'art. 1384, al. 1er, si elle ne dispose pas d'une action contre son transporteur.

Le cheminement de la pensée est le suivant: lorsqu'un accident ayant deux auteurs a causé des dommages à une troisième personne, la victime peut certes réclamer le tout à l'un quelconque d'entre eux en vertu de l'obligation *in solidum* pesant sur chacun d'eux. Mais cette obligation de payer le tout suppose que celui qui paie, tout autant pour son compte que pour le compte de l'autre, puisse se retourner contre ce dernier pour la part qui lui incombe, et un tel recours n'est possible que si la victime, dans les droits de laquelle le solvens n'est que subrogé, disposait elle-même d'une action contre cette personne. Or, en l'espèce précisément, la victime n'a pas d'action contre l'automobiliste qui la transportait bénévolement, ni sur la base de l'art. 1384, al. 1er, qu'il lui est interdit d'invoquer, ni sur la base de l'art. 1382, puisque, par définition, elle ne peut faire la preuve d'une faute de son transporteur. Dans ces conditions, estime votre deuxième chambre, la personne transportée à titre gratuit ne peut réclamer de l'autre automobiliste que la part qui lui incombe dans ce dommage, en fait la moitié.

Cette jurisprudence se heurte à la résistance de la grande majorité des cours d'appel. Si, dans les derniers temps, certaines d'entre elles se sont ralliées à la doctrine de la Cour de cassation, la rédaction des arrêts laisse à penser que c'est davantage par esprit de discipline que par conviction. Le système parait en effet d'autant plus surprenant que, si le passager, qui n'a aucunement contribué à l'accident ne peut obtenir de l'autre automobiliste que la moitié de son préjudice, son conducteur qui, lui, a contribué à la collision, pourra réclamer à ce même automobiliste la réparation intégrale de son propre dommage.

La solution ne semble pas non plus inéluctable en droit. Car il n'est pas certain qu'il faille faire appel, en l'occurrence, aux règles de l'obligation *in solidum*. Une telle obligation, a-t-on pu dire, suppose un ou plusieurs codébiteurs. Or, dans le cas considéré, la victime n'est pas en présence de deux débiteurs, mais d'un seul, puisque aussi bien l'automobiliste qui la transportait ne peut, en aucune façon, être tenu pour responsable à son égard et par conséquent, ne lui doit rien (v. Note Dejean de la Batie sous Civ. 2e, 21 déc. 1965 *J.C.P.* 1966, 2.14736; v. également *Rev. trim. dr. civ.* 1967, 170).

La question est délicate et l'occasion vous sera donnée de la trancher grâce à un autre pourvoi dont votre Chambre Mixte est saisie. Il n'est pas dans mes intentions d'en débattre maintenant. Si j'ai soulevé la difficulté, c'est dans le seul dessein de souligner qu'elle n'existe, au même titre que la précédente, que parce que la personne transportée, qui réclame réparation à son conducteur, est censée devoir se placer sur le terrain de l'art. 1382, L'une et l'autre disparaitraient si l'on autorisait cette personne à se prévaloir de l'art. 1384, al. 1er. Alors, d'un côté, rien ne s'opposerait plus à ce que la victime obtienne du tiers coauteur de l'accident une indemnisation totale. Et, d'un autre côté, il deviendrait sans intérêt de forcer la notion de faute jusqu'à l'extrême dans le souci d'aider la victime.

III. – J'approche, Messieurs, du terme de ce trop long propos.

Bien qu'ils n'aient pas été développés à la barre, les arguments qui militent en faveur d'un revirement de jurisprudence ont été exposés.

Il y a d'abord la fragilité de la construction juridique échafaudée en 1928, fragilité qui n'a fait que s'accentuer et devenir plus évidente au fur et à mesure que se développait et se consolidait l'édifice principal.

Il y a également le fait que l'intervention du législateur en 1958 a fait basculer l'argument moral qui permettait d'exclure le transport bénévole du champ d'application de l'art. 1384.

Il y a enfin ce fait que l'exception ainsi apportée à la règle générale n'est plus dans la grande majorité des cas – du fait de l'interprétation extensive de la notion de faute – qu'une simple fiction juridique.

Si l'on décidait, aujourd'hui, que l'occasion s'en présente, de mettre le droit en harmonie avec la réalité pratique, alors non seulement la conjoncture juridique serait assainie et clarifiée, alors non seulement disparaîtraient toutes ces 'inelegantiae juris' sur lesquelles je me suis permis d'appeler votre attention, mais, du même coup, un grand pas serait franchi dans la voie, tant souhaitée, de l'unification et de la simplification du droit de la responsabilité civile.

A n'en point douter, Messieurs, les avantages qu'il y aurait à consacrer la rupture avec l'ancienne jurisprudence sont considérables.

Il reste à en mesurer les inconvénients.

Qu'il ne s'en trouve pas quelques-uns, je n'oserais le prétendre. Quelle est la règle juridique qui, dans son application, ne rencontre pas quelque obstacle? Mais que ces inconvénients soient tels qu'ils contrebalancent les effets heureux de la solution préconisée et lui enlèvent son intérêt, voilà qui est plus que douteux.

Quels sont en effet les arguments que l'on oppose à l'arrêt de la Cour de Paris?

Certains sont propres à la matière du transport bénévole; il est un autre dont la portée est plus générale.

A. – En se plaçant sur le terrain du transport bénévole, Me Boré a présenté différentes objections dans la note qu'il a publiée au *Jurisclasseur* en suite de l'arrêt (*J.C.P.* 1968, 2.15487).

Les novateurs, écrit-il en substance, fondent toute leur argumentation sur le fait que l'assurance obligatoire a modifié les données du problème en reportant le poids de la réparation du transporteur bénévole sur la collectivité anonyme des assurés. Mais, c'est oublier qu'il y a tout un secteur important qui échappe à l'obligation d'assurance. D'abord, la loi de 1958 ne vise que les véhicules terrestres à moteur: elle ne s'applique pas en cas d'accident causé par une charrette ou un cycle. En outre, parmi les véhicules à moteur, il en est qui peuvent être soustraits à l'obligation d'assurance, pour ce qui est du transport bénévole: les véhicules à deux roues par exemple. Enfin et surtout, le législateur a exclu de l'obligation d'assurance les dommages causés aux membres de la famille de l'assuré. Dans tous les cas, le poids de la réparation n'est plus supporté par un fonds collectif, mais bien par le transporteur bénévole lui-même, sur son propre patrimoine. Voilà des situations, vous assure-t-on, où les motifs qui avaient inspiré la Chambre Civile en 1928 conservent leur plein intérêt.

En outre, – et c'est la seconde objection – appliquer la présomption de responsabilité au transporteur bénévole, c'est, dit-on, accroitre virtuellement, d'une fraction non négligeable, les primes d'assurance responsabilité automobile et voilà qui est fâcheux.

Il convient, Messieurs, de ramener ces différents arguments à leur véritable dimension.

Je ne m'arrêterai pas à l'exemple de la charrette, exclue du champ d'application de la loi de 1958: c'est un véhicule qui franchira bientôt le seuil de l'Histoire et qui n'offre guère plus qu'une hypothèse d'école. Je ne m'attarderai pas davantage à celui de la bicyclette, qui n'est pas un engin conçu pour le transport en commun et dont l'utilisation par un passager installé sur le cadre ou le porte-bagage peut être considérée comme une faute de nature à atténuer la responsabilité du transporteur.

Les exclusions méritant un examen plus attentif sont celles concernant les véhicules à moteur, qui sont l'objet même de la loi de 1958.

Il est bien exact que l'assurance obligatoire n'offre pas, à tout coup, sa protection au conducteur d'un véhicule à moteur lorsqu'il effectue un transport bénévole. Mais il faut voir ce qu'il en est exactement.

Le décret du 7 janv. 1959 a apporté deux limitations à l'obligation d'assurance: l'une figure à l'art. 10, l'autre à l'art. 8 de ce décret.

(*a*) L'article 10 permet d'exclure du contrat d'assurance, par clause expresse, les dommages subis par les personnes transportées sur un véhicule à deux roues, dans un side-car, ou sur un triporteur. Mais quelle est alors la situation de l'assuré?

Il paie une prime moins élevée, mais en revanche il s'engage à ne pas prendre de passager. S'il le fait néanmoins, et que son passager soit blessé, la question est de savoir si l'assureur ne sera pas, malgré tout, dans l'obligation de lui fournir sa garantie. La tendance manifestée par votre première chambre dans des arrêts récents (8 juil. 1968, D. 1968, 688, Note P.P.), me porte à croire qu'en application des art. 17, 21 et 22 de la loi du 13 juil. 1930, elle considèrerait volontiers cette situation, non point comme un cas de non-assurance, mais comme un simple cas d'aggravation du risque, que, moyennant un complément de prime versé par l'assuré, l'assureur est obligé de prendre en charge, sauf si son cocontractant était de mauvaise foi. Admettons cependant que la compagnie d'assurance soit dégagée de toute obligation vis-à-vis de son assuré et que l'indemnité reste à la charge de ce dernier. Faut-il pour autant le traiter avec une générosité particulière? Ne doit-on pas penser plutôt qu'il ne peut, dans ce cas, que s'en prendre à lui-même, puisqu'il devait normalement s'assurer contre ce risque, et que c'est volontairement et, en toute connaissance de cause, qu'il ne l'a pas fait?

(*b*) Passons au 'risque familial'. En vertu de l'art. 8 du décret du 7 janv. 1959, n'est pas comprise dans l'assurance obligatoire la réparation des dommages subis par le conjoint, les ascendants et descendants du gardien, ou du conducteur autorisé, lorsqu'ils sont transportés dans le véhicule assuré. Cette exclusion a été principalement dictée par des considérations financières – le législateur n'a pas voulu trop alourdir les charges des compagnies d'assurance et, par contrecoup, les primes imposées aux assurés. Cette fois, dit-on, il ne s'agit plus d'une hypothèse exceptionnelle. Les accidents sont fréquents, dont sont victimes les membres des familles. C'est là, par conséquent, que vous allez singulièrement aggraver la situation du transporteur en dispensant les victimes de la preuve de la faute.

L'argument n'emporte pas ma conviction.

D'abord, Messieurs, le transporteur peut se garantir contre le 'risque familial', en contractant une assurance, dite 'individuelle' qui, dans la limite d'un capital librement déterminé par les parties, garantit les tiers transportés même si la responsabilité du conducteur n'est pas engagée. Je concède qu'elle est assez onéreuse, mais elle est de plus en plus pratiquée.

En second lieu, on ne voit pas très bien pourquoi, en cas d'accident, les membres de la famille seraient, sur le plan juridique, moins bien traités que le premier venu.

En troisième lieu, il est incontestable qu'un scrupule moral, ou simplement la communauté d'intérêts, empêche le plus souvent l'exercice des actions en responsabilité entre membres d'une même famille. Leur permettre de fonder leur action sur l'art. 1384 au lieu de l'art. 1382 ne changera rien à cet état de choses. C'est le fait de demander réparation à un parent qui répugne, et non point le moyen juridique sur lequel la demande est fondée.

Enfin, dans les cas où néanmoins quelque conjoint en instance de divorce, quelque gendre, ou quelque bru, ou tel de leurs ayants droit n'hésitera pas à intenter une action contre le parent, auteur de l'accident, ou sa succession, il faut alors se demander quel avantage nouveau il retirerait du recours à l'art. 1384, alors que l'on sait de quelles facilités il dispose déjà grâce à la jurisprudence actuelle.

Et l'argument économique, dira-t-on?

En supprimant la nécessité d'établir la faute du conducteur, vous allez bien rendre plus facile l'action en indemnité et aggraver d'autant les charges des assureurs!

Là encore, Messieurs, il faut ramener les choses à leur juste proportion.

Précisons tout de suite que l'extension de l'art. 1384, al. 1er, aux dommages subis par les membres de la famille, aussi nombreux soient-ils, n'aura pas d'incidence sur les obligations assumées par les compagnies au titre de l'assurance responsabilité, puisque, nous l'avons déjà rappelé, le 'risque familial' est exclu de l'obligation d'assurance.

Par ailleurs, en ce qui concerne les dommages qui sont effective-ment couverts par l'assurance responsabilité, il me suffira de souligner, une fois encore, qu'en changeant la base juridique de l'action des victimes, on ne modifiera guère la situation, telle qu'elle se présente actuellement. L'interprétation extensive de la faute fait que l'on se trouve déjà pratiquement installé dans l'art. 1384, al. 1er, et les conséquences financières de cet accomodement sont déjà absorbées depuis plusieurs années. Sans doute existe-t-il des circonstances qui paralysent aujourd'hui encore l'action de la victime, et qui ne la paralyseront plus demain si l'on renonce au principe de la faute (prescription de l'action civile, démence de l'auteur du dommage, etc.). Mais il s'agit là de cas peu nombreux, dont on peut penser qu'ils n'obéreront pas le budget des compagnies. J'ai eu la curiosité de me renseigner sur ce que représenterait l'augmentation globale des charges pour les assureurs, si l'art. 1384, al. 1er, était étendu au transport bénévole. D'après les indications qui m'ont été fournies, cette augmentation serait de l'ordre de 1 à 2 p. 100, selon l'évaluation même des sociétés d'assurances.

Voilà qui me permet je pense, de clore ce chapitre.

B. – Il ne me reste plus qu'à examiner la dernière objection, qui, bien qu'inscrite en filigrane dans la plaidoirie de Me George, n'en est pas moins incisive, et qui élève le débat.

La jurisprudence traditionnelle, vous a-t-il rappelé, posait er principe que la responsabilité de plein droit des art. 1384, al. 1er, 1385, devait être écartée dans tous les cas où la victime avait participé à titre gracieux à l'usage d'une chose ou d'un animal resté sous la garde d'autrui. C'était traduire au plan du droit cette idée généreuse et juste que l'on ne doit pas accabler un homme qui n'a agi que par pure courtoisie et dans le seul dessein de rendre service à son prochain. En proclamant que le transporteur est responsable en dehors de toute faute de sa part, vous allez condamner cette idée générale et ruiner un principe juridique qui procédait pourtant d'une saine conception des choses. Que vous y dérogiez dans le cas du conducteur automobile couvert par une assurance obligatoire qui a pour résultat de faire supporter la réparation par un fonds collectif, passe encore, mais y a-t-il une raison valable de l'écarter dans toutes les autres circonstances?

Que ferez-vous demain quand vous sera soumis à nouveau le cas de la personne qui donne bénévolement une leçon de tennis ou d'équitation, ou qui initie au tir le fils d'un ami? Pénaliserez-vous cette personne complaisante en la rendant responsable de l'accident survenu alors qu'elle n'a rien à se reprocher?

Voilà, Messieurs, la mise en garde qu'en meilleurs termes, Me George vient de vous adresser.

C'est un langage qui, croyez-le bien, ne me laisse pas insensible.

Je pourrais, certes, répondre qu'à chaque jour suffit sa peine, que, pour l'instant, vous n'avez à vous prononcer que sur le sort du transporteur bénévole, que votre arrêt n'ira pas au-delà et qu'il vous appartiendra de dire ce qu'il y a lieu de faire dans les autres cas, lorsque la question se posera.

Je pourrais répondre également que dans les cas d'espèce cités en exemple, et dont on ne peut d'ailleurs pas prétendre qu'ils sont courants, une analyse judicieuse des éléments de la cause, sous l'angle de la garde, ou des causes possibles d'exonération (tel le comportement de la victime elle-même) devrait pouvoir permettre de rectifier ce qu'il y aurait d'injuste ou d'excessif dans l'application aveugle des régles de la responsabilité du fait des choses.

Maîs, pas plus que la précédente, cette réponse ne me satisfait entièrement.

Il y a bien un fonds de vérité dans l'objection présentée par le demandeur au pourvoi et il faudrait être un de ces froids 'technocrates du droit', qui sacrifient volontiers à la logique juridique le côté humain des choses, pour ne pas y être sensible.

A n'en point douter, la courtoisie, la générosité de cœur font partie de ces valeurs humaines que notre actuelle manière de vivre met en péril. Qu'il y ait intérêt à ne pas laisser dépérir ces valeurs et qu'il soit bon de les affirmer chaque fois qu'il est possible, j'en suis bien d'accord.

Cependant faut-il pour autant en fixer a priori les éléments, en déterminer par avance les effets sous la forme abstraite et figée d'une règle juridique de portée générale et de caractère absolu?

J'en doute sérieusement, tant l'entreprise comporte de risques.

La tentative qui en a été faite en 1928 le montre bien: pour avoir voulu être trop juste, l'on est tombé, en grande partie, dans l'injuste; pour pallier certaines conséquences fâcheuses d'un principe qui, en lui-même, était bon, était juste, l'on a voulu forger un autre principe qui devait fournir aux tribunaux la recette de l'équité. Mais l'équité ne s'accommode pas des formules abstraites et absolues. Elle exige une adaptation permanente aux nécessités mouvantes de la vie, et aux aspects changeants des rapports humains.

Qu'elle soit la préoccupation constante des juges, mais qu'on n'essaie pas de la mettre en équation.

Voilà pourquoi, Monsieur le Premier Président, Messieurs, je n'aurai pas de remords à voir disparaître de votre jurisprudence une règle qui, dans son inspiration, satisfait l'esprit de justice, mais, dans son application, le heurtera trop souvent.

Je conclus au rejet du pourvoi.

33 1re Espèce: *Cie d'assur. 'Le Continent' et Landru* c. *Dlle Schroeter* – Arrêt

La Cour; – Sur le moyen unique: – Attendu, selon les énonciations de l'arrêt confirmatif attaqué, que la voiture de Landru, dans laquelle demoiselle Schroeter était gratuitement transportée, quitta la chaussée dans un virage et alla se renverser sur le bas-côté; que demoiselle **Schroeter** fut blessée; qu'elle a assigné Landru et la *Cie Le Continent*, son assureur, en réparation de son dommage; – Attendu qu'il est fait grief à l'arrêt d'avoir accueilli la demande sur la base de l'art. 1384, al. 1er, CC, alors que ce texte, destiné à protéger en assurant, le cas échéant, leur indemnisation, les victimes du dommage causé par une chose à l'usage de laquelle elles n'ont point participé, ne saurait bénéficier à ceux qui ont accepté ou sollicité de participer, à titre gracieux, à l'usage de la chose, en pleine connaissance des dangers auxquels ils s'exposaient; – Mais attendu que la responsabilité résultant de l'art. 1384, al. 1er, CC, peut être invoquée contre le gardien de la chose par le passager transporté dans un véhicule à titre bénévole, hors les cas où la loi en dispose autrement; – d'où il suit qu'en statuant comme elle l'a fait, la Cour d'appel n'a violé aucun des textes visés au moyen;

Par ces motifs, rejette.

34 2ᵉ Espèce: *Cie d'assur. 'La Confiance'* c. *Epoux Zaroukian et autres* – Arrêt

La Cour; – Sur le premier moyen pris en ses deux branches: – Attendu qu'il est fait grief à l'arrêt confirmatif attaqué qui a condamné la Compagnie d'assurances *La Confiance* à garantir les conséquences dommageables de l'accident causé par son assuré Tarbouriec à la dame Zaroukian en la conduisant auprès d'un ami dont la voiture était en panne, d'avoir admis le caractère gratuit de ce transport, alors que celle-ci avait réglé un achat d'essence supérieur à ce qui était nécessaire pour le trajet, et d'avoir statué par un motif hypothétique et erroné en droit en retenant qu'un professionnel aurait demandé davantage, ce que rien n'établit; – Mais attendu que les juges d'appel ont relevé qu'à aucun moment une rémunération quelconque n'avait été envisagée, ni débattue entre la dame Zaroukian et Tarbouriec; que celle-ci avait spontanément réglé le coût du carburant pour manifester sa reconnaissance du service rendu et, par un motif non hypothétique, ont affirmé, ce qui pour eux était d'évidence, qu'un professionnel aurait exigé un prix infiniment supérieur; qu'au vu de ces éléments, ils ont estimé, sans la dénaturer, que jouait en l'espèce la clause de l'art. 4 du contrat stipulant que sont considérés comme tiers transportés à titre gratuit les passagers qui, sans payer de rétribution proprement dite pour le prix de leur transport, peuvent néanmoins participer occasionnellement et bénévolement aux frais de route; qu'ainsi les griefs invoqués ne sauraient être retenus; rejette le premier moyen.

Mais sur le second moyen: – Vu l'art. 1382 CC; – Attendu que pour attribuer la responsabilité de l'accident à Tarbouriec, la Cour d'appel, statuant uniquement sur le fondement de l'article susvisé, a retenu que le dérapage de l'automobile était nécessairement dû à un défaut de maîtrise du conducteur, dès lors que la preuve n'était pas rapportée que l'accident était imputable à une circonstance étrangère et que le fait que la chaussée était rendue glissante par la pluie, parfaitement connu du conducteur, aurait dû, au contraire, l'inciter à plus de prudence et caractérise encore davantage son manque de maîtrise; qu'en se fondant ainsi sur cette seule déduction purement hypothétique pour admettre l'existence d'une faute qui n'est pas directement constatée, la Cour d'appel n'a pas donné une base légale à sa décision;

Par ces motifs, casse..., renvoie devant la Cour d'appel de Nîmes.

35 3ᵉ Espèce: *Garantie mutuelle des fonctionnaires et Cothonay c. Durant et autres* – Arrêt

La Cour; – Sur le moyen unique: – Attendu, selon les énonciations de l'arrêt confirmatif attaqué, qu'à un carrefour, la voiture automobile de Cothonay entra en collision avec celle d'Atamaniuk; que Thomas, dame Costa et demoiselle Durant, transportés à titre gracieux par Atamaniuk, furent blessés; qu'ils ont assigné Cothonay et la Garantie mutuelle des fonctionnaires, son assureur, en réparation de leur dommage; – Attendu qu'il est reproché à l'arrêt qui a, sur la base de l'art. 1384, al. 1ᵉʳ, CC, retenu l'entière responsabilité de Cothonay, d'avoir condamné ce dernier et son assureur à réparer l'intégralité des dommages subis par les passagers de l'autre voiture, alors qu'une telle condamnation n'aurait dû être prononcée que pour moitié, les intimés ne pouvant agir contre leur transporteur bénévole que sur la base de l'art. 1382 du même code et, dès lors, indifféremment contre l'un et l'autre de leurs codéfendeurs dont la responsabilité découlait de textes différents; – Mais attendu que si, dans une disposition non attaquée par le pourvoi, la Cour d'appel énonce à tort que l'action récursoire de Cothonay et de la Garantie mutuelle des fonctionnaires contre un prétendu coauteur de dommage ne pouvait être exercée que sur le fondement de l'art. 1382 en raison du fait que les victimes avaient été transportées bénévolement, elle retient néanmoins que tout responsable d'un dommage en est tenu à la réparation intégrale 'tant sur le terrain de l'art. 1382 que sur celui de la responsabilité de droit de l'art. 1384'; que par ce seul motif, l'arrêt attaqué a justifié sa décision;

Par ces motifs, rejette.

36. Cour de cassation
Chambre Civile, 15 juin 1977
Sieur Cueff c. Dame Pivaut
(J.C.P. 1978,2.18780)

La Cour; – *Sur le moyen unique pris en sa troisième branche*: – Vu l'article 1384, alinéa 1, du Code civil; – Attendu que le gardien de la chose qui a été l'instrument du dommage hors le cas où il établit un événement de force majeure totalement exonératoire est tenu, dans ses rapports avec la victime, à réparation intégrale, sauf son recours éventuel contre le tiers qui aurait concouru à la production du dommage; – Attendu qu'il résulte des énonciations de l'arrêt infirmatif attaqué que, dans une agglomération, un jeune enfant, Cueff Thomas, sortant de la voiture automobile que sa mère avait arrêtée en face de sa villa de l'autre côté de la rue, traversa la chaussée, fut heurté par la voiture automobile de dame Pivaut et fut blessé; que son père, Cueff Armand, agissant en qualité d'administrateur légal, demanda à dame Pivaut réparation du préjudice subi par son fils; – Attendu que, pour exonérer partiellement dame Pivaut de la responsabilité par elle encourue en application de l'article 1384, alinéa 1, du Code civil, la Cour d'appel retient que dame Cueff, occupée à décharger sa voiture, avait commis une faute certaine en ne prêtant pas toute l'attention nécessaire aux faits et gestes de son enfant et que cette faute n'était pas plus imprévisible que celle commise par la victime; – Attendu qu'en retenant ainsi comme cause d'exonération partielle de la responsabilité du gardien une faute d'un tiers les juges du second degré ont violé le texte susvisé;

Par ces motifs, et sans qu'il y ait lieu de statuer sur les autres branches du moyen: – Casse et annule l'arrêt rendu le 18 novembre 1975, entre les parties, par la Cour d'appel de Rennes, et renvoie devant la Cour d'appel d'Angers.

37. Cour de cassation
Chambre Civile, 17 déc. 1963
Berthier et Caisse rég. de réassurance mutuelle agricole de l'Est central c. Veuve Lamende
(D. 1964,569)

Arrêt

Mais sur le deuxième moyen du même pourvoi, pris en sa seconde branche; – Vu l'art. 1384, al. 1er, CC, ensemble les art. 1147 et 1148 dudit code;

Attendu que le gardien d'une chose inanimée est, de plein droit, responsable du dommage causé par celle-ci, à moins qu'il ne prouve qu'il a été mis dans l'impossibilité absolue d'éviter ce dommage sous l'effet exclusif d'une cause étrangère qui ne peut lui être imputée, tel, s'il n'a pu normalement le prévoir, le fait de la victime ou d'un tiers; – Attendu que, selon l'arrêt infirmatif attaqué, de nuit, la voiture automobile conduite par Berthier, son propriétaire, passa sur le corps de Lamende, qui était étendu sur la chaussée, prés de son cyclomoteur, et le traîna sur une certaine distance; que Lamende décéda quelques heures plus tard; que sa veuve a assigné Berthier en réparation du préjudice par elle subi; que la Caisse régionaie de réassurance mutuelle agricole contre les accidents de l'Est central est intervenue au litige, sollicitant le remboursement des prestations versées en suite de ce décès; – Attendu que, pour accueillir cette demande, la Cour d'appel relève que Berthier avait aperçu, dans la lueur de ses phares, le corps de Lamende, qui était encore en vie et ne portait pas de blessures avant saigné; qu'il avait freiné pendant 20 mètres, mais l'avait cependant atteint et traîné sur une distance de 6 mètres entre les deux roues arrières de son véhicule; que la victime avait reçu alors des blessures qui avaient laissé d'abondantes traces de sang sur la chaussée; qu'après avoir remarqué que la voiture, dont Berthier avait la garde, était done intervenue dans la production du dommage, la décision énonce que, s'il est vrai que la présence d'un corps, étendu sur la route, constitue un fait imprévisible pour un usager de celle-ci, la preuve que cette présence constituait une faute à la charge de la victime, n'avait pas été rapportée par le défendeur à l'action et que, dès lors, celui-ci ne se déchargeait pas, même partiellement, de la responsabilité de plein droit, par lui encourue, sur la base de l'art. 1384, al. 1er, CC comme gardien de sa voiture; – Attendu qu'en subordonnant ainsi l'exonération de Berthler à la preuve d'une faute de la victime, alors qu'ils relevaient, d'autre part, un fait qui était susceptible, à la condition qu'il fût en relation de causalité avec le dommage, de constituer une circonstance étrangère propre à décharger en partie ledit Berthier de sa responsabilité, et même de l'en exonérer en entier si, normalement imprévisible pour lui, il avait été tel qu'il n'avait pas eu la possibilité de le surmonter, les juges du fond n'ont pas donné une base légale à leur decision;

Par ces motifs, et sans qu'il y ait lieu de statuer sur les autres moyens du pourvoi n° 62–11–074, non plus que sur le moyen unique du pourvoi n° 62–11–154, casse...

LIABILITY WITHOUT FAULT: VICARIOUS LIABILITY

38. Cour de cassation
Chambre Civile, 17 déc. 1964
Jacob c. Sté des Etablissements Millet
(*J.C.P.* 1965,2.14125 and Note R. Rodiere)

La Cour; – Sur le moyen unique: – Attendu qu'il ressort de l'arrêt infirmatif attaqué qu'au cours d'un transport de matériel effectué pour le compte de Barattre par un convoi automobile de caractère exceptionnel composé d'un tracteur appartenant à Jacob, conduit par son chauffeur Denis Millet et d'une remorque fournie par les établissements Millet, la remorque heurta et renversa Charpentier, qui circulait sur un cyclomoteur; que, Charpentier ayant été blessé, Denis Millet fut condamné pour délit de blessures involontaires à une amende et à des dommages-intérêts envers la victime, Jacob étant déclaré civilement responsable; que Jacob a assigné les Etablissements Millet en garantie de ces condamnations prononcées au profit de Charpentier; – Attendu que le pourvoi reproche à l'arrêt d'avoir rejeté cette demande aux motifs qu'un préposé ne pouvait avoir, dans le même temps et pour la même activité, plusieurs commettants et qu'il n'était point démontré que le chauffeur, préposé habituel de Jacob, fût passé sous l'autorité des Etablissements Millet, alors que, lorsque pour une tâche commune, des entrepreneurs emploient ensemble un même preposé, ils seraient responsables in solidum du fait de celui-ci, et qu'en l'espèce, Jacob et les établissements Millet, auraient joint leurs moyens respectifs, pour exécuter un transport sollicité par un client commun, l'un fournissant la remorque l'autre tracteur et le chauffeur, lequel agissant pour le compte des deux associés, aurait été leur préposé; – Mais attendu qu'après avoir rappelé qu'il s'agissait seulement de déterminer à qui incombait la responsabilité civile d'un accident, après condamnation pénale de l'auteur de celui-ci et que Jacob prétendait que le chauffeur du tracteur avait, ce jour-là, deux commettants, par suite de l'assocation de fait et de la communauté

337

d'intérêts ayant existé entre lui-même et les Etablissements Millet pour ce transport, la Cour d'appel remarque justement que la notion de profit n'est pas déterminante pour apprécier qui est le commettant, le lien de préposition résultant du pouvoir de commandement, du droit de donner des ordres et des instructions; que ladite Cour relève que Denis Millet était normalement et régulièrement employé comme chauffeur par Jacob, que celui-ci ne démontrait pas avoir, pour le travail réclamé par Barattre, transféré aux Etablissements Millet, le pouvoir de commandement et de direction sur ce chauffeur, qu'au contraire, en fournissant tracteur et conducteur, en sollicitant lui-même les autorisations administratives nécessaires et en réglant les conditions d'exécution du transport, Jacob avait conservé toutes les initiatives et notamment celle de commander le chauffeur chargé de la conduite; que la décision ajoute que la fourniture d'une remorque par les Etablissements Millet ne pouvait en aucune manière modifier cette situation; – Attendu que, de ces motifs, abstraction faite de tous autres critiqués par le pourvoi, qui peuvent être tenus pour surabondants, les juges de fond ont pu déduire que Denis Millet n'avait pas de lien de subordination qu'à l'égard de Jacob, et que, dès lors, ce dernier était demeuré un commettant pour l'exécution du transport litigieux; – D'où il suit que le moyen n'est pas fondé;

Par ces motifs: – Rejette le pourvoi formé contre l'arrêt rendu le 19 décembre 1962 par la Cour d'appel de Bourges.

39. Cour de cassation
Chambres Réunies, 9 mars 1960
Epoux Biehler c. *Huret*
(D. 1960, 329 and Note R. Savatier)

Arrêt

La Cour, statuant toutes Chambres Réunies; – Sur les deux moyens réunis: – Attendu que des motifs de l'arrêt confirmatif attaqué (Amiens, 15 janv. 1958), il résulte qu'Abos, ouvrier agricole au service d'Huret, profitant de l'absence de son patron, s'empara de la camionnette automobile appartenant à celui-ci pour se rendre dans une localité voisine où, après avoir perdu le contrôle du véhicule, il enfonça la devanture du débit exploité par les époux Biehler; que la dame Biehler fut blessée; – Attendu que le pourvoi reproche à la Cour d'appel d'avoir, sans rechercher si un lien de connexité permettant de rattacher le délit de blessures involontaires, commis par Abos, aux fonctions exercées par ce dernier, ne découlait pas des facilités que lui procurait son emploi, refusé de déclarer l'intimé civilement responsable du dommage causé par son préposé; – Mais attendu que les juges du fond, observant que la conduite de la camionnette ayant produit le dommage ne rentrait pas dans les attributions d'Abos, lequel, non titulaire d'un permis de conduire, avait utilisé ledit véhicule à des fins personnelles, au mépris des ordres et à l'insu de son commettant, la responsabilité de celui-ci ne pouvait résulter du seul fait qu'Abos avait accès, en raison de son emploi, au hangar où se trouvait l'instrument du dommage; que de ces constatations et énonciations qui impliquent qu'Abos avait accompli un acte indépendant du rapport de préposition qui l'unissait à son employeur, la Cour d'appel a pu déduire qu'Huret n'était pas civilement responsable des agissements de son préposé; qu'elle a ainsi, sans encourir les reproches du pourvoi, donné une base légale à sa décision;

Par ces motifs, rejette.

40. Cour de cassation
Assemblée Plénière, 10 juin 1977
Fonds de garantie automobile c.
Sté Albagnac et Florange et Gaulard
(*J.C.P.* 1977,2.18730)

La Cour; – Sur la demande de mise hors de cause de la Société Lyonnaise d'Exploitation de Véhicules S.L.E.V.E.: – Attendu que l'arrêt attaqué a constaté qu'était définitivement acquise la mise hors de cause prononcée par les premiers juges de la Société S.L.E.V.E., propriétaire du véhicule qui a été l'instrument du dommage; que cette disposition n'est pas attaquée par le pourvoi; que l'actuelle demande est donc dépourvue d'objet; – Sur le moyen unique, pris en ses deux branches: – Attendu que, selon les énonciations de l'arrêt attaqué, dans la nuit du samedi 12 au dimanche 13 février 1972. Gaulard, qui était alors chauffeur au service de la Société Albagnac et Florange et qui disposait d'une camionnette de livraison pour les besoins de son service, a utilisé ce véhicule pour effectuer, en compagnie de cinq camarades, une promenade au cours de laquelle il a occasionné un grave accident, l'un de ses camarades étant tué et les quatre autres blessés; – Attendu qu'il est reproché à la Cour d'appel d'avoir refusé de mettre les conséquences de cet accident à la charge de la Société Albagnac et Florange, alors, selon le pourvoi, que, d'une part, l'interdiction faite à Gaulard par son commettant d'utiliser le véhicule de service à des fins personnelles ne pouvait faire disparaître la responsabilité du commettant; que, d'autre part. Gaulard était le conducteur habituel du véhicule, qu'il l'utilisait pour aller au travail et en revenir, qu'il le garait à son domicile et qu'il en avait donc la garde continue; qu'enfin même s'il est sorti de ses fonctions en utilisant la camionnette à des fins personnelles, ce sont ses fonctions qui lui ont permis la réalisation du dommage, de telle sorte qu'en statuant comme ils l'ont fait, les juges du fond ont violé les dispositions de l'article 1384−5° du Code civil; − Mais attendu que le commettant n'est pas responsable du dommage causé par le préposé qui utilise, sans autorisation, à des fins personnelles le véhicule à lui confié pour l'exercice de ses fonctions; que, dès lors, la décision de la Cour d'appel est légalement justifiée.

Par ces motifs: − Rejette le pourvoi formé contre l'arrêt rendu le 20 novembre 1975 par la Cour d'appel de Bourges (2ᵉ Chambre correctionnelle).

Addenda

Additional note to German case 2

4. An interesting monograph (J. Taupitz, *Haftung für Energieleiterstörungen durch Dritte* (1981)) appeared in Germany after this manuscript had been sent to the printers, so here it can be mentioned only briefly. Its author argues that the acceptance of the new 'right of an established and operating business' makes the continued rigid distinction between physical damage and economic loss increasingly difficult to support. He argues that the typical defendants in these instances are 'professionals' in breach of *Verkehrspflicht*. Following a modern trend, strongly advocated by Professor v. Bar among others (*Verkehrspflichten* (1980)), the author argues that these *Verkehrspflichten* should be dealt with under para. 823 II BGB in order to enable victims to recover their economic loss. Though he admits that it may be economically cheaper to let the loss lie where it falls (a view taken in Germany by, *inter alia*, G. Hager, 'Haftung bei Störung der Energiezufuhr', *JZ* 1979, 53, 58, and in this country by Professor Atiyah, *Accidents Compensation and the Law*, 3rd edn (1980), 90–1), he feels that this argument should not, of itself, carry the day, given the defendant's 'unlawful' activity. Professor Kötz's insurance arguments are thus, implicitly at any rate, accepted (Zweiger and Kötz *An Introduction to Comparative Law* II (1979), 273 (trans. by T. Weir)). Nor is the 'floodgate' argument treated as being conclusively in favour of the *status quo*, since there are other devices (including that of contributory negligence) which could be used to keep liability within workable boundaries. Naturally, there are counter-arguments to most of these points; and the more cynically inclined could dismiss this as the latest in a long series of Ph.D. dissertations. And yet, quite apart from its merits, the work is a living proof of the fact that the pressures to change German law are not relaxing. And from a comparative point of view it is noteworthy in so far as it reveals the increasing willingness of German lawyers to approach issues not just through abstract concepts but also by means of the policy factors which lie hidden behind them and often determine the outcome of litigation (see vol. I, chapter 2). See also A. Bürge, 'Die Kabelbruchfälle, Eine rechtsvergleichende Untersuchung zum schweizerischen, österreichischen und deutschen Haftpfichtrecht', *Juristische Blätter* 1981, 57 et seq. In *Lexmead (Basingstoke) Ltd* v. *Lewis* [1981] 2 W.L.R. 713, the House of Lords implied that even English law may be open-minded about pure economic loss.

Additional note to German case 6

1. This formulation has also been accepted by the Bundesgerichtshof. As Larenz has put it (*Lehrbuch des Schuldrechts*, 11th edn (1976), 354–60): 'The value judgment underlying the theory of adequate causation is that the sphere of responsibility of the person liable should only include those harmful consequences of the event that is the basis for liability which would not appear wholly unlikely to occur from the standpoint of an experienced observer. Thus, liability can be avoided only when the harmful consequences are such that they occur because of a wholly unusual set of circumstances that such an observer would not have expected at all' (translation from v. Mehren and Gordley, *The Civil Law System*, 2nd edn (1977), 585). Larenz's words hint at the difficulties German lawyers have encountered in deciding how the probability of the harm is to be calculated. Professor Honoré (*Encyclopedia*, chapter 7, 'Causation and remoteness of damage', 51) has achieved an admirable summary of the divergent views in the following paragraph (notes omitted): 'Von Kries held that

the chance of harm must be estimated in the light of the alleged tortfeasor's knowledge at the time of his act. Others add to this the knowledge of a reasonable man in the position of the alleged tortfeasor at the time. Traeger included the knowledge available to a most prudent or exceptionally perceptive man [the 'optimal observer'], and his point of view has generally been followed in Germany. Rümelin included circumstances existing at the time of the conduct, then undiscoverable, which are discovered later, i.e., he adopted the hindsight principle (nachträgliche Prognose). Rümelin's view leads to a distinction between circumstances existing at the time of the conduct or defined event, for which the alleged tortfeasor is responsible, and later intervening events for which, if they occasion harm of a different type, he will not be.' It will be noted from the above that, to quote Larenz once again, 'If one takes the Bundesgerichtshof's standard of the optimal observer seriously, then the criterion of adequacy loses most of its ability to limit the area of responsibility of the person liable.' In consequence a more normative theory of causation had to be developed. See below, pp. 135–144, and discussion in chapter 3 of volume I.

Additional note to German case 10

1. These two cases give *some* idea only of the limitations of the 'scope of the rule' theories, and for further details one must consult the growing legal literature. The following may be of particular interest: Deutsch. 'Regressverbot und Unterbrechung des Haftungszusammenhangs im Zivilrecht', *JZ* 1972, 551 *et seq.*; Deutsch and v. Bar, 'Schutzbereich und wesentliche Bedingung im Versicherungs-und Haftungsrecht', *MDR* 1979, 536 *et seq.*; Huber, 'Normzwecktheorie und Adäquanztheorie', *JZ* 1969, 677 *et seq.*; idem, 'Verschulden, Gefährdung und Adäquanz', *Festschrift für E. Wahl* (1973), 301 *et seq.*; Stoll, *Kausalzusammenhang und Normzweck im Deliktsrecht* (1968). Two points, however, should he made. Firstly, these theories work well when the legislator has expressed his intention fairly clearly (for an example see pp. 166, 168, below); less well where the legislative intention is expressed in very general terms; and they reach a breaking point when applied to widely phrased provisions such as para. 826 BGB (or to our tort of negligence) where the ingredients of the wrongful conduct are only vaguely difinable. As Professor Honoré points out (*op.cit.* at p. 61) in these cases 'to attempt to settle the proper limits of recovery by inquiring into the scope of the rule is to invite the judge to fix them for himself'. The second point that should be made, though it does not emerge from the above cases, is that the 'risk theory' (which could be regarded as one variant) can also operate to *extend* liability where both the foreseeability and the adequate cause theory would not produce such a result. Thus Ehrenzweig in, *inter alia*, 'Negligence without fault', 54 *Calif. L. Rev.* 1422 (1966) has, for a long time now, been arguing that damage which is the typical consequence of the defendant's business or enterprise should be compensated irrespective of fault and of usual causal principles.

Additional notes to German case 17

1. Cf. J.A. Weir, 'Abstraction in the law of torts – economic loss', 1974 *City of London Law Review*, 15, 19: 'There is a difference between making a bad thing and making a

thing worse. No doubt the bad thing is worse that it should be, but it is not worse that it was, and it is only when you make a thing worse than it was that you can talk of property damage.' Contrast Lord Denning M.R.'s views in *Dutton* v. *Bognor Regis* [1972] 1 Q.B. 373 at 396, where he describes Mrs Dutton's harm as 'physical damage to the house' Extra-judicially, however, Lord Denning has, it is submitted more correctly, referrred to Mrs Dutton's harm as 'simply financial damage' *The Discipline of Law* (1979), 264.

2. The significance of the ruling that the plaintiff in such cases has only suffered pure financial loss is enormous for the law of products liability, for, in effect, it means that the manufacturer of a defective product will *not* be liable *in tort* towards the ultimate purchaser for the defect *of* the product but liable only for the damage caused *by* the product. The damage *to* the product rather than *by* the product is more of a 'sales' problem than a 'tort' problem and is actionable, if at all, in contract, not in tort. This was certainly true of English law until the decisions in *Dutton* and *Anns* and, *generally speaking*, it is also true of American law (e.g. *Seely* v. *White Motor Co.* 63 Cal. 2d. 9 (1965)), though some courts have extended *strict tort* liability even for economic loss (thus *Santor* v. *A and M Karagheusian, Inc.*, 207 A.2d 305 (N.J. 1965); purchaser allowed tort action to recover from a remote manufacturer value of poor-quality carpet). But damages for the defect in the product are widely recoverable under the provisions of the Uniform Commercial Code (§§ 2-314–18, on which see J.J. White and R.S. Summers, *Uniform Commercial Code*, 2nd edn (1980), 343 *et seq.*), which extend, often very considerably, the *contractual* warranties to persons who are *not* in any contractual privity with the manufacturer (thus, for example, *Mid Continent Aircraft Corp.* v. *Curry County Spraying Serv., Inc.*, 572 S.W. 2d. 308 (Tex 1978)). In between these two 'extreme' situations (defective product, damage caused to person or *other* property *by* the defective product) lies a grey area – the defect in the product may lead to further damage to the product itself. Some German courts have in these instances characterised the damage as property damage recoverable in a tort action under 823 I BGB so long as the defective part, which leads to the further destruction of the product, can be individually identified (BGHZ 67, 359, though in that case the manufacturer was also the vendor). Similar results have been reached by American courts, though the reasoning has varied a great deal. Recently, however, in *Russell* v. *Ford Motor Co.*, 525 P. 2d 1383 (Or. 1978), the Supreme Court of Oregon made an effort to abandon the property/economic loss distinction and make recovery in *strict tort* liability depend upon whether the loss resulted from a danger that threatened human safety.

The points briefly discussed here suggest that products liability has become a highly complicated area of the law that defies summary exposition. A cursory look at the American cases and books will immediately confirm this impression and also reveal an immense literature. Student case-books which give excellent accounts (and many references) include: Marc A. Franklin, *Injuries and Remedies Cases and Materials on Tort law and Alternatives*, 3rd edn (1979), 436 *et seq.*; W.L. Prosser, J.W. Wade and V.E. Schwartz, *Torts – Cases and Materials*, 6th edn (1976), 738 *et seq.*; D.W. Noel and J.J. Phillips, *Products Liability – Cases and Materials* (1976).